The Townsend Lectures

The Department of Classics at Cornell University is fortunate to have at its disposal the Prescott W. Townsend Fund—established by Mr. Townsend's widow, Daphne Townsend, in 1982. Since 1985, income from the fund has been used to support the annual visit of a distinguished scholar in the field of classics. Each visiting scholar delivers a series of lectures, which, revised for book publication, are published by Cornell University Press in Cornell Studies in Classical Philology.

During the semester of their residence, Townsend lecturers effectively become members of the Cornell Department of Classics and teach a course to Cornell students as well as deliver the lectures.

The Townsend Lectures bring to Cornell University and to Cornell University Press, scholars of international reputation who are in the forefront of current classical research and whose work represents the kind of close reading of texts that has become associated with current literary discourse, or reflects broad interdisciplinary concerns, or both.

CORNELL STUDIES IN CLASSICAL PHILOLOGY

EDITED BY

FREDERICK M. AHL ★ KEVIN C. CLINTON
JOHN E. COLEMAN ★ JUDITH R. GINSBURG
G. M. KIRKWOOD ★ DAVID MANKIN
GORDON M. MESSING ★ ALAN NUSSBAUM
HAYDEN PELLICCIA ★ PIETRO PUCCI
JEFFREY S. RUSTEN ★ DANUTA SHANZER

VOLUME XLIII

Artifices of Eternity
Horace's Fourth Book of Odes
by Michael C. J. Putnam

ALSO IN THE TOWNSEND LECTURES

Culture and National Identity in Republican Rome
by Erich S. Gruen

Horace and the Dialectic of Freedom
Readings in "Epistles 1"
by W. R. Johnson

Animal Minds and Human Morals
The Origins of the Western Debate
by Richard J. Sorabji

Socrates, Ironist and Moral Philosopher
by Gregory Vlastos

Artifices of Eternity

Horace's Fourth Book of Odes

Michael C. J. Putnam

Cornell University Press

Ithaca and London

First published 1986 by Cornell University Press.
First printing, Cornell Paperbacks, 1996.

Excerpts from "The Dry Salvages" and "Little Gidding" in *Four Quartets* by T. S. Eliot, copyright 1943 by T. S. Eliot; renewed 1971 by Esme Valerie Eliot. Reprinted by permission of Harcourt Brace Jovanovich, Inc., and Faber and Faber Ltd.

Library of Congress Cataloging-in-Publication Data

Putnam, Michael C. J.
  Artifices of eternity.

  (Cornell studies in classical philology ; v. 43.
The Townsend lectures)
  Bibliography: p.
  Includes index.
  1. Horace. Carmina. Liber IV. 2. Odes—History and criticism. I. Title. II. Series: Cornell studies in classical philology ; v. 43. III. Series: Cornell studies in classical philology. Townsend lectures.
PA6411.P8 1986   874'.01   85-25542
ISBN 0-8014-1852-6 (alk. paper)
ISBN 0-8014-8346-8 (pbk: alk. paper)

Printed in the United States of America

⊗ The paper in this book meets the minimum requirements of the American National Standard for Information Sciences—Permanence of Paper for Printed Library Materials, ANSI Z39.48-1984.

For my colleagues at Brown
and *in memoriam* A. G. E.

CONTENTS

Preface   9

Abbreviations   11

Introduction   15

Part One. The Loving Muse: Odes 1–3

Chapter 1. Ode 1   33

Chapter 2. Ode 2   48

Chapter 3. Ode 3   63

Part Two. Doctus Apollo: Odes 4–6

Chapter 4. Ode 4   81

Chapter 5. Ode 5   101

Chapter 6. Ode 6   115

Part Three. Time and Redemption:
Odes 7–9

Chapter 7. Ode 7   133

Chapter 8. Ode 8   145

Chapter 9. Ode 9   157

Part Four. Festivity's Musics: Odes 10–12

Chapter 10. Ode 10   177

Chapter 11. Ode 11   184

Chapter 12. Ode 12   198

Contents

Part Five. Sorcery and Song: Odes 13–15

Chapter 13. Ode 13   219
Chapter 14. Ode 14   236
Chapter 15. Ode 15   262

Conclusion   307
Appendix: Ode 15 and the Monuments   327
Bibliography   341
Index   349

PREFACE

In spite of extensive scholarly attention to Horace in recent decades (I single out the works of Commager, Fraenkel, and Reckford only because these have been most influential on my own thinking), there has been no comprehensive study of his fourth book of odes. In the present volume I attempt to fill that gap. My book serves in part as an act of rehabilitation. Published in 13 B.C., ten years after his universally acknowledged masterpiece, the collected first three books of odes, Horace's final gathering still suffers faint critical praise. The source of this disquiet is Suetonius' life of the poet, which, to all appearances, finds him yielding to Augustus' desire for Roman epinicia in his honor. The ready conclusion is that such poetry must be uninspired make-work, a gallimaufry plumped to completion by leftovers from earlier days. My view, by contrast, is that the fifteen odes which comprise Horace's last lyric offering are the rightful capstone of his accomplishment, beautifully crafted in themselves and shaped into a composition of exceptional power and brilliance.

My reading aims to elucidate the quality of individual poems and of the book as a whole, but it is also contextual in a dual sense. First, I have striven not to lose sight of the historical background of Augustan Rome against which these poems were written, and in an appendix I endeavor to trace a sympathy between many of the essential notions in Horace's final *elogium* of Augustus and what was to prove the ideological program of the emperor's forum. Second, the final flowering of Horatian lyric not only expands the intellectual horizon of his previous collection, but also absorbs and reacts to the

force of two other works of genius that appeared in the meantime—
Propertius' third book of elegies, dated most probably 22 B.C., and
the *Aeneid,* published soon after Virgil's death in September 19 B.C.
We will see Horace regularly co-opting and remolding the imaginative detail of his great predecessors as well as responding, in the
intensity of his own lyric acts of commitment, to the epic's multivalent narrative and to the evasions and yearnings essential to the
strategies of Propertian elegy. The conclusion of Horace's career is at
once a culmination and one of the great acts of origination in ancient
letters, and is so recognized in the pages that follow.

This book is an expanded version of lectures given at Cornell
University in the spring of 1985, under the aegis of the Department
of Classics and implemented through the generosity of Mrs. Prescott
W. Townsend. I am deeply honored to have inaugurated this series,
and remain grateful to the classics faculty and its staff for the many
gestures of kindness and courtesy tendered throughout my season in
Ithaca. Pietro and Jeannine Pucci, in particular, were unfailing
sources of generosity during my stay.

Freedom from academic duties and leisure to pursue research was
afforded me by the grant of a sabbatical leave from Brown University
and of a fellowship from the American Council of Learned Societies.
I owe thanks to many friends, especially Katherine Geffcken, William
Higgins, Kenneth Reckford, Charles Witke, and James Zetzel, whose
reading of my work in progress strengthened its initiatives while
helping to clarify the obscure and emend the faulty. Frances
Eisenhauer once again gave her usual care to the manuscript's final
preparation, and Emily Wheeler of Cornell University Press brought
both exactness and perspicuity to the process of editing.

Most of this book was conceived, and much of it written, in an
irenic setting of mutual support and encouragement which I have
enjoyed now for a quarter century. This indebtedness I happily ac-
knowledge on a separate page.

MICHAEL C. J. PUTNAM

Providence, Rhode Island

ABBREVIATIONS

In addition to standard abbreviations for ancient authors (and their works) and for modern journals, the following are used regularly in the notes:

CIL: *Corpus Inscriptionum Latinarum*. Berlin, 1863–.

Ernout-Meillet: *Dictionnaire étymologique de la langue latine*. Edited by A. Ernout and A. Meillet. Paris, 1959.

Lewis and Short: *A Latin Dictionary*. Edited by C. Lewis and C. Short. Oxford, 1955.

OCD²: *Oxford Classical Dictionary*. 2d ed. Oxford, 1970.

OLD: *Oxford Latin Dictionary*. Oxford, 1968–82.

Paulus-Festus: Sex. Pompeius Festus. *De Significatu Verborum* and its epitome by Paulus Diaconus. Edited by W. M. Lindsay, 1913.

RE: A. Pauly, G. Wissowa, and W. Kroll. *Realencyclopädie der classischen Altertumswissenschaft*. Stuttgart, 1893–.

TLL: *Thesaurus Linguae Latinae*. Munich, 1900–.

Save for one textual change and minor alterations in punctuation, I have followed throughout the Teubner text of Horace established by F. Klingner, 3d ed. (Leipzig, 1959). The publisher's permission to quote from this text is hereby gratefully acknowledged.

Artifices of Eternity

INTRODUCTION

> . . . he never exchanged praise for money, nor opened a
> shop of condolence or congratulation. His poems, there-
> fore, were scarce ever temporary.
>
> SAMUEL JOHNSON, *Life of Pope*

In late May and early June of the year 17 B.C. an event of some
moment occurred in the city of Rome: Augustus chose to revive the
secular games (*ludi saeculares*) after an interval of a century and a
quarter. For the citizens of the metropolis this meant three days and
nights of festive sacrifices followed by a week of *ludi honorarii,* games
paid for by the state.[1] For the *princeps* the significance went deeper.
The most recent celebrations of the *ludi* had taken place in 249, near
the end of the First Punic War, and in 146, a year which saw the
termination of the Third Punic War and hence represented a suitable
juncture at which to honor Rome's growing hegemony in the Mediterranean and the start of a new era in her imperial ambitions. In
fourteen years, however, the murder of the tribune Tiberius Gracchus introduced an element of violence into Roman politics that, in
retrospect, would take the shape of a century of sporadic civil war.
This bloodshed came to an end at the naval engagement off Actium in
September 31 B.C. when Augustus (still Octavian) routed the forces
of Antony and Cleopatra. The emperor then waited another four-
teen-year period before he set the time for his own ceremony to mark
a new beginning for Rome.

[1]On the *ludi saeculares,* see n. 20 to ode 6, below.

The interval between final struggle and proclamation of the start of Rome's new *saeculum* was a necessary testing period before peace could be pronounced assured, bringing with it an occasion to celebrate Rome's physical and ethical revitalization. There is evidence that plans were afoot to put on secular games in the late 40s, and Virgil's fourth *eclogue,* announcing that a new order of the ages is being born and that the reign of Saturn is returning, may reflect such a possibility. Certainly the accord between Octavian and Antony, reached at Brundisium in 40, the year of Pollio's consulship and the presumed date of the poem, seemed to augur well for a peaceful future for Rome. Such hopes were soon disappointed as a new term of warring began, to end only after Octavian's military success off the west coast of Greece nine years later. Yet even the Battle of Actium could not necessarily be seen, save in hindsight, as the end of civil strife, and the 20s had their moments of unrest. In the year 22, however, Augustus embarked on an extended tour of Sicily and the Roman east in the course of which the emperor received back from the Parthians, by diplomacy needing no recourse to arms, the standards they had taken from Crassus' legions at Carrhae in 53. And in the two years following his return to Rome in 19, Augustus effected the most far-reaching moral and religious reforms of his principate.

The resultant combination of peace, both abroad and civil, with an attempt at the moral regeneration of Roman citizenry, created an obviously appropriate moment to announce, with grand public display, that Rome was on the threshold of a renewed golden age. Horace was chosen to glorify the occasion in poetry, and the resultant *Carmen Saeculare* is as much a watershed in Horace's career as it is an imaginative confirmation of spiritual rebirth for his city and her world.[2] Just as the games symbolized stability for Rome, so Horace's poem sings his allegiance to Augustus and his accomplishment. This celebration for Rome's symbolic recommencement also presages a new burst of lyric brilliance on Horace's part which will take final shape in his fourth book of odes, published four years later, in 13 B.C., and the subject of the chapters that follow.

But before we look more closely at the *Carmen Saeculare* and the motifs it fashions which maintain their force in the subsequent book of poems, we should remind ourselves of how tempered was

[2]The authoritative discussion of the *Carmen Saeculare* is by Fraenkel (*Horace,* 364–82).

Horace's earlier vision of Augustus and his Rome, and how re-strained his response to the notion of writing about them. His first "refusal" ode, 1.6, addressed to Agrippa, disclaims the ability to sing what should be a topic for the epicist Varius, "the praises of splendid Caesar—and yours" (*laudes egregii Caesaris et tuas*). Horace's slender, unwarlike Muse edges away from the leaden ferocities of war to banquets, song, and love's nimble feuds. A later ode in the collection, *c.* 2.12, in which Maecenas is apostrophized, urges the great states-man to tell of Caesar's battles in the medium they apparently deserve, humdrum prose history (*pedestribus historiis*), leaving the poet-speaker free to expand on the musical talent and charm of Licymnia, pseudonym for Maecenas' wife Terentia. Even a poem on Caesar's homecoming from Spain, *c.* 3.14, serves as excuse for a private fes-tivity, not a public accolade. And the last ode in the earlier collections alluding to (still) "splendid Caesar," *c.* 3.25, a poem neatly balancing the first *recusatio*, *c.* 1.6, bursts with Bacchic enthusiasm to grant Caesar apotheosis. But no actual song of glorification is forthcoming.

Accompanying poems where generic incompatibility offers an ex-cuse for imaginative aloofness are *carmina* where misgivings about Augustus and the civil bloodshed enmeshed with his rise to power take over the poem. One has only to think of the ode placed second in book 1, following directly on the introductory priamel. The per-vasiveness of vengeance in Roman life is the central point of this meditation on decadence. Here Mars appropriately neighbors Venus in Rome's pantheon, and Caesar is urged to transfer Roman military energies away from attacking her guilty, dwindling populace to car-rying out a more seemly vendetta against the Parthians. Later in the same book, in an ode to Fortune, the speaker exclaims:

> heu heu cicatricum et sceleris pudet
> fratrumque. quid nos dura refugimus
> aetas? quid intactum nefasti
> liquimus? . . .

Alas, alas, the shame of our scars, our crime, our brothers. From what have we recoiled, a ruthless generation? In our evil what have we left untouched?

Or we have the searing lecture that opens the second book, asking

> quis non Latino sanguine pinguior
> campus sepulcris inpia proelia
> testatur auditumque Medis
> Hesperiae sonitum ruinae?

What field, enriched with Latin blood, does not with its burials bear witness to our unholy clashes and to the thud of Hesperia's collapse, heard even by the Parthians?

And there is the still deeper indictment of the six so-called Roman odes that introduce book 3. Here is their final stanza to which I will later return:

> damnosa quid non inminuit dies?
> aetas parentum peior avis tulit
> nos nequiores, mox daturos
> progeniem vitiosiorem.

What has our cursed age not demeaned? The era of our parents, worse than their fathers', has borne us, more evil, soon about to bear offspring yet more depraved.

Such negative sentiments, prominent as overtures, also find a place at a point of final climax. The penultimate poem of the collection, *c.* 3.29, urges Maecenas away from the "smoke, commercialism and noise" of Rome, away from her political cares, to enjoy the company of a self-sufficient speaker who prides himself on independence, however rough the seas through which his solitary skiff might sail. Antipathy toward Roman immorality and freedom of mind to pursue an intellectual course not necessarily to the liking of her ruling powers seem essential components of the Horatian spirit.

The change, then, that we sense in the *Carmen Saeculare,* a public gesture of applause for present Roman well-being and supplication for its continuance written six years after the first collection was published, is all the more remarkable. Horace's song, performed as day closed on June 3, the end of the initial triduum of festivities, imaginatively summarizes the interaction of human achievements with divine approval necessary to stabilize the values they extol. We learn of Rome's physical, moral and political prosperity, and we pay heed to the gods—Apollo and Diana; the Sun; the Ilithyiae, Parcae, and Capitoline triad—and to the terrestrial ruler, Augustus, who have brought it about and, the speaker prays, will maintain it.

It is a poem about birth and rebirth, beginnings and renewals, returns and reassurances. The young choristers sing of a nourishing Sun (*alme Sol*), about its bright daily restoration, and of the youth (*subolem, prolem*) of Rome, produced by Diana in her guise as goddess of childbirth but etymologically and assonantally linked with the sun's nourishment. They praise a law that is *ferax*, begetter of offspring and of moral quality, and Earth that is *fertilis*, productive in the land's goods, while reminding us of the still larger round of the *saeculum* itself that brings back (*referat*) singing and festivity. Complementing these manifestations of renewal is the cycle of the poet's own joyful music which takes us in its own course from Apollo and Diana at the beginning to their reappearance at the end.

Throughout the ode the focus is gently but clearly on the emperor himself. The center of the poem recalls the establishment of Rome by chaste Aeneas, fleeing the flames of Troy. But we are soon reminded that the impresario of the present celebration, offering a sacrifice of white cattle to Jupiter and his Capitoline colleagues, is also "the famous offspring of Anchises and Venus" (*clarus Anchisae Venerisque sanguis*). Rome's initial founder and present refounder are close kin.

But Horace finds a further analogy for the emperor that announces a continuity even grander than the repetitions implied in history's resemblances. Augustus not only has attributes of the nourishing Sun, he also resembles the Sun's alter ego, Phoebus Apollo. We hear at line 33, from apostrophe to Augustus' patron god, that he is "*condito mitis placidusque telo . . .*" (gentle and peaceful, his sword sheathed . . .), and the *princeps,* we soon learn, is

> . . . bellante prior, iacentem
> lenis in hostem.

superior to his foe, kindly when the enemy has fallen.

Apollo, warrior and lyre player, decorous with his bow but also beloved by the nine muses, has found his surrogate on earth, or at least poetry so professes. He is strong but merciful in war, and, one should add, the commissioner of a poet whose "charm" formalizes

the extraordinary qualities of the new age and prays for their continuity into the future.

Continuity exists in the mental life of Horace as well, for many of
these themes recur in the brilliant book of poems whose release follows four years after the performance of the *Carmen*. As we plunge
into a collection equally concerned with grace and charm, with the
broad meaning of education, and, most of all, with the creation and
performance of lyric song, we find Augustus ever-present, an object
of gratitude, on whom landscape, people, and poets, all depend, for
fertility of earth and of imagination. We will come again upon
Aeneas, appearing in a form of *recusatio* new to Horace. Instead of
refusing to tell of battles, the poet's persona proclaims that wars are
now over and hints that the singing of the *Aeneid,* with its extended,
probing analysis of men at arms and of the morally questionable
struggles that precede new political orderings, is replaced by odic
song praising a present worthy of lyric's concentrated acclaim. Finally, we will also see Apollo at work through his mouthpiece, fostering
the arts of peace, not war, inspiring and teaching the *Carmen Saeculare*
to a poet who in his turn instructs his world with much the same
songful music.

We are told something of the origin of the fourth book of odes
from the *Vita Horati* of Suetonius, excerpts from which are attached
to several manuscripts of the poet's writings. Since not only the facts
that Suetonius details but also the tone in which they are couched has
had a pejorative influence on the way critics of Latin letters have
treated these poems, it is well to review his testimony. Here is the
crucial sentence that seems to offer corroboration for a tradition of
negative evaluations of the poems themselves. The subject is Augustus:[3]

> scripta quidem eius usque adeo probavit mansuraque perpetua opinatus
> est, ut non modo saeculare carmen conponendum iniunxerit, sed et
> Vindelicam victoriam Tiberii Drusique privignorum suorum, eumque
> coegerit propter hoc tribus carminum libris ex longo intervallo quartum
> addere. . . .

[3] *E Suetoni Vita Horati* 2*, 20–25 (ed. Klingner).

Indeed he approved so highly of [Horace's] writings and was convinced that they would remain immortal that he bade him to compose not only the Carmen Saeculare but also a Vindelic victory [ode] for Tiberius and Drusus, his step-sons, and because of this compelled him, after a long interval, to add a fourth to his three books of odes. . . .

Two points are important here. First, Suetonius documents the unique occasion of Latin literature up to the conclusion of the Augustan Age where a poet is said to yield to the wishes of a patron.[4] Second, though it may look specifically to verbal usage of the second century A.D. when the life was written, there is no denying an element of coercion in the language Suetonius uses. If Horace, one of the most notoriously independent writers in our tradition, has surrendered his imagination to the emperor's compelling desires, what level of quality can we expect from the resultant poetry? For a poet to toady under any circumstances would indicate sufficient moral and intellectual weakness to stamp the results as tawdry. When the sycophant is Horace and his gifts appear willingly misused for purposes of public propaganda, then the critic's disquiet should be compounded.

Whether Suetonius' insinuations have proved prejudicial or merely seemed to validate what a thorough reading of the poems themselves advocated, the majority of critics have felt ill at ease before the fourth book, dismissing the political odes for their chauvinism and the private lyrics, with one or two exceptions, as so many fillers to flesh out the volume.[5] Critical opinion has been gradually changing toward

[4]Cf. also the contemporary *Epistles* 2.1. The most recent treatments of the effect of the patronage of Augustus on Horace's fourth book are by G. Williams ("Phases," 16–18) and Zetzel, 92.

[5]Babcock's excellent survey (1599–1602) of scholarship on book 4 since the Second World War points to a gradual revaluation upward of its quality. Readers are particularly in the debt of Fraenkel, (*Horace,* 400–53) for an assessment both magisterial and moving, and of Reckford (*Horace,* 123–45) for his sensitive treatment of Horace's poetic "Indian Summer." Negative voices are still raised, especially against the "political" poems, e.g., Wilkinson (85–86), Perret (135), Commager (*The Odes,* 228–34, 291), and G. Williams ("Phases," 17: "the poet's mind was no longer engaged in wrestling with real problems").

Kissel (1511–14) marshals the bibliography of work from 1936 to 1975 on book 4 as a whole and on individual odes.

more fruitful ways of reading Horace's final odes, and it is my purpose here further to redress this balance. Through close analysis of all fifteen odes I will offer evidence that, however the content and presentation of his verse may have altered during his career as lyricist, the excellence of his final masterpiece is fully equal to that of his first collection of odes.

Let us return to the matter of Suetonius' biography and to the completion of the sentence I began earlier. The subject is still the emperor himself:

> . . . post sermones vero quosdam lectos nullam sui mentionem habitam ita sit questus: *irasci me tibi scito, quod non in plerisque eiusmodi scriptis mecum potissimum loquaris. an vereris ne apud posteros infame tibi sit, quod videaris familiaris nobis esse?*

> Furthermore, after reading some of his "talks" and discovering no mention of himself he complained as follows: "Know that I am angry at you because in your several writings of this sort you do not speak with me above all. Are you afraid that your reputation will suffer before the judgment of posterity because you are seen to be my friend?"

Turning from Suetonius' third-person narrative to the actual words of Augustus' quoted letter, we observe a distinct change of tone. This is not the declaration of master to slave in a hierarchical relationship but the intimate, even jocular, interrogation of equal by equal or even of the person in power by his subordinate. It confirms what the *vita* had earlier made quite clear, that Horace had no hesitation on other occasions to refuse requests from the emperor and that, even when he did so, Augustus still pursued Horace's friendship, not the other way around: "*Neque enim si tu superbus amicitiam nostram sprevisti, ideo nos quoque* ἀνθυπερηφανοῦμεν" (For if in your pride you have scorned our friendship, we will not on that account treat you with *hauteur* in return). It is unlikely that the poet who early in his career turned down the post of secretary to the emperor would, in middle age with his reputation secure, suddenly accede to an unpalatable request for made-to-order poetry to whose contents he had no personal commitment. What happens in the *Carmen Saeculare* and in the fourth book of odes is something opposite. Rome's most politically powerful personage, one who publicly fosters art by engaging Horace's imagina-

[22]

tion to summarize the quality of the Roman present, becomes himself art's creature. To judge from the tone of the letter just quoted, it is a role he seems to crave.

Moreover, if Augustus were given to demanding the superficial homage of flattery for whatever reasons or, more negatively, had been troubled by what we have seen to be a less than enthusiastic approach on the poet's part to the public affairs of Rome, he would have been expected to manifest his feelings early in his career, when his own fortunes were still in doubt and uncertainties remained. But Horace is outspoken against Roman immorality, especially against civil war, from the beginning of his political statements. There is every reason to believe, in fact, that Horace means exactly what he says in book 4, that his praise of Rome and Augustus is genuine, and that, paradoxically, in the very idealistic spirit of community which emanates from these poems lies the continuing possibility of independence for the individual imagination.

But arguments based on biography are at best speculative. If we turn to the poems themselves we are on firmer ground. Not only the excellence of the individual odes but the extraordinarily moving structure of their sum suggest a decisive awareness on Horace's part of his poetic, and therefore of his intellectual and moral, design. That is to say, he is fitting Augustus to his own mental vision, not his plan to Augustus' design. He is inventing, and we continue to reinvent through him, his own version of the Augustus of 13 B.C.[6]

The placement of the long poems to Drusus and Tiberius, odes 4 and 14, which have most elicited the displeasure of critics, is a case in point. I will look at these odes later in detail, noting their ironies and assaying the various ways in which Horace makes lyric of epic's intransigent material, expanding its emotional possibility or calming its vehemence by framing it within a hymn. Here it must suffice to observe that their respective positions as fourth and penultimate in the book's progress are in neither case climactic. Each is followed by

[6]I abide by 13 B.C., traditional date of publication for *Odes* 4. The emotional focus of the book, from the second to the penultimate poem, is on the return of Augustus from his campaigning in Gaul during the summer of that year. The attempt by G. Williams (*Horace,* 44–49) to date the collection to 8 B.C., the year of the poet's death, raises more problems than it solves. For instance, would it have been suitable to publish two odes in which Drusus plays a prominent role in the year after his death?

a lyric eulogy of Augustan stabilities, and the fourth, in particular, fits carefully into a larger pattern of poems on human mutability and personal loss, so that we are forced to restudy it in a way its Pindaric surface does not at first demand.

I practice here what I hold as a basic premise, that a book of poems should be read as a developing entity, to be analyzed as it evolves from poem to poem. This does not mean that I will forgo the scrutiny of themes, motifs, images, and the like that permeate the book— my work is dependent on critics who have already done so. It is merely that I put the emphasis, literally, on consequences. I will watch, as I follow out such a linear "reading," not only how themes recur and are reviewed and reexamined over a series of very different odes, but how the friction of poem against poem in context can help expand on previous interpretations and generate new approaches, both to individual lyrics and to the book as a whole. The structures that I sense in the collection, therefore, have arisen from examining it as a sequence and not because I have traced certain notions—love, death, patriotism, poetry, and the like—or patterns of imagery— birds, fire, water, and so forth—and attempted to group the poems under such headings.[7] These ideas and their poetic embellishments are, I need scarcely add, crucial to the poems and to the discussions of them which follow. The change of emphasis will, I trust, both reconfirm their presence and illuminate further both content and expression because of this new angle of critical vision.

To read linearly is, paradoxically, to demand of a book that it stand as a cycle as well. We unroll the papyrus, or turn the pages of a book, as we advance from poem to poem. But what we learn as we follow out such a narrative of lyrics is a cumulative matter. It is a process of discovery which never reaches an end. It forces us, once we have

---

[7]Analysis by theme has been the critical principle of Fraenkel (*Horace,* see n. 5 above), Ludwig (*passim*), Becker (*Das Spätwerk,* 116–93), and La Penna (136–47). The numerological schema of Ludwig (8) is modified by La Penna at 139–40. Porter's detailed analysis of the manifold images that adorn these themes ("The Recurrent Motifs," *passim*) is most sensitive to the nuances of the book as a whole. Though he groups the poems by category and, save for the three central odes, in an apparently haphazard though climactic order (he ends with odes 5 and 15), Fraenkel (*Horace,* 410) is quite correct when he states that no other extant poetry book of the Augustan period "shows so refined an arrangement."

finished any such gathering of poems, to begin over again, with earlier questions answered and beauties elucidated, but with new issues, needing explanations, being raised, and new areas of connotation ever opening out.

Both of these mutually indispensable ways of reading, the linear and the cyclical, put special stress on the beginning and concluding poems of a sequence. The former must be programmatic and outline, in however idiosyncratic a manner, what is to follow; the latter, in its act of closure, must summarize the preceding poetic performance. But it must also remain suggestive enough of new ways of considering the total book that it returns our attention, here with the help of meticulous verbal allusions, to the opening poem, leading to the act of rereading and to a richer mastery of the whole.

The contents of the first ode forewarn us, as critics have noted, that we may expect among the lyrics that follow poems concerned with love, with the pressures of temporality and its results (loss of youthful bloom and desirability, age and death), and with the personages of contemporary Rome, most particularly, as it turns out, Augustus himself. By the time we conclude the last poem we discover that we have been reading a series of poems about artistry and its many forms, about grace and its manifestations, especially in the acts of speaking and writing, and about the importance of festivity and ritual, whether specific or general, in human life. This in turn recalls for us how important these notions are to ode 1. But the conclusion of ode 15 is also sensitive to the renewal and fostering of traditions of poetic performance, and this, too, reminds us that the initial ode is devoted to love-making, which is also to say poetry-making, in a tradition of erotic lyric that is amply illustrated—and alluded to in the ode itself—from Sappho to Catullus to Horace himself.

Just as the initial poem, ironically, is a leave-taking from the writing of private amatory lyric (a metaphor for its plot which sketches an end to love-making except in a dream), so the concluding ode offers a series of novelties and of new starts. It varies the tradition of encomium, of refusal-poem and of the *sphragis,* the poetic "seal" through which the creator imprints the stamp of his own "I" onto his book. It revitalizes old vocabulary and invents new words. Above all it seeks to refresh ways of poetic expression which hark back hypothetically to a communal, public lyric in the Roman past, to be sung now in the Roman future. It is an epilogue that is also a prologue, to song in the hereafter and to a reexamination of the collection it concludes.

In sum, both poems 1 and 15 look to past and present poetic achievements, to origins and renewals, whether the tradition in question is to be dismissed—itself an act of renewal—or espoused, whether the poet adopts a private or a public persona. And this regard for the conception and refreshment of poetry and its heritage calls to our attention the fact that the book's circularity, and the lyric tradition of which it is a major example, reinforce in its very mode of composition what is perhaps the book's primary ideological theme. This is, first, the ability of Rome to renovate itself, be it in the immediate moment of Augustus' return from a period abroad or on the deeper level of moral and secular refurbishment. Such a motif is complemented by the concomitant, essential capability of poetry's ritual to effect continuous renewal for itself, for its imaginer, and for his chosen subjects, especially Rome and the wielders of her power.

It is a dictum of Robert Frost that "A poem is best read in the light of all the other poems ever written," and I endeavor here to practice a very limited version of this difficult maxim. Some poets—Donne, for instance—do not readily betray direct influence from the literary past they knew so well. Horace, like most of his Latin colleagues, is different, for his poetry is rich with references to his Greco-Roman heritage. I will consider this allusiveness a critical tool, and use it to denominate many of the traditions from which Horace's multifaceted versions of lyric spring and to appraise their originality. Though Horace's intellectual ancestry in these poems stems from Homer and extends through many of antiquity's major literary figures, I am particularly interested in two areas: Horace's use of his earlier work and his attraction to, and reevaluation of, the work of his great contemporaries, Virgil and Propertius.

Self-referentiality in Horace's fourth book is, as we would expect, largely limited to bows toward the *Epodes* and the first collection of odes, and is of importance to a critic in evaluating both the ongoing evolution of lyric genres in Horatian practice and the ideological mutations in Horace's career as it progresses toward its conclusion. Since, for Virgil and Propertius, we are dealing not with lyric but, in the first case, pastoral, georgic, and especially epic, in the second, elegy, I will focus chiefly on the influence of content rather than form.

Though the presence of Virgil's *Eclogues* and *Georgics* is felt in *Odes* 4, and will be noted in the pages which follow, I am particularly interested in the power exerted by the *Aeneid*. We must remember that if the *Aeneid* was published shortly after Virgil's death in September 19, as is most plausible, then, with the possible exception of Propertius' final book of elegies, *Odes* 4 is the first masterpiece of Roman letters to betray the effect of viewing the epic as an entity. (There is little doubt that in his earlier grouping of odes, published in 23, Horace exhibits interest in, and influence from, Virgil's poem in progress. To read and react to the complete text is a different matter.) I am not bent on cataloging yet again Horace's nods toward Aeneas, the translation of Troy to Rome, and the hypothetical beginnings of the Julio-Claudians (the most obvious references are to be found in odes 4, 6, 7, and 15). What I will pursue is a moral dialogue between poets whereby, to put the situation too simply, the idealized future time of the *Aeneid* becomes the lyricist's Augustan present, and the dubious uses of force in the epic's foreground yield to Horace's portrayal of an era of peace in which even the problematic military excursions of Drusus and Tiberius, aimed at the consolidation of empire, are safely harbored by contexts of eulogy and prayer.

The creative interchange with Propertius is not dissimilar. Here I will be attending primarily to his third book of elegies, published, according to received opinion, in 22 B.C. soon after Horace's first collection of odes whose influence marks it clearly. It is Horace's turn, in his fourth book, to rethink many of the subjects which claimed Propertius' attention, ranging from the immortalizing power of poetry (and the immortality of poets), in the initial elegies of book 3, to the power of the poet-seer to predict and implement the process of aging in the last elegy of the book. The emperor is never far distant from these poems. But Propertius' contemplation of Augustus and the morality of his politics, either of themselves or as potential subjects for poetry, always elicits ironic treatment of the one or rejection of the other. In the next decade, as he writes his fourth book, Horace looks thoughtfully at these poems of the elegist while crafting an opposite estimation of contemporary Rome. (I cannot condone the opinion prevalent among literary historians that Horace viewed

Propertius with disdain, and that the portrait of the Roman "Callimachus," in *Epistles* 2.1, who is surely Propertius, is treated with any greater irony than that which Horace expends on himself, a latter-day Alcaeus. That the two poets carefully built on and revised each other, as work succeeded work, argues for a mutual respect that surmounts any superficial distinctions of tone or content.)[8]

I argued earlier that the quality of individual poems, including the so-called occasional pieces, and of the whole book is proof of the combination of independence and commitment that lay behind its production. This integrity is further confirmed by the cohesion of the intellectual "biography" that the fifteen poems present. I am not here advocating a return to the autobiographical fallacy; however, the portrait that emerges of the creative mind which formulated the fifteen diverse "masks" of *Odes* 4 is a remarkably consistent composition. Speakers subject to age and losing the battle against temporality are sporadically and then finally replaced by other singers who preach the triumph of the Augustan moment and its poetry over time, and therefore of art over life. Yet both sets of speakers are obverse and reverse of the same coin. These Janus-like personae are much like what we would expect Horace to fashion for himself as, in his final lyric maturity, he became the praiser of Rome's immortality as well as the swan singer of his own private farewells. The social lyricist counterpoints and eventually replaces the vanishing chanter of the self's sensualities. I have therefore from time to time, especially when the narrating "I" details facts that harmonize with what we know to have been the poet's lived experience, yielded to the temptation to label his individual speakers, as well as their inventor, "Horace," though this is out of present academic fashion. Let me offer a few brief comments on this approach to unity as final preparation for prodding the poems into speaking for themselves.

What is initially most moving as one reviews the fourth book's linear strategy is the change from private to public voices. This mutation is not accomplished with sudden drama. No lightning bolt of conversion strikes a speaker already venturing unwittingly on the road

---

[8]The relationship is treated by Flach (92–97) with a review of past opinion and its two basic divisions (93, n. 58; cf. also, most recently, Babcock, 1607, n. 129). The proper call to dismiss the notion of a quarrel between the two poets is made by Ross (136, n. 2). It is not heeded by Luck (414) who speaks of "the slightly foppish elegist caricatured" by Horace, if this happens to be Propertius.

to Rome and Augustus. Rather the change from the first poem—a lyric devoted to youth and age, love gained and lost—to the last—a grand eulogy of the emperor—is a microcosm of the whole, as odes on the encroachments of time on individual speakers punctuate, and finally give way to, encomia on Augustus and the contemporary world at large. It is as if Horace, in his parade of personae, was deliberately forgoing the human body, with its dwindling passions and vulnerability to temporality and death, as a source of inspiration, and replacing it gradually, then climactically, with the more enduring entity of historical Rome and the godlike restorer of its golden age.

But if poetry of private loss defers to poetry of community and social responsibility, it also, as we will see, gives place regularly to odes on the immortality of poetry and through it of the poet and his subjects, even if the subject is his own evanescence. Even in the private poems where this power is least in evidence, the speaker is always revealing the truth—about himself to us, about others to themselves (as well as to us)—and in one remarkable instance (ode 13) he actually spurs the arrival of senescence. The five poems, which round off each grouping of three as the book unfolds, strongly proclaim and demonstrate this strength of the poet and his artifact. In two of these, odes 3 and 9, the birth of the poet-singer not only contrasts with the meditations on aging and death which precede each but also offers evidence for his own continuing rebirth in the first of these poems, for that of Lollius, in the second. The sixth ode, about the crafting of the *Carmen Saeculare,* promises perpetuity to Rome through the perpetuity of poetry. The twelfth ode rounds out a duet that pledges to sequester the speakers' guests from the pressures of time each knows so well. The immediate means of achieving this relief from temporality is festivity, but the deeper remedy is poetry's ritual of song and music. Finally we have the extraordinary ultimate poem, on the surface a many-sided *laudatio* of Augustus, but also a summary of past poetry and a revision of its traditions, particularly that of lyric. It presents itself as an example of what its last lines crave, namely, a poetry that through the imagination's wit recalls to the memory and therefore projects into the future what is worthy to be repeated from the past.

Song, quite literally, has the last word. If praises of Augustus and Rome supersede, in group after group, poems on private bereavements, the final position and the final potentiality are given to poems

[29]

on poetry. If any one notion pervades the book as a whole it is the idea of return, reintegration, revitalization, whether it be of Augustus, of the seasons, of historical Rome.[9] And the dynamism to accomplish these magical acts stems from the grandeur of poetry which conjures their possibility before the audience of our imagination.

[9]I disagree here with Porter who considers the idea of return a "minor motif" in the book as a whole ("The Recurrent Motifs," 226, n. 74, with reference to Fraenkel, *Horace,* Commager, *Odes,* and Dyer).

PART ONE

The Loving Muse:
Odes 1–3

[Nobility] is the imagination pressing back against the pressure of reality. It seems, in the last analysis, to have something to do with our self-preservation; and that, no doubt, is why the expression of it, the sound of words, helps us to live our lives.

Wallace Stevens, "The Noble
Rider and the Sound of Words"

[1]

ODE ONE

Intermissa, Venus, diu
  rursus bella moves? parce precor, precor.
non sum qualis eram bonae
  sub regno Cinarae. desine, dulcium

mater saeva Cupidinum,   5
  circa lustra decem flectere mollibus
iam durum imperiis; abi,
  quo blandae iuvenum te revocant preces.

tempestivius in domum
  Pauli purpureis ales oloribus   10
comissabere Maximi,
  si torrere iecur quaeris idoneum.

namque et nobilis et decens
  et pro sollicitis non tacitus reis
et centum puer artium   15
  late signa feret militiae tuae,

et quandoque potentior
  largi muneribus riserit aemuli,
Albanos prope te lacus
  ponet marmoream sub trabe citrea.   20

illic plurima naribus
  duces tura lyraque et Berecyntia
delectabere tibia
  mixtis carminibus non sine fistula;

illic bis pueri die   25
  numen cum teneris virginibus tuum
laudantes pede candido
  in morem Salium ter quatient humum.

me nec femina nec puer
  iam nec spes animi credula mutui   30
nec certare iuvat mero
  nec vincire novis tempora floribus.

sed cur heu, Ligurine, cur
  manat rara meas lacrima per genas?
cur facunda parum decoro   35
  inter verba cadit lingua silentio?

nocturnis ego somniis
  iam captum teneo, iam volucrem sequor
te per gramina Martii
  campi, te per aquas, dure, volubilis.   40

Venus, are you again stirring wars long in abeyance? Have pity, I pray, I pray. I am not such as I was under the reign of kindly Cinara. Cease, merciless mother of honied Lusts, to twist with your soft sway someone calloused by a near half-century. Away, whither the soothing supplications of the young hail you back.

Aloft on purple swans, you will revel more timely to the abode of Paulus Maximus, if you search to sear a fitting heart. For he is both noble and gracious, and vocal in defense of worried wards. Boy of a hundred arts, he will carry afield the banners of your service, and when he will laugh, triumphant over the largesse of a spendthrift rival, he will establish you in marble beneath a citron roof beside the lakes of Alba. There your nostrils will sniff abundant draughts of incense, and you will be gladdened by songs blending with lyre, and Berecyntian flute, and pipe as well. There, twice a day, boys, chanting your divinity in company with gentle girls, will with spotless feet thrice set the ground to shake, compliant with the Salian rite.

Neither woman nor boy delights me now, nor the beguiled hope for a responding mind, nor vying in our cups, nor binding brows with fresh flowers. But, alas, why, Ligurinus, why does a fitful tear trickle across my cheeks? Why does my eloquent tongue amid its words fall into a less than graceful silence? Now I clasp you, grasped in my dreams at night, now I pursue you, aflight through the grasses of Mars' field, you, callous, through the fluent waves.

For guidance in choosing the subject matter for the initial ode in what proves to be his final collection, Horace could turn to many exemplary models, not least to his own past accomplishment. The initial astonished question, directed by apostrophe to the unexpectedly present love-goddess, draws the reader into the time-frame of the speaker's life. The number of years in Horace's biography, which his speaker leaves vague with the metaphoric *intermissa bella* and *sub regno Cinarae,* we know to have been almost exactly a decade, from 23 B.C., when he probably released his first collection, to 13, when the fourth book of odes was most likely published. But to meditate on a lyricist's past life means also to ponder past poetry and to reflect on how Horace chooses here to project himself, especially by comparison with the introductory poems of the initial collection. Each of the earlier three poems announces a distinction between the speaker and other ways of thinking and living. The priamel that initiates the first book pits the poet-seer against partisans of other careers that range from Olympic driver to soldier and hunter. The first poem of book 2 addresses Pollio, poised to write the treacherous horrors of civil war, an intellectual endeavor as unsuitable to the poet's "lighter plectrum" as it is sharply detailed by it. Finally the grand statement that initiates the "Roman" odes of book 3 juxtaposes the speaker's moral and stylistic restraint, practiced in a Sabine retreat, with more expansive ambitions and their consequent trials.

By contrast to these earlier prologues the fourth book's initial ode is a far more initimate, revelatory poem whose essence looks to self-definition not by contrast with others but by distinctions within the experience of the speaker himself. The figure of speech that helps divine these differences is oxymoron. In confronting the battles renewed by a harsh love-goddess whose progeny are sweet desires, the speaker acknowledges the division between his "hardness" to love and her "soft" imperatives, between the age of him who must plead for her forbearance during her unwonted epiphany and the youth of those whose prayers should seduce her into their more suitable presence. It is a brilliant poem about love put into the mouth of someone who apparently has the power and the desire to command love away.[1] Of these three jurisdictions presided over, respectively, by Venus, aging speaker, and charming youth, time and appropriateness combine only the first and the last. The richly metaphoric opening stanzas dwell only on interior emotional space. If we search for detail about a literal scenario, we learn only that Venus has suddenly appeared before the speaker and that she should return to those who summon her back whither she belongs.[2] For the central five stanzas of the poem the speaker restores Venus in the mind's eye to her correct realm, that of young Paulus Fabius Maximus. It is a setting as palpable as it is symbolic. The military metaphors remain. Unlike the reluctant speaker, Paulus will carry Venus' standards into battle and defeat a prospective rival, and we are reminded by mention of his liver, which she roasts, that synecdoche also shares in detailing the onslaught of youthful love.

Yet, as the poem changes orientation from the speaker's inner world to the *domus* of Paulus, we enter a sphere where immediate external detail is paramount. We watch Venus, winged on purple

---

[1]The interpretation of ode 1 as an ἀποπομπή is proposed by Fraenkel (*Horace,* 412). This view is disputed by Lefèvre who sees the poem as a *recusatio* whereby the poet states his own inability to write further love poems while positing more suitable singers for Venus elsewhere. That the poem is essentially cultic is argued by Weinreich, but even the ancient commentators saw it as an allegory concerned with poetic themes (Porphyrion on lines 1–2; pseudo-Acron on line 1). Pasquali (146) recognizes the ode's role as preface and Fraenkel (*Horace,* 413) defines it as an "overture" to a series of love poems and of portraits of great men. Perret (135) finds the book possessing "no real prologue." Rudd (382) views the poem as anticipating "several themes which occur later, viz. love, aging, poetry, and the praise of a distinguished contemporary." The themes of youth and age are discussed by Porter, "The Recurrent Motifs," 198. Bradshaw (especially 146) examines details of the portrayal of Paulus Fabius Maximus, seeing in it evidence for an *epithalamium.*

[2]Syndikus (289, 294), discusses the opening and closing of the poem as mimetic of passionate speech. He also points out the novelty of the initial stanzas being given from the point of view of the old man (286, 293). The poem's first word, *intermissa,* is a declaration of novelty. Like *comissabere* (11), it is first used here in Latin poetry, with the exception of its appearance in comedy.

swans, ready to participate in his revelry. Then we learn of Paulus himself—aristocratic, graceful, a notable lawyer and artist, broadly defined. He embodies one of Venus' standard characteristics, for he will smile after besting his competition at love's games.[3] He will also use his aesthetic talent to enshrine his patroness's marble statue in a richly sensuous setting, in view of the Alban lakes, sheltered with beams of citron wood. And, as this vision of the future expands still more graphically, the temple becomes the locale for celebrations in her honor, with incense adding to the fragrance of the citron and with songs accompanied by lyre, flute, and syrinx to delight the ear. There festivity will do her continuous homage, with boys and girls, twice a day in triple Salian beat, dancing her praise.

From the vivid center, into which he has imagined his unwelcome visitor, we return for the poem's concluding stanzas first to the musings of the speaker. His litany, which balances the earlier details of her worship, briskly catalogs the losses time brings. Not for him any new amours, male or female, who inspire hope of mutuality, nor the wine and flowers that attend love-making. Then, with an unexpected reenactment of interrogative statement and the excited diction with which the poem opens, the speaker suddenly offers contravening evidence. Venus is, after all, still present in his life in the person of the boy Ligurinus, her emblem. As her surrogate he receives a further set of apostrophes that balance the opening address and bring the poem to a cyclic finale with the announcement that there is a second person still emotionally vivid in the poet's life, even if only in his nocturnal hallucinations.

The center of the poem envisions a Venus stabilized apart from the poet, courted by Fabius Maximus. Framing this core is the emotional truth of her immediacy, emotionally conveyed. But there is a distinction between the poem's beginning and end which suggests further interpretations. At the poem's start winged Venus has lodged herself with the speaker who orders her off. By the conclusion the dreaming speaker is wishing to capture Ligurinus or to follow him as he practices swift sports in Rome's center or flees toward waters as fickle as his speeding form (the alliteration from *volucrem* to *volubilis* urges the connection).[4] And we now find the same speaker, who initially styled himself *durus* to Venus' importunities, labeling his young phantom-

---

[3]Horace has his own smiling Venus at *c.* 1.2.23 (*Erycina ridens*).

[4]To visit the *campus Martius* is to survey the area where Ligurinus would have been sporting himself, with the entranced speaker no doubt watching his athlet-

lover equally *durus* for not softening to his desires. Winged Venus comes unbidden to the poet, and at the poem's end her symbol, Ligurinus, takes flight, attracting the somnolent, aging lover in his wake.

This active, emotional, centrifugal outline, as the speaker succumbs, at least in thought, to the allure of evanescent youth and fleeting love, contrasts with the anchoring of Venus at the poem's core where she belongs. In dealing with Paulus, *nobilis, decorus,* and a good rhetor, the tone is itself decorous and well-spoken, even a bit baroque. In looking at himself, suddenly afflicted with unexpected emotion, the speaker's tone is excited and brisk, the rhetoric filled with repetitions and parallelisms. Venus' effect on the speaker in lines 35–36, for instance, is carefully plotted. Line 35 is hypermetric, exemplifying in its unusual excess the lack of spoken fluency (*facunda cadit lingua*) and the graceless silence (*parum decoro silentio*) that her advent brings to the aging speaker.[5] If she were to accept a position in marble at the focus of Paulus', and of the poem's, life, she would be the firm emblem of stability in a setting fully appropriate to her, one that complements her as she complements it. By contrast with the (ironically) stumbling speaker at the end, Paulus Fabius Maximus is both *decens,* seemly in behavior, and an eloquent lawyer.[6] As a *nobilis* and a "boy of a hundred arts," he knows presumably the *artes* of political endeavor. What the poem also tells us, in anticipation, is his appreciation of the sensory beauty—visual, olfactory, aural—neces-

---

icism. We think of Sybaris in *c.* 1.8.3–4, whose athletic life on the *apricum campum* has been disrupted by Lydia's charms, or Enipeus in *c.* 3.7.26, whose equestrian prowess on Mars' turf (*gramine Martio*) should not distract Asterie from her absent lover (cf. also *A. P.* 162). Horace makes the connection of *volubilis,* water and time's passing at *epi.* 1.2.43 when he speaks of a stream as *in omne volubilis aevum,* forever rolling on. See also Porter, "The Recurrent Motifs," 198, n. 13.

[5]The metrical irregularity is treated by Commager, "Some Horatian Vagaries," 65–66.

In connection with the distinction between speech and silence that runs through the poem, the pun on *volubilis,* the poem's final word, is particularly noteworthy. The waters are rolling but also fluent, for young Ligurinus, by a type of hypallage, is still, and finally, associated with what the aging, tongue-tied speaker now claims to lack—the ability to speak readily.

[6]On the importance of propriety for the poem as a whole see Reckford, "Some Studies," 29–30.

sary to create a suitable habitat for the goddess of passion. Paulus' worship of her is in several senses "decorative."

In sum, her potential monumentalization, stabilized at the center of the poem and of Maximus' life, is a visual counterpart to the abstractions that secure him so firmly to Roman greatness—*nobilitas* of character as well as ancestry, *decus* of spirit and of physique, eloquence (*facundia*) placed at the disposal of his world, and an aesthetic appreciation that enhances its beauty. Venus' liaison with the speaker, whatever his lingering regrets at the end, is unsuitable for both, an unbecoming attempt to turn back the clock that deprives the speaker (again ironically) of his raison d'être, the communication of intense feelings in lyric verse.

This last lingering glimpse of youth and love by the speaker is also a farewell to the poetry of love and youth by the creator of the speaker, Horace himself. He is contemplating not only the Roman tradition of subjective elegy but also the lyric past as he glances back via Catullus and Anacreon, who bemoan the passing of time, to Sappho. Sappho's creative presence is felt from the poem's start. In the lyric that commentators place first in her collection, the speaker, who is addressed by Aphrodite as Sappho, prays to the goddess of love to visit her. "Beautiful swift sparrows whirring fast-beating wings" had brought her once before at a time of need.[7] Now she must return and revenge the speaker by making the girl, who is unresponsive to her, fall in love and suffer the same emotions that the speaker is presently experiencing.[8]

From what we can tell, Sappho's tour de force is an extraordinary leap from the origins of lyric in communal prayer directed to a transcendent divinity whose epiphany was occasioned for society at large, and in the imagination alone. In Sappho 1, the solitary speaker prays in confidence to her personal Aphrodite whose apparition is graphically described and whose epiphany is made still more palpable in the address by which she assures her devotee of her imminence and of her willing understanding of Sappho's plight. The very intimacy the poem projects is a form of meiosis, a witty subversion of naive social belief in epiphanic divinities through the speaker's special audience with her heavenly friend and abettor.

Horace humorously responds to his Sapphic inheritance by pre-

[7]The translation is by Campbell, in *Greek Lyric*, 53–54.
[8]I follow the interpretation of Giacomelli, 136–38.

suming a Venus really, and annoyingly, at hand, who must be importuned not to pay heed and appear but to go elsewhere, responding to the *revocatio* of those with whom she fits. Sappho's "realization" of transcendence, her pronounced humanization of the awesome, and Horace's clever variation of her apparent invention, whereby Venus' diminution is the equivalent of his loss of creative speech and her inappropriateness mirrors his, must be reversed. Looked at, therefore, as an epigone to Sappho's masterpiece, Horace's ode is a prayer for the reritualization of Venus. From a goddess who socializes with aging mortals and demeans them along with herself, she is asked to regain a fitting status and station elsewhere, intimate with her proper worshipers in the formal semblance of a marble replica. She should become a decorous adjunct to their decorousness.

This very propriety, which includes the sensuality of incense and music, and the thudding wildness of Salian rhythms, creates an exotic scenario from which the no longer young speaker is outlawed. But, to add still another level of irony, the very self-awareness the speaker now possesses (and which youthful Paulus implicitly lacks in the charmed world the speaker invents for him) makes his love all the more profound, and his final love poetry all the more moving. Venus, in fact, is still essential in his life, is still, for one last moment, his Muse.

The Sapphic tradition exerts itself for a final time in the manifestations of love, the occasional tear, the tongue dropping into unseemly silence, which the astonished speaker is forced to scrutinize as his own in the next to last stanza. The poet is perhaps alluding to Catullus' clinical evaluation of the symptoms of passion (51.9–10):

> lingua sed torpet, tenuis sub artus
> flamma demanat. . . .

. . . but my tongue grows numb and a slender flame drips under my limbs . . .

But Catullus is only gently varying the Sapphic original (31.9–10, 13):

ἀλλ' ἄκαν μὲν γλῶσσα †ἔαγε λέπτον
δ' αὔτικα χρῶι πῦρ ὐπαδεδρόμηκεν,

. . .

κὰδ δέ μ' ἴδρως κακχέεται, . . .

. . . but my tongue is broken, and a gentle flame has forthwith coursed
under my skin, . . . and sweat pours down me, . . .

In Sappho the lover's tongue is shattered, in Catullus, numbed.
Horace's falls into a silence striking for its absence among the properly loquacious partisans of Venus earlier in the poem. As for the
image of falling liquid, Sappho's mixture of figurative (fire racing)
with literal (sweat streaming down) is concisely turned by Catullus
with the extraordinary oxymoron *flamma demanat*. Horace looks back
to both, yet this time it is neither flame nor sweat that pours down,
only an occasional tear, as if plenitude of emotion were no longer
possible or as if love brought forth tears not only of yearning but of
sorrow because fulfillment is now scarcely retrievable, and only then
in a dream.

One of the reasons the ending is so moving is exactly this last grasp
at the tradition of private lyric. If the beginning of the poem, by
allusion to Sappho, looks to the (near) renunciation of those individual desires that are at the root of lyric, so the final spasm of love at
the end, by furthering the remembrance of the lyric past, is also a
final clutching at that same past, which is to attempt, humanly and
poetically, to stay young and remain able to articulate the poetry of
love. Ligurinus is to Horace what Octavian is to the Marschallin or
Tadziu to Aschenbach, at once real and symbolic. We will watch
both Ligurinus and Venus undergo their own very different metamorphoses as the book unfolds.

In beginning his book, then, with a poem devoted to the tension
between temporality and eroticism in the life of the aging speaker, the
poet takes cognizance of two influential figures from his lyric past.
Thus, here at least, to contemplate the effect of the passage of time on
amatory experience is to measure oneself against lyric expression of
that experience over a length of literary time, to contemplate the
speaker's human, and the poet's literary, past. Horace adds a new
dimension to his poetic inheritance at the same time as his persona

divulges the novelty of late, troubling love, purging himself of the tradition of amatory lyric and yet renewing it as well.

Horace also makes a careful and, for him, unusually conspicuous bow to his own creative past by incorporating, as line 5, the whole opening verse of *c.* 1.19.[9] Even in that poem, as he prepares to soften the force of Venus' arrival by offering her a calming sacrifice—victim for victim—the speaker claims to be finished with love (*finitis amoribus*). Yet, beyond his control, he is comically pulled back into the erotic life by Venus' power, which exerts itself over what he might say as well as do:

> in me tota ruens Venus
>   Cyprum deseruit nec patitur Scythas
> et versis animosum equis
>   Parthum dicere nec quae nihil attinent.

Venus has left Cyprus behind, rushing upon me with all her might, nor does she allow me to sing of the Scythians and the spirited Parthian, his horses turned in flight, nor of anything that has no bearing.

To write erotic lyric is, for a poet, equivalent to embarking on an affair of the heart, the situation in which the speaker nearly finds himself in ode 1. But the Venus of ode 1, instead of making a powerful arrival, is already unexpectedly present and must, somehow, be exorcised. In the process, however, the speaker's own lyric past momentarily floods in on him, for it, too, must be remembered in order to be prayed away as concomitant with love itself and with the fierce goddess who presides over love's adventures. Different *bella* loom in the poet's imminent future.

This literary self-consciousness, as the poet places himself in the line of his lyric inheritance and in relation to his own past, will prove of equal importance in the two poems that follow, and I will have more to say when I survey all three as a group. Beyond this direct interest in poetry and beyond the prominent place given to the themes of love and time, there is much else in this initial poem that is programmatic for the book as a whole. From the erotic plot that

---

[9]The placement of *c.* 1.19 is, in its way, as important as that of ode 1 here. It comes at the conclusion of the first half of book 1 of the *Odes* and precedes an address to Maecenas which initiates the second half.

frames the poem Horace will abstract the figure of Venus and change her notably at the end of his collection, and the tension the story line suggests between motion and stability, arrival and departure, absence and return, fickleness and steadfastness, insecurity and certainty, will be put through a series of mutations in the subsequent odes. But ideas that we find literally central in this poem, in the depiction of Paulus Fabius Maximus, one of many notable contemporaries whom the poet will proceed to address, will be equally dominant throughout the book. We can subsume this material under the general title of artistry, for the poems that follow are often concerned with the conditions for and achievement of monumentality. Ode 1 introduces us to the fine arts through the temple of Venus and her statue, but, fittingly enough, it is to words and their use that Horace most expansively attends. We find the poet's concern, of course, manifested in the natural eloquence of Paulus (eloquence the speaker soon claims to have lost, in stanzas of particular rhetorical brilliance), as appropriate for love-making as the speaker's self-styled hesitancy is awkward. We see it in the songs and sounds offered for Venus' delectation. Words and music, as the essence of lyric verse, will be a frequent subject in book 4, culminating in the lyre, flute, and *carmina* that accompany the ceremonies of communal pride, in the collection's final poem. Last, there is the attendant idea of ritual festivity, to the meaning of which song most notably contributes. We have celebrations of triumph and of restoration, of occasions as grand as secular renewal and as limited as a birthday, of a private feast to distract its participants from life's trials or of a public rejoicing for Augustus and for the multivalent splendor of his accomplishment.

In ode 1 the special emotions of the speaker surround the imagined depiction of a ritual celebration in which the speaker should have no part. In the next poem, the speaker is also involved with a moment of rejoicing in which he can partake in a way that maintains his own sense of decorum. But before I look ahead I would like to turn back to ode 1 and examine possible reasons for the poet's choice of the name Ligurinus for his boy-love. I draw my suggestion from the *Aeneid* where one of the few prominent Ligurians is Cupavo who shares the leadership of their contingent coming to the aid of Aeneas.[10] His ancestry is of interest to readers of Horace:

[10]*Aen.* 10.185–93. The other Ligurian in the *Aeneid* is the unnamed son of Aunus who fails in his attempt to dupe Camilla (11.699–724). There is a sim-

Non ego te, Ligurum ductor fortissime bello,
transierim, Cinyre, et paucis comitate Cupavo,
cuius olorinae surgunt de vertice pinnae
(crimen, Amor, vestrum) formaeque insigne paternae.
namque ferunt luctu Cycnum Phaethontis amati,
populeas inter frondes umbramque sororum
dum canit et maestum musa solatur amorem,
canentem molli pluma duxisse senectam,
linquentem terras et sidera voce sequentem.

Nor would I pass by you, Cinyras, bravest leader of the Ligurians in battle, and you, Cupavo, accompanied by your small troop, from whose crest swan feathers arise, a badge of your father's shape (the reproach, O Love, belongs to you). For they say that Cycnus, mourning for his beloved Phaethon, while singing and with poetry consoling the sadness of his love amid the shade of his sisters' poplar boughs, took to himself whitening age with soft feathers, abandoning the earth and following the stars with his cry.

Cupavo's father Cycnus, the swan, was in love with Phaethon.[11] At his death he underwent metamorphosis into the bird that bears his name, and Cupavo wears swan's plumage on his crest as a remembrance. Ovid describes the mutation,[12] and Servius, in his note on Virgil's lines, gives a brief biography: "There was a Ligurian, Cycnus by name, gifted by Apollo with song's sweetness, lover of Phaethon."[13] This "sweetness," with which the god of poetry favored him, is based on an etymological play between Ligur-Ligus and λιγύς, "clear-voiced." Pausanias alludes to the connection when he mentions a musician named Cycnus who was king of the Ligurians.[14]

---

ilarity here, too, with Ligurinus as trickster, the phantom deceiver who relies on speed but who also stands, no doubt, for the speaker's bemused self-deception. The speaker is fickle because of his indecorous pursuit of the unfitting. Ligurinus is fickle, swift, and full of transformations, because he represents young love.

[11]Most recently, Ahl (esp. 389) treats the Phaethon–Cycnus myth and includes a full bibliography on the symbolism of swans in literature.

[12]M. 2.367–80.

[13]Servius on Aen. 10.189 (fuit etiam Ligur, Cycnus nomine, dulcedine cantus ab Apolline donatus, amator Phaethontis. . .).

[14]1.30.3.

The relationship of the myth of Cycnus to ode 1 is manifold. First, on the level of plot, is the association of homosexuality with each relationship. Second, Ligurinus is envisioned as a bird, *volucris*, speeding off over land and sea. Yet, as we noted earlier, Ligurinus is a synecdoche for Venus whom, therefore, the somnolent speaker does in fact pursue at the poem's conclusion, though he prays her away at its start. Now Venus' arrival, winged on her purple swans (*purpureis ales oloribus*), has never been satisfactorily explained. She had been awarded the adjective "purple" (πορφυρῆ) by Anacreon,[15] and Horace himself, no doubt in emulation of the sparrows to whom Sappho gives the task, invents her swan-drawn chariot.[16] But for the first time in literature not only are her swans purple but she herself is winged, akin to the creatures who bear her aloft.

We may debate the meaning of *purpureus* here. It is not unlikely that Horace was thinking of passages such as *Aeneid* 1.590–91, where Venus sheds the "purple light of youth" (*lumen . . . iuventae purpureum*) on her hero son, and that he was using purple as the color of youth and love, appropriate both for the goddess of love and for her self-extension, Ligurinus.[17] What I think clarifies the poem's texture more directly is the connection between Venus, winged on her swans, and the birdlike Ligurinus, made through the myth of Cycnus, the swan of Liguria. Finally one can speculate, especially in a poem so attuned to the act of speaking and to the inheritance of lyric discourse, on the meaning of Ligurinus as "clear-voiced" and on the association of the swan not only with Venus and love but with Apollo and song. As the speaker's unexpected, youthful love, Ligurinus serves as a reminder of exactly what he appears to be, evanescent youth and eroticism. For the poet, however, this attractive dulcet-toned, winged creature is also the lure of the lyric past, the pull toward the voice and song of private desire that once was, but can no longer be, his. Ligurinus is very much the speaker-poet's former self.

For the epilogue of his second book of odes Horace had imagined himself changed into a swan, surveying from on high the terrestrial domain his imagination had conquered, so assured of immortality

[15]357.3("a unique epithet," according to Campbell, *A Selection*, 319).

[16]*C.* 3.28.15.

[17]In his comment on *Aen.* 1.590, Austin defines *purpureus* as "the bright glow of youth and health." To his citations add Cat. 45.12 and *c.* 3.3.12. (Schoonhoven [200] treats *purpureus* as a possible *adunaton*.) At *c.* 1.30.7 *Iuventas* is a member of Venus' entourage as she is asked to approach the house of Glycera.

that there was no need for a tomb to mark his earthly remains. The prologue of his last book offers us no such certitudes. The call of the swan elicits what is in fact a moving swan song to his human and imaginative past. Ode 1 is the first of a series of carefully placed poems that meditate on the losses, usually incurred by time, that afflict the lives of individual mortals. The center of the poem proclaims what will prove central to the book as a whole, that Horace's relation to Rome and Romans will now become his chief emotional focus. But what remains at the end is a reflection on human aging with only a wistful dream of escaping time's ravages.

Yet perhaps there is even here a hint at a reversal of this negative process. If we view Ligurinus as an actual youthful lover, then on the level of mere story the inappropriateness of the speaker's reverie is apparent. If, however, he stands for the speaker's lost, or better vanishing youth, then the Ligurian swan becomes an emblem of the speaker himself, something he wants to be or remain, but cannot. From this point of view the metamorphosis of the swan image in the next two closely allied poems should be closely watched. In ode 2, Pindar is the Dircaean swan whose expansive style the ironic speaker dares not emulate. Ode 3, by contrast, finds the speaker, ward of Melpomene, praising his Muse for giving the sound of the swan to mute fish, should she choose. At the end of the book's opening trilogy, "swan song" betokens neither the foolish allure of lost love and youth nor the sublime utterance of an inimitable Greek poet but the music of poetry itself, something the now modest speaker subtly takes to himself. To follow the Sirens' melody of dwindling eroticism is to dream the impossible, to point up the passage of time in the speaker's life. To take to oneself the emblem of song, to adopt the sound of the swan, in pursuing one's vocation as poet is, by contrast, to announce one's immortality, to incorporate duly the voice of eternal rebirth rather than manifest a foolish hankering after a human status no longer feasible. The change from one realm to the other, from one speaker involved with aging and loss to another, plying the poet's trade and presuming himself immortal and capable of immortalizing others, will prove a consistent motif of the book as a whole.

In brief, by ode 3 we will find a poet-speaker who is himself associated with the bird of Apollo Μουσαγέτης. As creature of Melpomene, singer of μέλος, he will now assure for himself and his subjects the youth which, in the different, experiential guise he

adopts in ode 1, could no longer be his. Appropriately for its novelistic context, ode 1 looks on the surface not to any misguided, revi-
sionary permanence, untoward for senescent mortals, but only to one
last melancholy imagining of time past. But, after all its appearance as
an adieu to youthful love, the book's initial poem also carefully anticipates odes on the crafting of poetry and the calling of the poet, to
which Horace now turns.

[2]

ODE TWO

Pindarum quisquis studet aemulari,
Iulle, ceratis ope Daedalea
nititur pinnis, vitreo daturus
    nomina ponto.

monte decurrens velut amnis, imbres   5
quem super notas aluere ripas,
fervet inmensusque ruit profundo
    Pindarus ore,

laurea donandus Apollinari,
seu per audacis nova dithyrambos   10
verba devolvit numerisque fertur
    lege solutis,

seu deos regesque canit, deorum
sanguinem, per quos cecidere iusta
morte Centauri, cecidit tremendae   15
    flamma Chimaerae,

sive quos Elea domum reducit
palma caelestis pugilemve equomve
dicit et centum potiore signis
    munere donat,   20

flebili sponsae iuvenemve raptum
plorat et viris animumque moresque
aureos educit in astra nigroque
 invidet Orco.

multa Dircaeum levat aura cycnum,   25
tendit, Antoni, quotiens in altos
nubium tractus: ego apis Matinae
 more modoque,

grata carpentis thyma per laborem
plurimum, circa nemus uvidique   30
Tiburis ripas operosa parvos
 carmina fingo.

concines maiore poeta plectro
Caesarem, quandoque trahet ferocis
per sacrum clivum merita decorus   35
 fronde Sygambros,

quo nihil maius meliusve terris
fata donavere bonique divi
nec dabunt, quamvis redeant in aurum
 tempora priscum;   40

concines laetosque dies et urbis
publicum ludum super inpetrato
fortis Augusti reditu forumque
 litibus orbum.

tum meae, si quid loquar audiendum,   45
vocis accedet bona pars et "o sol
pulcer, o laudande" canam recepto
 Caesare felix.

tuque dum procedis, io Triumphe,
non semel dicemus, io Triumphe,   50

civitas omnis dabimusque divis
    tura benignis.

te decem tauri totidemque vaccae,
me tener solvet vitulus, relicta
matre qui largis iuvenescit herbis   55
    in mea vota,

fronte curvatos imitatus ignis
tertium lunae referentis ortum,
qua notam duxit, niveus videri,
    cetera fulvos.   60

    Whoever strains to rival Pindar, Iullus, depends on wings waxen after the scheme of Daedalus, soon to lend his name to the glassy sea.

    Careening like a stream down a mountainside, which rain-storms have nourished over its familiar banks, Pindar seethes and, beyond measure, rushes with fathomless sound, to be rewarded with the laurel of Apollo, whether he whirls down new words in the boldness of his dithyrambs and is carried along by rhythms freed from restraint, whether he sings of gods and kings, the blood of gods, at whose hands the Centaurs fell in a deserved death, the fire of the dread Chimaera fell, or chants of those, whether boxer or steed, whom the palm of Elis has brought home turned divine, and bestows a tribute more sturdy than a hundred statues, or laments a youth torn from his wailing bride and exalts to the stars his strength, his courage and his golden ways, and grudges them to dark Death.

    Many a gust lifts the swan of Dirce whenever, Antonius, he presses toward the lofty reaches of the clouds. I, in the way and manner of a Matine bee, culling tasty thyme, with toil on toil, around the grove and banks of moist Tibur, in my small style I sculpt my effortful songs.

    Poet of a grander strain, you will celebrate Caesar when, graced by the garland he has won, he will lead the savage Sygambri up the holy incline. (The fates and kindly gods have conferred nothing greater or better on the earth, nor will they bestow, even were the times to return to a past of gold.) You will celebrate days of joy, and the city's public games for the long-craved return of brave Augustus, and the forum rid of disputes.

    Then, if I cry anything worthy to be heard, the fit part of my voice

will join in, and I will sing "O beauteous sun, deserving of praise,"
happy at Caesar's homecoming. And, as you lead the way, all we
citizens will shout, again and again, "Hail, God of Triumph," "Hail,
God of Triumph," and we will proffer incense to the kindly gods.

Ten bulls and as many cows will fulfill your pledge, mine a slim calf
who, now that he has left his mother, grows young on swelling grasses
to implement my vows, imitating on his brow the bowed flames of the
moon as she brings back her third rising, snowy to the sight, where he
has claimed a mark, for the rest tawny.

The second ode of book 4 begins as the first had concluded, with a
figurative use of the image of flying. Now, however, the speaker is
initially concerned with the mind, not the body, with poetics, not
with desire and temporality. His advice to Iullus has a moralistic ring.
To rival Pindar is to follow the pattern of Icarus the overreacher,
attempting to be something or, in this case, someone that he was not.
In general this means for earthbound man foolishly to claim metamorphosis into a creature of the air. It also indicates reliance on the
fraudulent and the borrowed, on the wax wings that melt as their
possessor pursues his immoderate course and on the potency that
comes from Daedalus, not from within himself.[1]

But we also find ourselves observing one poet commenting on
another. (I am assuming that the scholiast is correct in attributing
twelve books of an epic *Diomedeia* to Iullus Antonius.[2] I am also,
again, presuming much of Horace himself behind the speaking persona.) For a poet to imitate Pindar is to emulate not Daedalus but
Icarus, to opt for the fake instead of the true and for the artificial over
the natural, the mimetic over the spontaneous and automatic. It is
also to forgo a primary privilege of the creative writer, one that is a
major concern to Horace in book 4, for which this poem is also
programmatic. To renounce self-reliance is, in the mysterious processes of creativity, to renounce the possibility of immortalizing others through the full realization of one's own gifts, of projecting them

[1]The influence of Pindar on Horace is treated, with particular reference to ode
2, by Steinmetz, and Wimmel ("Recusatio-Form"), more generally by Highbarger (224–25) and Wilson (98–99).

[2]Pseudo-Acron on line 33: "*Iullus Antonius heroico metro Diomedias duodecim
libros scripsit egregios*" (Iullus Antonius wrote twelve outstanding books on Di-
omede in epic meter).

to fame by one's own achievement. The imitative poet, in his Icarian feebleness, can name only himself, not those beyond him. He can egotistically make himself, perhaps, into a legend, but he lacks the authority to offer the solace of a future reputation to his subjects. Even what he names, the glassy sea, does him little service. Horace elsewhere speaks of "glittering reputation" (*vitrea fama*),[3] and the adjective carries a similar ambiguity here. What is glassy is arresting yet colorless. It is alluring but transparent and therefore insubstantial. Incautious rivalry for the unique can, for a poet, result only in the unoriginal and solipsistic, in suicidal self-naming, which is to abrogate the artistic autonomy that alone can save others from death.

Pindar himself is no imitator of nature but, in Horace's analogy, nature itself. In the initial stanza the reader's imagination is turned heavenward to contemplate not only the failure of Icarus but also the heroic accomplishment of Daedalus whom Horace had called to our attention in an earlier ode:[4]

> expertus vacuum Daedalus aera
> pinnis non homini datis; . . .

Daedalus made trial of the empty air on wings not given to man.

The comparison of Pindar to a mountain stream also moves implicitly from high to low, but the energies of imagination detailed are urgent and continuous. We attend to inspiration (*imber*), tradition and the ordinary bounds of genre and technique (*notas ripas*), content, style, and expression (*inmensus, profundo, audacis*), lexical choice (*nova verba*), and meter (*numeris lege solutis*).[5]

It is an "epic" simile and as such offers metaphorical reasons for Pindar's Daedalian generic achievement.[6] Equipped with an imagination equivalent to an elemental force, Pindar broke with his inheritance of lyric and, through his own form of wildness and lawlessness, made something new and vital of his poetic past. He is an epicizing, heroic reshaper of lyric verse, fearless before his own novelty. He is

---

[3] *Sat.* 2.3.222.

[4] *C.* 1.3.34–35.

[5] The elaboration of the metaphor is noted by Fraenkel (*Horace,* 435) who rightly stresses the bias of Horace's portrait of Pindar toward *ingenium* rather than *ars,* the inspirational rather than the craftsmanly.

[6] Cf. Virgil's similes at *Aen.* 2.305–8 and 12.523–25.

worthy of Apollo's laurel which means that he assumes for himself the same emblem of victorious courage earned by the athletes whom he celebrated. In his third Nemean epinicion, for instance, Pindar draws a protracted metaphoric comparison between the accomplishment of Aristokleides as competitor and of himself as maker of verses.[7] The achievement of each defines different forms of individual heroism which, paradoxically, must be interdependent to receive the due honor of survival.

For Horace it is Pindar who is the re-creator. Surveying the Pindaric career typologically in three successive stanzas, he first alludes to "bold" dithyrambs. Their position within the simile's evolution into metaphor expands their frame of reference to include not only the first genre of a catalog but a stylistic exuberance that marks not only dithyramb but Pindar's oeuvre as a whole. The list continues with hymns and paeans, victory odes, and, finally, dirges.[8] Each précis has a different orientation. In summarizing Pindar's hymnic verse Horace looks primarily at the offspring of the gods and at the exploits that confirmed their ancestry. Those named are not the demi-gods themselves but monstrous creatures they subdued, the horse-men Centaurs and the Chimaera, part lion, part snake, part she-goat. To rid the world of the "unnatural," the primitive, irrational and animalistic, is the civilizing role of semidivine heroes. Horace leaves for treatment in later poems the fates of the heroes themselves, Theseus and Pirithous among others from the first adventure, Bellerophon riding Pegasus, from the second.

The view of the conquering athletes looks to matters of more immediate moment. It is the palm of victory that divinizes the returning hero but the poet who assures the permanence of the accolade. Horace will come back to Pindar's emphasis on the return home of the victorious when, in the poem's second half and in several subsequent odes, he will concern himself with victorious Augustus' arrival in Rome and the series of "renewals" that accompany it—the expansive, Roman, military equivalent of the ludic progress of Pindar's subjects.[9] The eternal endurance of words in comparison to the de-

[7]Cf. Crotty, 31.

[8]Freis examines with insight Horace's catalog of Pindar's poetry, showing in particular why the Roman poet alters the order of Pindar's work established in Alexandria, putting dithyramb first and *threnoi* last.

[9]The importance of the hero's *nostos* for Pindar is treated at length by Crotty in chap. 4.

ceptive longevity of monumental statuary is also a theme that will occupy Horace in the book's central odes. Here the specific reference to a "tribute more sturdy than a hundred statues" (*centum potiore signis munere*), which the gifted poet himself bestows, looks not only forward but backward to the preceding poem where Paulus Fabius Maximus was "triumphant over the largesse of a spendthrift rival" (*potentior largi muneribus . . . aemuli*).[10] Moving from the successes of amatory rivalry and their artistic results, we are now involved first in competitions over primacy in physical prowess, then in the power of poets to render such feats immortal and, finally, in the rivalrous search between poets for a means to express glory adequate to immortalize doer and bard alike.

As Horace turns to the suffering of private deprivation, his treatment of Pindar's response grows increasingly involved, with two hypermetric lines.[11] These mimic Pindar's stylistic extravagance and reveal a parallel emotion in Horace's speaker who can, when he will, not only absorb Pindar's feelings but also duplicate their "enthusiastic" manner. Of gods and demigods he sings (*canit*), of victors in the games he tells (*dicit*), for a youth dead before marriage he weeps (*plorat*). It is for him that Horace reserves the strongest manifestation of Pindar's power. As we shall see, especially in ode 4, it is through the efforts of the imagination that a man's courage, spirit, and moral behavior endure beyond his own span of existence, and that brilliance of righteous living survives the blackness of Orcus. Only a speaker who has himself surmounted the envy of others can dismiss for himself and the subjects with which he empathizes the envy of death.

---

[10]1. 17–18. The connection is noted by Porter, "The Recurrent Motifs," 211. Horace's use of *comissor*, at 1. 11, which calls attention to itself, suggests another link between the two initial odes. The verb is borrowed from κωμάζειν to join in a κῶμος, a celebratory revel. In Pindar's hands, the κῶμος is a poetic celebration of an athletic victor's excellence, and κωμάζειν means to applaud that excellence in choral song. In the initial ode Horace's speaker cannot join the *comissatio* appropriate for Venus and young lovers. In the second he disclaims the ability to emulate Pindar and direct a κῶμος for Augustus. He can only share in the crowd's shouts of joy. Yet, however self-ironic, the ode is in fact Horace's own κῶμος for the emperor, just as its predecessor proves finally to be a last, pensive look at the possibilities of erotic "revelry" in his own life. In both instances the κῶμος seems to be relegated elsewhere yet is actually being created before our eyes.

[11]See Commager, "Some Horatian Vagaries," 66–68.

Pindar's ability to raise human accomplishment "to the stars" draws the reader's vision with it up from Orcus and back to the opening myth. This return to origins is reaffirmed as the poem reaches its center. In apostrophizing Iullus Antonius again and completing his name, Horace reminds us once more of Pindar's soaring spirit, this time seeing him as Apollo's swan, associated still with elemental nature but now also with high reaches of buoying air rather than the depths of swirling water. For Horace to adopt for himself such an emblem of inspired spontaneity would be, in terms of poetics, to claim the manner and mode of a Pindar, a gesture as perverse and Icarian stylistically as the speaker's yearning for the birdlike Ligurinus at the end of ode 1 was erotically. Pindar is to Horace as swan is to bee, the minuscule fashioner of polished works of art engendered with great effort.[12] Pindar is the inspired "artless" genius, Horace, the humble, earthbound craftsman. We are right to think of the Melissae, the bee priestesses (or perhaps merely bees), who at the end of Callimachus' Hymn to Apollo carry water "from a sacred fountain, pure and unpolluted,"[13] and of the dainty, winged cicada in whom the same poet finds an analogy for himself at the end of the prologue to his *Aetia*.[14] In the poetic credo of his great Hellenistic forbear Horace discovered the model for stylistic control and refinement which would distinguish him from the "boundless" afflatus of Pindar's rich genius. Pindar's stream surges over its wonted banks; Horace's bee plucks its thyme only near the banks of wet Tibur.[15] Pindar is nature, Horace would only seem to be supported by it.

But, paradoxically, the analogy suggests Pindar as well in its very elaboration, teaching us much about the *ego* who apparently preaches self-containment. In place of the solitary allusion to Thebes in *Dir-*

[12]The image of the sculpting bee may seem at first to demean Horace's speaker in contradistinction to Pindar's soaring swan. (At N. 5.1ff. Pindar himself abjures the image of sculptor.) The metaphor seems to confirm a hierarchy already suggested by the statement of lines 19–20, that Pindar's gift surpasses a hundred statues. But this very "bee" is in the process of offering a splendid example of Pindarizing, while disclaiming its ability to do so. It thereby both takes to itself, and marshals, Pindar's skills.

[13]Call. *H.* 2.110–12. Pfeiffer's final judgment (*History of Classical Scholarship*, 284) eliminates the priestesses in favor of bees.

[14]Call. *A.* 1. fr. 1.29ff.

[15]Horace's relationship with Callimachus, with special reference to ode 2, is treated by Wehrli, Wimmel (in particular 268–71), and Syndikus (302–3).

caeum, we follow the biography of our eloquent bee from his native Apulian beginnings to his presence at Tibur.[16] We remember that Pindar, more directly even than Callimachus, compared the thematic structure of his poetry to the artifact of a bee[17] and that Virgil found enough in common between the technology of Daedalus and of bees to show them "fashioning their Daedalian dwellings" (*daedala fingere tecta*).[18] In this poem concerned with originality and inspiration, the natural and the artificial, with degrees of imaginative inventiveness and technique in the process of creativity, how would Horace have us now define him? The second half of the poem continues to keep these polarities before us, but the conclusion places Horace firmly, and not unexpectedly, on the side of the natural.

In the meantime the speaker imagines the future career of Iullus. Though the details seem specific, no actual date for such a putative triumph for Augustus can be proposed. It is helpful in this instance to remember the historical facts. After Lollius' defeat in Gaul in 16 B.C., Augustus went north to pacify the Sygambri and did not return to Rome until July 13 B.C., the year in which Iullus was praetor. Though the Senate at that time voted the *Ara Pacis Augustae* in the emperor's honor, there was no such triumphal procession as the poet here envisions.[19] Horace imagines a future event of importance to the book as a whole which can be read as an extended *revocatio* of Augustus, who is mentioned here in the third person, addressed in absentia in the fifth ode, and only apostrophized as if present in the concluding two poems.

What Horace foresees is Iullus' participation in the actual moment of celebration. This would be appropriate, first, because as husband of Marcella Maior he was married to a niece of Augustus and was thus a prominent member of the imperial family. More important for

---

[16]See Porph. on *c.* 1.28.3 for the meaning of Matinae: "*Matinus mons sive promunturium est Apuliae*" (Matinus is a mountain or promontory of Apulia).
  [17]*P.* 10.53–54.
  [18]*Geo.* 4.179. Callimachus' Pindarizing is examined in detail by Newman, 45–48.
  [19]*C. D.* 54.25. The absence of 13 B.C. is conspicuous in Barnes' list (26) of the official victories of Augustus. Their allusions to the Sygambri and to the events of 16 B.C. provide important *termini* for dating both Propertius' fourth book of elegies (see commentators on 4.6.77) and the first edition of the *Amores* of Ovid (cf. Cameron, esp. 331–33).

the present context would be his pretensions as a poet to something "grander" than what small Horace could supply. These are Horace's only two uses of the verb *concino*. More than the simple *cano* that he had used in connection with Pindar at lines 13, the compound underscores the double sense of involvement Horace imputes to Iullus, both as part of the ceremony and as singer, with others, of the exploits it honors.

Because of this sense of community, Iullus' claims as poet smack more of Pindar than of an epicist, distanced from his material. Augustus is in the position of conqueror, feted upon return to his homeland, but Iullus, as Pindar often also imagines himself, is not only the producer of the victory hymn but a sharer in the triumphal procession that it creates and re-creates. As such he could assert the validity of the parallel the poem suggests between himself as Pindar, *laurea donandus Apollinari,* and the *triumphator, merita decorus fronde.*

Iullus, of course, as far as we know, never pursued the poetic venture Horace outlines for him. It is to Horace himself, as imaginer of a speaker imagining Iullus' career, that the reader should attend. Despite the speaker's disclaimers, he knows matters of significance for the poems that follow. One such, as I mentioned, is the idea of Augustus' return which here is paid a striking compliment. The lexical resonance of *redeant* in *reditu* links the emperor's arrival back in his capital with the renewal of a golden time, something even more remarkable than any earlier era that the gods have bestowed on Rome. Moreover, as in the first ode, feast days are pivotal for the poet's thoughts on temporality, whether they dwell on loss, on restoration, or only on vivifying the moment.

The speaker's own role, as his hypothetical celebration continues, remains modest. The few words he will utter further the impression of an unassuming bystander, content to enhance the obvious. In lines 45–48 he exclaims on the beauty of the sun, which is, ambiguously, both to praise the day itself and to flatter Augustus with an attribute fit for Alexander the Great and his *epigonoi. Recepto* strikes the same note by reinforcing the idea of a golden age restored by Augustus alluded to previously. In lines 49–52 the speaker expands on the distinction between himself and Iullus. While Iullus marches with the procession, which is in effect to share the triumph, the speaker withdraws into the communal "we," acknowledging the triumph and offering due thanks, not as an individual but as part of the general citizenry.[20]

The creator of this retiring speaker has placed him in an imagined situation with a rich heritage in Roman poetry to which we must turn before analyzing the poem's conclusion. I refer to poems in which the poet represents someone like himself, contemplating the emblems of a returned or returning victor and offering the reader his meditation thereon. The tradition begins with the newly discovered epigram of Gallus, probably addressed to Julius Caesar, and continues with poetry by Propertius and Horace himself.

Gallus' lines present, appropriately, the most apothegmatic as well as the most abstract version of such an event:

> Fata mihi, Caesar, tum erunt mea dulcia, quom tu
> maxima Romanae pars eri[s] historiae
> postque tuum reditum multorum templa deorum
> fixa legam spoleis deivitiora tueis.

My fate, Caesar, will then be sweet to me, when you will be a most important part of Roman history and when, after your return, I survey the temples of many gods richer from the hanging of your spoils.

I take Gallus' words to be a straightforward accounting of his joy in realizing that Caesar's deeds will be part of history. He offers as proof his autopsy of the victor's booty adorning temple walls.[21] The conceit is expanded and dramatized, with verve and irony, by Propertius in the fourth elegy of his third book. His subject is Augustus whose triumphal procession, after an anticipated defeat of the Parthi, Propertius finds himself contemplating as he "reclines on the lap of his dear girl."[22] Augustan pretensions toward military glory, the central

---

[20]In spite of the warning of Kiessling and Heinze, 397–98, and the arguments of Fraenkel (*Horace,* 438–39), I read the second person addressed in 33, 41, 49, and 53 in all instances as Iullus. I have therefore adopted the reading *tuque* from Klingner's *recentiores* instead of the major manuscripts' *teque* where "you" would be an address to the procession of triumph.

[21]The *editio princeps* is by Anderson, Parsons, and Nisbet. I have slightly modified Nisbet's reading and offered further evidence for Propertius' imitation in "Propertius and the New Gallus Fragment." Though I take Julius Caesar as the addressee, a strong case can also be made for reading Octavian as the poem's recipient.

[22]3.4.15.

topic of the poem, are demeaned in two ways. One is the direct moral lecture of the final couplet:[23]

> praeda sit haec illis, quorum meruere labores:
> me sat erit Sacra plaudere posse Via.

Let this booty belong to those whose efforts have deserved it. It will be sufficient for me to have the chance to applaud on the Sacred Way.

The results of campaigning in the east are not defined through any larger political or ethical goals but merely through the resultant plunder. Though the speaker will congratulate the procession, his elegiac posture, leaning on his girl, also suggests less than total commitment to any chauvinistic ideals.

In a closely contemporary ode, *c.* 3.14, whose dramatic date is 24 B.C. Horace honors the return of Augustus from his successful campaigning against the Cantabrians (13–20):

> hic dies vere mihi festus atras
> exiget curas: ego nec tumultum
> nec mori per vim metuam tenente
>   Caesare terras.
>
> i pete unguentum, puer, et coronas
> et cadum Marsi memorem duelli,
> Spartacum siqua potuit vagantem
>   fallere testa.

This festal day will surely rid me of my black cares. While Caesar possesses the earth I will fear neither upheaval nor death by force. Go, boy, seek out unguent and garlands and a cask recalling the Marsian war, if any jug could elude the roaming of Spartacus.

Propertius had constructed a public scene only to mock it with a richly ironic presentation. Horace by contrast retreats from the hazards of a public gesture.[24] His poem makes Augustus' grand moment an excuse for private festivity and possible love-making (is he too

---

[23]3.4.21–22.
[24]Brink (540–43) discusses the connection between the two poems.

old?). In so doing he shies away from any moral or rhetorical difficulties that description of a civic solemnity might entail and maintains a posture that is at once complimentary to his honorand and aloof. Even his playfulness has its serious side. Mention of Spartacus suggests how uncertain such celebrations can be. Horace has a stake in a public event, but it is purely personal and very fragile.

Ode 2 is a variation on this inheritance. Gone is the Propertian and (earlier) Horatian allusion to eroticism which hints, overtly or subtly, that there are worthier things to do than fete a conqueror (or that such an occasion could be put to a more comfortable use than communal praise). Gone, too, is Propertius' direct criticism of the ethos behind Augustus' militarism. Horace's speaker imagines himself in the very public scenario that Propertius demeans and Horace earlier avoids. And yet, though the ode develops the dramatic setting wherein two poets gather evidence for a *laudatio* of Augustus which would explicitly offer him due respect, the reader knows that the poem in one case will not, and in the other cannot, be written. Horace's refusal, then, to sing Augustus' praises, his apparently polite yielding before the mightier talent of Iullus, more adapted to such a poetic venture, seems to lack any Propertian acerbity. Following Virgil's statement of refusal in his sixth *eclogue* and Callimachus' rhetoric of tact, our poet relies on his own stylistic moderation at once to explore and then graciously to reject, apparently, any Pindarizing on Augustus' behalf.

The poem's ending, therefore, both satisfies and surprises. The votive offerings of the two poets, which symbolize the gifts their poeticizing will present as thanksgiving to Augustus, seem at first wholly suitable. Grandiloquent Iullus, given to epic and perhaps to Pindaric dithyramb, is imagined as tendering twenty grown cattle, creatures as noteworthy for their number as for their size. Horace, advocate of lyric refinement, proffers only an immature bullock. But the rhetoric of the conclusion turns this easy distinction unexpectedly about. Since Iullus' extensive gesture is given one line and Horace's limited effort is allotted the poem's final seven, it is to the latter, as to the bee at lines 27–32, that we chiefly, and paradoxically, attend.

First the calf is immediately eye-catching. The shape of its horns resembles the crescent moon. We see the lunar outline but also the moon's rising, fiery brightness against the evening sky. The calf's skin, tawny, with snow-white spots, shares the same color contrast of light with darker. The poet's graphic offering, in other words, is visually appealing and shapely. Miraculously for an animal, but suitable for an Horatian artifact, despite its expansionary proclivities, it grows young (*iuvenescit*) rather than old.[25] It also has a quality that confirms its presumably Callimachean background while complementing the extended manner of its presentation: it retains its youth *the vitulus* on "swelling grasses" (*largis herbis*), on nourishment proper for a fat victim though not a slender muse.[26]

This enigmatic final self-portrayal calls into question or, better, alters the balance between the two poet-protagonists of the poem. If the speaker claims through broadened metaphor the same kinship to Pindar that Iullus does through the content and scope of his verse, then we must interpret the role of the Theban poet as a poetic touchstone in a richer light. On the one hand the "I" of the poem downplays Pindar by reducing his extraordinary versification to the more gentle repetitiveness of Sappho's meter, by imagining the Roman exemplar of his heroic language as someone other than himself, and by proclaiming his own adherence to a calmer stylistics. Yet all this is accomplished by someone who was at the same time sufficiently knowledgeable about Pindaric poetics that he could brilliantly re-create them for his Roman audience, imputing to Iullus the power of projection that he himself possesses and, in fact, offering him a model of its use.

Through the word *referentis* and the power it implies in the speaker's words to renew themselves and their subjects, the ending leads us back into the center of the poem, to the vocabulary of "return" (*redeant, reditu, recepto*) that is part of Iullus' putative Pindarizing and of the speaker's slighter voice. The ending also takes us back to the poem's beginning to bring out its ideas still further. At the start, we remember, the emulator of Pindar was deemed parallel to Icarus, naming in his downward fall only the translucent and the bodiless. His poetic behavior, I suggested, was self-involved, synthetic, spurious. The speaker at the end makes a poetic offering that is as solid as it is colorful. He can do this because he imitates not another master's inimitable genius, whose resources are beyond his, but nature herself,

[25]This is usually said to be the first use in Latin of *iuvenesco* with the literal meaning "grow up," "become a youth." For my more metaphorical reading, cf. Ovid's usage at *Am.* 3.7.41.

[26]Horn (238–39) interprets the ending differently, seeing the delicate offering as only "playing" with Pindar's pathos.

the young bull mirroring the very rising of the moon. His poetic achievement is as natural as the rival of Pindar's would be false. In being honest to himself—in being true to his own nature—the speaker and, let us assume, his creator can, enigmatically, expand in his own original imaginative fashion. He can also pay the ultimate compliment to Augustus. By being truest to himself and responsibly measuring his own gifts against his varied inheritance, he will finally be most faithful to and creatively supportive of those whose future depends on his present wise expenditure of his talent. Though he may treat the equation ironically, he is Pindar, but he is Callimachus, too, and (at least as Horace chooses to see them) the earlier poet's devotion to *mania* and the later one's to *techne* are here fused into a novel genius going about the work of reexamining his world.

Pindar's poetry may have the power to lead "golden customs" to the stars, and Augustus' political genius may bring us back into a time of "ancient gold," but Horace's poetic offering also reproduces both heaven's brightest nocturnal body and the color of gold.[27] It is through him that poetry's incandescence will function both to refashion Pindar along the lines of a more modern poetics and to immortalize what Augustus, the sun, will renew for Rome.

[27]Cf. Var. *R. R.* 1.37.3 for the moon as an *astrum;* Tib. 1.1.1 and Vir. *Aen.* 7.279, 10.134, and 11.776 for gold as *fulvus.*

[3]

ODE THREE

Quem tu, Melpomene, semel
   nascentem placido lumine videris,
illum non labor Isthmius
   clarabit pugilem, non equos inpiger

curru ducet Achaico   5
   victorem, neque res bellica Deliis
ornatum foliis ducem,
   quod regum tumidas contuderit minas,

ostendet Capitolio:
   sed quae Tibur aquae fertile praefluunt   10
et spissae nemorum comae
   fingent Aeolio carmine nobilem.

Romae, principis urbium,
   dignatur suboles inter amabilis
vatum ponere me choros,   15
   et iam dente minus mordeor invido.

o testudinis aureae
   dulcem quae strepitum, Pieri, temperas,
o mutis quoque piscibus
   donatura cycni, si libeat, sonum,   20

totum muneris hoc tui est,
   quod monstror digito praetereuntium
Romanae fidicen lyrae;
   quod spiro et placeo, si placeo, tuum est.

Whom you, Melpomene, have once regarded at his birth with peaceful eye, no struggle at the Isthmia will illumine for his boxing, no racing steed will lead in victory on Achaian chariot, nor will the turns of war exhibit him on the Capitolium, leader adorned with laurel wreaths, for having crushed the bloated threats of kings, but the waters which flow past fertile Tibur and the dense foliage of its forests will sculpt him into nobility by his Aeolian song.

The offspring of Rome, chief of cities, deigns to establish me among the loveable choirs of bards, and now I am less gnawed by envy's fang. Pierian, O you who soften the sweet roar of the golden lyre, O you who, should you desire, could tender music of the swan to soundless fish, all this is your bounty, that I, player of the Roman lyre, am pointed out by the finger of passers-by. That I breathe and please, if please I do, is yours.

After apostrophes to Venus, who should figure in the amatory life of Paulus Fabius Maximus and no longer in that of the speaker, and to Iullus Antonius, a Pindarist more fit to sing in elevated lyric of Augustus than the poet's more reticent persona, Horace turns to address the Muse herself, Melpomene, inspirer of *melos*. In one long sentence embracing half the poem, we learn what her kindly glance means for the newborn poet. The extraordinarily sweeping definition, from *quem* to *nobilem,* apparently impersonal and abstract but in fact oriented toward a speaker not unlike Horace himself, clarifies at its climax the nobility of the poetic vocation by contrast with three other careers that its rhetoric embraces.[1] These callings—boxer, chariot driver, *triumphator*—grow in intensity with phrases of increasing complexity. They share in the opening image, explicit or implicit, of

---

[1]The unique qualities of the priamel of ode 3 in comparison with others in Horace are discussed by Estévez (287–88) in an important essay that studies the poem's originality against its own Horatian background (see also Becker, *Das Spätwerk,* 180–84; Fraenkel, *Horace,* 408). In his view, the absence of an intensive first-person speaker in the priamel contributes to a tone of generality which typifies the poem as a whole.

seeing and being seen. Effort at the games will bring bright fame to the successful boxer, his prowess in battle will make the conquering general the cynosure of his public, and presumably the same holds true for the charioteer.

But the development is also hierarchical. Topographical references configure a specific focus, taking us from Corinth, to Greece in general, to the Capitolium at Rome's center. References to *homo ludens* grow increasingly intricate: we move from boxing to the speed of the racer who must maneuver his horses; and, as the games change to politics and war, we have still further detail. The victorious hero's adornment, the threats of his (now regal) opponents, which he suppressed, and the triumphal procession mimic in verbal amplitude the extent of the protagonist's assertion of supremacy in Roman activist *Realien*. Even here, however, Greece is not forgotten, for the laurel of Delian Apollo bedecks the conquering Roman as it would have his Hellenic athletic prototype.

All of these dynamic, competitive, martial lives, illustrious as they are, contrast with the quiet, peaceful eye that Melpomene casts on the neonascent poet—Melpomene, whose qualities he absorbs in his distinctive career.[2] Greek and Roman elements share also in its designation. But it is neither symbolic Apolline laurel nor Roman civic applause that fashions our poet. The waters and groves of Tibur are the formative element of an imagination that charms through the melody of Lesbian lyric. Our poet's nobility is sculpted by the inspiriting amalgam of very real enrichments from the Tiburtine landscape and of the creative inheritance of Aeolia, both of which, literally and figuratively, abstract him from Roman effortful affairs.

This composite self-definition carefully complements parallel formulations in the preceding ode, to which it is closely linked. We are twice reminded of the subjects Pindar, in fact, and Iullus, potentially, celebrate. Mention of the *pugilem,* whom Isthmian struggle glorifies, and of the "eager horse" (*equos inpiger*) that leads his Achaian chariot to success, recalls the Greek boxer or horse, *pugilemve equomve,* immortalized in Pindar's epinicia.[3] The third figure in the list, the *triumphator* shown to the Capitolium crowned with laurel for suppressing the threats of foreign powers, generalizes the picture of Caesar in

[2]Such divine emanations of light and the blessings they bring are discussed by Pöschl ("Die Dionysosode," 212) who compares Call. *H.* 2.9ff.

[3]See 2.17.

the preceding poem, climbing the Sacred Way, adorned with the victor's chaplet he duly earned, drawing the conquered Sygambri in his wake.

But what are topics for song in ode 2 here become emblematic of callings based on athletic or bellicose rivalry from which Melpomene's blessing deflects her spiritual fosterling. The speaker differentiates himself from the contents of his and others' song, and his apartness brings with it both a touch of pride and an overt admission of dependence. To distinguish his own métier from Augustus' profession, while leaving it to others to praise Augustus in verse, is to hint at imaginative authority over political might. But any note of self-importance is softened in the further acknowledgment that genius is not ungoverned by its surroundings. Horatian eminence may be at variance with that which accrues from pugilistic heroism or military exploits, but it, too, is the fashioned as well as the fashioner. In the preceding ode, the Horatian artisan-bee occupies itself sculpting *operosa carmina* at Tibur. In the present poem, though Aeolian song marks the speaker's prestige, it remains itself crafted by inspiring landscape.[4] Melpomene and Aeolia suggest the speaker's Greek heritage, but it is an Italian setting that actually molds Horace into an artifact.

Though this final item of the priamel at first appears a deflection from the world of "doing" into a passivity where the creative speaker is himself structured by nature, the very differentiation of Rome and Tibur promotes a climax of a subtler sort. For Horace the two loca-

[4]These are Horace's richest allusions to an explicit landscape in *Odes* 4 and among the most evocative in his poetry, real and symbolic at once. The interconnection is noted by Troxler-Keller (155–58) and by Lee ("Everything Is Full of Gods," 259) who also sees the importance of the "liquid and vegetative" imagery as well as that of artisanship.

The relationship of Tibur and Rome within the poem underscores a major paradox—the need to escape from Rome for creativity (see, e.g., *c.* 3.29 and *epi.* 2.2.77–78) and the ultimate necessity of an appreciation by Rome for survival (a point humorously put in *epi.* 1.20). It is another way of looking at the tensions between private and public, privacy and publicity, country and city, between independence, individuality, freedom, quiet, and the necessity for community and the awareness of power among the perquisites for immortality. Estévez (293) suggestively locates a parallel polarity between the need that *nobilis* implies to be associated directly with Rome and the "descriptive understatement" that characterizes the poem, be it in treatment of landscape or in the suppression of the grand symbols his tradition would have associated with a poet's initiation.

tions are antithetical, and the antithesis has both a real and a meta-phoric side. We have the distinction between city and country, be-tween the smoke and noise of the metropolis and the calm of a rural retreat. Tibur, with the orchards on its hillside wet from its abundant water, is fertile, shady, and quiet.[5] Yet, in *c.* 1.7, the same shade offers a contrast to war camps with their gleaming standards, which are the present lot of Plancus, and in *c.* 2.6 the quiet which Tibur boasts is afforded the speaker after a limit has been set to his seafaring and battling. The damp Tibur, which the speaker conjures up for Maecenas in *c.* 3.29, is likewise meant to attract the statesman away from the complexities of Rome's political agenda.

Yet in all these instances there is implicit another aspect of Tibur made explicit elsewhere. When, in an epistle also addressed to Maecenas, Horace announces

> . . . mihi non regia Roma
> sed vacuum Tibur placet aut inbelle Tarentum. . .

> . . . not royal Rome but empty Tibur or peaceful Tarentum gives me pleasure . . .

he gives *vacuus* a double edge.[6] Negatively it defines the absence of the tangled ambitions of Rome's ironic pretensions to regality, the new age of Romulus that squashes the threats of kings. Put positive-ly, this world apart connotes for the speaker the freedom to be a philosopher-poet and to pattern his thoughts in verse. It is with sloping Tibur, not teeming Rome, that Horace elsewhere associates his Muse.[7] Her inspiration is his life of the mind and its poetic ex-

---

[5]Tibur is mentioned thirteen times in Horace's poetry, the earliest occasion chronologically being *sat.* 1.6.108 (the *via Tiburtina*) and *sat.* 2.4.70 (its famous apples), the latest in odes 2 and 3 in book 4.

[6]*Epi.* 1.7.44–45. In the epistle that follows (1.8.12) Horace makes his affection for both places a humorous example of his own fickleness: "*Romae Tibur amem, ventosus Tibure Romam*" (At Rome I love Tibur, inconstant at Tibur I love Rome). But the same serious antithesis, between the country as the place of spiritual sustenance and Rome as the source of vapidity and easy power, lies just beneath the surface. For Horace here it is the natural world, not urban preciosity, that engenders both the artist and his art.

[7]*C.* 3.4.23.

pression. In proposing Tibur to Maecenas he is urging on his patron both his external landscape and his inner sacred spirit.

If, then, the move from Corinth to Rome blends game with reality, the change from Rome to Tibur postulates the still grander leap from body to spirit, from the physicality of Greco-Roman competitive energies expended under the public glare to the poet about his equally Greco-Roman work of contemplation and writing, shaded from shallowness by the thick foliage of his animating grove. What seems at first a humble turning aside from Rome's grandeur is in fact a culmination that transcends Rome and forces us to redefine *nobilem*, the last climactic word of the sentence that comprises the poem's first three stanzas. Horace will be known, uncharacteristically for a Roman, for his words, not his deeds. With an understatement that advertises its opposite, Horace modestly professes a lack of outward ambition that in fact proclaims the securing of a more valuable inner worth.[8]

In an earlier ode, Tibur was singled out for its tractable soil that produced the wine of forgetting-life's-turmoil.[9] By now, as Horace gives to his very autobiographical speaker this last mention of his beloved spot, Tibur's soil has become fertile not only with wine, and poems about wine, but with the poet himself. His quality of soul is not so much different from Rome, as country, say, is from city, as superior to it because of the mind's more powerful assets. Instead of ending in an antithesis that implies equality, if dissimilarity, Horace's priamel concludes paradigmatically, as it should, with the model of a poet and the truth of his special integrity.

The surface tone of humility and deference continues in the second half of the ode, though the "I" of the speaker enters for the first time. Rome, the city, now dominates the poem, helping frame the final three stanzas. The offspring of Rome design to suggest that the speaker can be considered the player of her lyre (*Romanae fidicen lyrae* again

[8]I cannot here agree with Estévez (293) that for Horace Tibur is "a public locale" which "commits him to his public, making him *nobilis;* and to be *nobilis,* one must be out among men." The symbolism of Tibur makes it a private spot, distinct from Roman practicality, begetting a nobility not to be measured by standard political definitions of the word. In the second half of the poem the speaker appears honored by his newfound acclamation from the capital. What cannot be stated, in a poem where no manifestations of pride are overt, is that the final triumph belongs not to Romans but to him, because of the successful efforts of his own special nobility to raise their sensibility to meet and understand his.

[9]C. 1.18.2.

places a Greek word in a Roman context). Melpomene, called Pieris as a further reminder of her Hellenic origin, still rules the speaker and conditions his acceptance by Rome. She "moderates" the lyre and, if it is her wish, she grants the gift of beautiful sound even to the voiceless. If the poet is an agent of pleasure it is because of her. Even in these two roles, as poet of Rome but in the service of Melpomene, he treats himself as enduring, not acting on, life. He is no longer bitten by envy's tooth (*mordeor*) and is now shown (*monstror*) to passers-by.

He brings Tibull to Rome [handwritten marginal note]

Devotion to Melpomene has other ramifications. She first looked at him with an indulgent eye (*placido lumine*) and the resultant grace is what allows him in turn to give enjoyment to his audience (*placeo*). The word *placeo* has intimations of the erotic, especially when juxtaposed with *spiro*.[10] The *munus* of the Muse to her poet is that he have life as well as enliven others by his imagination. But Horatian usage of *spiro*, though it looks to life's "spirit," will help us see in the verb a meaning still richer than "breathe divine inspiration."[11] Its only other appearances in Horace's lyric poetry are both in book 4 and both concern love.[12] The first is in the ninth ode where the speaker, dealing with the permanence of poetry, assures us that Sappho's love still breathes in her verse (*spirat adhuc amor . . . Aeoliae . . . puellae*).[13] The second context, in ode 13, looks back to Lyce's beautiful former self "who breathed loves" (*quae spirabat amores*).[14]

The reader of the fourth book expects a connection between *amor* and *spiro*. But any aura of love which emanates from the poet in the third ode inspires mental, not physical, affection. What pleasure issues from his lyre causes him to be ranked *inter amabilis vatum . . . choros*, among choirs of bards, loved for the beauty of their song. This *amor*, offered and reciprocated, is therefore the opposite of the unrequited carnal desire to which the aging speaker yields in his imagination at the end of the first poem.[15] In that poem, bodily

[10]Cf., for example, *c.* 3.7.27.

[11]This is the rendering of *OLD s.v.* 1e (the only example offered).

[12]Apart from the examples in the lyrics Horace uses the word only at *epi.* 2.1.166.

[13]9.10–12.

[14]13.19.

[15]On the strong emotional tone of *amabilis*, see Fraenkel (*Horace*, 408, n. 3), and Porter ("The Recurrent Motifs," 207), who rightly sees that "the greatest object of his affection has become poetry."

yearning lures the speaker to follow his swan-lover away from his Roman focus. Here the speaker, taking on attributes of a statue, through the metamorphic power of Melpomene and of the countryside of Tibur, is the quiet center of dynamism past which Rome moves in approbation. As love changes from erotic to spiritual, the speaker instead of being centrifugal is himself the center. Instead of tracking his lover, he now shares, if Melpomene is agreeable, in the power of the swan given in the preceding poem to Pindar. He becomes the producer of enchanting, enduring *melos* rather than the mesmerized pursuer of the passing and the vanishing. He is one with the permanence of his lovely song, an example of the highest form of eros, with art constantly renewing itself.

The speaker's view of himself seems a model of discretion and understatement. The generalized poet is defined by others. He is a creature of Melpomene and a creation of the personified Tiburtine landscape. When a first-person speaker does enter the poem at line 15, it is to maintain that his *dignitas,* instead of being blazoned as the product of his own persistent labors, is given him by the offspring of Rome. Even the two conditional clauses, *si libeat* and *si placeo,* placed at the same metrical position in the last lines of the final stanzas amplify the sense of fragility and contingency that the earlier stanzas scrupulously outlined. But there is a difference between these clauses and the condition with which Horace's first ode, to Maecenas, draws to a conclusion:

> quodsi me lyricis vatibus inseres,
> sublimi feriam sidera vertice.

But if you rank me among lyric bards, I will strike the stars with my lofty head.

There the speaker, with the prospect of a career as lyricist still imagined, foresees a moment of prideful exuberance dependent on Maecenas' approval. Now, in retrospect, with a masterpiece of odes behind him, pride need not be publicly anticipated but merely presumed, and unstated.

Nevertheless the very impersonality of the poem's opening stanzas and the passivity of the speaking "I" in the last three indicate a modesty that deftly mitigates what his words also imply. The speak-

er's profession is not only differentiated from those of boxer, charioteer, and general but climactically surpasses them. His love affair
with the Muse has made him, and no one else, Rome's lyre player, as
famous a sight as any *triumphator*. Far from seeking analogies for
himself in preceding poetic careers and continuing to load himself
with the baggage of poetic symbols that separate him from more
pragmatic vocations, he is successful enough that he can now gener-
alize a definition of the poet from the particularities of his own life.
Though to all appearances indebted to his world, he is also the standard against which the curricula of other poets will now be measured.
Such a stance is above, and beyond, pride.

I will return shortly to additional points of unity among the book's
first three odes. I would like now to look again at the third ode, in
particular at its literary heritage, for further help in adjudicating a
balance between pride and humility as our poet defines his nobility.
The opening two lines, for instance, have an illustrious pedigree that
begins with Hesiod. Early in the *Theogony* the poet speaks of the
Muses and the power they offer:

> Whomsoever of god-minded princes the daughters of mighty Zeus
> honor and oversee at his birth, they pour sweet dew on his tongue, and
> gracious words flow from his mouth. All the people look toward him as
> he settles cases. . . . And when he makes his way through a gathering
> they greet him as a god with gracious reverence.[16]

In Hesiod it is the Muses who honor the child at birth, in Horace it is
the landscape that ennobles him. Hesiod pictures the honorand as in
motion, walking through an assembly to be greeted like a god. For
Horace, the creature nourished by the Muses is himself statuesque,
pointed at by passers-by. But the major difference is that Hesiod's
Muses bless a prince, Horace's Melpomene commends a poet. By
arrogating to the poet in his initial allusion the posture of prince, the
speaker adroitly puts himself on a par with the Augustan *triumphator*.
He thus, through literary allusion, treats with further irony the stance
of modesty and deference the speaker seems to adopt, just as at the
end of the preceding poem he had astutely reversed his posture of
restraint.

[16]*Th.* 81–85; 91–92. On the primacy of Hesiodic influence, see Syndikus 314
and n. 10.

Callimachus varied Hesiod in lines he uses twice:[17]

> . . . Μοῦσαι γὰρ ὅσους ἴδον ὄθματι παῖδας
> μὴ λοξῷ πολιοὺς οὐκ ἀπέθεντο φίλους.

. . . for whomever the Muses do not look askance at as children, they do not abandon them as friends when white with age.

Preceding lines in each case speak of envy.[18] In the prologue to the *Aetia* Callimachus commands envy to be gone and in his father's epitaph he speaks of his own songs as "stronger than envy." Envy, of course, appears later in Horace's poem, as a creature by whom the speaker is now less frequently nagged, but its absence from the ode's beginning is one of Horace's several changes of Callimachus. *Placido lumine* does not translate ὄθματι . . . μὴ λοξῷ which Horace renders *limis [oculis]* or *obliquo oculo*.[19] Horace forgoes his predecessor's litotes for a positive statement. He replaces the absence of envy in this aslant glance with the favoring look that makes its recipient favorable. But the major change from Callimachus concerns time and merely confirms the primacy of Hesiod. Callimachus takes the poet from childhood to old age. Horace, as Hesiod, looks only at his birth. The speaker-poet as lover may suffer and yearn to escape from temporality in the first ode. In the third only his birth is mentioned, as if the muse's monumentalizing set her protégé beyond time, or as if it touched him only at his nativity.

To court, or at least accept, the approval of the public at large is a change from Callimachean reserve and from an earlier Horace who could, as priest of the Muses, avow hatred of the profane mob from the safety of his Sabine retreat. But it is against recent formulations by Propertius, himself a dedicated adherent of Callimachus, that Horace seems to have measured himself when contemplating his future. The elegist ends the final poem of his second book, a poem

---

[17]Callimachus' allegiance to Hesiod needs no documentation. Allusion to the *Theogony* frames the *Aitia* (1. fr. 2.1–2 and 4. fr. 112.5–6). *Ep.* 27 (29) = *AP* 9.507 states the admiration directly. For further bibliographical references, see Pfeiffer on *Aet.* 1. fr. 2, Kambylis 79–81, and, specifically for the connection between the *Aitia* prologue and *Theogony* 81ff., Reinsch-Werner, 327–29.

[18]Call. *Aet.* 1.1.37–38. The lines as quoted are identical with Call. *ep.* 23 (= *AP* 7.525), 5–6.

[19]*Sat.* 2.5.53; *epi.* 1.14.37–38.

written in 26 B.C. or soon thereafter, with a list of poetic forbears leading from Varro of Atax to the recently deceased Gallus. It concludes:

> Cynthia quin etiam versu laudata Properti,
>   hos inter si me ponere Fama volet.[20]

Yes and Cynthia has been glorified by the poetry of Propertius, if Fame will wish to establish me among these [poets].

The members of this illustrious catalog would no doubt help form the "loveable choirs of bards" among which Horace now ranks himself. The next poem in the collection of Propertius, the initial elegy of the third book, also has remarkable thematic parallels to ode 3: an initial address to the shades of Callimachus, mention of "Greek choruses" as part of Propertian stylistics, and later apostrophe to the Muses.[21] The surmounting of professional envy—

> at mihi quod vivo detraxerit invida turba
>   post obitum duplici faenore reddet Honos; . . .

But that which the envious throng has reft from me in my lifetime Honor will restore with double interest after my death . . .—

and the approval of Rome's citizenry—

> meque inter seros laudabit Roma nepotes.
>   illum post cineres auguror ipse diem.

Rome will praise me at last among its descendants. I myself predict this day after I am become ashes.—

are also subjects in common between the poems, and new to Propertius. Here, too, Horace varies his past. What will occur to Propertius

---

[20]The reminiscence of Propertius 2.34.79–80 at ode 3, lines 17–18, is further proof that Horace had this elegy of Propertius in mind as he wrote. Both allusions are noted by Becker (181, n. 14; 183, n. 19).

[21]Observe how we are dealing with poems that begin and end poetry books, as will also prove to be the case with Horace surveying his own past.

only after his death, the disappearance of envy and the endorsement of Rome, is already beginning to happen to Horace while he is yet alive.

Hence we may summarize Horace's alterations of his poetic past in Hesiod, Callimachus, and Propertius. From the first he expropriates with the blessing of the Muses the prestige of princes, and by distinction with the latter pair he looks only to birth, not to the process of aging, and to the concession of immortality by his contemporaries while still living. The apparent conditionality of Melpomene's involvement is therefore quietly modified through an allusiveness that grants to the poet a full share of dignity not only from his fellow Romans but also from his chosen pantheon of illustrious ancestors. Through gentle but unequivocal reference to his poetic heritage he heralds his own immortality.[22]

The poems, or sections of poems, from his past to which Horace most often refers constitute beginnings and endings, introductions and conclusions. It is reasonable, therefore, to claim for ode 3 a similar position wherein one expects a table of contents and proclamation of poetic credo or a warrant that each has been fulfilled or justified. This claim gains substance in two ways, both now connected with Horace himself. The first is the strong presence of the opening and closing poems from the first collection of odes. From *c.* 1.1 Horace appropriates the form of the priamel to define his own calling and stresses the provisional quality of his world, beholden to the Muses Euterpe and Polyhymnia for initiation into the "nimble choruses of Nymphs" (*Nympharum . . . leves . . . chori*) and, as we have seen, to Maecenas for ranking among "lyric bards" (*lyricis vatibus*). Connections with *c.*3.30 are closer still. Each poem is concerned with time, the earlier with the immorality of the poet's opus, the later with the birth and prestige of the poet himself. Both use the Capitolium in analogies, in *c.* 3.30 as emblem of endurance of Rome's (metaphorically) triumphant past, in ode 3 as center of power for a literal *triumphator* whose relation to Rome is markedly different from the poet's. Both are concerned with *Aeolium carmen,* the poetry of Aeolia, and both address Melpomene, at the poem's conclusion (*c.* 3.30) or start (ode 3).[23]

[22]For further details on Hesiod, Callimachus, and the notion of the poet's immortality, see Scodel, *passim* but especially 318–19.

[23]Estévez (281 and 294–95) notes connections as well between ode 3 and *c.* 2.20, the final ode of the second book.

Horace's attention, then, to other "framing" poems, especially the boundary poems of the first collection, during the writing of the third ode of his book confirms that the poem itself should be considered delimiting and should be read closely with its two predecessors as part of a continuum, with the trio serving to introduce the new collection. The first and third poems instance Horace's only uses in book 4 of the fourth Asclepiadean meter which suggests that the two poems are interconnected while the second ode acts as bridge. In the course of my analyses I have proposed several thematic ways by which the poet harmonizes the progressive development of the poems. These I will now summarize and briefly reappraise to put the whole into perspective. First, the themes of time and eroticism. In the initial poem the aging speaker betrays his humanness and wishes away an epiphany of Venus, though the ode ends with a spasm of yearning to follow final love and fleeting youth. The third finds the poet illuminated by Melpomene at birth, honored by the young, replacing waning individual sexuality with spiritual, public "eroticism" that now co-opts attention to the speaker himself and assures him of a permanent place in the "lovable" communion of bards.

The production of song and the placement of the singer comment on these themes. The first ode finds the stricken poet tongue-tied, while decorousness and nobility belong with the *puer* Paulus Fabius Maximus. The lyre and song remain adjuncts of Venus whom he, not the speaker, enshrines centrally, and properly, in his life. In the third

---

On the originality of ode 3 in relation to *c.* 1.1 and 3.30, see Becker, 180–82, and Fraenkel, *Horace,* 408. Because of their common apostrophe to Melpomene, in their last and first lines respectively, ode 3 could be read as continuing where *c.* 3.30 left off. If so the surface modifications of tone and content between one poem and the next are astonishing. Gone are all the approximations of power and pride, along with the symbols of poetic accomplishment. They are replaced by a sense of restraint and a different topography. Arrogance toward Melpomene becomes deference, and allusion to a literal birthplace "poor in water" (*pauper aquae, c.* 3.30.11) changes to a new "fashioning" landscape of "waters which flow past prosperous Tibur" (*quae Tibur aquae fertile praefluunt*). The Capitolium that the speaker had made symbolically his own in *c.* 3.30 now belongs to others of a more superficial bent, while the poet, once *princeps* (*c.* 3.30.13), cedes his position to Rome, *princeps urbium.* This remaking of the language of power, which now separates from the speaker words such as *princeps* and *Capitolium,* puts special emphasis, which rhetorical closure abets, on *nobilis.* Horace's speaker is distinguished for the loftiness of his character, not for the immediate notoriety of public heroism.

poem, Horace's persona finds himself monumentally "fashioned" at Rome, assured of a metaphysical nobility of his own that makes him Rome's lyre player and song maker. Instead of being subject to time, and in motion away from the stabilities of youth and external beauty no longer his (as the mortal creator of song), Horace's speaker is himself the quiet pivot, the "artifact" venerated by folk who must move past a (now decorous) version of the poet-maker's self, assured of endurance.

In the second ode the fashioned is the fashioner, and in his world, too, motion and rest play their part. The politics of Rome become a subject for the first of many times in the fourth book. Political might concentrates on Augustus as *triumphator,* the passage of whose procession the speaker merely joins in acclaiming, leaving the celebration of triumph in more capable hands. Ode 3, where the speaker seems to be dealing most closely with his own vocation, mentions only a nameless *triumphator,* emblem of one out of several careers not destined to be his, as if to purge himself of practical heroism and opt only for honor given to the imagination.[24]

But the major unity behind the three personae Horace creates of, or for, himself in these initial odes is their common devotion to poetry, its influence and its creation. Together they sketch the outline for an *ars poetica* that is at the same time an apology for a *vita contemplativa* strangely like what we might be tempted to ascribe to Horace himself, designing this remarkable last set of odes in the late teens of the first century B.C.

All three are poems of retrospect and prospect, of testing against origins in the past and toward possibilities in the present, of envy at last mollified, of decorousness. They form a series of redefinitions of the poetic self. The first, put in the mouth of a speaker passing his prime and renewing the erotic only in his dreams, appears to dismiss, or nearly dismiss, the tradition of Sappho, Catullus, the elegists and the amatory poems of Horace's own lyric past as fit models to kindle and satisfy his own imagination, while in fact revising and reenlivening it. In the second, more overtly concerned with the life of the mind, the speaker assesses the talents of his own lyric genius against the grandeur of Pindar. Though he finds them wanting—he is only

[24]In fact all three poems deal in varying degrees with *carmina,* with the meaning of *munus,* and with emulation, imitation, and envy.

an industrious bee devoted to Callimachean smallness in comparison to the effortless winging of Pindar's swan—he can, nevertheless, brilliantly recreate heroic *virtus* in the lofty Pindaric mode and in fact eulogize those whose glorification he claims to leave to the greater gifts of others. The final ode of this opening trinity engages most directly with inspiration and the inner life of the poet. It is addressed to the muse and makes a series of bows to past poetic prologues and epilogues, placing the speaker firmly in the linked tradition of Hesiod, Callimachus, and Propertius. He seems then, as his dependence on the Muse would imply, to sanction a poetics of elegance and refinement and an apolitical ethics of moderation and retreat. But there is also scarcely hidden pride in this accomplishment and in the approval of Rome, a pride sanctioned by the particular allusions chosen. He, too, with Melpomene's blessing, has a kinship with Pindar's swan.

As we turn from an ode on the inevitability of physical aging to one on the constancy of spiritual rebirth, we move, in terms of influences, chronologically from Sappho's crystalline privacies (rehearsed in her Roman imitator, Catullus), to Pindar's bounteous inspiration and heroic content, to Callimachus' more tempered imagination with its emphasis on the craft and crafting of verse and on the blessing of a calmer Muse. All three lyric modes will reappear, in suitably varied forms, in the odes that follow. Sappho, Catullus, and the tone of elegy will lie behind a series of poems on personal decline, while the challenging amalgamations in the second and third odes— between the manner of Pindaric sweep and Callimachean artfulness, in the one, and between matter appropriate to Callimachean restraint and the acceptance by and of the immediate world of Rome, in the other—will be most at Rome's service, though still very much under Horace's jurisdiction, in the subsequent poems.

PART TWO

Doctus Apollo:
Odes 4–6

How but in custom and in ceremony
Are innocence and beauty born?
Ceremony's a name for the rich horn,
And custom for the spreading laurel tree.
                                    W. B. YEATS,
                            "A Prayer for My Daughter"

[4]

ODE FOUR

Qualem ministrum fulminis alitem,
cui rex deorum regnum in avis vagas
    permisit expertus fidelem
        Iuppiter in Ganymede flavo,

olim iuventas et patrius vigor   5
nido laborum propulit inscium
    vernique iam nimbis remotis
        insolitos docuere nisus

venti paventem, mox in ovilia
demisit hostem vividus impetus,   10
    nunc in reluctantis dracones
        egit amor dapis atque pugnae,

qualemve laetis caprea pascuis
intenta fulvae matris ab ubere
    iam lacte depulsum leonem   15
        dente novo peritura vidit:

videre Raetis bella sub Alpibus
Drusum gerentem Vindelici; quibus
    mos unde deductus per omne
        tempus Amazonia securi   20

dextras obarmet, quaerere distuli,
nec scire fas est omnia; sed diu
   lateque victrices catervae
      consiliis iuvenis revictae

sensere, quid mens rite, quid indoles   25
nutrita faustis sub penetralibus
   posset, quid Augusti paternus
      in pueros animus Nerones.

fortes creantur fortibus et bonis;
est in iuvencis, est in equis patrum   30
   virtus neque inbellem feroces
      progenerant aquilae columbam.

doctrina sed vim promovet insitam
rectique cultus pectora roborant;
   utcumque defecere mores,   35
      indecorant bene nata culpae.

quid debeas, o Roma, Neronibus,
testis Metaurum flumen et Hasdrubal
   devictus et pulcher fugatis
      ille dies Latio tenebris   40

qui primus alma risit adorea,
dirus per urbis Afer ut Italas
   ceu flamma per taedas vel Eurus
      per Siculas equitavit undas.

post hoc secundis usque laboribus   45
Romana pubes crevit et inpio
   vastata Poenorum tumultu
      fana deos habuere rectos,

dixitque tandem perfidus Hannibal:
"cervi, luporum praeda rapacium,   50
   sectamur ultro quos opimus
      fallere et effugere est triumphus.

gens, quae cremato fortis ab Ilio
iactata Tuscis aequoribus sacra
   natosque maturosque patres   55
      pertulit Ausonias ad urbis,

duris ut ilex tonsa bipennibus
nigrae feraci frondis in Algido,
   per damna, per caedis ab ipso
      ducit opes animumque ferro.   60

non hydra secto corpore firmior
vinci dolentem crevit in Herculem
   monstrumve submisere Colchi
      maius Echioniaeve Thebae.

merses profundo, pulcrior evenit;   65
luctere, multa proruet integrum
   cum laude victorem geretque
      proelia coniugibus loquenda.

Carthagini iam non ego nuntios
mittam superbos: occidit, occidit   70
   spes omnis et fortuna nostri
      nominis Hasdrubale interempto.

nil Claudiae non perficient manus,
quas et benigno numine Iuppiter
   defendit et curae sagaces   75
      expediunt per acuta belli."

    Like the winged wielder of the thunderbolt, to whom Jupiter, king of
the gods, allowed domain over feckless birds, once blond Ganymede
had proved him loyal—at first youth and inheritance of energy prodded
him from the nest, ignorant of toils, and, once the storm-clouds are
dispelled, the winds of spring have taught him in his fear unwonted
lunges; soon an onrush of strength has pitched him down, a foe against
sheep-folds, now love of food and fray have launched him against strug-
gling serpents—or like a lion, newly thrust from the rich milk of his

tawny mother, whom a roe, obsessed with the luxury of her pasturage, saw, about to perish from his young tooth: the Vindelici saw Drusus as he waged his wars under the Rhaetian Alps. (Whence custom, drawn down through all length of time, arms their right hands with an Amazon's axe I have deferred exploring. It is not right to know all things.) But the hordes, conquering over long time and space, reconquered by the youth's wisdom, felt what an intelligence, what a nature duly nurtured within a fostering household, what the fatherly spirit of Augustus toward the Nerones, could realize.

The brave and good create the brave. The courage of their fathers remains with bulls, remains with steeds; savage eagles do not beget the timorous dove. But teaching advances ingrained might and proper refining confirms the heart. Whenever morality has been derelict, faults disgrace the innately good.

O Rome, to what you owe the Nerones the river Metaurus bears witness, and Hasdrubal vanquished, and that glad day for Latium, with blackness routed, which smiled in cherishing glory first since the fell African galloped through the cities of Italy like fire through pitch-pines or East wind through Sicilian waves.

Thereafter, their efforts ever thriving, the Roman young advanced, and sanctuaries ravaged by the Carthaginians' profane rampage have held upright gods, and treacherous Hannibal at last cried: "Deer, the prey of gluttonous wolves, ourselves we attend upon those whom it is a premier triumph to baffle and elude. The brave race which from the embers of Troy bore its relics, storm-tossed on the Tuscan sea, and children and patriarchs through to the cities of Ausonia, like an ilex shorn by axes' hardness on Aufidus, fecund in dark foliage, through hurt, through carnage draws resource and resilience from the iron itself. No hydra with its body hacked grew sturdier against Hercules, smarting at his defeat, nor did the Colchians or Thebes of Echion rear a greater prodigy. Drown it in the deep, it leaps forth more valiant. Wrestle with it, it will throw an undefeated champion to great applause and will spur combats for wives to tell of. Now I will not send proud messengers to Carthage: darkened, darkened is the whole hope and fortune of our name with Hasdrubal's downfall. There is nothing that Claudian arms will not effect, which Jupiter guards with gracious majesty, and wisdom's carings maneuver through the hazards of war."

Coming after protestations of inability to rival Pindar's exuberant majesty and of Callimachean dependence on the Muse's blessing, the opening of the fourth ode is doubly surprising. Gone is a highly individuated speaker examining his place as aging lover or as lyric genius in a more public context. Gone, apparently, is the entire presence of a shaping first person. As we commence one of Horace's three longest odes, we seem to be in an intellectual world as impersonal as it is expansive, one that derives its impulse as much from epic's discursiveness as from Pindaric sweep.[1] The success of Nero Claudius Drusus, son of Tiberius Claudius Nero and Livia Drusilla, and therefore stepson of Augustus, as warrior against the Vindelici in 15 B.C., is the initiating subject.

To begin a lyric with an extended simile is a Pindaric gesture. The most famous example of such elaboration is the opening of *Olympian* 7 where the Muses' nectar distilled into the poet's fancy is compared to a golden bowl proffered as loving cup by a bride's father to his future son-in-law. But the presence of the poet as artisan and gift-giver is prominent in what follows; the analogy bolsters the "I" behind producer and product. The absence of Pindar's first-person speaker suggests, then, that Homer or Virgil might offer closer parallels for equating the victorious hero's prowess, without authorial intrusion, to the physical strength of the mighty of the animal kingdom. It is true that Homer, as part of the narrative of the *Iliad,* describes a conflict between eagle and snake,[2] and Virgil has two similes in books 10 and 11 of the *Aeneid* in which, respectively, a lion is slathered with the blood of a roebuck or a stag whose inwards he is devouring, or an eagle struggles with a serpent, claws against coils.[3] With one exception to be discussed shortly, each simile gives parallel space to the two protagonists, whether seen as equals or as master and victim. As such they expand on the military encounters they enhance. But duality is of as little importance to Horace as narrative flow. Victims are mentioned as in Virgil—sheepfolds and snakes for the eagle, a roebuck for the lion—but only apparently for documentation. They offer external proof of what is the speaker's chief concern, the development of *virtus,* inner strength and courage. The details are novelistic, and time does pass, but Horace is finally concerned with

[1]*C.* 3.27 equals ode 4 in length. Only *c.* 3.4 is longer.
[2]H. *Il.* 12.200f. (*cf.* Cic. *Div.* 1.106).
[3]Vir. *Aen.* 10.723–28, 11.750–56. Virgil uses a pair of similes at *Aen.* 4.469–74 and 12.521–25. G. Williams (*Figures,* 78) discusses their particular power in ode 4.

defining a single psychic abstract in a single individual. As such he has no parallel in either the epic writers or in Pindar.

Horace begins with a scarcely disguised compliment to Augustus and his stepson.[4] Drusus will prove his virtuosity by feats of arms against the Vindelici, but the emperor will offer the opportunity for such corroboration. Jupiter, the king, shares his royal prerogatives with the eagle, bearer of thunderbolts and of Ganymede. Augustus, incarnation of divine omnipotence on earth, will partition his juris-diction with the "eagle" Drusus by charging him with the "eagles" of legions he led successfully against the Gallic invasions of Italy. Early fidelity earns increased authority to curb the undisciplined. The timing is outlined in four nearly equal stages, demarcated by conjunc-tions, *olim, iam, mox,* and, finally and most immediately, *nunc.* In the first stage, youth and paternal vigor, time of life and inherited poten-tial, are the operative principles. However inbred the eagle's natural impulse to leave the nest, it is still *laborum inscium,* ignorant of life's demands. Nature of another sort, the spring winds of external reality which, as the poet will later imply, are emblematic of the respon-sibilities asked of his eagle by Augustus, do in fact teach the un-schooled by fostering what is instinctive. It is not far, etymologically, from *vigor* to the lively (*vividus*) impulse that now rules the eagle's actions. But the teaching winds of life have intervened, and as a result of their tutelage the quality of inherited inner abstractions is further confirmed in the eagle's formal development. Fear yields to courage. As the eagle's quarry changes from helpless sheep to snakes who return the struggle, so *impetus* changes to *amor,* excited inclination becomes settled attachment to battle and its rewards.

The first simile complements Augustus' power and discretion while openly alluding to Drusus' paternal inheritance from Tiberius Claudius Nero. In the shorter lion simile, fledging has become wean-ing, and father is replaced by mother (a passing reminder that her second son received the name he was known by from Livia, whose

---

[4]Horace equates Augustus directly with Jupiter at *epi.* 1.17.34 and 1.19.43. Perhaps, given the parallel with the opening of ode 4 and the suggestive com-parison in *c.* 3.4 of the followers of Augustus with Olympians and of Antonians with giants, we are meant to see Augustus as sharing in the potential of Jupiter at *c.* 3.1.6–8. Yet, even should he realize his godlike capabilities, he will be subject to the king of the gods (see *c.* 3.5.1–4).

father was M. Livius Drusus Claudianus). Here comparison with
Virgil will be helpful in illustrating Horace's meaning. Mezentius has
just sighted as prey purple-clad Acron:[5]

> impastus stabula alta leo ceu saepe peragrans
> (suadet enim vesana fames), si forte fugacem
> conspexit capream aut surgentem in cornua cervum,
> gaudet hians immane comasque arrexit et haeret
> visceribus super incumbens; lavit improba taeter
> ora cruor—
> sic ruit in densos alacer Mezentius hostis.

Even as often an unfed lion, roaming through his deep dens (for raging
hunger urges him), if by chance he has sighted a fleeting roebuck or a
high-antlered stag, rejoices with mouth hugely gaping, and raises his
mane, and clings bending over the guts; and foul gore slavers his greedy
lips—so eager Mezentius rushes into the thick of the foe.

Though the victim, its corpse and gore, is integral to the simile, it is
on the feelings of the lion that the narrator dwells. Mezentius' spying
of Acron becomes the hungry lion's scouting of his target and rejoicing in his conquest. Horace's simile is different in two respects. First,
his newly weaned young lion is well fed and has no need to eat.
Instinct for self-survival must be imposed (*depulsum*). In the case of
the eagle, innate energy pushed him from the nest (*propulit*). For the
lion, the mother must force nurture to yield to nature.

The second alteration from Virgil modifies any possible interpretation of Horace's victims as mere documentation. In Horace we see
the narrative possibilities, literally, from the viewpoint of the victim,
who looks up, too late, from her feeding. Virgil's bloodied lion
exults in its meal. No emotion is imputed to Horace's cub. It is the
roebuck, ironically following its own instinct for pasture, who be-
holds and is about to die. This gentle turning of emphasis from victor
to conquered operates as we turn from vehicle to tenor. Because of
the forceful reiteration of *vidit* in *videre,* the reader sees Drusus mak-

[5]*Aen.* 10.723–29.

ing war through the eyes of the Vindelici, and the resonance of *laetis . . . pascuis* in *Raetis . . . Alpibus* is a reminder that the battling occurs in their home territory, not in Rome's. The Alpine tribes, whose conquest was a vindication of Drusus' military expertise, may have posed a threat to Rome, but nothing in Horace's words suggests either their menace or his glory. There is no catalog of successes to demonstrate the realization of the eagle-lion's capability, only a two-line announcement that the Vindelici looked while Drusus fought.[6]

This meiosis prepares us for the *coup de théâtre* that follows as the first-person narrator takes control of the poem. The sudden appearance of the speaking "I," which has shocked many critics, is usually seen as a further instance of Horace's Pindarizing in ode 4, and indeed the Theban poet offers two parallels.[7] One is in *Nemean* 5 where, in praising the Aeacidae because of the victory of Pytheas of Aegina, he refrains out of shame from telling of the murder of Phocus by his half-brothers Telamon and Peleas.[8] *Isthmian* 1 contains a further example, where the tallying of all Herodotus' victories is impossible, given the limits of the speaker's song. Pindar supplies precedents for a speaker's unwillingness to pursue possible directions for his song, whether from ethical reticence or rhetorical decorum.[9] But his contexts in no way approximate the abrupt change from the high epic tone of the opening similes to a first-person speaker blazoning the postponement of an evidently pedantic search into an obscure piece of aetiology.

[6]Doblhofer (100) comments on the unexpected absence of telling detail in what we expect to be a panegyric. The poem is seen as a disguised critique of Augustan expansionist foreign policy by Ambrose ("Horace on Foreign Policy"). Whatever the case, the reader questions the nature of the victory of lion over deer. True glory and nobility require that only equals engage in duels.

[7]In their important analyses of ode 4 Reckford ("The Eagle and the Tree") and Johnson ("Tact in the Drusus Ode") discuss in further detail Horace's variations on Pindar, especially his stress on *doctrina* and (implicitly) *ars* in contradistinction to the Theban poet's primary concern with natural endowment in the make-up of heroism. See also Syndikus (321, n. 17, 322, and 325) for comment on Horace's replacement of Pindar's use of myth with Roman history for purposes of analogy.

[8]*N.* 5.14ff.

[9]*I.* 1.60ff., noted by Kiessling and Heinze on line 18. G. Williams (*Tradition and Originality*, 753–54) sees the parenthesis as evidence for the poet's "desire to insert his own personality" into the ode.

From one point of view, then, the startling authorial interruption continues to diminish the opening's epic pretensions, which are initiated by the succinct mention of Drusus and the Vindelici. The soaring Pindaric eagle is fastened by a tether partially of his own devising. From another viewpoint, the intrusive "I" and the use of Pindar against himself, helped by the coinage of a new word (*obarmet*), only underscore the attention the speaker now claims for himself.[10] He thus deflects the poem away from an impersonal outline of Drusus' exploits, an outline he will present judiciously in ode 14, and toward himself as lyric persona. He reminds us that we are in fact not involved with impersonal narration but with a strong-willed individual voice, carefully choosing and disposing of its own material.

The persona Horace unexpectedly adopts is that of inquisitive scholar, and the mode of the poem becomes briefly didactic. In *c.* 1.11 the speaker warns Leuconoe not to attempt to learn some facts:

> Tu ne quaesieris, scire nefas, quem mihi, quem tibi
> finem di dederint . . .

Do you not seek—it is wrong to know—what end the gods have allotted to me, what end to you . . .

In ode 4 the poet's mask finds only claims of omniscience to be sacrilegious; he merely defers necessary inquiry into the long-term arming habits of the Vindelici. But the postponement of more confined investigation into the meaning of a singular custom and even the forgoing of omniscience betray the speaker's interest in the study of origins and in teaching, in what he as imager of knowledge can and cannot, should and should not learn and tell. We are to have, as the first simile adumbrates, a poem about education. It will suggest the union, in the formation of one individual's *ethos,* of what Horace merges in the preceding poems when he combines the poetics of Pindar and of Callimachus: imagination and craft, shading, as we turn from versification to morality, into the amalgamation of instinctive nature and its training by education and upbringing. The

---

[10]Altogether in ode 4 there are some twenty words that Horace employs only in this poem and three others (two of them proper names) he only utilizes in book 4. *Indecoro* (36) appears elsewhere only once (Accius *Trag.* 459R) and *progenero* (32) is first used here in Latin poetry.

speaker's assertive stance reminds us that the process of education involves not only Augustus as molder of the natural inheritance of the Nerones but also the speaker-poet himself. He is the re-creator of this praxis in poetry; his words share a subtle but vital part in it as well.

The momentary authorial dislocation, then, shatters any expectation of epic sequences and anticipates explicit confirmation that the opening similes were metaphoric not for heroic action but for the formation of inner personal characteristics that attend the hero. The teacher-speaker knows, or knows not to know. The Gallic hordes only sense, physically, the results of Drusus' strategies, which are also his wise uses of intelligence. The sources of these *consilia* are reached in two climactic namings. We expect from the triple use of *quid* in lines 25–27 that the speaker will enumerate three corresponding gifts with which Drusus and Tiberius are endowed. However, their quality of mind (*mens*) and natural disposition (*indoles*) lead not to notice of a further inherited characteristic but, with an unexpected twist, to the animating spirit of Augustus, the wise fosterer of instinct, who serves as begetter of their minds, not of their bodies. The naming of Augustus is a rhetorical culmination for another verbal pattern that begins with *rite,* is elaborated in *faustus penetralibus,* and reaches its peak only with the mention of his *paternus animus.* What is done "duly" has, given the context, a religious significance that is specified in the well-omened, cherishing "shrine" where the youths have the good fortune to be reared. At the focus of this hallowed spot is the divine majesty of the emperor, whose tutelage, if we follow one strand of the rhetoric as well as the meaning of his name, is the greatest resource that they could possess.

But the second, final climax is in the mention of the Nerones. Ancient sources are exact about the etymology of the name. Among the various *cognomina* assumed by the Claudian *gens,* Suetonius lists *Nero* "the meaning of which, in the Sabine tongue, is brave and strong" (*quo significetur lingua Sabina fortis ac strenuus*).[11] And the cognate Nerio or Nerienis, warrior goddess wife of Mars, according to Aulus Gellius, "is a Sabine word which has the meaning courage and bravery" (*Sabinum verbum est, eoque significatur virtus et fortitudo*).[12]

---

[11]Suet. *Tib.* 1.2. The etymology is noted by Reckford ("The Eagle and the Tree," 28, n. 9) and documented in detail by Ernout-Meillet *s.v. Nero.* Virgil's Clausus ("from whom both the Claudian tribe and *gens* are spread through Latium," *Aen.* 7.708–9) is from Cures (*Aen.* 10.345).

[12]Gell. 13.23.7.

The "significance" and signifying of this name, Horace's speaker goes on to explain, is important for what it tells us both of the Nerones and of the poem itself. The opening simile, with its uses of *vigor* and *vividus,* had prepared us for *virtus* as an abstraction essential to the Nerones. The double use of *fortes* and *fortibus* and the abstract *virtus* along with *vis,* to which the ancients closely linked it, further substantiate the speaker's interest in the meaning of the name.[13] To determine and explicate the etymology of a name is to authenticate the possessors of it. To define their name linguistically is to define those named as living beings with a prescribed inheritance to admire and to enhance. Their actions verify (or betray, as the case may be) their nomenclature.

Once more, as in the initial simile's use of *docuere,* we find the speaker interested in what one learns from *doctrina,* from the civilizing instruction that molds the natural. And it is not surprising that the metaphors he uses of grafting (*insitam*) and strengthening (*roborant*) come from didactic, in this case georgic, literature.[14] We expect the brave to beget the brave, but only education will bring them knowledge of proper Roman behavior, of the wisdom, as Horace says elsewhere, to combine *vis* with *consilium* in an intelligent, rational use of the power that fashions and sustains an empire.[15] The speaker, then, has not allowed us to forget his interest in aetiology which his self-projection into the poem had called to our attention. What he considers valuable is not the origin of a custom peculiar to the Vindelici but an etymology of direct bearing on the endurance of Rome, not an arcane *mos* but the *mores* that must refine and guide this Neronian energy and whose loss means the loss of *decus* and the advent of *culpa.*

In the central stanza of the poem, where Horace's speaker apostrophizes the city of Rome for the only time in his poetry, we turn to the past. In this education by poetry, which is to say by exemplification, the speaker looks backward for his evidence. The victory of Gaius Claudius Nero, during his consulship in 207, over Hannibal's

---

[13]Cf. Ernout-Meillet *s.v. vis* ("Les anciens ne separaient pas *vis* de *vir, virtus*"). Livy on Camillus (6.22.7) offers a good example of the interconnection between *vividus, vigor* and *vis*: "*sed vegetum ingenium in vivido pectore vigebat virebatque integris sensibus*" (but a spirited intelligence flourished in his lively breast and he remained sharp in all his senses).

[14]This is Horace's only use of the participle *insitus.* Virgil's is at *geo.* 2.33.

[15]Cf. *c.* 3.4.65–68.

brother at Sena, on the Umbrian river Metaurus, was a turning point in the Second Punic War. What Rome owes Claudius Nero is what it owes and will owe Augustus' stepsons. The model for them to follow is located in their own past, and the poetry supports the interconnection in several ways.

As in the opening similes and in the speaker's brief disquisition on differentiation through inherited traits, we contemplate hierarchies of power. Before the battle at the Metaurus, Hannibal against Rome possesses the force of nature—fire against wood, air against wave. His strength is, metaphorically, that of a horse to which the energy of flame and east wind are added by simile. Claudius Nero broke this power and caused one of the celebratory moments, the bright "days," that are so important to Horace in these poems. The mastering of Hasdrubal (*devictus*) is an earlier parallel to the vanquishing of the Gallic hordes (*revictae*), and the removal of the clouds (*nimbis remotis*) which in the initial simile allows the Neronian eagle to perceive and assume its full potential corresponds to the Punic darkness (*fugatis tenebris*) routed by the great Claudian.

Here, too, the teacher-poet has not forgotten his role as deviser, renewer, and explicator of words. The meaning of *adorea,* the nourishing glory that enhances this new Roman dawn, was debated in antiquity, but the glosses that we have preserved, including Porphyrion's comment here, link it with the verb *adorare* (pray to) and explain it as *laus bellica,* praise won on the battlefield.[16] Servius, for instance, in making this same equation, reasons that people "addressed [*adloquebantur*] the man with thanksgiving who has behaved bravely [*fortiter*] in war."[17] This association between *adorea* and martial bravery is borne out by the contexts of its rare uses, in Plautus' *Amphitruo,* for instance, where it is conjoined with *virtus,* and in two places in the *Metamorphoses* of Apuleius, the first tying it to *virtus,* the second to *fortibus factis,* brave deeds.[18] Horace, in a splendid example of *callida iunctura,* the "clever joining" of words which the *Ars Poetica* lists as a poet's duty to discover,[19] places this lexical rarity where it will illuminate not only the prowess of Gaius Claudius Nero but his *cognomen,* once more, as well. This initial instance of courage proved

[16]Pliny (*H. N.* 18.14) and Paulus-Festus (3.22) derive the word from *ador.*
[17]Serv. on *Aen.* 10.677.
[18]Pl. *Amph.* 193; Ap. *M.* 3.19, 7.16.
[19]*A. P.* 47–48.

the aptness of his naming as will the expertise of his descendants nearly two centuries later. The poet, through his enlivening way with words, promotes the correspondence.

The nature (*indoles*) of Drusus and Tiberius had been fostered in the Augustan household, and it is a "nourishing" Neronian glory that anticipated the growth of an earlier generation of Roman youth, when Hannibal admitted defeat.[20] I will return shortly to the authenticating force of Hannibal's long monologue. Even at the start its artistry exhibits a marked similarity to the content and expression of the preceding stanzas. Horace's Hannibal also analogizes through rankings of power. He who shortly before, in the poem's and history's time, appeared like fire to the vulnerable pine woods of Rome becomes, in his own imagining and along with his fellow Carthaginians, a stag at the mercy of ravening Roman wolves. The Claudians have visited on their enemies a reversal of roles which the poetry reflects in simile. Hannibal also betrays his Horatian origins by sharing with his creator a fascination with words. According to the lexica, this instance is the first time in Latin that the adjective *opimus* is used metaphorically; ordinarily we would expect an explicit reference to a triumph subsequent to the death and despoiling of an enemy chief.[21] The nearest to such a triumph Hannibal can come is via metaphor and a show of pusillanimity. His success is only that he slips away and escapes.

Horace may, however, hint at the standard meaning of *opimus* which would explain why Hannibal is given the unexpected attribute *perfidus* immediately preceding his speech. Perhaps the closest Hannibal came to fulfilling the conditions of a Roman triumph involving *spolia opima* was in 208 B.C., the year before Hasdrubal's defeat at the Metaurus. Fearing that he was no match for both consuls together and practicing, as Livy puts it, his wonted "artistry" of treachery and deceit, he ambushed and killed near Venusia another great early Claudian, Marcus Claudius Marcellus.[22] Allusion to *spolia opima* would remind any Roman that Claudius was the last of three recorded gen-

---

[20]*Indoles*, etymologically derived from *alo* and glossed by Paulus-Festus (94.12) as *incrementum*, is therefore connected with both *alma* (41) and *crevit* (46, 62).

[21]See *TLL s.v.* 709.60–61.

[22]Livy records Hannibal's *insidiae* at the time of Marcellus' death (e.g., 27.26.3). Cf. 21.4.9, on his treachery (*perfidia plus quam Punica*), and 21.34.1, on his military "arts" of *fraus* and *insidiae*.

erals to have won the honor, in his case for killing the Insubrian chief Viridomarus at Clastidium in 222 B.C.[23]

If this explains Hannibal's perfidy and his allusion to an abortive *opimus triumphus,* Horace is too discreet to say so directly. Such outspokenness would mean mention of the death not only of a great member of the Claudian *gens* at the hands of Hannibal but also of his descendant and namesake, nephew and heir of Augustus, dead at the age of nineteen in 23 B.C. He does so, with extraordinary tact, through allusion to Virgil. At *Aeneid* 6.855–59 Anchises, concluding the colloquy with his son, points out both Marcelli, beginning with the elder:

> "aspice, ut insignis spoliis Marcellus opimis
> ingreditur victorque viros supereminet omnis.
> hic rem Romanam magno turbante tumultu
> sistet eques, sternet Poenos Gallumque rebellem,
> tertiaque arma patri suspendet capta Quirino."

"Behold how Marcellus makes his way, a cynosure for his 'rich spoils' and as a victor looms over all the men. This horseman will steady the Roman state when a great uproar will trouble it, will lay low the Carthaginians and the rebellious Gaul, and for the third time will hang up captured arms to father Quirinus."

The proximity of *Romana, Poenorum,* and *tumultu* in ode 4, 46–47, where the context also involves *spolia opima,* makes imitation a plausibility. Through his reference to the elder Marcellus, then, Horace touches on another example of Claudian military genius. At the same time he deflects attention away from Rome's public loss and from Augustus' private sorrow, which Virgil so movingly portrays in his description of the younger Marcellus' funeral, and toward Hannibal's defeat and Rome's renewal.

[23]The triumph is recorded in *CIL* 1.² 47. Ogilvie discusses the meaning of *spolia opima* in his note on Livy 1.10.7. It is noteworthy that in a poem devoted to Claudian *virtus* and Hannibal's loss of *fortuna,* a temple to *Virtus* was vowed by M. Claudius Marcellus at the battle of Clastidium and attached by him to an already existent shrine to *Honos* built by Q. Fabius Maximus Verrucosus after his war with the Ligurians (Cic. *N. D.* 2.61; for the dedication of the *aedis Virtutis,* Livy 27.25.7–9 and 29.11.13). It was in front of this temple, outside the Porta Capena, that the Senate consecrated the *Ara Fortunae Reducis* at Augustus' return from Sicily, Greece, and Asia in 19 B.C. (*R. G.* 11).

The *Aeneid* was also once again much on Horace's mind as he found words for Hannibal who sweeps us, in a summary of Virgil's grandeur, from Troy to Italy. We begin in the epic's first book, with Aeneas "tossed about" (*iactatus*)[24] and with Juno asking Aeolus for help in destroying Troy's remnants:[25]

> "gens inimica mihi Tyrrhenum navigat aequor
> Ilium in Italiam portans victosque penatis . . ."

"a race hostile to me sails the Etruscan sea, carrying Ilium and its conquered gods to Italy . . ."

The reader of the *Aeneid*'s second book remembers Aeneas' great act of *pietas,* leading his son and carrying his father into whose hands he has put Troy's *sacra:*[26] "'*tu, genitor, cape sacra manu patriosque penatis; . . .*'" ("father, do you clasp the holy objects and the nation's gods in your hand; . . ."). Horace's Hannibal, moving from particular to general, turns Aeneas and his symbolic action into a representative race that bore its sons, fathers, and holy emblems toward a new destiny. Line 55 documents Horace's only use of the adjective *Ausonius,* which, though frequent in Virgil, is coupled with *urbes* by him only once, in *Aeneid* 7.[27] That Horace was thinking not only of Virgil's look at the Trojans' departure from their homeland and subsequent trials but also at their arrival in Italy is confirmed by his bow to further words Virgil there gives the vengeful queen of the gods:[28]

> ". . . num incensa cremavit
> Troia viros? medias acies mediosque per ignis
> invenere viam."

"Did the conflagration of Troy make ashes of its men? In the midst of battle-ranks, in the midst of fire they have found their way."

---

[24]Re. *Aen.* 1.3; 4.14 (Dido speaking), 6.693 (Anchises speaking) for *iactatus* attached to Aeneas, and 1.629 where it is given to Dido, comparing her past with that of the Trojans.

[25]*Aen.* 1.67–68.

[26]*Aen.* 2.717.

[27]*Aen.* 7.104–5.

[28]*Aen.* 7.295–97; see Kiessling and Heinze (on line 53). One should also compare *Aen.* 11.305ff.

Repetition of the adjective *fortis* does not allow us to forget the Sabine Claudii, yet they do not have a monopoly on bravery in the Roman background. If Claudian heroism stemmed Hannibal's destructive tide and now turns back a Gallic menace, the original act of renewal and restoration was the translation of Troy to Rome. This was accomplished, as the name *Ilium* reminds us, not by an earlier Clausus but by Aeneas himself, ancestor of Augustus and therefore source of the Julian *gens* and its contemporary glory.

The poetic heritage of the second simile Horace puts into Hannibal's mouth—the Romans as a holm-oak unharmed by a shearing from the blows of double-bladed axes—stems from two predictable sources. The first is from Pindar's fourth *Pythian* ode where the poet likens the exiled, but faithful, Damophilus, yearning to return to Cyrene, to an oak that maintains its essence even when transformed:[29]

> If a man, with keen-edged axe, were to hew all the boughs of a mighty oak, and mar its comely form; even although its fruit may fail, it nevertheless giveth proof of itself, if ever it cometh at last to the wintry fire; or if, having left its own place desolate, it resteth (as a beam) on the upright pillars of some palace, and doeth slavish service amid alien walls. [Sandys]

The second is Virgil's comparison of Ilium sinking into flames to a mountain ash hacked at and felled by farmers:[30]

> ac veluti summis antiquam in montibus ornum
> cum ferro accisam crebrisque bipennibus instant
> eruere agricolae certatim, illa usque minatur . . .

[29]*P.* 4.263–69. The Pindaric allusion is discussed by Fraenkel (*Horace,* 430) and Johnson ("Tact in the Drusus Ode," 178), among others. It is possible, because of *roborant* (34) and the *ilex* simile, that Horace may be suggesting a connection between Drusus and δρῦς, oak. The ancients, however, derived the name from Drausus, a Gallic chief slain by a Livius who adopted it as a surname (Suet. *Tib.* 3).

[30]*Aen.* 2.626–28. It is interesting for the relation of lines 33–34 to the *ilex* simile that within a few lines in *Aeneid* 2 Virgil can co-opt the simile's essential metaphor by looking at the sturdy Trojan remnant "whose strength stands firm to its core" (*quibus . . . solidae . . . suo stant robore vires* [638–39]).

just as when farmers vie with each other to bring down an aged ash tree amid mountain peaks, they gird it with iron and attack it with many an axe blow, ever it threatens . . .

In each case the alterations are telling. Horace exchanges Virgil's *ornus* for an *ilex* placed not in an anonymous setting but on Algidus, the eastern spur of Mons Albanus, known for its shrine to Diana and its oak forests, and therefore very much surviving and in Italy. Instead of being toppled for some final unstated purpose, its trimming furnishes continual foliage, presumably for food or bedding.[31] From Pindar's comparison Horace adopts the idea of *usus* (the wintry fire) and, though in a more practical sense, of artistry (the oak's placement as a prop) against whose modifications inner vitality remains immutable. Horace's point is the steadfastness of the living heart of oak, which survives, and in fact supports the georgic efforts of others. Horace means us to review lines 33–34:

> doctrina sed vim promovet insitam
> rectique cultus pectora roborant. . .

It is Claudian *vis* that is grafted on to the tree of Julian *doctrina,* not the other way around. Only from Augustus' cultivation does the oak of the Claudii gain its strength. Augustus provides both nature and nurture for his stepsons. Like Rome, their martial spirit thrives on the challenges of battle, but the "spirit" thus gained needs the determining vigilance of Augustus' *animus* as well.

Hannibal's second analogy for Rome varies many of the same themes. From *ilex* to *hydra* we change from inanimate to animate, land to water, Italian reality to Greek myth. There is a touch of irony, especially by comparison to the preceding stanzas, when the Carthaginian attributes to himself the civilizing heroism of Hercules about his labors—and, implicitly, of Cadmus—clearing Thebes of monsters. But essentially we have a symbol of Rome similar to that of the ilex tree—gaining strength as its body is cut, growing as its youth "grew" after the defeat of Hannibal, conquering (*vinci, victorem*), like Gaius Claudius Nero and his newly tested descendants. The mention of "much praise" (*multa laude*) looks back specifically to

---

[31]The latter use is suggested by Cato (*Agr.* 5.7).

the *adorea,* the *laus bellica,* that accrued to the victor at the Metaurus and that comes now to the young Nerones from their heroism and through a poet's praise.

But a note of sadness has gradually crept into Hannibal's words. Hercules grieves, albeit at his temporary loss, and wives tell of battles not only because their husbands performed gloriously but because they died. It is on the idea of his personal loss as well as of Claudian accomplishment that Horace has Hannibal conclude his speech and the poem.[32] This highly emotional moment, bordering on threnody, is pointed up by the repetition of *occidit* in asyndeton. Because of Hasdrubal's death, there is no Punic future, no hope and no possibility of good fortune. He is named, but the larger naming of reputation that ensures transcendence is lost. It is this very "naming" of the Nerones that Horace has projected in his great ode, starting with etymology and endorsing its propriety by the documentation of history. It is on the reassurance of Claudian, and therefore Roman, futurity that Hannibal ends. Once more, through the contrivance of his speaker's words, Horace looks back into his poem to bring it full circle. Claudian military artistry, like the development of Claudian character, will depend on two things; the blessing of those in power and their own canny instincts.

Cicero defines *sagire* as *sentire acute,* a sharp sense of discernment.[33] Their ability to surmount the crises of war comes from the Claudians' inheritance. But inheritance, at least in their case, must be supported by approval from heaven. From Hannibal's point of view this means the favor of the king of the gods. In the larger context of the poem as a whole, however, reference to Jupiter takes us full circle and reminds us that it is Augustus as Jupiter who fosters this present generation of Nerones, prosecuting the persistent work of renewing Rome.

In the unfolding pattern of book 4 as a whole, ode 4 looks in one of two directions. How one interprets its major element of structural continuity, namely the poet's constant recourse to bipolar analogies that pit strong against weak, enduring against ephemeral, is decisive. Judged from the point of view of epic or of Pindaric sublimity, these

[32]Fraenkel (*Horace,* 428, n. 1) argues decisively in favor of having Hannibal's speech continue until the end of the poem.
[33]Cic. *Div.* 1.65. Line 76 offers the first use in Latin of *acutus* as a substantive with meaning equivalent to "crises" (*TLL s.v. acuo,* 468.3–4).

enhance the glory that is Augustan Rome. The poet's privileged simultaneity, which looks at the layers of Roman history from Troy to Augustus, stresses what remains abiding and static through Rome's ability to regenerate and reenliven its heroism. As such the poem fits into a series of what are to all appearances eulogistic poems that do honor to Augustus and his burgeoning principate. But as he molds history into lyric, especially by conceiving a soliloquy for Hannibal in defeat that praises Rome more convincingly than any open encomium from the creating "I" could, Horace casts a cold eye on Rome's epic by dwelling on victims as well as victors, brothers who lose as well as those who win, families splintered as well as reinforced.[34] It is to the misfortune and death that war brings to Hannibal in Italy that the poet gives the next to last word. And in this we will find the ode clinging to another pattern of poems more private and personal than first glance reveals.

Finally, through its stress on youth and youthfulness, ode 4 serves to introduce the book's second triad. The opening trio ended with the poet's birth in the special charge of the Muse and with his acceptance by Rome. The second pays special heed to the rejuvenation and education of Rome. We see this emphasis on youth in ode 4 not only in the prominence given the relationship of parents to children but also in the young age of Drusus (*iuvenem*) together with his brother (*pueros*), and of Rome after Hasdrubal's defeat (*pubes*).[35] It is *iuventas* that first propels the eagle Drusus from his nest. As a general notion youthfulness was important for Augustan propaganda. Though he was close to fifty when it was apparently completed in the middle teens of the first century B.C., the statue of Augustus found at Prima Porta depicts him as vigorously heroic. Likewise the appearance of children on the Ara Pacis, dedicated in 13 B.C., because not ordinarily included in early Roman reliefs, demonstrates their importance now for domestic legislation as well as dynastic succession.

[34]Through the eyes of Horace's Hannibal it is Rome that is partially unnatural and monstrous, while he takes for himself the role of Hercules who became the epitome of civilizer and with whom Augustus was closely associated (cf., for example, *Aen.* 6.801–3 and Galinsky, *The Herakles Theme,* 138–41). Just how kindly are we to take these wolves and eagles, Nerones who kill deer and sheep, who are driven by *amor,* who fight snakes but are themselves snaky hydras? The speaker and his Rome seem to know a great deal, but it is Rome's victims who feel (*sensere* [25])!

[35] Etymologically *iuvencis* (30) also comes from the same root as *iuvenis.*

There was a particular association between Augustus and *Iuventas* which reminds us that Romans interpreted their equivalent of the Greek Hebe not so much as a goddess of youthful beauty as patroness of the *iuvenes* or men ready for military service.[36] The so-called *Feriale Cumanum* informs us that Augustus assumed the *toga virilis* on October 18, the same day on which there was a *supplicatio Spei et Iuventati,* a propitiatory celebration for Hope and Youth.[37] We also know from his *Res Gestae* that Augustus restored (the exact date is unknown) the temple of *Iuventas* which had burned in 16 B.C.[38] The origin of this temple has a vicarious bearing on ode 4, a poem concerned with both *iuventas* and the *virtus* manifested by those whose initiation into manhood began in her shrine. Its construction was vowed on the battlefield at the Metaurus in 207 B.C. by Marcus Livius Salinator, co-victor with Gaius Claudius Nero in that crucial conflict.[39] Horace, then, while more directly noting Augustus' concern with *iuventas,* by inference reminds us that a direct ancestor of Livia, mother of the young lion Drusus from whom he took his name and also a Claudian, was likewise instrumental in enhancing a cult much on Augustus' mind at the time Horace was accomplishing his own formidable act of poetic rejuvenation.

[36]Ogilvie (on Livy 5.54.7) discusses in further detail plausible reasons for Augustus' interest in the cult of *Iuventas.*

[37]*CIL* 10.8375.

[38]For the burning, C. D. 54.19.7; for the restoration *R. G.* 19 (and cf. *app.* 2).

[39]The *ludi Iuventatis,* which Livius Salinator also vowed, are mentioned by Cicero (*Brutus* 18.73). The temple, located at the edge of the Circus Maximus, was begun by him when censor in 204 and dedicated by C. Licinius Lucullus in 193 B.C. (Livy 36.36.5–6).

[5]

ODE FIVE

Divis orte bonis, optume Romulae
custos gentis, abes iam nimium diu:
maturum reditum pollicitus patrum
    sancto concilio, redi.

lucem redde tuae, dux bone, patriae.   5
instar veris enim voltus ubi tuus
adfulsit populo, gratior it dies
    et soles melius nitent.

ut mater iuvenem, quem Notus invido
flatu Carpathii trans maris aequora   10
cunctantem spatio longius annuo
    dulci distinet a domo,

votis ominibusque et precibus vocat
curvo nec faciem litore dimovet,
sic desideriis icta fidelibus   15
    quaerit patria Caesarem.

tutus bos etenim rura perambulat,
nutrit rura Ceres almaque Faustitas,
pacatum volitant per mare navitae,
    culpari metuit fides,   20

nullis polluitur casta domus stupris,
mos et lex maculosum edomuit nefas,
laudantur simili prole puerperae,
    culpam poena premit comes.

quis Parthum paveat, quis gelidum Scythen,   25
quis Germania quos horrida parturit
fetus incolumi Caesare? quis ferae
    bellum curet Hiberiae?

condit quisque diem collibus in suis
et vitem viduas ducit ad arbores;   30
hinc ad vina redit laetus et alteris
    te mensis adhibet deum.

te multa prece, te prosequitur mero
defuso pateris, et Laribus tuum
miscet numen, uti Graecia Castoris   35
    et magni memor Herculis.

"longas o utinam, dux bone, ferias
praestes Hesperiae" dicimus integro
sicci mane die, dicimus uvidi,
    cum sol Oceano subest.   40

Sprung from gracious gods, finest warden of the race of Romulus, you are absent now too long. Return, since you promised a timely return to the sacred council of the fathers. Noble leader, render again your brilliance to your fatherland. For when your countenance, like spring, has beamed upon your people, the day courses more pleasantly, and suns better their gleam.

Just as a mother calls with vows and omens and prayers her young son—the South wind with envious gale estranges him, lingering longer than a year's span, from his sweet home across the reaches of the Carpathian sea—nor does she turn her face away from the curved shore, so stricken with the yearnings of loyalty, the fatherland seeks its Caesar.

For the cow saunters safely through the fields, the fields Ceres and nourishing Well-being sustain, sailors sweep through a sea at peace, Faith fears to suffer blame, chaste homes are befouled by no stain, custom and law have tamed blotched evil, women in childbirth are praised for likeness to their offspring, punishment presses hard on blame.

Who might cower before the Parthian, who before the chill Scythian, who before the whelps that bristling Germany spawns, with Caesar safe? Who would be troubled by war with wild Hiberia? Every man on his own hills puts the day to set and weds the vine to widowed trees. Hence joyously he returns to his wine-draughts and invites you as a god to the main course. You he accosts with many a prayer, you with libation poured from his goblets; he mingles your divinity with the gods of his household, just as Greece stays mindful of Castor and of mighty Hercules.

"Noble leader, please grant long holidays to Hesperia," this is our prayer, sober in the morning when the day is whole, this is our prayer, mellow, when the sun sinks into the Ocean.

Augustus was imagined absent in the second ode of the book. In the fifth ode he is still away while Horace addresses him directly for the first time in the collection. The second poem had been concerned in part with Augustus' triumphant homecoming from Gaul which, we remember, would surpass even the restoration of ancient golden times, should this be among the bequests of the "good gods." The *boni divi* stand at the head of Horace's new ode, hymnic confirmation that this renewal has now occurred, even if the vitalizing figure remains elsewhere.

The force of this initial compliment can be judged by comparison with the passage from Ennius which critics agree Horace was revising:[1]

> Pectora . . . tenet desiderium, simul inter
> Sese sic memorant "O Romule, Romule die,
> Qualem te patriae custodem di genuerunt!
> O pater o genitor o sanguen dis oriundum!
> Tu produxisti nos intra luminis oras."

Desire clings to their hearts, as soon as among themselves they thus recall to mind "O Romulus, blessed Romulus, what a guardian of the

[1]Ennius *Ann.* 110-4V³, noted by Fraenkel (*Horace*, 441–42, and 442, n. 1) and Syndikus (332 and n. 7).

fatherland did the gods beget in you! O father, o begetter, o blood sprung from the gods! You have led us within the shores of light."

The eulogistic apostrophe that Ennius weaves into his epic context is chanted by Horace's speaker directly to its recipient as a hymn: Augustus, like Ennius' Romulus, is sprung from the gods, to be a guardian of his country.[2] The poet's archaising use of *optume* not only enhances the reverential tone but draws us back through linguistic time to Ennius himself.[3] Just as Augustus is the new Romulus, protecting by his saving power what Rome's first king had originated, so the teller of his tale reminds us of his lexical heritage, beginning majestically again. But there are major differences between Ennius and Horace. The context of Ennius' fragment in Cicero's *De Re Publica* calls one of these to our attention. The great orator is illustrating a people's bereavement at the passing of a just and excellent (*optimus*) king.[4] Horace, by contrast, deals not with a *rex* but merely with a *dux bonus,* and not with death but merely with absence. In place of Ennius' exclamation on the apotheosis of Romulus we have the speaker's imperious attention to return (*reditum, redi*) which resonates into his second command (*redde*). His hymn (and Horace's book) is a *revocatio* that succeeds only in its final poems. But unlike prayers that crave a divine presence to turn away evil or revive the moribund, the setting here already is renewed. It lacks only Augustus, its living focus of continuity.

These stanzas dwell on an aspect of time that further distinguishes their content from Ennius. *Maturum* looks to the completion of a span of linear time, but *orte,* while explicitly defining Augustus' divine ancestry (as *oriundum* did that of Romulus), hints at origination of another sort. Romulus had led his people into the shores of light. Augustus, by contrast, is not only good, like the gods from whom he emanates, he is light itself for his people. Though, as we will see, land and society thrive, the Roman world, at the start of Horace's en-

---

[2] Norberg ("La divinité") offers a good survey of Horace's varying treatments of the divinity of Augustus.

[3] Horace is not afraid of juxtaposing the archaic with the novel here and elsewhere in the poem, as if to show, *in parvo,* that his poem is an unprecedented variation on the encomiastic tradition. At 5–6, for instance, the archaic *vultus* neighbors *adfulsit,* used for the first time in Latin poetry, and at 18–19 the coinage *Faustitas* appears one line before the archaizing *navitae.*

[4] Cic. *Rep.* 1.64.

comium, still awaits the emperor's bright rising. This brightness takes several forms. His face is like spring, but not the spring of later poems which contrasts human evanescence with the recurrence of the seasons. This spring has something of the preceding ode's Jovian spring breezes that foster the eagle's growth into its full potential. The face of Augustan spring is soon associated with the day's glad course and with the gleaming suns that categorize its clarity.[5] Once Augustus returns, complex (*reditum, redi,* again) yields to solemn simplicity (*it*), as the day's continuous brightness certifies his continuous presence. The connection is substantiated by the use of *melius* where we expect instead a word such as *candidius.* Augustan suns shine "better" because they qualify someone who is both the best guardian (*optume custos*) and a good leader (*dux bone*). The poem will show this gleam working a double magic on Rome's people, preserving both the exterior and interior quality of their lives, landscape and ethics at once.

Horace defines Rome's emotion through simile. It has been proposed that the literary source of the yearning mother, who serves as analogy for Rome, lies in the deserted heroines of Greek myth, an Ariadne or a Phyllis waiting in vain for their lovers to return.[6] I suggest that Horace's imagination was triggered by something nearer to hand. Shortly after he had issued his initial collection of odes, Propertius, whose influence on odes 2 and 3 of book 4 I have already touched upon, published his third book of elegies. Among its masterpieces is the extraordinary seventh poem devoted to one Paetus, driven by avarice and drowned at sea, his body devoured by fish. In counterpoint to this tale of ambition revenged is the picture of the youth's dear mother whose name was often on the dying swimmer's lips:[7]

> et mater non iusta piae dare debita terrae
> nec pote cognatos inter humare rogos,

[5]Pöschl ("Horaz und die Politik," 141) duly notes the importance of spring as an element in the Hellenistic–Oriental figuration of the savior in the background throughout ode 5.

[6]Kiessling and Heinze (on l. 9), working backwards from a passage in Oppian (*Hal.* 4.335ff.) which recalls Ovid's treatment of Phyllis in *Heroides* 2 (121ff.), suggest a common source in a lost passage of Callimachus (cf. the apostrophe to Demophoon in *Aet.* fr. 556Pf.).

[7]Prop. 3.7.9–12 (and cf. 17–18, *cara mater*).

> sed tua nunc volucres astant super ossa marinae,
> nunc tibi pro tumulo Carpathium omne mare est.

but your mother cannot offer the rites due the holy earth, nor bury you among the tombs of your relatives, but now sea birds stand over your bones, now the whole Carpathian sea replaces your burial mound.

These are the only occasions on which each poet uses the phrase *Carpathium mare*.[8] It seems more than coincidental that a mother and son are in each case involved. Propertius' speaker reproves his subject's depravity. Had Paetus heeded his words,[9]

> viveret ante suos dulcis conviva Penatis,
> pauper, at in terra nil nisi fleret opes.

he would survive as a loving comrade before his household gods, poor, but on land he would weep for nothing except his wealth.

In Horace death from innate greed is replaced by absence caused by an outside force of nature, and censure becomes a parent's prayers, which are but a variation of the speaker's own evocative words of longing.

Use of *desiderium* suggests that Ennius also remained on Horace's mind. But this further reminiscence points up another distinction with his epic predecessor as well as a major unifying theme of these four stanzas. For Ennius, Romulus is *patriae custodem, pater* and *genitor*. In death he has become *pater patriae,* a title that was first awarded to Julius Caesar and bestowed, by universal accord, on Augustus in 2 B.C. It was inscribed on the *quadriga* standing at the center of his forum which was dedicated that same year. Horace here takes a different tack, more subtly complimentary. The parenthood of the state links these lines, leading from *patrum concilio* (3–4) to *patriae* (5) and *patria* (16), with *mater* an important figure in the intervening simile. But, unlike Romulus, Augustus is not made to share in the communal dignity given to age. Horace's speaker treats him implicitly as son, explicitly as *iuvenem*. He is not so much the person-

---

[8]Propertius refers to *Carpathiae undae* at 2.5.11 and Horace to *Carpathium pelagus* at *c.* 1.35.8.

[9]Prop. 3.7.45–46.

ification of *pietas* as of *Iuventas,* incorporating what Horace had imputed to the Nerones in the preceding poem. From the *paternus animus* of a special father cherishing and rearing his stepsons, he has become a more general symbol of youth whose vital presence is essential for the extended rejuvenation of the state. He epitomizes the stalwart heroism upon which the well-being of his "fathers" depends and on which their familial love concentrates. It is this spiritual eroticism, not the fading, private sexuality of ode 1, which gradually becomes paramount as book 4 evolves.

The preceding ode also enters briefly into the expansive vision of the golden time Augustus has effected.[10] Ode 4 concentrates on the particulars of an education by Augustus and on the instincts of the Nerones nourished within his fostering domain (*indoles nutrita faustis sub penetralibus*). In the wider dispensation of an Augustan peace it is the goddess of the harvest who does the cherishing together with *Faustitas,* an abstract personification of a new fostering spirit abroad in the land.

Faustitas is an invention of Horace, apparently receiving her only literary mention here, but she has one interesting Horatian antecedent. Lines 17–20 bear a resemblance to a love poem (*c.* 1.17) in Horace's first collection in which he invites the singer Tyndaris to share the sequestered beauty of his Sabine retreat.[11] Menace and fear are unknown in this sheltered haven which the girl enlivens with her music (5–8):

> inpune tutum per nemus arbutos
> quaerunt latentis et thyma deviae
> olentis uxores mariti
> nec viridis metuunt colubras . . .

without harm the wandering consorts of the rank he-goat seek hidden arbute and thyme through the safe woods, nor do they fear green watersnakes.

---

[10]Fraenkel (*Horace,* 443) observes the change of style at line 17 and Syndikus (337) notes the important influence of Hesiod (*W. and D.,* 225ff.) who associates a country's peace with the presence of a righteous judge.

[11]Syndikus (337–38, n. 44) sees the relation among ode 5, 17–20, *c.* 1.17.5–8, and *epode* 16.43ff.

The external cause of this innocence, according to the opening stanza, is the kindly presence of the god Faunus, the Roman Pan, country god of many shapes, who protects the speaker's flocks from summer's fiery heat and rainy winds. Now Faunus and Horace's coinage, *Faustitas,* are allied lexically, each having its origin in the verb *favere,* to be propitious.[12] Their Horatian contexts suggest a further parallel. The earlier poem shows Faunus preserving the speaker's private *locus amoenus* from danger. The later bow to Augustus invents, as an appropriate spirit for his age, an abstract variant of Faunus who not only cherishes a newly revived Roman outer world of land and sea but also apotropaically thwarts any corrupting moral tendencies.

The enemy of the natural world, which seems to have held it motionless in history's version of winter, is war. With peace comes the freedom of cattle to roam at will and of sailors to fly the seas. In the moral warfare waged at home, the victorious abstractions *fides, castitas, mos, lex,* and *poena* are pitted against *culpa, stupra,* and *maculosum nefas,* a beast of many stains.[13] In the preceding poem, with its more particular setting, we pondered what might happen in a family situation when *mores* failed and *culpae* disgraced innate quality.[14] Ode 5 looks to broader exemplification of Augustan *doctrina* at work. Horace may mean to remind us, as the emperor himself duly noted, that by 13 B.C. Augustus had already twice been appointed *curator legum et morum* and would soon receive the title once again.[15] But even amid the plethora of abstractions that dot this wider moral landscape, it is still on the home and on childbearing and offspring that Horace has his moralist speaker concentrate. Fittingly, he does so in these poems on Roman fathers and sons, whose center is ode 5.

To underscore the high tone of his speaker's magisterial pronouncements in these stanzas, Horace uses vocabulary that might have surprised even his ancient reader. *Faustitas* he invents, as we have seen, and *volitant* is unique in his works, but lines 21 and 22 contain the greatest cluster of verbal novelties in book 4 and perhaps in his entire poetic output. *Polluitur, stupris, maculosum* and *edomuit* all

---

[12]On the relation of *Faunus* and *faustus* with *faveo* see Ernout-Meillet *s.vv.*

[13]The particular meaning of *fides,* "sanctity" in making contracts, for an agricultural and commercial context is pointed out by MacKay.

[14]Ode 4, 35–36.

[15]R. G. 6. The dates were, respectively, 19, 18, and 11 B.C.

appear for the first and only occasion in Horace's work.[16] All are rare words in poetry (*edomuit,* unusual in itself, finds its first poetic use here). In the speaker's perception, their presence vivifies the abstractions whose domination over Roman life Augustan moral reforms have brought to an end by suppressing the corrupt.

In terms, then, of lexical usage that combines archaism with novelty, Horace's ode stands as metaphor for the Augustan Age itself. It revives the old and discovers the new, carefully incorporating the past into a present that, for all its facade of conservatism, has its share of bold invention.

Horace summarizes the essence of these two stanzas devoted to country peace and civic moral fortitude near the opening of his epistle to Augustus where he speaks of the emperor's ensuring the safety of Italy with arms, adorning it with customs and emending it with laws.[17] Ode 5 in particular seems to be sketching an Italian landscape secure and productive again after the disruptions of civil war. Only after noting the outer and inner health of Italy does Horace turn to foreign enemies. The point is universal in antiquity: the safety of a people regularly depends on the well-being of its leader. For Rome this means freedom from fear of enemies surrounding the empire: Parthia and Scythia covering the extent of the east, Germany to the north, and Hiberia on the west. It is appropriate, as the poet re-addresses the theme of proper birth and education, that, were it not for Augustus' tutelage, what Rome might fear is the offspring that uncouth Germany and, presumably, primitive Spain might engender. Such barbarian births would lack the *recti cultus* afforded the growing Nerones and would not stem from the chaste homes of Rome.[18] Yet against them Caesar provides immunity just as he had furnished re-creative norms for his own populace.

For the focal showplace of this stability Horace's eulogist chooses country, not city. The idea of renewed continuity of landholding or usage (the force of *suis*) is put in terms of daily time and the regularity

[16]This is the first and only use, until Tertullian, of *maculosus* with an abstraction that it therefore helps personify. Its meaning ("blotched," "spotted") elicits the etymological connection of *polluitur* with *lutum* ("mud"), and together they contrast with the imagery of light the poem associates with Augustus.

[17]*Epi.* 2.1.2–3: "*res Italas armis tuteris, moribus ornes,/legibus emendes. . .*"

[18]Ode 4, 34.

of viticultural tasks. Just as the imminent, majestic reappearance of Augustus assures the brightness of Rome's day, so his return finds its synecdoche in the restored quotidian regimen of the farmer, taking advantage of the day to do his own "leading," and returning to make obeisance to the divinity upon whom the perpetuation of this routine relies.

This daily cycle of work and rest encapsulates one strand of nature's productivity, as we move from the hills, where vines were planted, to the vines themselves and their actual supports, to the utilitarian results of the farmer's efforts (*vina*). In line 30 Horace is thinking of the second of Catullus' wedding hymns in which the boys remind the girls that a virgin who remains unmarried is "like a companionless vine which springs up in an empty field" (*ut vidua in nudo vitis quae nascitur arvo* . . .).[19] It is the farmer's duty to "marry" vines with elms to corroborate the potential of nature to renew itself. But behind the performance of such tasks lies marriage itself, in the presumption of continuity of the rustic home life Virgil so movingly portrays at the conclusion of the second book of the *Georgics*. Virgil ends by jolting us out of what he imagines was once the beatific reality of rural domesticity into the truth of the present, when war trumpets blare and swords are forged on creaking anvils. According to Horace's encomiast, Augustus has led Rome through this time of war and renewed in the countryside a manner of living which for Virgil was practiced in a past recalled only through a poet's dream.

Horace may have been thinking of Virgil in another way. His use of *condere* in line 29, meaning to finish a certain stretch of time, has only two antecedents in extant Latin poetry. One of them is in Virgil's ninth *eclogue,* a poem concerned with the loss of poetic power and with the departure of poet-shepherds from the countryside because of war's displacements. One of them, Moeris, as he leaves, thinks back to the time of his youth whose long days he would see to their conclusion (*condere soles*) as he sang.[20] In the preceding lines his

---

[19]Cat. 62.49. There are other connections between Catullus 62 and ode 5, among them the echo of 62.46 (*cum castum amisit polluto corpore florem*) at 21 (*nullis polluitur casta domus stupris*).

[20]Ecl. 9.52. The other, still earlier parallel use of *condere* is at DRN 3.1090 (*condere saecla*). The model for Moeris' language at line 52 is Call. *Ep.* 34(2) = AP 7.80, lines 2–3, an epigram that deals with the enduring power of immortal verse.

colleague Lycidas has recalled a snippet of former song which chron-
icled the appearance of the comet said to represent the divinized spirit
of Julius Caesar—[21]

> astrum quo segetes gauderent frugibus et quo
> duceret apricis in collibus uva colorem.

the star at which the wheat grows glad with grain, at which the grape
draws in its color on the sun-drenched hills.

If Horace wants his audience to recall these lines it is in order to say
that war is over and that Julius Caesar's great-nephew has in his own
person fulfilled for the countryside what is proposed for the star of his
uncle only after the latter's death and in a singer's nearly forgotten
words. Augustus has returned prosperity to the countryside. He has
also restored to its denizens the capability of song.

About the time of the publication of the fourth book of odes, in 13
B.C. or soon thereafter, Horace addressed the epistle to Augustus we
mentioned earlier. In it he treats the emperor as a *divus praesens*.[22]

> praesenti tibi maturos largimur honores
> iurandasque tuum per numen ponimus aras, . . .

to you in your own person we bestow due honors and we establish
altars for oaths to be sworn by your divinity, . . .

We also know from inscriptions that as early as 12 B.C. altars were
dedicated to the *Genius Augusti* and placed for worship together with
the images of the *Lares Compitales,* a practice institutionalized in 7
B.C.[23] In ode 5 the imagined ceremony is carefully located in the
country and remains private. The rustic's prayer reechoes the prayers
(13) of the fatherland as "mother," yearning for her absent son. He
uses the vintage he has produced for offering, and the speaker trans-

---

[21]*Ecl.* 9.48–49.

[22]*Epi.* 2.1.15–16. In line 5 he had already been linked with Romulus, Liber
Pater, Castor and Pollux.

[23]On the origins of libations to Augustus, see C. D. 51.19.7. Latte (306–8),
Frazer (4:15–16, on *F.* 5.146), and Brink (553–54) discuss in detail the association
of the *Genius Augusti* with the *Lares Compitales.*

fers fact to metaphor as he describes the act of worship (*miscet*) which establishes Augustus among the protecting deities of his own dwelling.

The leap to Greece and the analogy drawn between Augustus, Castor, and a Hercules now identified is imputed to the learned speaker, not to his chanting comrades. The compliment is multi-faceted. Like Romulus, with whom he is connected in the poem's opening lines, and the two Greek heroes, Augustus is worthy of apotheosis for accomplishing heroic exploits. Yet unlike them he is deified while still alive. Moreover he combines in himself their separate spheres. Along with Castor he guarantees the safety of the now pacified seas. He shares with Hercules the ability to purge the earth of monsters that challenge civilization's order, the Hercules of the preceding ode. The hero's link with Augustus has its particular propriety here. As divinized husband of Hebe, with his earthly victories behind him, he has close associations in Rome with *Iuventas*.[24] He shared a feast day with Ceres[25] and, as grandson of Silvanus, was worshiped as an averter of evil from the countryside.[26] This apotropaic quality extended to his role as protector of possessions. Hercules *Custos* is to the well-being of the domestic microcosm what Augustus is to the empire at large.[27]

The eulogy reaches its climax and conclusion as third person changes to first and the speaker, joining the other celebrants, quotes the actual words uttered during the communal country feast. He has imagined one honorific song within which he re-creates a further moment of song-making, as if the prolongation of rural festival offered the final reassurance for the permanence of his own song, and vice versa. Both song about festival and festival-song depend, of

[24]In this connection, and thinking back to ode 4, we should remember that in the year 218 B.C., with Hannibal in the north, a *Lectisternium* and *Supplicatio* were offered to *Iuventas* in the temple of Hercules (Livy 21.62.9).

[25]Macr. *Sat.* 3.11.10 mentions a common sacrifice to Hercules and Ceres.

[26]Hercules and Silvanus are often connected on inscriptions (e.g., *CIL* 6.288 and 295ff.). See also *Carm. epig.* 23 Buecheler (= *CIL* 6.30738): "*Hercules invicte, sancte Silvani nepos, hic advenisti: ne quid hic fiat mali*" (Unconquered Hercules, holy grandson of Silvanus, you have made your way here, lest any evil happen here).

[27]On *Hercules custos*, see the comments of Pseudo-Acron and Porphyrion on *Sat.* 2.6.15 and Latte (219 and n. 3). Wissowa (281–82) also discusses in detail the role of Hercules as household divinity. Cf. also Bayet (372–79) for the relationship of Hercules, Faunus, and Silvanus.

course, on continuity of setting, on the peace and stability which Augustus, even in absentia, can promote.

The words themselves are a synecdoche for the tale they tell, mirroring the reiteration of the event and what it stands for (and, therefore, bringing it perpetually into being). It is a hymn making more timeless still the act of hymning, and the events hymned, within the poem. As he writes Horace may be hearing Virgil's beautiful account of Orpheus mourning for his beloved Eurydice.[28]

> te, dulcis coniunx, te solo in litore secum,
> te veniente die, te decedente canebat.

he sang of you to himself on the lonely shore, you, sweet wife, you, as day came, you, as it departed.

Here, too, verbal repetitions simulate song poured out unceasingly against the backdrop of the changing daily round. Yet, richly emotional as Virgil's epic evocation is, its narrative cannot claim the intensity of the lyric "we" singing a hymn within a hymn. The manner in which the two poets look at time in these passages underscores this distinction. For Virgil's Orpheus the day arrives and withdraws, like the seasons, or love, or life. Its motion echoes our emotional risings and fallings. Horace's lyric speaker steadies day's brightness, symbol of a yearning beyond Orpheus' very human needs, before our thoughts. Night does not fall. Nothing comes or goes. The sun is under the ocean only momentarily. What alternates is merely the sobriety or inebriation of the singers as they pursue their honorific task.

The last stanza also brings the poem full circle. The reiteration of the apostrophe *dux bone* from line 5 associates quoted song with the ode that gives it context, and the concluding *die* and *sol,* by picking up *dies* and *soles* from the same earlier stanza, offer one final reminder of the interassociation or, better, interdependence of the radiant days Augustus extends to Rome and the festal song that enduringly ritualizes their praises. Augustus is the sun, only temporarily absent.[29]

The final act of homage is, of course, the extraordinary poem itself

---

[28]Vir. *geo.* 4.465–66.

[29]*Mane,* l. 39, is also cognate with *maturum,* l. 3 (see Ernout-Meillet *s.vv.*). A helpful comparison with 5.40 is provided by 2.46–48. In each instance Augustus is associated with the sun.

which by its very indirection avoids the bombast that so readily invades panegyric poetry. Ode 4 subverts our expectation of a catalog of bold deeds and dwells instead on the molding of the inner quality of heroes as well as on the emotions of those who suffer their dynamism. The present poem re-creates the Augustan peace not from the viewpoint of urban Rome and its glory but from the quieter remove of the rural world whose celebration it imagines.[30] As such it is at once a special *laudatio* of the emperor and a gentle *recusatio,* true to the love of privacy and of freedom for self-reflection which the countryside so often symbolizes in Horace's poetry.

[30]Doblhofer (100–101) is correct in seeing the poem as a litany more in praise of peace than of Augustus, the peace-bringer ("Über den Kriegstaten stehen ihm die Friedensleistungen des Herrschers, über den Friedensleistungen—der Friede"). Bergson discusses the influence of Pindar, especially the conclusion of *Pythian* 8, as well as of Hellenistic precedent—Theocritus 17 is the most salient example—on Horace the encomiast.

[6]

ODE SIX

Dive, quem proles Niobaea magnae
vindicem linguae Tityosque raptor
sensit et Troiae prope victor altae
    Pthius Achilles,

ceteris maior, tibi miles inpar,   5
filius quamvis Thetidis marinae
Dardanas turris quateret tremenda
    cuspide pugnax—

ille, mordaci velut icta ferro
pinus aut inpulsa cupressus Euro,   10
procidit late posuitque collum in
    pulvere Teucro;

ille non inclusus equo Minervae
sacra mentito male feriatos
Troas et laetam Priami choreis   15
    falleret aulam,

sed palam captis gravis, heu nefas, heu
nescios fari pueros Achivis
ureret flammis, etiam latentem
    matris in alvo,   20

ni tuis flexus Venerisque gratae
vocibus divom pater adnuisset
rebus Aeneae potiore ductos
    alite muros:

doctor argutae fidicen Thaliae,   25
Phoebe, qui Xantho lavis amne crinis,
Dauniae defende decus Camenae,
    levis Agyieu.

spiritum Phoebus mihi, Phoebus artem
carminis nomenque dedit poetae: 30
virginum primae puerique claris
    patribus orti,

Deliae tutela deae, fugacis
lyncas et cervos cohibentis arcu,
Lesbium servate pedem meique   35
    pollicis ictum,

rite Latonae puerum canentes,
rite crescentem face Noctilucam,
prosperam frugum celeremque pronos
    volvere mensis.   40

nupta iam dices "ego dis amicum,
saeculo festas referente luces,
reddidi carmen docilis modorum
    vatis Horati."

    O god whom the offspring of Niobe suffered, as revenger of a brash
tongue, and the seducer, Tityos, and Achilles of Pthia, nearly conqueror
of tall Troy: he was a soldier mightier than the rest, but not your equal,
no matter he was sea-nymph Thetis' warrior son, shaking the towers of
Troy with his awesome spear.
    Down, like a pine gashed by gnawing iron, or a cypress blasted by the
eastern wind, he plunged, and lodged his neck in the dust of Troy.
    Chambered in the horse that lied of its sanctity to Minerva, he would
not deceive the Trojans at their foolish festivities and the palace of Priam

blithely bent on dancing, but all openly, a bane to his captives, would burn in Grecian flames—woeful, woeful crime—children ignorant of speech, even one hiding in its mother's womb.

But the father of the gods, bending to entreaties from you and kindly Venus, approved for Aeneas' regime walls reared under a securer sign:

Phoebus, lyre-playing mentor of clear-voiced Thalia, who bathe your locks in the stream of Xanthus, guard the grace of the Daunian Muse, smooth-cheeked Agyieus.

Phoebus granted me breath, Phoebus the art of song and the repute of poet. Illustrious girls and boys sprung from fathers of renown, charges of the Delian goddess who checks with her bow fleeing lynx and stag, maintain the rhythm of Lesbos and the strumming of my thumb.

Duly hymn the son of Latona, duly, the Night-gleamer, burgeoning with her torch, encourager of crops and swift to propel the plunging months.

Now when married you will boast: "As the age was restoring days of celebration, I myself performed again a song friendly to the gods, I, instructed in the modes of the bard, Horace."

Horace begins his hymn to Augustus with a look at the emperor's divine antecedents (*Divis orte bonis*) and with a complimentary equation of his creative presence with light, spring and the bright days and suns associated with it. The neighboring hymn to Apollo commences, strikingly, with the same word, *Dive,* but instead of looking at immortal ancestry or at a Herculean hero's pretensions to divinity we are addressing a god himself. When he is finally named, three times in the poem's seventh and eighth stanzas, it is through his epithet *Phoebus,* the light-bringing sun-god, suitable patron overseer of Augustus and his renewal.

The first half of the poem, however, concentrates on a different side of Apollo.[1] We are introduced to him as the far-darting archer god, known for his prowess at arms. The tradition in myth and epic from which Horace draws sees Apollo as a god of vengeance, against the boasts of Niobe, the brute force of Tityos and, above all, Achilles,

[1]The opening stanzas of ode 6 have troubled critics. Fraenkel feels that the first six stanzas of the poem "have little to do with the concluding part" (*Horace,* 400) and deal with "a theme on the periphery." Williams (*Tradition and Originality,* 64), though noting the poem's Pindaric complexity, finds its mythological references "rather calculated" and "abstruse."

whom the *Iliad* subtly conceives as a prime rival and antagonist to him.[2] Though Homer does not describe the event directly, he twice alludes to Achilles' death, which was accomplished either by the god himself or through the medium of Paris.[3] They are pitted against each other, soldier for soldier, might for might. But the threats of the famous spear of the contentious (*pugnax*) hero are no match for the biting (*mordax*) of the weapon that fells him.[4]

Horace gives the moment a special "epic" intensity. We think of the several tree similes in Homer and his successors which depict heroes fallen in battle, and lines 11–12 refer specifically to the last book of the *Odyssey* where Achilles and Agamemnon meet in the afterlife of heroes. The son of Atreus remembers his mighty comrade, fallen mightily in the swirl of Troy's dust and celebrated with funeral rites.[5] All of this is couched in a stanza of nearly Ennian flair where almost every word plays upon the other through assonance or alliteration. The language, mirroring the event itself, builds climactically toward *pulvere Teucro,* and the picture of Achilles' corpse. If we look only at the framing words of the preceding lines, *pulvere* draws on *pinus* and *procidit* while *ferro* and *Euro* prepare, in the verse's melody, for its powerful conclusion in *Teucro.*

The third stanza, by documenting the grandeur of fallen Achilles, is the decisive tribute to his divine adversary's martial preeminence, but the ode's initial stanzas establish two themes that will be important for the poem as a whole. The first is the speaker's concern with

---

[2]The death of Achilles at the hand of Apollo is also treated by Pindar in his sixth paean, a poem Horace may well have had in mind as he wrote. The antagonism-equation of Apollo and Achilles, touched on most directly by Homer at *Il.* 20.447ff. and 21.6ff., has been treated by Burkert, Chirassi Colombo (esp. 251) and most recently in detail by Nagy (esp. 61–65, 121 and 142–45).

[3]*Il.* 19.410–17 and 22.358–60 (Hector's dying words). The usual reasons given for Apollo's need for vengeance are Achilles' boasts over the body of Hector and his killing of Apollo's son Troilus.

[4]Since this is apparently the first use in Latin of *mordax* to mean "sharp," the reader should hear the expected metaphor "biting" in the word. Horace uses the word twice elsewhere, of a caustic personality (the speaker) at *sat.* 1.4.93, of Diogenes the Cynic, at *epi.* 1.17.18. The verb *mordeo* is associated in ode 3 (16) with envy, which the speaker may mean to suggest here as an aspect of Apollo's motivation to kill.

[5]*Od.* 24.39–40. Homer uses tree similes at *Il.* 5.559–60 and 13.389–91 = 16. 482–84. The double simile conveys a deliberate air of matter-of-fact detachment absent, say, at *Aen.* 2.626–31.

the relationship of children and parents, especially of mothers and sons. He begins the poem with allusion to two events in Apollo's life when the god comes to the defense of his mother Leto. In the first he is her, and in a sense his own, avenger by killing the offspring of Niobe who are victims of their mother's prideful boasting of their superiority to Leto's twin progeny. Tityos he killed for sexually assaulting his mother. And Leto figures indirectly even in the conflict between Apollo and Achilles. The latter may be the son of a sea-goddess and thereby have partial claim to pit himself against Apollo's divinity. Nevertheless he is still Pthian, fathered by the mortal Peleus, and ultimately no match under Troy's walls for his completely immortal rival.

The second theme is only touched upon in the opening lines, through a play on words. It is because she misused her tongue, because of a perversion of words, that Apollo sought revenge on Niobe. His role, reciprocal to hers, is that of *vindex,* someone, to follow out the etymology, who asserts force through speaking and then, often, acting. This hint at Apollo's interest in proper and corrupt use of language surfaces when the speaker offers reasons for his hatred of Achilles. We first learn who Achilles is not and whom he does not directly attack. He is not treacherous Odysseus, taking advantage of the unsuspecting Trojans, deceived by joy. Unlike his wily colleague he is not concerned with the hidden and counterfeit, with a horse that speaks calculated untruths about its holiness, nor with those who rely naively on ritual. Since *feriatos* is a cognate of *fari* (to utter), as well as with *fas* and *nefas,* it further defines his avoidance of those who are making disastrous use of ceremonial language.[6]

Achilles' intent is both public and singularly ugly. His hypothetical violence is directed against the helpless, those already captive, children, the unborn. Horace underscores this intent as Achilles' by imputing to him notions Homer reserves for Agamemnon addressing his brother in *Iliad* 6: "Of them [the Trojans] let not one escape steep destruction at our hand, not even the boy-child that the mother bears in her womb." Such infants are to be ἄφαντοι, unseen and therefore unknown.[7] For Horace's speaker to ascribe such thoughts to Achilles

[6]On the lexical interrelationship of *fas-nefas, festus,* and *fari,* see Varro *L. L.* 6.29–30, Paulus-Festus 76.17 and 78.5, and Ernout-Meillet *s.vv. fas* and *feriae.*

[7]*Il.* 6.57–58, 60. The fact that Apollo himself is, from the poem's start, defined as a killer of children compounds the irony of the ode's initial stanzas. His sister is

is doubly appropriate in the context he has established for them in ode 6. He would draw down the wrath of Apollo because he would destroy the parent–child relationship in a particularly depraved manner, offering violence not to soldiers concealed in the lying belly of a wooden horse but to those lurking where safety would be most natural, within the protection of their mother's womb.[8]

There is a difference from Homer that suggests a second reason why these words are fitting for Achilles. Horace calls it to our attention by allotting his singer a double exclamation of horror, and a pun. Achilles would decimate Trojan children before they have the capability of speech (*nescios fari*). In itself this is an unspeakable act (*nefas*), enlivened verbally for the reader in the telling by the echo of sound as well as by the etymological figuration. To twist familial relationships and to deprive the powerless of speech are acts equally un-Apolline, and worthy of Apollo's vendetta. Because the physical act of revenge has already taken place, the pivotal, central stanza of the poem can dwell on the god's words. The bending of Jupiter by Apollo and Venus, of a father by his divine son and daughter, a mother on behalf of her son, is also the bending of the poem: from Achilles dead to Aeneas surviving, from the ill-omened walls of Troy to the auspicious ramparts of Rome, from the mythic past to the lived present. It also initiates the metamorphosis of Apollo, as poetry of action yields to poetry about poetry. When the speaker at last apostrophizes the poem's deity, it is no longer in the guise of avenging Far-darter (ἐκηβόλος) that Apollo is addressed but as Lyre-Player (κιθαρῳδός) and Leader of the Muses (Μουσαγέτης). He is now *doctus,* inspiring patron of music and poetry, not *heroicus,* destructive engineer of war.[9]

Apollo plays a many-sided role as lord of the imagination, when

---

also said, later in the poem, to make use of the bow, but now against animals, and only to restrain, not kill.

[8]Virgil uses parallel vocabulary in his description of the wooden horse in *Aen.* 2: *includere* (19, 45, and 258), *alvus* (51 and 401; cf. *Aen.* 9.152), *latere* (48, and cf. *latebrae,* 38 and 55). Horace's dependence in lines 13–20 on the imagery of pregnancy and ruinous birth which Virgil associates with the horse deserves separate study. The horse is mentioned in Homer at *Od.* 4.271ff. and 8.493.

[9]The change in Apollo is varied by Horace at *C. S.* 33ff. and *c.* 2.10.18–20. Pfeiffer ("The Image") treats the bow and the Graces, which Delian Apollo holds in his usual sculpted form, as emblems of the balancing principles in his ethics.

his martial weaponry gives place to the lyre. He is smooth cheeked, with flowing locks, and therefore a symbol of youth.[10] He is also closely involved with both a Greek and a Roman muse, who are felt presences in what follows. He is first a teacher, the educator of the songstress Thalia whose name, based on a root meaning "growth" and "fullness," connects her specifically with festivity and celebration.[11] Furthermore he is called upon to protect the grace of the Latin Camena to whom ancient etymologists assigned an earlier form, namely Casmena, cognate with *carmen* and often linked with *cano*, hence with notions of prophecy and magic as well as song.[12]

The Muse, whose grace Apollo is called on to protect, is Daunian, from the birthplace of Horace himself. At this moment in the poem the reader presumes that the poet is her *decus*, her emanation of honor and glory. As the poem unfolds toward its conclusion we realize that Horace also intends the Muse to refer directly to himself. He is the one who will twice refer to a *carmen* of his own making. He not only acts as Camena, he resembles Thalia as well, creator of and presider over a prestigious festal moment. Finally, in the most notable boast, he is a metonymy for Apollo himself, not only student of the god who stimulates song but a teacher of students, tendering in turn his own form of inherited inspiration.

After the single command to Apollo and its hint that the speaker not only graces the Daunian Muse but is actually her claim to fame, Horace reorients the poem away from any further aretology of the

[10]At the mouth of the Xanthus was Patara with its famous oracle of Apollo (cf. *c.* 3.4.64). Hence Horace may be deliberately associating him here with prophecy and *carmina* put into the mouth of *vatis Horatius*. When Apollonius Rhodius compares the physical beauty of Jason with that of Apollo, he places the god "by the streams of Xanthus" (*Arg.* 1.307–10). Perhaps, however, it is the Trojan Xanthus that more exactly enhances Horace's point. If so we are meant to imagine the striking juxtaposition of Apollo fiercely slaying Achilles and then washing his golden hair in a nearby stream as he prepares to assume his role as god of song.

[11]The most recent discussion of the lexical background of Thalia and θάλλω is by Lowenstam. The four semantic contexts he lists for their root meaning are weeping, porcine fat and feasts, youth and fertility, and the plant world. At *O.* 14.15–16 Pindar labels Θαλία, one of the Graces observing the chorus of triumph, "lover of song" (ἐρασίμολπε). Cf. Sappho 2.15, and Horace's pun on the name Thaliarchus at *c.* 1.9.8.

[12]For the etymology, see Varro *L. L.* 7.27 and Paulus-Festus *s.vv. dusmoso* and *pesnis.* At *Aen.* 8.336–40 Virgil connects the name *Carmentis* with *cano.*

god and toward the first-person narrator, as author and preceptor of song. Apollo is now distanced as the third-person source of the artistry and reputation he was called upon to defend. He is replaced by a different, plural set of addressees, the girls and boys who are being prepared by the poet to perform what critics universally agree is the *Carmen Saeculare,* written, as we have seen, by Horace at the request of Augustus for inclusion in the ceremonies of the *ludi saeculares* of 17 B.C. What we have, then, is a song by its maker about song, and about its source in Apollo and its performance at Rome.

The song chants prayers as much to Diana as to her twin, and it is suitable, because so much of the ode has been devoted to Apollo, that the essence of Horace's summary be devoted to Diana as patroness of wild animal life, of the moon, and of earth whose fertility is conjoined with the passage of the months. Apollo may inspire the poet, but it is Diana who civilizes and enriches his setting, seeming, here, to restrain the feral and to sustain the energy of crops which emulate her own lunar patterns of growth.

Yet this ode is neither a restatement of the *Carmen Saeculare* nor a new hymn in praise of the events of 17 B.C.[13] It is a hymn about the genesis and communication of a hymn, as much about the *pueri* who are instrumental in the praising as about the *puer* who is object of praise. Above all, it is about the creator of the *carmen* as "Horace" directs those who project his words (*canentes*). Yet one of them is given the last word. Time passes in the life of the young chorister as she changes from *virgo* to *nupta,* but the speaker anticipates in the future her song about song which itself documents an enduring present. Withstanding the temporal variability in the singer's life is the counterthrust of the cyclicity of Roman secular time based on the rendering of a song in its honor. If human time passes toward the responsibility of marriage, in the present context the implication is that the result will be children who will continue to re-create through art the rituals that refresh and renew the community. In this instance the gestations of poets are dependent on the voices of children, and literal Roman endurance is contingent on the imaginative ceremony of art and music which both together engender.

Yet as so often these dependencies are based on mutuality. It was the speaker's earlier boast that Apollo had given him *nomen,* reputation, yet for the only time in both collections of odes the Horatian

[13]The opposite view is taken by Cairns, 443–44.

speaker has himself literally identified.[14] The poet has the final word, designating himself in a context that would seem to assure immortality both to himself and to his subject, named and namer alike. The singer's words, by which she helps us in the future to remember her past, also help tighten the poem. In labeling herself *docilis* she reminds us that she has been taught by Horace who in turn is the student of *doctor* Apollo. As a *vates,* Horace is the mouthpiece of the god both of poetry and of prophecy, pronouncing incantatory verses, fabricating the *carmina* that themselves fabricate the Roman secular present and guarantee its future.

Horace is here creating a song about the contexts of song and about the sources of creativity. We are made to sense the speaker's posture as learner, the communicant who receives divine inspiration and in turn communicates it to his pupils, becoming their *vates.* He is the explainer of a ritual. At the same time he is the preserver of the setting behind the ritual, watching a spiritual moment—the change in Apollo—of some importance to Rome. He is therefore thrice-over practicing the vatic art, as teacher-priest of the modes and rhythms of poetic utterance, as explainer and interpreter of the intellectual reasoning behind the occasion to which he alludes, and as crafter of the poem that brilliantly merges lyric and didactic elements. Eschewing epic's grand pattern in favor of lyric precision, he can claim Apollo as his inspirer, not his punisher. And yet, in his climactic art of self-naming, he pointedly has the last word, preserving his own originality in the course of memorializing others.

But the Varronian etymology of *vates,* from *fari,* to speak, draws us back into the ode on its most essential level.[15] In this poem devoted to the making of a poem, the *poeta,* as he fashions this public version of himself, is most engaged with the occasions of speech. On this interest the poem turns. Its first half, as we have seen, finds Apollo extracting revenge from Niobe for her evil tongue and from Achilles who would deprive unborn Trojan *pueri* of speech. In the second segment Apollo, as god of music, instructs Horace who becomes his intermediary in training Roman children in the art of song.

The moment of speech is as important as what is spoken, and in this connection the root of *fari* plays an important role. On it is based

---

[14]Horace's only other use of his nomen is at *epi.* 1.14.5. His *cognomen* occurs at *sat.* 2.1.18 and *epode* 15.12, and he has himself addressed as *Quinte* at *sat.* 2.6.37.
[15]Varro *L. L.* 6.52 (cf. Isidore *Et.* 8.7.3).

the etymology not only of *nefas,* but, as we saw earlier, of *feriatus,* and *festus.* The second book of the *Aeneid* offers graphic evidence for the destruction that comes to those given over to wrongful celebrations (*male feriatos*) and to round-dances ill-conceived.[16] However, this poem is not only about the multiple aspects of Apollo but about the metamorphosis of Priam's Troy into Augustan Rome, about disruption, symbolized by song misused, become stability in those festival days (*festas luces*) honoring Roman secularity. These are days, as the etymology reminds us, in which good speaking and the proper use of well-omened words are essential, and during which cities are re-founded, not destroyed.

Achilles is a tree, stricken (*icta*) by a blow from Apollo's weapon. It is the beat (*ictum*) of the poet's thumb that the chorus in new Rome must follow. Legendary Apollo exacts revenge for misuse of voice from an Achilles who would eliminate the possibility of utterance in the young. Horace's chorus, as the bride muses in retrospect, epitomizes proper song that arouses not enmity but friendship in the twin gods whose blessing is crucial for the continuance of both song and secular revival.

I have left until now treatment of the epithet Agyieus which Horace gives Apollo in line 28, for it too has powerful implications understood only in the framework of the poem as a whole. The word appears only once in Latin literature and as such deserves special scrutiny.[17] The title, which derives from a Greek word for road, ἀγυιά, associates Apollo specifically with the city and the streets.[18] Since his altars were set up in front of housedoors, Macrobius equates

[16]Note especially the ironic juxtaposition at 2.237ff. of the horse climbing the walls of Troy and the boys and girls chanting holy songs around it (*pueri circum innuptaeque puellae / sacra canant*), a description that looks to the whole of ode 6.

[17]The epithet has puzzled commentators, e.g., Kiessling and Heinze ("an ihre Bedeutung . . . soll gar nicht gedacht werden"). Syndikus (351, n. 32) finds a "fremder Klang" in the word. For ancient discussions of its meaning, see Varro in Porph. on line 28; Hesychius *s.v.* ἀγυιεύς; Harpokration *s.v.* 'Αγυιᾶς; the Suida *s.v.* Ἀγυιαί and Eustathius on *Il.* 2.12. Borzsak, who rightly interprets the two sides of Apollo as a major unifying factor of the poem, views Apollo *Agyieus* as a patron of the young coming to adulthood.

[18]For general treatments of Apollo Agyieus see Farnell, 148–51; Cook, 143–68, esp. 161–68 and figures 100–108; commentators on Aes. *Aga.* 1081, Aristophanes *Wasps* 875, Eur. *Ph.* 631, Paus. 10.25.6. Farnell's conjecture, that the epithet means "protecting the tribe on its migratory journey" (150) and that Apollo is as much a "deity of colonization" as a guardian of the community,

him, along with Apollo Θυραῖος, with Janus as god of exits and entrances, comings and goings, the turns and changes symbolized in the threshold.[19] He is an apotropaic god who wards off evil from the city and its dwellings, and who, presumably, protects and nurtures families and especially the young. The renewals that time brings to life are part of his province, be it the daily refreshment the sun's orb provides or the spring that renovates the year.

Ode 6 touches on all these roles, but it charges Apollo in particular with the power to bless the still larger act of Roman secular renewal instituted by Augustus in 17 B.C. His position as a patron god of Roman secularity, which the *Carmen Saeculare* makes richly clear, gives further point to his hatred of Achilles which at first seems inordinately prominent in the poem's first half. The last book of the *Iliad* shows gods and men together for the last time, feasting at the wedding of Peleus and Thetis, and at the end of the *Odyssey* the Olympians unite to mourn Achilles, the heroic product of that marriage. The great sixty-fourth poem of Catullus, which deals with the same union and its progeny, varies the Homeric tale in one important respect: Apollo and Diana do not deign to attend the ceremony.

Originally the chief divinities worshiped during the performances of the *ludi saeculares* were Dis and Proserpina, gods of the underearth and of terrestrial revivification.[20] By the year 17 B.C. Apollo and Diana, of course, were the chief divinities. Catullus 64, written around 55 B.C., defines the first oblique instance of the shift from one pair to the other. The second, more direct illustration is the fourth *eclogue,* whose dramatic date is 40 B.C. Students of the *ludi saeculares* have seen this poem as marking a movement to celebrate the games in the middle or late forties. Certainly Diana and Apollo figure prominently in the poem as divinities under whose auspices the new *saeclorum ordo* is going to be

---

aptly explains the change in the poem from Troy destroyed to Rome founded and renewed. In the end Apollo presides over the city spaces and over the saving rituals in them that honor him.

[19]Gagé (*Apollon romain*) treats the Macrobius passage (*Sat.* 1.9.5–7) in his discussion of the relationship between the cult of Apollo Agyieus and Janus.

[20]For surveys of the development of the *ludi saeculares* see the articles by M. P. Nilsson ("Saeculares Ludi," *RE* 2.2.1696–1720) and L. R. Taylor ("Secular Games," *OCD*[2] 969–70). Aspects of the poetry of Roman secularity are treated by Kukula. The ancient epigraphical evidence for the celebration is *CIL* 6.32323.32 and 6.32323.139.

born, and Horace, as he composed the *Carmen Saeculare,* was often
reflecting, whether deliberately or not, on the phraseology of his great
predecessor. For the purposes of commentary on poem 6 it is important to note the negative posture of Achilles in each poem. In the first
he symbolizes the blind brutality of the warrior greedy for slaughter.
He seems to offer the poet obvious evidence for civilization's decline,
sketched at the poem's conclusion, from a more, though not totally,
perfected era when gods mingled with men. The fourth *eclogue* gives
him prominence as symbol of a heroic age of fighting to which men
must once more succumb before a golden time can be restored. In each
case the lust for war typifies him as emblematic of the antisecular. He is
thus a prime antagonist of Apollo, whether literally at the gates of
Troy, or symbolically, as Rome celebrates its renewal at the hands of a
god who averts evil from its revitalized citizenry.

There is another reason for the epithet Agyieus here. The icon
associated with the worship of Apollo Agyieus is the *betylos,* a con-
ically shaped column of stone set upon an altar base.[21] Scattered
examples remain from the Greco-Roman world: among others, one
from Corfu; another from Apollonia, where Octavian was studying
at the time of his great-uncle Caesar's murder.[22] It is also represented
on coins found along the Illyrian litoral, from Apollonia south to the
Ambracian Gulf. Octavian took the emblem for himself.[23] *Betyloi* are
prominent in the wall decoration of both the "Casa di Augusto" (the
so-called Room of the Masks) and the "Casa di Livia" (south wall of
the triclinium) on the Palatine.[24] Apollo Kitharoedos faces his sister,
Diana, as huntress, across a *betylos* on one of the terracotta plaques

---

[21]For general discussions of the *betylos,* see Zuntz, Picard-Schmitter,
Thompson 62–69 and Balestrazzi (esp. 127–29, 136–38, 146–53). Picard-Schmitter (77–79) makes the connection between Augustus, Apollonia, and Actium.
She also hazards that the spear leaning against the *betylos* in the decoration on the
walls of the "Casa di Augusto" is an emblem of the spear of Augustus, marking
the place where the temple of Apollo was founded after the earth was struck by
lightning. The suggestion is adopted by Gagé ("Apollon impérial," 567 and n.
15). See also the important discussion by Simon ("Apollo in Rom," esp. 218–
20).

[22]Balestrazzi (128) discusses the Corfu and Apollonia columns.

[23]See Franke (312–24) and Balestrazzi (180, n. 39).

[24]For the "Casa di Augusto" see Carettoni, "Due nuovi ambienti," and, more
recently, Balestrazzi (128 and fig. on 146) and Carettoni, *Das Haus* (27 and pl. 6
and pl. F); for the "Casa di Livia," see Künzl (371 and pl. 30). His treatment of
the *betylos* (352–58) is also especially helpful.

that decorated the temple to Apollo on the Palatine, dedicated on October 9, 28 B.C.[25]

The temple was vowed during the campaign against Sextus Pompeius in 36 B.C., but the most conspicuous part Apollo takes in Augustan mythology is at the battle of Actium:[26]

> Actius haec cernens arcum intendebat Apollo
> desuper; omnis eo terrore Aegyptus et Indi,
> omnis Arabs, omnes vertebant terga Sabaei.

Beholding these things Actian Apollo stretched his bow from above. Frightened by that, every Egyptian and Indian, every Arab, every Sabaean turned his back [in flight].

The temple seems to memorialize this even more crucial sea-battle as well, fought in the Ambracian Gulf. But the battle is commemorated in another way of still greater interest to readers of poem 6, for in Roman coinage minted in 28 B.C. and after, we find the prow of a ship on which a *betylos* is prominently placed.[27] Apollo Agyieus is also Apollo Actius, the averter of evil and turner of the tide of war at a grave moment in the history of Rome. Agyieus, as we have seen, implies many aspects of Apollo, all with ramifications for ode 6. None would have been more important to Augustus than the epithet's reminder of Actium. Without that victory against Antony and Cleopatra fourteen years earlier, no reason would exist to celebrate the games of 17 B.C. Without that turning point, the larger moral and artistic refurbishing of Rome, which the secular games symbolized and over which Apollo, in his many guises, would appropriately preside, would not have occurred. Ode 6, by touching on that moment, reminds us of the instant after victory when Apollo could justly change from war god to god of the spirit, inspirer of poets who in turn inspire by their own creativity.[28] But even from the poem's

[25]The terracotta was discovered in 1968 and first published by Carettoni ("Terrecotte 'Campana'," 129 and 131, fig. 5). Andreae furnishes a large color reproduction (pl. 40).

[26]*Aen.* 8.704–6.

[27]See Küthmann *passim* (pl. 12 for illustrations). He links Apollo Agyieus and Actium (76–77).

[28]The battle of Actium and the change of Apollo from war god to god of song is the subject of another extraordinary, contemporary poem, Propertius 4.6 (is the numbering coincidental?). See, for example, 69–70: "*bella satis cecini: citharam*

start Apollo, god of the bow, is forceful guardian of the right to proper speech, a synecdoche of the civilizing function he and the vatic poet he protects perform. Together they regenerate and stabilize an era that turns away from violence to peace. This affirms that Rome prospers as much from the artistry that poets teach, and gods inspire, as from the decisive military prowess that allowed it to develop.

Reference to the aftermath of Actium serves to adumbrate further the presence of Augustus in ode 6. The *princeps,* once himself the ward of Apollo, is now the sponsor of a majestic act of civic renewal and of the poet whose *carmen* praises the god and his sister, in prayer for their enduring tutelage.[29] His presence provides an important link with the two preceding poems. We have already noted how their initial words link poems 5 and 6, and their endings confirm the connection. The last stanza of each poem contains quoted speeches that lend the power of direct statement to their respective conclusions. One is put in the mouth of the poem's speaker, as sharer in a communal wish; the other is imputed to a protagonist of the *Carmen Saeculare.* Each concerns festivity, the first devoted to the *longas ferias* that will be Rome's upon Augustus' arrival, the second to the *festas luces* during which the life of Rome started anew and which the bride and her poet revivify with remembering words.[30]

In each case the ideas of peace in the wake of war, of return, recurrence, and regeneration, of customs and ceremonies, however differently proposed, are paramount. The intensely Roman and particularly Augustan focus of the two poems is paralleled in their predecessor in the book's second triad which can now be seen to introduce many of the later poems' major themes. Ode 4, like its successors, ends with a speech and centers on a day pivotal to Rome, when the darkness of Hannibal's war clouds was put to flight. This renewal could occur because of the presence of the great families of Rome, like the Claudii, upon whom her survival depends. But Rome and

---

iam poscit Apollo/victor et ad placidos exuit arma choros" (Enough of wars have I sung. Victorious Apollo now claims his lyre and doffs his arms for the quiet of choruses). The interaction of the two poems deserves separate treatment.

[29]Lambrechts surveys the role of Apollo in the propaganda of Augustus.

[30]The word *lux,* of course, was attributed to the features of Augustus at ode 5.5 where the emperor serves as the equivalent of daylight and its powers.

her families thrive because of the rapport of particular parents with particular children, in this instance Augustus and his Claudian stepsons. The relationship is reversed and made symbolic in ode 5 where Augustus, himself sprung from the gracious divinities, is the saving youth upon whom the mothers and fathers of Rome rely for survival. Finally ode 6 dwells first on the youthful god Apollo's concern for proper treatment of parents and children, then on the illustrious young girls and "boys sprung from famous fathers" (*pueri claris patribus orti*) who will sing Rome's secular hymn on a day of extraordinary communal celebration. The bride who has the poem's final words will presumably reinvigorate both her family, by further generation, and the incantatory words, along with the civilization they bespeak, by their repetition.

The involvement with teaching and teachings which the framing poems demonstrate complements this interest in the origins and education of youth, in how the past affects the future, in the many masks of history, whether linear, cyclical, or immutable. The *doctrina* Augustus bestows on the Nerones is reinforced by the teachings of *doctor* Apollo and the *docilis* student of the seer-poet who reiterates his words. The permanence of Rome is their common goal. The poet would accomplish this by acts of naming. The Nerones authenticate their inheritance of nomenclature and of familial exploits by their own present accomplishments. But the final validation is neither of Rome nor Augustus nor even Apollo but of the poet himself, *vates Horatius,* who, in imagining Rome's secularity, has fashioned a futurity for himself of a different temporal magnitude.

Closely knit as these three poems are, they follow and vary a pattern established in the initial triad which will be repeated for the remainder of the book. Poem 4, in the company of its two successors, is in praise of Augustus and the Nerones, of Rome's past and present. Its conclusion, however, on the "death" of Hannibal's hopes and name, associates it with the book's opening ode and its concentration on the private losses time brings the aging speaker. The sixth ode also looks to Rome and Apollo's attendance, as god of the bow and of the lyre, on her destiny. But it is equally devoted to the writing of poetry and to the position and authority of the Apolline poet in society. It stands therefore as a fit companion piece to the third ode where the nascent poet is fostered and made acceptable to his world only through the indulgence of the muse Melpomene. In between, in these two instances, are odes devoted to the absent Augustus, the first ode to his appropriateness, in himself and to the poet, as a subject of song, the second to his significance as the essential figure for Rome's physical and moral well-being.[31] Both sets of poems have carefully crafted verbal links between them, but the second and third of each triad are most closely conjoined. This pattern, too, will be modulated and strengthened in the poems that follow.

[31]Two connections between odes 2 and 5 deserve mention here. First, the *boni divi*. At 2.38 it is the "good gods" who neither have given nor will give anything greater or better than Augustus' return, even were a renewal of the golden age conceivable. At 5.1, with Augustus, though not imagined to be physically present, at least in the speaker's mind's eye, he is apostrophized as *Divis orte bonis,* while the speaker contemplates his return. Second, the notion of *dies,* meaning the light of day and the particular celebratory moment this brightness represents. It occurs at 2.41 and 5.7, 29, and 39. It will also prove a focal word at 11.15 and 14.36. In poems 2, 5, and 14 the sun is an important ingredient in this clarity (2.46, 5.8 and 40; cf. 14.5). This outer gleam is replaced, in poem 11, by the glimmer of Phyllis herself (*fulges,* 5; cf. *adfulsit* at 5.7) and by the flames of the speaker's festive hearth which, for a moment, obliterate the cares of real life. In odes 2, 5, and 14 it is implicitly the whole Roman world that would be dark without his effulgent, enlivening presence. On "the motive of fire and light" in the book as a whole, see Porter, "The Recurrent Motifs," 217–20. We should observe also the change from the single, future *dicemus* (2.50) to the repeated, present *dicimus* (5.38–39). Ceremony, for Augustus, imagined potentially in the first poem, is now said to be actually taking place in the second. The futurity of a still larger ceremony is guaranteed at 6.41 (*dices*) where the verb carefully echoes both previous uses.

PART THREE

Time and Redemption:
Odes 7–9

"I play for Seasons; not Eternities!" Says Nature.

MEREDITH, *Modern Love*

"Visual art reaches its goal in the finite; that of the imagination . . . in infinity."

SCHILLER, *Über naive und
sentimentalische Dichtung*

[7]

ODE SEVEN

Diffugere nives, redeunt iam gramina campis
    arboribusque comae;
mutat terra vices, et descrescentia ripas
    flumina praetereunt.

Gratia cum Nymphis geminisque sororibus audet   5
    ducere nuda choros.
inmortalia ne speres, monet annus et almum
    quae rapit hora diem.

frigora mitescunt Zephyris, ver proterit aestas,
    interitura, simul   10
pomifer autumnus fruges effuderit, et mox
    bruma recurrit iners.

damna tamen celeres reparant caelestia lunae:
    nos ubi decidimus
quo pius Aeneas, quo dives Tullus et Ancus,   15
    pulvis et umbra sumus.

quis scit an adiciant hodiernae crastina summae
    tempora di superi?
cuncta manus avidas fugient heredis, amico
    quae dederis animo.   20

cum semel occideris et de te splendida Minos
    fecerit arbitria,
non, Torquate, genus, non te facundia, non te
    restituet pietas.

infernis neque enim tenebris Diana pudicum   25
    liberat Hippolytum
nec Lethaea valet Theseus abrumpere caro
    vincula Pirithoo.

The snows have scattered, grass now returns to the meadows and foliage to the trees, the earth transfigures her changes, and subsiding streams wash past their banks. With Nymphs and her twin sisters, Grace dares unclothed to lead the dance.

"Hope not for immortality" warn the year, and hour, which snatches the nourishing day. Frosts mellow in the western wind, summer tramples down spring, to perish the moment that fruitful autumn has lavished her bounty, and soon shiftless winter recurs.

Nevertheless scurrying moons replenish their losses in the skies. We, when we have waned toward good Aeneas, toward rich Tullus and Ancus, we are dust and shade. Who knows whether the gods of heaven will append tomorrow's times to the total of today? All which you lavish on your own dear spirit will escape the greedy clutches of your heir.

When once your sun has set and Minos has decreed his flash of findings about you, neither your ancestry, Torquatus, neither your eloquence nor your goodness will restore you back. For Diana does not release chaste Hippolytus from nether dark, nor does Theseus' strength shear Lethaean shackles from his beloved Pirithous.

Although the fourth ode dwells on the misfortunes of Hannibal and many shades of violence imbue the sixth, the mood of the second triad of the book is essentially positive. Rome's *saeculum* is renewed and assured by Neronic youth; by the quality of Augustus, the prosperity of whose domain lacks only his bodily presence; by Apollo and Diana; and by a poet's rejuvenating words given to a young chorus in their praise. The extraordinary seventh poem reminds us, with a sudden change in virtuosity, that time passes and that there is another temporal mode, another system of recurrence, an uncompromising aspect of nature measured against which the accomplishments of individual man are diminished. That is the cycle of the year, signaled by the rotations of its seasons, which puts into relief the linearity of human time and the inexorability of our passing.

Horace begins with the disappearance of winter.[1] The power of nature, nature's rhythmic energy expended in constructing her own circularity, is apparent from the ode's first phrase. A lesser poet might have written of vanishing winter or melting snow. The metaphoric "flee," replacing the expected "thaw," personifies winter at the start, and the plural "snows," in synecdoche, expands the humanizing of nature suggested by the verb. When applied to inanimate objects, *diffugio* means only to disperse. The personification attaches an element of emotion to the verb which, when concerned with mankind, regularly means to take to flight in terror before some looming menace.[2] The snows of winter neither liquefy nor evaporate. They merely scatter their collective strength before the vigorous manifestations of spring. Though their time will come again, at present they are replaced by the return of creatures whom they had once dispelled, the similarly personified grass come to fields and leaves to trees. The arbiter is earth, *terra mater,* who rings her changes on wet as well as dry, on streams swollen from the snows' departure, which now also lose their diminishing power to destroy by passing along, rather than over, their banks.[3]

Divinities close to nature, Grace and Nymphs, celebrate this renewal of spring with their own form of motion. But even such naked dancing as lends elegance to spring's revived beauty and bestows fertility upon the land is an act of daring, to be perpetrated only as the larger schema of seasonal progress allows.[4] For a mortal, contempla-

[1]Porter ("The Motif of Spring") looks at Horace's treatment of that season in poem 12 as well as in the present ode. Cf. also his "Recurrent Motifs" (200, n. 18) for a summary view.

[2]For *diffugio* in situations involving fear, see Cic. *Phil.* 2, 108; Lucr. *DRN* 5.1338; Vir. *geo.* 3.150, *Aen.* 2.212 and 4.123. Führer (206) catches specifically military overtones in the word.

[3]Horace describes the streams not through a word associated with liquid but with a verb linked with passage through time as well as in space. *Decresco,* used by Horace only here, is in earlier Latin more connected with the waning moon than any other natural phenomenon.

[4]In lines 5–6 of *c.* 1.4, which Horace is here varying, Venus is not mentioned nor is there reference to the nakedness or the daring of the Grace. The two poems are compared briefly below.

tion of the challenges that the twists of nature present, even to those who symbolize its flowering, provokes a grander meditation, one that in due course will directly apply to mankind. That nothing even in nature is deathless is the warning of both the year and the hour, of which the one embraces the seasons with their cautionary mutability while the other does violence to those bright particular days honored by the preceding poems.[5] In Greek iconography, the Horae parallel the Graces, sustaining the natural world by their attendance.[6] In Horace's enclosing stanza, the Grace can take courage to dance, but the Hora, complementing the personified, admonitory Annus, only snatches away the nourishment day's light offers the world. The still unspecified addressee should take heed: nature's seasonal and quotidian changes provide sufficient evidence against immortality to assure man of his own temporariness.

But first the temporality of nature. Horace expands on the hint of the poem's opening phrase. Seasonal nature, intensely vivid in her various manifestations, oppresses herself unceasingly as she pursues her round. Winter's chills become appropriately mellow before the creative Zephyrs. Summer tramples spring, like corn to be threshed,[7] yet she passes away when autumn yields up her produce. With autumn's energies expended, listless winter returns.[8]

Yet Horace's only other use of the verb *protero* suggests that the metaphors should be read in a still harsher way, as war imagery. In the fifth "Roman" ode, *c.* 3.5, Horace has Regulus chide his fellow Romans on their cowardice:

> si pugnat extricata densis
> cerva plagis, erit ille fortis,

[5]Cf. ode 4.40–41 (*dies, alma adorea*), ode 5.7 and 39 (*dies, die*), ode 6.42 (*festas luces*), *et al.* Horace's only uses of *tenebrae* are at 4.40 and 7.25, an important link between the poems.

[6]On the Graces see Deonna, *passim;* for bibliography on the *Horae,* see G. M. A. Hanfmann in *OCD²* *s.v.*

[7]Cf. Columella's use of *protero* at 2.20.3.

[8]The verb Horace allots to autumn, *effundo,* means both "pour forth" and "expend," "use up." This secondary sense associates even nature's most fruitful period with the *damna* that seasonal time imposes. We should also compare the context of Horace's only other use (the first in Latin, it should be noted) of *pomifer* at *c.* 3.23.8 ("*pomifero grave tempus anno*" [the sickly season of fruit-bearing autumn]) where the play on the meanings of *gravis,* "pregnant" or "ill," makes a parallel point.

qui perfidis se credidit hostibus,
et Marte Poenos proteret altero,
qui lora restrictis lacertis
sensit iners timuitque mortem.

If a doe fights back when unravelled from thick nets, he will be brave who has entrusted himself to the treacherous foe, and he will wear down the Carthaginians in another war who has listlessly felt lashes on arms tied back, and feared death!

The feelings of winter's cold become less fierce not only for but in the face of the Zephyrs. Summer dies after having trodden on spring as if it were a defeated foe.[9] Cowardly winter can hurry back only because her unrelenting enemy, spring, is momentarily displaced. But as the etymology of *bruma* implies, such happenings are only momentary.[10] The snows take flight, and *redeunt* begins again what *recurrit* had ended. Nature, like the metaphoric structure of Horace's verses, returns to its starting place and readies its renewal.

We are soon disabused of any notion that seasonal nature's inimical expense of energy against herself is more than passing. The swift lunar months—province, as we were reminded in the previous poem, of swift Diana, and by appearance as continuous as the seasons are disjointed—recover for heaven any economic losses incurred by annual variations. Heaven's "deaths" are recurrent but transitory. Our "fall" has only metaphoric relation to sun or moon. It is final and irrevocable, locating us in the constant present of death. The personifications that seem to affirm a rhetorical equivalence between nature and man prove only a poet's protreptic device to expose their differentiation. Paradoxically, were we to share in nature's self-inflicted violence and death, we would be ourselves deathless. But human life has no part in nature's dynamic fluctuations, which, for all their declines, presume always resuscitation of strength. Her alterna-

[9]Cf. Virgil's only use of *protero,* at Aen. 12.330, where Turnus, in the heat of battle, tramples entire throngs of the enemy with his chariot (*agmina curru proterit*).

[10]This etymology (*bruma* = *brevissima*) is one reason why Horace uses a word for winter which alludes to time, not to the sensation of cold (*hiems*). Nature's brevity is only momentarily consequential. It is the truth of our brevity, as *c.* 1.4.15 warns, that forbids us to fancy "long hope." Norden (*Aeneis Buch VI,* 167–68) examines in detail the equivalence of *bruma* with the winter solstice.

tions—waxing and waning, setting and rising, losing and restoring, fleeing and returning, dying and reviving—are ours to contemplate, not possess.

This constancy, as any potential becoming is lost in eternal being, is reflected sonically in the repeated use of the letter *s*. In the span from *nos* to *sumus,* nine words end in that letter, and each of the three lines in question concludes with the syllable *us* so that unusual rhyming complements persistent sibilance and the impressive alliteration of *u* in line 16 to create a verbal imitation of the uniform fate of all mortals. Monotony of sound mirrors the loss of individuality to which we insubstantial humans are forever subject. This invariability, which levels every uniqueness into a general community of shades, serves to illuminate the three names Horace chooses to mention and their characteristics while still alive.

The first is Aeneas, founder of Rome as noted in ode 6, whose *pietas* Virgil's *Aeneid* had recently celebrated. Tullus, placed second, is known for his riches with which he cannot barter his way into the realm of heaven's gains and losses. Ancus, third in the list, is awarded the epithet *bonus* in a similar context in Lucretius (who is at least partially imitating Ennius).[11] The tag is unnecessary here because between them *pius* and *dives* cover both internal and external ambitions, the moral and the economic. What unites all three is the idea that the powerful become powerless. The originator of Rome and two of her subsequent early kings are as subject to death as anyone.

If Rome herself is gifted with recurrence through secularity and through the magic of her vatic educator, those who hold sway over her from era to era remain as far outside this recurrence as they rest beyond seasonal renewal. Artless, violent, relentless nature is what recurs. Nature, without designs of its own invention, triumphs over man's patternings, his aspirations toward singularity and survival. Even the vatic pronouncer of secularity in ode 6 becomes, in the subsequent poem, spokesman for the common "we." The "I" who names himself and controls the teaching and singing of verses that

---

[11]*DRN* 3.1025, harking back to Ennius *Ann.* 149V³. The Lucretian context, which deals with the powerlessness of the mighty when confronted with death, was a probable stimulus for Horace (see, e.g., the use of *occiderunt* at 3.1028).

Lucretius' list of the mighty dead, leading from kings and generals to poets and philosophers, culminates in Epicurus, but we are surely meant to include in our own thinking the philosophical poet Lucretius himself as well.

renew Rome, has become mortal everyman, joining his once salient subjects as they accept metamorphosis into dust and shade. Even for the good poet death impends.

There is one escape from the unremitting sameness to which we are condemned by this somber philosophizing. It comes from proper treatment of the lived present. This very Horatian attitude—make the most of the given occasion—is tinged with irony, because it must be based on ignorance, not knowledge. To know the future is to be divine, to wish to know it, foolishly human. Only daily time, today's time, is manageable, and only what we give to ourselves will escape the greed of those to whom our property will pass.

Horace enhances his point by continuing the metaphor from economics and attaching to it the image of height. Heaven repairs its losses, but we can expect a set sum of todays beyond which none will be further affixed.[12] But *summa*, substantive from *summus*, is in form a superlative of *super*. Lexically and ideologically, therefore, we are allowed to amass a certain reckoning of time for ourselves, but this totality may be seen to depend on creatures defined by loftiness itself, the gods (*superi*) who dictate what will or will not be added to our aggregate of temporality.

Interrogation becomes statement as the speaker turns to what he can pronounce on with validity, the possessions we have in hand. This secure wholeness is best served by being lavished on our own *animus*. The philosopher's self-love is in one view the only untainted form of *amicitia* because it is completely unbeholden to the demands of others. It posits a responsive yielding to the desires of the inner spirit, and a truth to one's talents and inclinations. As long as the gods dispense life, the "fleeing" and the "giving" that form part of this solipsistic commitment are man's to dictate and not contingent on celestial mutability.

The distinctiveness that defines the individual psyche is what is lost in death. As if to emphasize the point for one final time, the speaker at last names the unspecified "you" of the preceding stanzas. In *epistle* 1.5 Horace invites a certain Torquatus to dinner. The communality of context with ode seven implies that the speaker is here addressing the same man:[13]

---

[12]In line 17 Horace uses the adjectives *crastinus* and *hodiernus* for the only times in his writing.

[13]*Epi.* 1.5.7–9, 12–15.

iamdudum splendet focus et tibi munda supellex:
mitte levis spes et certamina divitiarum
et Moschi causam: . . .
quo mihi fortunam, si non conceditur uti?
parcus ob heredis curam nimiumque severus
adsidet insano: potare et spargere flores
incipiam patiarque vel inconsultus haberi.

For a long time the hearth is gleaming and the furniture brightened for you. Away with fickle hopes and the struggles for riches, and Moschus' case. . . . Why possess a fortune if I am not granted its use? One who restrains himself out of responsiveness for his heir, and is too puritanical, neighbors a madman. I shall begin to drink and scatter flowers and allow myself to develop the reputation of a fool.

Each poem meditates on man's hopes and on the competitions wealth foments. Each urges the exploitation of good fortune, even at the expense of one's heir and even if the resultant banqueting, to which the poem summons Torquatus, appears to the imperceptive as the proclivity of an uncontemplative mind. From the beginning of the epistle we learn that Torquatus is a lawyer, and the conclusion urges him to elude his client by sneaking out the back door toward Horace's party. It is to his judicial talent that Horace also directs his present thoughts. When the sun of Torquatus' life has set, what remains for him to appreciate are the resplendent judgments that Minos, permanent arbiter of subterrestrial souls, passes upon him and against which his earthly eloquence will have no sway.[14]

Moreover, neither his family background nor, in place of prominence, his *pietas* will carry any authority once he is dead. Just as *occideris* echoes *decidimus,* so Torquatus' useless triple traits link him with his three famous predecessors, Aeneas, Tullus, and Ancus, who are now where he soon will be. His *pietas* makes him a modern-day representa-

[14]The uselessness of *pietas* for both Aeneas and Torquatus leads Dyer to interpret the poem as anti-Augustan. (My reading supports *pius* in line 15, as printed by Klingner, rather than the alternative *pater,* which has slightly less manuscript authority.)

tive of *pius* Aeneas, an example, perhaps, of Rome's renewal under Augustus.[15] Yet even this illustrious characteristic has no saving potential. The thrice repeated *non,* negating each quality before the concluding *restituet,* is a last reminder that even gifted humans have no share in the primaveral return of grass to the fields (*redeunt*) or the monthly restorations of heaven's swift moons (*reparant*).

Nor does intervention by god or demigod effect any change. Though the lot of each mortal is in a sense now atemporal, the deathless station of the gods is incompatible with the final destiny of humans who have suffered their doom. Even love, that intense attempt to procure ecstasis out of time, whether it be the heterosexual, chaste affair of Diana and Hippolytus or the implicitly homosexual liaison of Theseus and Pirithous, cannot bend the rigidity of mortal death. The gods are on high, associated with the heavenly bodies—Diana with the moon, for instance—whose appearance and reappearance betokens the continuity of immortal and, for Horace's present purposes, inanimate nature. The dead remain prisoners of darkness below (*infernis tenebris*).[16] Their attributes are the polar opposite of the height and brightness belonging to the celestial gods, and their frozen bondage serves as antonym for the energetic, varied motion that seasonal nature vouchsafes to man as an emblem of recurrence.

It is in this treatment of sexuality that Horace distinguishes himself from one of the two poems of Catullus that he has in mind as he creates. Catullus, before he asks thousands of kisses from Lesbia, muses for a moment on death's final slumber:[17]

[15]*Restituo* also has a legal ring when it means "restore one's due." Life is not due Torquatus, for all his talent. The poem does end, however, with a suggestion of restoration inherent in its very structure. The exact same metrical pattern of the first stanza is repeated again only in the last. Prosodic cyclicity may offer a metaphoric suggestion, through the poet's reinvention of his material, that man does partake somehow in nature's immortal renewals. In fact the poem as a whole is a "warning," a *monumentum,* that builds in its own immortality even as it cautions us on human mortality.

[16]Horace lends force to his depiction of hell's bondage, from which there is no breaking free, by using the verbs *abrumpo* and *libero* for the only occasions in his career.

[17]Cat. 5.4–6.

soles occidere et redire possunt:
nobis cum semel occidit brevis lux,
nox est perpetua una dormienda.

Suns can set and return. When once our brief light has set, it is one
unceasing night of sleep.

Catullus allows himself only for an instant the philosophizing that
dominates Horace's poem. When love enters the ode, briefly at its
center and at its conclusion, it is to underline the importance of self-
love in this life and the futility of expecting sexual reciprocity after
reaching the underworld, even when one's beloved is a god. For
Catullus the moment's physical rapture constitutes an escape from
thought. To scrutinize, to "know" the number of kisses the lovers
share, is to shatter the illusion that passion can be perpetually extended in life just as sleep is enforced after death, and that such
counterfeit continuity can serve to deflect the truths derived from any
realistic appraisal of nature's temporal modes. The aging Horace
would have Torquatus, and us, recognize otherwise.

Horace's borrowing also suggests that he has been reexamining
another Catullus poem, 46, which begins

Iam ver egelidos refert tepores,
iam caeli furor aequinoctialis
iucundis Zephyri silescit auris.

Now spring brings back chill-less warmths, now the frenzy of the
equinoctial sky is hushed with the gentle gusts of the Zephyr.

For the remainder of the poem Catullus, by insistent anaphora, draws
an analogy between spring and his own mind. Just as the season
brings back renewed heat, so the desire to wander that his thoughts
now arouse will bring him back physically to Rome. Catullus' speaker, ever alive to the excitement of the immediate, imagines a con-
gruity between human and seasonal nature whereby we seem, for the
nonce at least, idealistically to partake in its cyclicity. It is not Catullus' purpose, as it is Horace's, to remind us that summer soon tramples on spring, and that mortality unremittingly exacts its human
toll.

Finally it is surely correct, as most critics maintain, that Horace was also meditating on that extraordinary "spring" poem that he had placed fourth in his first book of odes.[18] Both odes begin with the end of winter and the idea of change, but the earlier poem, which concentrates more on the season itself, centers on but one annual mutation with which man is potentially and actually involved, as sailor, shepherd, or ploughman. It is very much a poem concerned with the present, with the immediacy of Venus and her choruses, with proper festive wreaths and sacrifice to Faunus, with the final love Lycidas now claims for himself from youths and will soon extort from girls. Against the nimble beat of spring is the steady thud of universal death, which, as in ode 7, warns of the folly of hope and of the imminence of our habitation in the underworld. Spring and death form a counterpoint but only to highlight the eroticism in nature, as the divine couple Venus and Vulcan reenliven their dependencies, and in man, as happy Sestius, though forewarned of death, still drinks wine and remains entranced by a young love. And this love, unlike the tight categorization with which ode 7 ends, is in the process of change, from male bonding to heterosexuality. For a moment life's spring and nature's spring are at one.

Ode 7 expands in several ways on this tension between youth's season and the catholicity of death. First, its temporal and spatial purviews are grander.[19] Against the harsh cycle of nature in all its seasons is placed the linearity of man whom the speaker locates on the vertical plane between heaven and hell, and to whom he offers only the downward descent to darkness.

In the second place, the addressees are treated quite differently. Lucius Sestius, *consul suffectus* of 23 B.C., the year Horace published his first three books of odes, is honored with the fourth poem in a collection whose earlier three apostrophes were to Maecenas, Augustus, and Virgil. Yet in the poem itself he appears only in the role of anyone blessed with wealth and youth, whom the speaker places in a larger continuum. Whatever the strength of its generalities, the

[18]The two odes have been compared in detail by Levin, Quinn (*Latin Explorations,* 14–28) and Woodman. The last two agree that *c.* 1.4 is the better poem. Woodman, criticizing ode 7, speaks of "patchwork character" (765), "lack of structure" (766), and "crude technique" (778).

[19]Nor is there the concern for daily time that Horace evinces at the earlier ode's conclusion.

poem is essentially immediate and private. One man's primaveral eroticism is posed against the ineluctability of every man's death. The situation of Torquatus is, by contrast, more public. As befits his entrance into book 4, we sense his Romanness, not only because he was a lawyer of good breeding but because his characteristic piety makes him a latter-day Aeneas, an analogy in the present to a major figure in the historical past. Yet the general Roman renewal of the preceding poem does not save him from the loss of his own Roman distinctiveness in the face of dogged nature's ever-changing change-lessness.

There is also special prominence in the later poem given to both speaker and addressee as part of a universal "we." The first poem used *nos* only once, at line 15. The commonality of our mortal doom is the subject of the central stanza of ode 7, as "we"—speaker, hearer, and reader—are dust and shade. In these pivotal lines mortality embraces Rome's historical past. The concluding verses expand our vision into the world of myth, as absent as is historical allusion from the earlier ode, to lend final paradigmatic emphasis to the uselessness of life, however grandly lived, and to death's omnipotence.[20]

[20]*Lethaea* reminds us of our forgetfulness, and of the forgetting of us, in death. Yet myth and poetry remember. For all the pessimism of its truths, it is primarily because of our ode that Torquatus still lives. And, along with Virgil and Livy, Horace's poem recalls for us, immortally, the mortality of Aeneas, Tullus, and Ancus.

[8]

ODE EIGHT

Donarem pateras grataque commodus,
Censorine, meis aera sodalibus,
donarem tripodas, praemia fortium
Graiorum, neque tu pessuma munerum

ferres, divite me scilicet artium   5
quas aut Parrhasius protulit aut Scopas,
hic saxo, liquidis ille coloribus
sollers nunc hominem ponere, nunc deum.

sed non haec mihi vis, nec tibi talium
res est aut animus deliciarum egens: 10
gaudes carminibus; carmina possumus
donare, et pretium dicere muneri.

non incisa notis marmora publicis,
per quae spiritus et vita redit bonis
post mortem ducibus, [non celeres fugae   15
reiectaeque retrorsum Hannibalis minae
non incendia Karthaginis inpiae
eius qui domita nomen ab Africa
lucratus rediit] clarius indicant
laudes quam Calabrae Pierides, neque   20

si chartae sileant quod bene feceris,
mercedem tuleris. quid foret Iliae
Mavortisque puer, si taciturnitas
obstaret meritis invida Romuli?

ereptum Stygiis fluctibus Aeacum   25
virtus et favor et lingua potentium
vatum divitibus consecrat insulis.
[dignum laude virum Musa vetat mori]
caelo Musa beat. sic Iovis interest

optatis epulis inpiger Hercules,   30
clarum Tyndaridae sidus ab infimis
quassas eripiunt aequoribus ratis,
[ornatus viridi tempora pampino]
Liber vota bonos ducit ad exitus.

Gladly would I present the gift of bowls and shapely bronze to my
comrades, Censorinus, gladly present tripods, prizes for the bravery of
Greeks, nor would you carry away the least of the rewards, if only I
were affluent in the artistry which either Parrhasius or Scopas advanced,
the one with stone, the other with liquid pigments, clever to devise now
a man, now a god.

But this is not my forte, nor does your station or your instinct crave
such delicacies. You delight in songs. We have the power to offer songs
and are able to tell the worth of the reward.

Neither marbles carved with entries plain to all, through which
breath and life return to noble leaders after their demise, nor the swift
flights of Hannibal, nor his threats reversed into retreat, nor the fiery
razing of godless Carthage broadcast more brightly than the Muses of
Calabria the praises of him who returned with his name enhanced from
the Africa he had subdued. Nor if the chronicles were reticent about
your noble deeds, would you earn recompense.

What would the child of Ilia and Mars be if envious silence checked
Romulus' meed? The prowess and support and voice of powerful bards
wrested Aeacus from Stygian waves and hallowed him on the Rich
Isles. The Muse forbids death to a man worthy of praise, the Muse
devotes him to heaven. Thus eager Hercules shares Jupiter's hoped-for
banquets. Thus the sons of Tyndareus, bright constellation, wrest

shaken ships from the sea's depths, and Liber, his brow adorned with a tendril's green, brings vows to happy consummation.

The speaker of the seventh poem links himself with loss. As small particulars in a communal "we," it is our fate, as we relinquish our bodies, to abandon the characteristics, ethical or erotic, by which we are distinguished while alive, in exchange for mortality's formless dust and shade. And with disintegration goes memory. Yet, for all its gloom, the poem itself is a multiform act of remembrance, of Torquatus and of past poets, of Rome's historical continuum from foundation to present and of the writer's literary heritage. Each recollection suggests sequence and development through a time that in the end does not yield total submission to death. Poem 8 turns this glimmer of hope into a proclamation that the stuff of poetry is atemporal and that it is within the capacity of artistic language to salvage quality from time.[1] To redeem one's subjects is to presume self-redemption as well.[2]

The central poem of the collection opens, therefore, with a speaker who is very much dominant. The topic on which the initial lines ruminate is the uniqueness of his power to reward and the tangible results of such power. Looking first to Greek athletic competition, the speaker sees himself as neither the producer nor the bestower of works of art which serve as honorific reminders for victories accomplished and a degree of immortality achieved. Though an artist, he is implicitly viewing himself also as a patron, even if neither the artistry nor the form its patronage takes is his own.

The second form of patronage from which the speaker distinguishes himself is still more potent. He is not a fine artist, a Parrhasius or a

[1]Ode 8 is the only exception to the rule propounded contemporaneously by Meineke and Lachmann in the early nineteenth century that the number of verses in each of Horace's odes is always divisible by four (see the discussion by Lachmann, 84–86). Since then most criticism of ode 8 has been spent on tracking down the errant lines that make the poem asymmetrical. Most recently Dornseiff would eliminate verses 17 and 33, and Becker ("Donarem Pateras") 15b–19a, 28, and 33. Elter, who argues (77) that the poem is not strictly lyric and that therefore the Lex Meinekiana does not apply, considers genuine the whole of the received manuscript tradition. It is so treated in my analysis.

[2]The notion that song immortalizes begins with Homer and the early lyricists (Sappho 55, Ibycus 282a, and cf. Theognis 237ff.), and extends to Pindar (see Bundy, 11) and Theocritus *Id.* 16.24f.

Scopas, who can perpetuate his subject by the value, real and symbolic, of a memorializing gift as well as by his attempted re-creation of it in painting or sculpture. Yet, though names are named and forms specified, this latter form of valuation also depends on viewing the artist as patron. In using the word *artes* for the "arts" in which he is not gifted, the speaker means not only types of artistry but also, by synecdoche, the works of art produced by this diversity of talents. The metaphors used further validate this dualism of abstract and concrete, spiritual and physical. Each artist is appropriately *sollers,* given over fully to his ingenuity, but his commitment remains twofold. Just as his display of inner genius obliges him to exhibit his actual works of art (*protulit* bears both connotations), so he could be bidden not only to express himself in art but also to set up the tangible works that result (*ponere* accommodates both senses), for public estimation and for the glory of the subject. In sum, the speaker will not reward his subjects with palpable works of art, whether they are emblems of athletic prowess offered by presiding judge or whether they in fact resemble the receiver and are produced by the giver himself, as creator and then purveyor of his wares.

Horace's speaker is a realist where Pindar in similar contexts might be called a symbolist. When the Theban poet begins a poem "I am no sculptor, ready to carve images doomed to stand resting quietly on their pedestal," he is not differentiating his poetry from sculpture but merely revealing his impatience toward an art form that lacks the movement of his winged words.[3] Nor is the speaker using the literal figuratively as does Pindar when he compares the rich vessel of his song to a golden bowl brimming with poetic wine.[4] Poetry is Horace's art. His mouthpiece does not meditate on any difference between visual and verbal artistry, on the truth of inner versus outer "seeing." He merely lays straightforward claim to songs as his province.

The word *carmina*, repeated forcefully, is the climax of these opening lines. The strong iteration of one word highlights a progress that begins with a list of triple prizes and continues with the alternatives Parrhasius and Scopas offer the viewer. But the process of appraisal, which ends by giving place of honor to the heard and read, with

---

[3]N. 5.1ff.
[4]O. 7.1ff. On bowls and tripods as victory prizes, see also *I.* 1.19–20.

subjects to be contemplated by the mind's eye rather than externally seen, is more complicated than first appears. It involves both the poet and his addressee, Censorinus, whose *cognomen* implies the practiced critic's ability to compose proper aesthetic judgments. To offer one's allegiance only to the fine arts is to yield to the static and, one might imply, the superficial. The word *res* could bend either way, to mean the literal possessions for which Censorinus does not now opt or the mental inclination, which is presently his, for Horace's invisible handicraft. In choosing the latter, Censorinus benefits from a giving that is inwardly rich, if not always immediately perceived as such. The *munera* that come his way from a poet are at once valueless and invaluable. The poet's intangible gifts, ironically and paradoxically, are the ultimate treasure, and his inner force, which creates them, can also evaluate them for what they are worth vis-à-vis tripods and statuary. The singer of songs is in the end the authentic patron with the most lasting power to enrich. For poems talk, statues and paintings do not. The statesman Censorinus would well understand that speech, in setting man apart from all other creatures, makes politics possible. But it is the superior quality of poetic speech that provides a more lasting fame than that which accrues even to the most gifted orator in the arena of government.

Though he dismisses any analogy between himself and a patron or practitioner of the fine arts, between his words and their dispensations, nevertheless Horace's lines have a lapidary quality that mimics more concrete examples of monumentality. I will turn later to the larger role of meter in abetting this tone, but some details deserve mention here. The first Asclepiadean is one of only two meters (the other is the fifth Asclepiadean) used by Horace in his odes which is stichic, that is, one in which the same metrical line is repeated for the entire poem. This in itself imparts a certain *gravitas* that more rhythmically varied ensembles lack. But there is a peculiarity to the first, lacking in the fifth, that redoubles this solemnity. The line of the fifth Asclepiadean contains sixteen syllables and has two regular caesuras after the sixth and tenth syllables. The metrical line of ode eight is dodecasyllabic with one natural pause after the sixth syllable dividing it into two equal halves. The rhythmic repetition within lines therefore compounds with mathematical precision the effect of stately, straightforward directness that the lines themselves convey.

Horace adds still further compulsion to this inevitability by a remarkable rhyme scheme, embracing both the center and the final syllables of each line. Of the twenty-four syllables in question during the initial twelve lines, all but three end in *s* or *m,* and in seven lines—that is, in fourteen instances of these two dozen—the same letter used at the middle is repeated at the end.[5] This urgent reassertion of sound complements the number of verbal repetitions unusual for Horace. Both devices help center on line 12 where the initial word *donare* picks up *donarem,* which begins lines 1 and 3, and the concluding *muneri* echoes *munerum,* which finishes line 4. This combination of rhythmic and sonic repetition, with carefully demarcated lexical enclosure, fabricates an utterance that in its intense patterning serves as verbal metaphor for any more tangible artifact that might have honored Censorinus. He possesses the *donum* and *munus* of an artist, excelling (so he would have us witness) any creation whose shape was scanned with the eye and not the imagination's ear. In his use of words Horace can engender a feeling for space framed and filled which gratifies both senses.

Yet, in the grand example of a poetic "gift" which occupies the core of the ode, Horace does not lose sight of palpable monumentality. As we turn from Greece and its varied memorializing to Rome, we can compare for ourselves Horace's point when applied to one of the most famous individuals in the Roman past, Scipio Africanus Major.[6] We might gauge the effect on a Censorinus of Horace's distinction between a poet's literary offering to his subject and the legacy of painter or sculptor by the way the reputation of Scipio, whose accomplishment engaged the genius of each category of artist, was and presumably will be preserved. In Scipio's case it is a question of degree, not of total differentiation. Marble statues of the great, with their *elogia* inscribed beneath, of which I will have more

---

[5]The exceptions to this schema are *tu* (4), *me* (5), and *muneri* (12). Since *muneri* echoes *munerum* (end of 4), particular emphasis is given to *tu* and *me.*

[6]Horace magnifies the heroism of Scipio by imputing to him the burning of Carthage in 146 B.C., which was in fact the accomplishment of Scipio Aemilianus and about which Ennius, who died in 169 B.C., could not have known. The prominence of Scipio here reminds us that he also appears importantly in *DRN* 3.1034, the same Lucretian context that exerts such a strong influence on ode 7 (see above, p. 138 and n. 11). This commonality helps give a strong feeling of continuity and contrast between the two poems.

to say during my analysis of the book's final ode, compete with the verses of Ennius to assure a deathless future for their subject.

The facts that are "known to the public," the glorious deeds against Hannibal which evoke the proper response of praise, can be projected in two ways, by marble statuary or by the Muses of Calabria. The distinction reveals the poet's partiality. Each is a form of metonymy, marble as material for effigy and inscription, Muses standing for the poet and poetry they inspire. But the compliment lies not in turning individuated statues back into their unwrought origin but in raising Ennius to the level of the divinities who quicken his imagination.[7] He is both poet and source of poetry, living and immortal, unlike marbles that deal only in semblance. It is no wonder that Ennius and his patrons "disclose more clearly" (*clarius indicant*) the worth of Scipio. Marbles, no doubt, brightly yield their facts to passers-by, but both adverb and verb gain added richness when partnered with speech, with those who proclaim words equally solemn and "sonorous" (the original meaning of *clarus*).[8]

Scipio is not named but the manner in which we are made to attend to his *laudes* helps place him as a figure of importance in the book as a whole. The routing of Hannibal is the pivot of the fourth ode. Here it is the concerted emphasis on returns and returnings which looks beyond its immediate context. The fifth ode deals with the return of Augustus, essential for Italy's preservation, the sixth with secular renewal. Ode seven dwells on our inability to bring our bodies back to life after death, no matter how virtuous our existence has been. Here the "returns" are both positive and negative, momentary and eternal. They are negative for Hannibal whose threatening self is turned doubly back whence he came. Scipio's homecoming has a more expansive temporality. On the one hand it is a single documented occasion, now long past (*rediit*). But that unique act is made

---

[7]Horace indulges in parallel self-praise at ode 6.27 (*Daunia Camena*).

[8]It is ironic for Horace's point that the Scipios repaid Ennius' honorific verse by monumentalizing him in their own way. Cicero (*pro Arch.* 22) and Livy (38.56) offer evidence that a statue of Ennius was associated with their sepulcher between Via Latina and Via Appia outside the Porta Capena. These and other citations are discussed in detail by Coarelli who would place Ennius' statue on the facade together with those of Scipio Africanus and Scipio Aemilianus.

forever present by the works of art, visual or verbal, that afford a continuous return of breath and life (*redit*) to the doer.

In this connection the speaker allows himself an ironic twist on the word *lucror*. Valerius Maximus attests to a remark of Scipio's that he came back from Africa enriched only by an addition to his name.[9] The context Horace gives the word reverses this potential bitterness with another irony. The dowry that will immortalize the great comes not from an expanded name or from the palpability of wealth, but from the esteem of poets, who themselves eschew the immediately lavish to embrace, and bestow, values of a different quality. When the speaker again looks to Censorinus, after his central analogy from the life of Scipio, he keeps the economic image alive. True "payment" for Censorinus' services to Rome comes not from the results of the deeds themselves but from their recounting. Poetry offers a name for all time, incorporating and therefore eternalizing less durable nomenclature gained from politics, even transforming the facts of history and the ambitions history enshrines to suit its own purposes.

Here, and for the remainder of the poem, the competing but less authoritative profession of sculpting is dropped. Only the resonance of the written word speaking from the poet's page will be sufficient for Censorinus, as it was for Romulus. The speaker turns from a question to a statement whose force puts to rest any doubts the interrogative might have raised. For all the impersonality of the pronouncement—this is what poet-seers in general accomplish, not the handiwork of a particular Horace fashioning a particular persona—in one brisk act of the imagination's magic, the words justify by example the claims of the poem as a whole.

From Plato on in Greek literature and Cicero in Latin, Aeacus is a judge of the dead in the underworld, often in consort with Minos, Rhadamanthus, and (once, at least) Triptolemus.[10] It is in the act of

---

[9]Val. Max. 3.7.1.

[10]Plato *Apol.* 41a and *Gorg.* 523e (with Minos and Rhadamanthus), Cic. *Off.* 1.97 (with Minos) and *Tusc.* 1.98 with (Minos, Rhadamanthus, and Triptolemus). In Prop. 2.20.30 and 4.11.19 and in Ovid *M.* 13.25 he is simply a judge, but at *M.* 9.435–40 he is again associated with Minos and Rhadamanthus. Kiessling and Heinze (on l.22) interpret Horace's repositioning of Aeacus as merely a "symbol of undying fame," but this rings strangely because of the juxtaposition of *Stygiis fluctibus* which in the case of Aeacus must, at least initially, be seen as literal. Alteration of inherited myths by poets goes back at least to

judging (*iudicantem*), as part of the kingdom of somber Proserpina, that Horace places Aeacus (and that his quasi-autobiographical speaker nearly sees him) in *c.* 2.13.22. In that same ode Horace startlingly reverses inherited myth by assigning Prometheus, along with Tantalus and Orion, also to the realm of the dead. The transposition of myth here is equally vigorous and especially apt. The power of the poet can succeed where Diana and Theseus failed in the preceding poem. Their lovers remained imprisoned in the darkness below by the fetters of forgetfulness. By contrast the omnipotent poet co-opts the authority to immortalize. His words, both literally and figuratively in this case, wrest their prey bodily from death and deify him (*consecrat*). The islands on which the blessed are placed are rich, but the etymology of the word *dives* makes it cognate with *divus,* divine.[11] The richness of apotheosis stems from virtue recognized and rewarded by the strength of a poet's tongue.

Apotheosis through poetic will is the theme of the poem's finale. The patronage of the poet-muse, the power of words to stir the imagination and mold the myths by which we live is what raises the civilizing attributes of any mortal to the status of divine. This status, in turn, allows Castor, Pollux, and Bacchus to continue their services to mankind from a different vantage point. But the activism of these new gods, as they go about their kindly tasks, has its parallel with the poet's imagined power to alter our world. The sons of Tyndareus may snatch ships from the sea's depths because of the luminosity of their star, but it is a poet's clear words, manifesting his ability to snatch Aeacus from Stygian floods, that effects deification in the first place. Though Bacchus can secure for mankind the righteous fulfillment of prayers, the wizardry of the poet allows him this perquisite by granting him his privileged position. The poet is the final god.

Stesichorus on Helen (see fr. ed. Vürtheim, 64–72) and to Pindar on Pelops (*O.* 1). The preceding poem offers an example of the procedure in reverse. Though it had already been alluded to in the *Naupaktia* (Apoll. 3.10.3) and treated by Callimachus (*Aet.* fr. 190Pf, drawn from Servius on *Aen.* 7.778), Virgil in *Aeneid* 7 dwells on an abstruse aspect of the Hippolytus legend by having him restored to life by Aesculapius. Woodman (765) finds Horace's change back to the more traditional legend unfortunate, but this authorial self-assertion may be exactly Horace's point.

[11]Varro *L. L.* 92 and *OLD s.v.* Horace is apparently the first to name the blessed or fortunate islands *divites* in *epode* 16.42, but the etymology has particular point here.

Meter plays a significant role in this monumentalizing, and in no other Horatian work is its symbolic significance more forthcoming. Horace uses the first Asclepiadean only twice elsewhere, for the first and last poems of his earlier collection of odes. They provide, therefore, the bordering frame for that remarkable poetic gathering, and the self-consciousness of their content emphasizes this careful calculation. The introductory priamel, addressed in its initial word to Maecenas, dwells on a variety of careers the speaker forgoes in favor of his role as bard, provided his patron approves. The "seal" poem announces the completion of this imaginative edifice raised by the creative "I," admonishing Melpomene to offer the architect his due honor only at its conclusion. By contrast, the present ode, instead of helping form an outline, is pivotal, thus centering a major theme in this tightly interwoven fabric of poems (and words). If the earlier terminal poems delineated the majesty of what the speaker has executed, which is also to say of the speaker himself, the core poem of the fourth book broadcasts directly the ability of the poet to memorialize and monumentalize others than himself. Though the ultimate glory no doubt rests with the maker of poems as his words forge their own illusion of continuity, the immediate myth is that the imagination eternalizes its subjects. In this grand fantasy poetry tames temporality, and life, at least the residue of values memory salvages after we cast off our mortal coil, is resubstantiated through the efforts of the imagination. The permanence of art seems to triumph over nature's mutability.

The tone of the poem that pronounces such heady possibilities for itself and its companion pieces is appropriately solemn.[12] Though the speaker does have *sodales* and gives poems as gifts, and though the addressee is rewarded accordingly, nevertheless in the prolonged obeisance to Scipio and in the concluding elaborations of Greco-Roman myth the poem becomes impersonal as it supports its abstract claims. For all the initial interplay between speaker and addressee, we learn little explicit information about the poet and nothing about his addressee except his name, Censorinus. For the latter's identity, since

---

[12]The number of lexical and formal archaisms in the ode abets this majestic tone. *Mavors* (23) appears only here in the lyric work, *beo* (29) only elsewhere at *c.* 2.3.7, and *Graius* (4) only at *c.* 2.4.12 and 2.16.38. Line 4 also contains Horace's only use of *pessuma* (cf. *pessima* at *sat.* 2.7.22).

the poem tells us nothing, we must go to secondary sources. Two candidates have been proposed. The first is Gaius Marcius Censorinus, consul in 8 B.C., the year of Horace's death. Horace would no doubt have perceived him readied for this honor in 13 B.C., but his youth (he would not yet have been thirty) and what little we know of his career is incompatible with the respectful position the central poem's dedicatee holds in book 4. More specifically, the words of lines 21–22 imply deeds already done of such magnitude as to be celebrated in panegyric verse.[13]

A more likely candidate for the honor was the by then probably septuagenarian Lucius Marcius Censorinus, arguably the father of Gaius, praetor in 43 B.C. and consul in 39 B.C. He was one of two senators who attempted to defend Julius Caesar on the Ides of March, in 44 B.C. Whatever his subsequent political vagaries, the memory of this deed and perhaps others remained with Augustus. In the year 17 B.C. he was given the special compliment of serving together with the emperor's most trusted friends as one of the *Quindecimviri* who adminstered the *ludi saeculares*. On the inscription that preserves for us the *acta* of that event, his name comes second after that of the revered Marcus Agrippa in the first listing of the celebration's overseers.[14]

It is tempting to conjecture that this accolade is the basis for the place of prominence with which Horace honors Censorinus, and that the *sodalicium* the two enjoyed stemmed from their mutual participation in that festivity. For all its impersonality, the eighth ode shares with the *Carmen Saeculare* and the occasion it graces a concern with the future of Rome. Rome's historical recurrence was on Augustus' mind, and Rome, her leader, his family, and supporters were equally the beneficiaries of Horace's genius, here and throughout book 4, for his lyric fixes time and stabilizes heroic individuality. In the subsequent poem we learn a great deal more about the poem's creator and its recipient than we do here, but nothing, outside of important verbal parallels, unites the two poems more closely than the fact that Marcus Lollius, addressee of ode 9, was also a lieutenant of Augustus and member of the same *Quindecimviri*.[15] The *sodalicium* was to bring

---

[13]Details in *RE* 14.2.1551.

[14]For his life see *RE* 14.2.1554–55. The inscription is reproduced in *CIL* 6.32323. (Censorinus is named at 44.)

[15]*CIL* 6.32323.45 and 6.32323.107.

him a poet's tribute as well, but it would remain less forceful without the brief for his own, and any hero's, immortality through poetry which Horace offers in homage to Censorinus.[16]

[16]We should note here, as often in book 4, the particular appropriateness of the poem's last word, *exitus*. The ode ends with a vision of immortal endings, a final nod at its own immortality and consequent ability to fulfill its own promises of constancy. This will prove typical of the book as a whole which, in its conclusion, will posit a series of new beginnings and openings out.

[9]

ODE NINE

Ne forte credas interitura quae
longe sonantem natus ad Aufidum
    non ante volgatas per artis
        verba loquor socianda chordis:

non, si priores Maeonius tenet   5
sedes Homerus, Pindaricae latent
    Ceaeque et Alcaei minaces
        Stesichorique graves Camenae,

nec, siquid olim lusit Anacreon,
delevit aetas; spirat adhuc amor   10
    vivuntque conmissi calores
        Aeoliae fidibus puellae.

non sola comptos arsit adulteri
crinis et aurum vestibus inlitum
    mirata regalisque cultus   15
        et comites Helene Lacaena,

primusve Teucer tela Cydonio
direxit arcu, non semel Ilios
    vexata, non pugnavit ingens
        Idomeneus Sthenelusve solus   20

dicenda Musis proelia, non ferox
Hector vel acer Deiphobus gravis
   excepit ictus pro pudicis
      coniugibus puerisque primus.

vixere fortes ante Agamemnona   25
multi; sed omnes inlacrimabiles
   urgentur ignotique longa
      nocte, carent quia vate sacro.

paulum sepultae distat inertiae
celata virtus. non ego te meis   30
   chartis inornatum silebo
      totve tuos patiar labores

inpune, Lolli, carpere lividas
obliviones: est animus tibi
   rerumque prudens et secundis   35
      temporibus dubiisque rectus,

vindex avarae fraudis et abstinens
ducentis ad se cuncta pecuniae,
   consulque non unius anni,
      sed quotiens bonus atque fidus   40

iudex honestum praetulit utili,
reiecit alto dona nocentium
   voltu, per obstantis catervas
      explicuit sua victor arma.

non possidentem multa vocaveris   45
recte beatum; rectius occupat
   nomen beati, qui deorum
      muneribus sapienter uti

duramque callet pauperiem pati
peiusque leto flagitium timet,   50
   non ille pro caris amicis
      aut patria timidus perire.

Lest you chance to believe that the words are prone to perish which I, born near the far-resounding Aufidus, utter in consort with strings, through skills never before divulged: though Maeonian Homer claims pride of place, the Muses, of Pindar and of Cea, threatening for Alcaeus and solemn for Stesichorus, do not lie concealed, nor has time expunged whatever Anacreon once trifled. The love still breathes, the passions still survive, which the Aeolian girl entrusted to her lyre.

Helen of Sparta was not the only woman who glowed agog at her lover's patterned locks, at his gold-daubed garments and his regal stance and retinue, nor was Teucer the first to aim arrows from Cretan bow, nor was Troy but once hard pressed, nor did stalwart Idomeneus or Sthenelus alone fight battles worthy of the Muses' words. Neither savage Hector nor fierce Deiphobus was the first to encounter weighty blows for chaste wives and children.

Many brave men lived before Agamemnon but, unwept and unknown, all are burdened by night's length because they lack a sacred bard. Courage unrevealed differs but little from shiftlessness entombed. I will not in silence fail to array you in my pages nor, Lollius, will I suffer the spites of darkness to pluck scatheless at your deeds. Yours is a spirit cautious before its tasks and upright, whether occasions favor or perplex, an avenger of greed's conceit, and aloof from wealth that lures the universe to itself; your spirit, consul not for a single year but for the host of times a noble and trusted judge has preferred the decent to the expedient, rejected with glance of scorn the bribes of the guilty and carried its arms of victory through the thronging crowds.

You would not brand a well-propertied man as truly happy. He more truly claims the title happy who has the will to employ wisely the rewards of the gods and to endure grievous poverty, and who fears iniquity worse than death, a man unafraid to die for his beloved friends or for his fatherland.

The detachment that characterizes the conclusion of poem 8 is appropriate for a celebration of poetry's ability to memorialize. As the center of a chiasmus of poems it is crucial in Horace's creation of a complex verbal structure that offers symbolic proof to the reader of the veracity of its individual claims. The book as a whole is a monument to Horace's own potential to monumentalize the components of his world as he chooses, person by person, poem by poem. Yet at the moment of centrality we learn little of himself, still less of his subject, Censorinus. The subsequent poem makes amends for this layered objectivity by dealing closely with each item. Instead of comparing art forms, the speaker situates himself in a strictly poetic heritage, and in place of an addressee of whose *facta* we remain ignorant, we have an exemplification of the qualities a poet interested in the ethics of community would be expected to glorify. Poem 9 is lively proof that the professions of its predecessor are true, and that in Augustan Rome there exists a present master poetic strategist, who absorbs and adds luster to the poetic past and who possesses subjects of new value worthy of his eulogizing.

First, the heritage of the poet. In the speaker's "autobiographical" self-placement, origin and originality, the Aufidus and the artistry that ultimately stems from its precincts, each complements each other. This birth takes form through synecdoche, in the words that are the poet's self-extension and that unlike death-ridden (*interitura*) summer in the seventh ode, escape mortality.[1] There are no claims for the poet himself, only for what he speaks. These separate enlivenings share one special characteristic. Each is associated with sound. The wide-echoing Aufidus is a topographical representation of the poetry that results from the alliance of words and music forged by its nursling.[2] It provides the initial pattern that the poet will sym-

---

[1] Horace's only two uses of the participle *interitura* are these two instances (lines 10 and 1 of their respective odes).

[2] This is Horace's only use of the verb *socio* and the first instance, according to *OLD*, of its meaning to combine or associate things together (but cf. the use of *consociare* at *c.* 2.3.10). Yet the "politics" of poetry is important here because it is a politician who is to be the subject of the present union. Here *verba* and *chordis* are paired to publicize Horace's deathlessness, and at lines 11–12 *calores* given to the lyre define the work of Sappho. (*Chordae,* the strings of the lyre, from the Greek χορδή, gut, are virtually equivalent to *fides,* which seems to derive from the Greek σφίδες, defined by Hesychius as χορδαὶ μαγειρικαί, guts for cooking.) *Verba* and *calores* are as metonymical for the poem itself (means of construction for the object constructed, effects of emotion for the description of it) as *chordis* and *fidibus* are for its manner of communication. It will not be long before the conjunction of Lollius with Horace's *chartae* will assure the former's presentation from oblivion. Horace will have his similarities with Homer and the Greek lyricists, but Horace and Lollius are united, the first as creator of, the second re-created in, words. Lollius, too, as noted below, is as much a metonymy as the *chartae* that prolong his existence.

bolically reproduce, for unlike our dying selves poetry has its equivalence in nature. The constant resonance over time which it shares with the Aufidus assures the durability of those subjects fortunate to share in this double engendering.

Horace's speaker plays on this dual importance of place and time as he begins his overview of the Greek poetic past. Like Daunian Horace, Homer too, at the start of western poetic tradition, has a location—Lydia—and is named accordingly. But the phrase *priores sedes* looks two ways. A Roman reader would think of the seats of honor at theatrical performances, in the orchestra and the initial rows of the *cavea,* given to the nobility. Homer occupies the front ranks of poets, and is seen by viewers of all categories and venerated accordingly. But *priores* can also refer to priority in time, and in this category, too, Homer comes first. In neither case, however, does Homer completely surpass his progeny. Horace has just told us that artistry of his own sort has never been publicized before (*ante*). And the reverential public treatment metaphorically granted Homer does not overshadow the talents of succeeding poets. Horace will continue in what follows to review this distinction between the open and the hidden, especially in regard to the poet's ability to illuminate and darken his universe, by promulgating or suppressing possible topics for song.

Just as Horace's birth is inextricably tied to the immortality of his words, so Homer, famous author of the *Iliad* and the *Odyssey,* is also a metonymy for the content of his writing. It is on the individual essences of later Greek poetry that the speaker now dwells with growing excitement. The Muses of Pindar and Simonides of Ceos are, like Homer, merely named and placed, but the inspirers of Alcaeus and Stesichorus, who stand for their inspired words and works, are threatening and majestic, as we imagine them seen, along with noble Homer, and as we understand their influence in the tone of verses read. No muses are mentioned for Anacreon or Aeolian Sappho, placed though not named, yet the language grows increasingly figurative.[3] *Ludere,* to play, is, as Catullus notably demonstrated, to make love and to create amatory verses:[4]

---

[3]Becker (*Spätwerk,* 139) well notes the gradual change from poetry per se to content.

[4]50.4–6. Cf. *epi.* 1.1.3 (*ludo*) and 10 (*ludicra*).

scribens versiculos uterque nostrum
ludebat numero modo hoc modo illoc,
reddens mutua per iocum atque vinum.

Writing little verses, each of us teased now in this meter now in that,
with give and take as we jested over our wine.

And, as *scribens* marks, this duplex mental and physical action likewise involves the act of writing:[5] "*multum lusimus in meis tabel-
lis, . . .*" (we sported richly in my writing-tablets, . . .). Horace
takes the immediate day and night of Catullus' amatory intensity and
expands its purview to embrace the larger *aetas* of time's passage. But
something of Catullus lingers in his play on *delevit* as well. Time, the
great leveler, will not destroy either Anacreon or his erotic amuse-
ments, imagined or otherwise, because it is unable to expunge the
immortal writing that resulted from them.[6]

Sappho's work is even more vividly presented. In the poet's climactic metonymy Muses and the play of writing about play yield to the
contents of poetry—the loves and, still more immediate, "warmths"
that Sappho confides to her lyre. Not Homer, the initiating poet, or the
Muses, personifying inspiration and the tonalities of its results, but the
concentration and passion of poetry itself are now alive before us.
These qualities may have been entrusted to the lyre for future singing,
as Anacreon's sporting was implicitly confided to writing and to a
continuing existence through reading. Whatever the means of communication, it is brilliance of content that lives on and that is the final
self-preserver for time to come.

But though epic narrative in general lacks the immediacy of the
lyric first person and his dense poetic energies, the subject matter of
Homer, to whom Horace now turns, is far from dispassionate.[7] On
the surface, Horace's point in these stanzas is that primacy and singularity in the annals of human events as catalogued by poetry are
only apparent. The lines are carefully regimented to illustrate that the
extraordinary cast of characters in early Greek epic is not unique. *Non*

[5]50.2.
[6]On the confusion of *deleo* and *delino,* see Ernout-Meillet *s.vv. deleo* and *lino.*
[7]Kiessling and Heinze (436) speak, misleadingly, of "die zwischen v. 12 and 13
klaffende Lücke des Gedankengangs."

sola, which begins line 13, is echoed by *solus* at the conclusion of line 20, and *primus,* which initiates the second stanza of this Homeric overview, is balanced by its iteration at the end of the third. The careers of Helen, Teucer, Sthenelus, and Deiphobus document a historical truism that the poetic statement, for all the care of its structuring, seems only further to support. The four uses of *non,* coupled with *-ve* and *vel,* reinforce the rote that, on the level of rhetoric, partially flattens the distinctiveness of the personages tolled.

Yet Horace uses other means to leave with us the memory of this very uniqueness. Sappho's lyricism may brilliantly imagine the flames of her private loves, but it is the burning of Helen for Paris, and the responsive genius of Homer in the telling, that at once sparked the Trojan war and gave western literature its initial impetus. Horace's catalog is in fact a remarkable survey of the saga of Helen, taking us from Sparta to the heroism on her behalf at Troy. It begins in Greece with her seduction by Paris. Even though the speaker uses irony at his expense with the word *inlitum* (is Paris' charm all surface?),[8] we are, like her, awestruck by his beauty. Sappho's *calores* served as transition to Helen's ardor, yet as we follow her eager response, we gradually turn away from Paris—first his hair, then his gilded clothing, then his finery in general—and toward his comrades in his journey of seduction. Thence Horace takes us to her new home, where the Greeks are active, Troy and the Trojans passive, troubled, and receiving blows. The list turns from former suitors to a brother-in-law fighting to regain Helen, to a new brother-in-law and still another consort, challenging their onslaught.[9] To conclude with Deiphobus is a masterstroke. As Virgil's *Aeneid* powerfully reminds us, he was Helen's husband after the death of Paris and was viciously murdered by Menelaus, whose wrath she feared, with her assistance during Troy's final night.[10] So what Horace also gives us is a chro-

[8]Horace is varying Virgil's satire of Roman pretension in dress at *geo.* 2.464 (*inlusas . . . auro vestis*).

[9]At *c.* 1.15.24–26, Teucer, Sthenelus, and Meriones, charioteer of Idomeneus, are listed among those who will revenge themselves on Helen. The first two are named as suitors of Helen in Apollodorus (*Bib.* 3.10.8). Hyginus (*Fab.* 81) lists Sthenelus and Idomeneus who also figures in the list at Hesiod *Cat.* fr. 204–56 (Merkelback and West).

[10]Deiphobus tells his own tale to Aeneas (*Aen.* 6.509–34). The death of Deiphobus is touched upon in the *Iliu Persis* of Demodocus at *Od.* 8.516ff.

nology of the Trojan war based on the amatory life of Helen. The speaker leaves us, teaching with Homer's teachings, to ponder the word *pudicis*. Andromache's chastity would not be questioned, but what of Helen's? The survey has an erotic cast and the final exercise asked of the reader is to offer a moral judgment on that eroticism as well as to consider the possibility that poets can deceive.

The immediate reason Homer's heroes survived is because the Muses found a mouthpiece to tell of their bravery. This is the nub of the poem's central *dictum*. There is continuity in the existence of bardless heroes, even when their life is past, but it persists in a gloom that never turns to day because listeners neither know about nor respond to their deeds. To know is to weep, and in the tearful emotions of the recaller stems the very knowledge that assures the endurance of the doer of deeds. As commentators note, Horace is thinking of Pindar who warns that[11]

> . . . μεγάλαι . . . ἀλκαὶ
> σκότον πολὺν ὕμνων ἔχοντι δεόμεναι · . . .

great acts of bravery possess only deep darkness, if they lack songs.

But Horace varies his powerful model by seeing heroes and their heroism as one. It is people themselves who survive in the words of the poet, sequestering them from night.

The apothegm of lines 29–30 reviews the thought. The human who lacks *ars* is buried, incapable of the recurrence the seventh ode allows even *bruma iners*.[12] Courage, when it is hidden, partakes ironically in unmanliness because it is lost to understanding, which is to say all but dead. It is the imagination's *artes* that in their turn have the power to re-create heroism and distinguish it from cowardice, the morally artful from the artless, because, like quotidian nature itself, they can elicit day from night and make the hidden visible.

This is exactly the service that Horace performs for his addressee, Marcus Lollius, who has been a part of the poem since the opening

---

[11]*N.* 7.12–13.

[12]Ode 7 (12), where, as we observed, Horace also plays on the double meaning of artlessness and sloth, the formless and the cowardly.

credas but who is only named during the second half, which belongs to him. The theme of sound versus silence is not new to the poem, nor is the triumph of light over darkness or of memory over forgetfulness, but their synaesthetic conjunction, combining hearing and seeing, is. The speaker's word choice emphasizes the moment. This is the only documented occasion in classical Latin where *inornatus* means "unhonored," "uncelebrated."[13] Ordinarily the word applies to a person and, by transference, to a style lacking in elaboration and embellishment. As so often in Horace, novelty embraces and points up standard, expected usage. Lollius will indeed be glorified in Horace's verses, but this poetic consecration occurs because he becomes incorporated into the poet's words and modes of expression. He is the climax in a sequence of metonymies for poetry extending from Homer's initial *verba* to the menacing, severe Muses of Alcaeus and Stesichorus, to the warmths of Sappho and the adorned locks and gold-smeared garments of Paris (synecdoche of Homeric epic), to the *chartae* that at once hold, and are, the lyrics of Horace. The adorning of Paris and the adorning of Lollius have their parallels as do Homer and Horace. Each gives honor to his subjects by writing of them, but that honor is conveyed in the decoration of the poetic statement itself.[14]

The words *lividas obliviones,* linked by enjambment and alliteration, also have a special richness. Personified "forgetfulnesses" are "spiteful" of accomplishment and attempt, ironically, to speak out against them, to use words to dull words. Yet they are also dark and darkening, kin to the underworld and sharing its lack of memory. Since etymologists connect *oblivio* with *lino,* meaning to smear, we have a further instance of the saving aspects of poetry, first overpowering the efforts of time to smudge its words and now, similarly, assuring

[13]OLD *s.v.* 2 and *TLL s.v.* 1763.6–8 (*de homine laude non illustrato*). Horace's only other use of the word is as an attribute of *nomina* (*A. P.* 234). The only instance of it *de hominibus* before Horace, Cic. *or.* 78, is in an analogy between an unadorned woman and a spare style. Otherwise, examples are only connected with style ([Cic.] *ad Her.* 4.69; Cic. *de or.* 2.341).

[14]*Chartis* is appropriately both locative and instrumental. Lollius, as a historical figure treated by Horace, will be honored in parchments containing poems. As a concatenation of verbal elements become a poem, he will be ornamented by the poetry itself.

Lollius that he will escape through Horace's help the erasures of oblivion.[15]

The first half of the poem gives Homer and his creatures a conspicuous place. The *laudatio* of Lollius, which brings the ode to a conclusion, is Horace's Roman equivalent. In forming epic deeds to the contour of Alcaeus' "menacing" rhythms, he does not so much demean Homer as, in his own lyric way, place Lollius on a par with the champions around Troy. Yet there is an impressive difference. Though a hint of moralizing overlays the way Horace epitomizes Iliadic Homer, observable in the story line (*adultera, pudicis*) and in metaphor (*inlitum*), the essence of his characterization is in the prowess of physical heroics, with bows and arrows, fights battled out, blows received, all to summarize bravery in action. The *virtutes* for which Horace segregates Lollius are of another sort.

Roman heroism, for which Horace had earlier found a paradigm in Regulus, is largely of the mind, not of the body, to be treated in ethical, not physical terms. The précis of the *Iliad* is a history of literal events, looking to the savagery of Hector, Deiphobus' ferocity, and brave Agamemnon. The handling of Lollius focuses, in one ambitious synecdoche, on his inner life. The expansive analysis of its characteristics surveys those courageous qualities of mind that lend value to the daily existence of a Roman statesman and that in turn enhance the spiritual excellence of the community which he serves.[16]

Throughout the encomium Horace differentiates between the superficial and the lasting in Lollius' acceptance of life. *Res* (political or economic bases of power) and *tempora* (the mutable moments that

[15]On *oblivio* and *lino* see Ernout-Meillet and *OLD s.v. obliviscor. Oblivio* and *oblivium* are linked with Lethe, the fountain of forgetfulness, by both Virgil (*Aen.* 6.714–15) and Horace (*epode* 14.2–3, where *inertia* does the pouring of oblivion). Virgil's only use of *lividus* is to describe the waters of the underworld (*Aen.* 6.320). Horace's use of *lividus* may look back to Call. *H.* 2.105–13 and the personification of Φθόνος in a context dealing with the creation of poetry. *Livor* is first personified in Latin poetry by Propertius (1.8.29; cf. Ovid *Am.* 1.15.1, *R. A.* 389).

[16]Fraenkel (*Horace,* 426), who does not think that Horace found in Lollius "a congenial topic," speaks of these lines as occupying "a decent minimum of space." He comes to the poet's defense in a way that undermines, rather than extols, his quality: "If . . . the eulogy sounds somewhat laboured, this is clearly not the poet's fault" (425–26). The heroism of Regulus, confirmer of standards for the Roman Senate, is the subject of *c.* 3.5.

change brings) find him prudent and straightforward. He is, in epithets given structural prominence, *vindex, consul,* and *iudex,* but the playing of roles finds him treating them more deeply and seriously than we might expect others would. His consulship is not a passing moment of political opportunity but a continuous practice of counsel.[17] In his life, and in the poet's etymological play, this takes the form of words, not action. The "speaking" of *vis* and the "speaking" of *ius,* which the suffix *-dex* implies, exemplify in his case the persuasion of moral, not physical, force. That very judiciousness shies away from both the superficiality and the capability of money (he is as *abstinens* as wealth is *ducentis,* in the speaker's sharp enjambment) and from the gifts of those guilty of crime.[18]

Yet there is one moment of activity, at the end of this philosophical characterization, that in fact further distinguishes Lollius from his Homeric antecedents. As an effective jurist, a judge of both immediate and long-term high-minded intentions, he deploys his armory so as to rout victoriously the opposing squadrons. For him, whether the language documents an actual case in progress or is only symbolic of a steadfast mental outlook, these are not palpable weapons unleashed against rapers of wives, only the figural panoply of implicit eloquence exercised against the injudicious, whether abstract or concrete, inanimate or alive (*fraudis, pecuniae, nocentium*). In the case of Lollius, legal and moral victories are one and the same, and the public manifestation of justice is only an aspect of the judicious *animus* at work.

It is not Lollius the noteworthy jurist or even his conduct itself which receives Horace's panegyric, but his *animus,* the spirit that makes him a Stoic sage, whatever the ethical choices before him. Lollius' intellectual well-being provides the vital part that for the poet defines the whole. But the personification of the protagonist's *animus* becomes a special, nearly abstract form of *consul* and *iudex.* The "you" that Horace praises is a disembodied entity. As Lollius reenters the poem at line 45, Horace once again leans on generalization.

As the poem draws to a conclusion, we are left purposely unsure of the role the poet is having Lollius play. Apparently Lollius shares

---

[17]On the early connection between *consul* and *consulo,* see Acc. *Praet.* 39R, Cic. *Leg.* 3.8, and Varro *L. L.* 5.80 (which also contains the Accius citation).

[18]*Nocentium,* which ends line 42, is another of several participles in these stanzas whose location makes them salient.

with the speaker the ability to describe the blessed—in other words, to define a state of bliss—by the actions of the wise. The striking repetitions at lines 46–47, which emphasize the importance of truth in this designation, leave out even a generalized addressee at the crucial moment of naming. Are we to understand an everyman "you," or even a specific Lollius, from line 46 to the end, joining with the speaker to agree on the meaning of happiness? Are the characteristics of wisdom, endurance, uprightness, and patriotism to be read as Lollius' own or as part of a larger portrait of the good man? The answer is probably yes in both cases. Just as Lollius' *animus* is the motive force behind a re-creation of the whole man, so Lollius himself now becomes an abstract *exemplum* of the Stoic saint, illustrating the speaker's definition of happiness by the motivations of his own career.

Lollius is immortalized not for the specific valiant feats Homer imagines for his characters but for the general, inner pattern of his life. It is true that the language suggests a parallel between the blows received by Hector and Deiphobus and the fearlessness of a Stoic worthy before an intrepid death. The first two suffer *pro pudicis coniugibus puerisque,* the second *pro caris amicis aut patria.* Immortality is in each case achieved by the proper acceptance of morality. In Horace's Homer, the code of ethics values loyalty to wife and children, and hence adherence to proper sexual behavior. For the contemporary Roman saint of Horace's imagination, Lollius *beatus,* there is no challenge from eroticism. The potential suffering and death, against which he is fearless, stem from love of friends and fatherland, from *amicitia* toward those who embody the abstraction and then from the abstraction itself. His innerness, like the feelings of a poet or his characters, a Sappho or a Helen, becomes a symbol created by those other symbols, the words of a poet. It is finally through them, and not so much because of the model pattern he has been abstracted into, that Lollius is as deathless in his Roman way as any previous plaything of the imagination.[19]

[19]Marcus Lollius suffered defeat in Gallia Comata at the hands of the Sygambri in 16 B.C. Since the event was an embarrassment on several counts—Lollius lost the eagle of a legion in conflict and yet survived—it is possible to interpret Horace as ironizing against Lollius as he does against his vision of Helen (see Ambrose, "The Ironic Meaning," *passim*). Since Syme, however, has demonstrated ("Some Notes," 17–18; *Roman Revolution,* 429) the insignificance of the

In its context in *Odes* 4, the ninth ode is a suitable companion piece to its predecessor and carefully linked to it by the poet. Both concern the power of a *vates* to immortalize and the *chartae,* whose lack of silence provides the tangible means to this end. The earlier ode reminds us that it is not public statuary that restores breath and life (*spiritus et vita*) to good leaders after death. The second twists the thought around to prove what does survive, the loves and ardors of Sappho:

> . . . spirat adhuc amor
> vivuntque conmissi calores
> Aeoliae fidibus puellae.

In the first we look at the affairs and soul (*res . . . aut animus*) of Censorinus for what they do not need. The second, following the same pattern as before, speaks of what Lollius is and has:

> animus tibi
> rerumque prudens . . .

Ode 8, in sum, looks more abstractly at poetry as an art in relation to other arts and at its ability to monumentalize and deify with the

---

defeat from a military point of view, it is equally plausible that Horace, writing between 16 B.C. and 13 B.C., was bent on a different form of mythmaking. For Horace to find in Lollius the personification of bravery, despite the *clades Lolliana,* is to treat any political loss as insignificant; it is also to create a version of Lollius and to define his special Roman heroism in such a way as to anticipate and undermine later writers who might in due time attempt to denigrate his career, for example, the Tiberian Velleius Paterculus (2.97.1) and Suetonius (*Tib.* 12.13; cf. Tac. *Ann.* 3.48). Though Velleius uses the word *clades,* the phrase *clades Lolliana* is from Tacitus (*Ann.* 1.10.4), part of a negative survey of the career of Augustus. Cassius Dio (54.20.4–6) gives a dispassionate account of the event itself. Velleius' claim that Lollius was a man "more desirous in every respect of money than of proper behavior" (*in omnia pecuniae quam recte faciendi cupidiore*) seems a direct echo of Horace's statement that he was "aloof from wealth that lures the universe to itself" (*abstinens ducentis ad se cuncta pecuniae*). Whatever the truth or falsehood of each portrait, the fact that Velleius mimics Horace's words in order to claim their opposite only proves their power. Horace's verses have their "vengeance" (*non . . . inpune*) against not only the grander pressures of oblivion but future Roman derision as well.

Muses' help. Ode 9 exemplifies this dynamism at work, opening with a close look at poetry's survival in the great variety of its contents, and concluding with a specific act of immortalizing. The integrity of a Roman statesman, whose inner values shape his actions, is preserved for us as previous poets had saved a Scipio or a Hercules from being forgotten. The abstract principle of a poet's *virtus*, central, like the eighth ode, to the book as a whole, is followed by concrete examples of poetry's singularity and of the individuals who are remembered because of it.[20]

The seventh ode, which introduces this focal triad of poems, lays the groundwork for much that follows in the subsequent odes.[21] It portentously announces the inevitability of death for all humans by contrast with the restorative capability of yearly time. The next of its companion poems offers contrary evidence for the triumph of art over temporality, of the endurance of mortal *animi,* be it those of poets or of their human creations, through the timeless brilliance of the imagination. Summer dies only momentarily. A poet's words never do. Winter's artlessness prevails, but only for its allotted span. A poet's *artes* grant assurance that the genius of his subjects is beyond any mortal linearity and in fact partakes in the very power inanimate nature has to restore itself. Bodies may vanish and with them the possibilities of sexual love, but a higher form of eroticism, a poet's love, replaces it and promises an escape from human sexuality's limitations.

There are several ways in which this splendid trio of poems shows such a modulation in action. I will offer two illustrations. The first links poems 7 and 9. At the end of the earlier ode we learn that Diana cannot free chaste Hippolytus (*pudicum Hippolytum*) from darkness nor Theseus break the bonds of forgetfulness for his dear Pirithous (*caro Pirithoo*). Yet redemption from oblivion's dark night is exactly the poet's promise in ode 9. It is no accident that Homer and the Homeridae preserve Hector and Deiphobus for us, fighting *pro pudicis coniugibus,* or that Horace's speaker, during a counterbalancing moment at the poem's end, glorifies Lollius, hypothetically perishing *pro caris amicis.* What a god or demigod cannot do for his beloved remains

---

[20]Other possible connections: *Tyndaridae* (8.31) and *Helene* (9.16); *ornatus* (8.33) and *non . . . inornatum* (9.31); *obstaret* (8.24) and *obstantis* (9.43), these last the only instances of *obsto* in book 4.

[21]Fraenkel (*Horace,* 426) speaks correctly of a "central triad, firmly linked together," though he dissociates the poems from those that precede and follow.

within the province of a poet's fancy, able not to refurbish bodies but to eternalize minds.

My second illustration concerns the act of judging. In ode 7, the speaker, his addressee, and the ode's readers are all soon to become dust and shade, beholden to the (ironically) gleaming settlements of Minos. Torquatus cannot expect to move Minos with eloquent pleas. In the next poem, the speaker, who is now artisan of poems and molder of myths, can, by the stroke of a word, remove Aeacus, another judge of souls, from the underworld to the Rich Isles of the blessed. Finally, as the speaker comes closest of all to mirroring Horace his sponsor, he becomes the most immediate, helping the *animus* of Lollius, now become both idealized *consul* and *iudex,* to outlast time. The potential slave to judgments in the afterlife becomes, first, the aloof transformer of arbiters, and then the more personal imaginer of the proper judicial spirit. In all instances, the poet is the ultimate *iudex,* assessing the prospects of himself and his clients in their confrontation with death and holding out for the select few the chance of remaining longer in memory through the reverberations of his words.

As in the case of the initial two groups of odes, poems 7 through 9 can stand by themselves. Since they deal in essence first with human subjection to time, then with the charm of poetry and poets finally to circumvent it, they follow easily after sets of odes devoted to the speaker's self-placement among poets and to his role as educator and preserver of Rome, especially of its youth. But in the emotional architecture of the book as a whole, there are close connections between all three sets as each in its own way progresses from explorations of individual loss to firmer assurances of survival for poetry and for the communal values of Augustan Rome.

The seventh ode, for instance, shares with the first its meditation on the deprivations, especially sexual, that time brings to the speaker and his world.[22] The losses of Hannibal, as outlined in the fourth ode, are of a different sort:

[22]Among other verbal echoes we should note the reflection of *gramina Martii campi* at the conclusion of ode 1 (39–40) and *gramina campis* in the opening line of ode 7. The particular place where young Roman athletes exercised has changed to the more generalized manifestation of nature's renewal of her youth in the spring. In the first instance the aging, somnolent speaker imagines himself fruitlessly in the setting of youth, which is to say into youthfulness. In the second, the more philosophical speaker sees himself with no share in nature's cycle of rejuvenation.

The forgoing of the erotic within the course of ode 9 makes it a microcosm for the pattern followed by the book as a whole.

> . . . occidit
> spes omnis et fortuna nostri
> nominis . . .

Hasdrubal's death means for him the renunciation of hope, fortune, and reputation. His luck has waned, Rome's bright new day arisen. Much the same will happen to Torquatus, the "you" of ode 7, *cum semel occideris,* "when once your sun has set." Unlike nature's sun, our metaphoric day once darkened will never dawn again, no matter how noble our family or our private gifts have been. *Immortalia ne speres,* the speaker warns suddenly of the disparity.[23]

The middle poem of each sequence switches to the poet as artificer and encomiast. When, in the second poem of the book, the speaker says of Pindar,

> . . . centum potiore signis
> munere donat, . . .

his words could equally apply to the poet's crafting power as it functions in poem 8. By contrast to the giver of bronzes and the painter or sculptor, the poet grants songs:

> . . . carmina possumus
> donare, et pretium dicere muneri.

One of the specific beneficiaries of this potential is Augustus, twice addressed in ode 5 as *dux bone,* who in the eighth ode is absorbed into the more general number of *bonis ducibus* resuscitated after death by a poet's words. In the prayer for Augustus' return at the end of ode 5, imputed to a farmer and then voiced by the speaker, Augustus is linked with Castor and Hercules, just as he was at the ode's start with Romulus. In the more general, pivotal poem of the book, "good leaders" are linked again with the same Greek and Roman heroes, among others, as worthy of the grand divinization that the style and the content of poem 5 only suggest.

---

[23]Note that Horace's only two uses of *tenebrae* are at 4.40 and 7.25, and that two of the three instances of *damnum* in the lyrics (and Horace's only two examples of the form *damna*) are at 4.59 and 7.13.

Finally, the concluding ode in each sequence deals with the speaker and his construction of song more specifically than any others in the collection (except poem 8 which in any case is conjoint).[24] In the third poem he is blessed by Melpomene at birth, presumably to share in the melody of the swan because of her benison. The ninth sees him again at birth, this time affiliated with the resonance of the Aufidus. The poem continues, placing him in the context of other immortals previously inspired by the Muses. In between, the sixth ode supplements those *biographiae litterariae* by showing the speaker as lyre player under the patronage of Apollo who grants him breath, the art of song and name. While the ode takes us from Troy to Rome, it is the latter's recurrence that the poet stabilizes in his verse. The ninth ode, which also sweeps from Homer to a very Horatian speaker glorifying a leader of contemporary Rome, reminds us yet again not only of the poet's dependence on the gods for inspiration but of the inheritance against which his originality is measured and which, not least, perpetuates himself and, through him, Rome.

[24]The only uses of *vates* in book 4 are at 3.15, 6.44, 8.27, and 9.28. Likewise, the only example of *fides* (lyre) in book 4 is 9.12, while two out of Horace's three instances of *fidicen,* lyre player, are at 3.23 and 6.25 (the other is *epi.* 1.19.33).

PART FOUR

Festivity's Musics: Odes 10–12

In sweet music is such art,
Killing care and grief of heart
Fall asleep, or hearing die.
SHAKESPEARE,
King Henry VIII

[10]

ODE TEN

O crudelis adhuc et Veneris muneribus potens,
insperata tuae cum veniet pluma superbiae
et quae nunc umeris involitant, deciderint comae,
nunc et qui color est puniceae flore prior rosae,
mutatus, Ligurine, in faciem verterit hispidam,   5
dices "heu", quotiens te speculo videris alterum,
"quae mens est hodie, cur eadem non puero fuit,
vel cur his animis incolumes non redeunt genae?"

O cruel, still, and sovereign from Venus' largesse: when unexpected
plumage will sprout on your arrogance, and the locks, which now swirl
about your shoulders, will lie fallen, and your complexion, which now
surpasses the blossom of a crimson rose, Ligurinus, has turned its altered features into shag, you will cry "Alas," as often as you face in the
mirror the other you, "why, when I was a boy, was my inclination not
the same as today, or why, with these feelings, do my unblemished
cheeks not return?"

Poems 8 and 9 depend for their power on the shared revelations of
the speaker as maker of verses, which is to say as an imagination
claiming to eternalize the concerns worthy of its bravura. The love of
Sappho still breathes because we as readers relive, and therefore constantly reenliven, her experiences, conflating *amor* with its telling.
With the extraordinary tenth poem, Horace relieves us of this en-
veloping fabric of poetics to present a speaker who is simply a new

Sappho, sharing an instant of intense private feeling, without any diverting self-consciousness about what it means for writer or reader to structure a poem.

Not that either the reader as literate entity or the speaker as philosopher-teacher is entirely absent. The word *adhuc,* for instance, in this context gains its full potential from nearer and more distant literary events. Eight varied lyrics have intervened since we first encountered a speaker infatuated with the boy Ligurinus, abetted by his metonymy, Venus.[1] And the intellectual time the reader takes in making this progress is metaphoric for the continuance, in the speaker's emotional life, of Ligurinus' lack of response, which in the book's opening ode was imagined only in the receiver's brief final fantasy. A further literary prospect, which has a momentarily generalizing effect, is gained from the opening exclamation, *O crudelis.* These are the initial words that Virgil, in line 4 of his second *eclogue,* puts into the mouth of the shepherd Corydon. His uncouth (yet amazingly well-read) courting of the young Alexis, addressed to his beloved but directed at mountains and woods, contains an admonition similar to the present speaker's warnings to Ligurinus.[2] Its careful recollection here, postulating a prototype for Ligurinus in Roman literary precedent, has the effect of expanding still more broadly the reader's time-frame. We are not dealing now with one speaker's emotional diffi-

[1]Ode 10 is also closely related to its predecessor. The only two uses of *adhuc* in book 4 are at 9.10 and 10.1. *Prior* also appears in book 4 only at 9.5 and 10.4. At 9.47–48 the poet bases the immortality he offers Lollius as Stoic sage on the latter's wise use of the gifts of the gods (*deorum muneribus*). In the more intimate subsequent ode, Ligurinus relies on Venus' gifts (*Veneris muneribus*) for his ascendancy, but the framing context of poets offering poems as *munera* (see also 8.4 and 12), and therefore treating as their own the power of the gods, is gone. Ligurinus' *munera,* though bestowed from heaven, will prove as fickle as the love-goddess herself and as short-lived as any mortal moment.

[2]The reminiscence is noted by pseudo-Acron. There are several other thematic parallels between the poems, but some (for instance, the loss of color in an adolescent equivalent to a flower's fall, or the prayer of the lover not to flee) are commonplaces in pederastic literature from Theognis (1299–1304) on. Cf., as do most commentators, among others Theocritus 23 *passim* (esp. 28–32), Alcaeus (*AP* 12.30 = 8 Gow and Page), Meleager (*AP* 12.33 = 90 Gow and Page), Diocles (*AP* 12.35 = 4 Gow and Page), and Automedon (*AP* 11.326 = 10 Gow and Page).

culty stretched over the partial extent of a poetry book, and therefore of the reader's contemplation of it, but with the circumspect, hidden writer's reminder that much the same emotion, similarly reproduced, has been part of a previous literary event. The perception of Ligurinus and his tale as part of the history of poetry prolongs not only the cruelty of the youth to the speaker, or the story of that cruelty protracted in the spacings of poems; it also evokes the imagination of Virgil in the wit of its offspring, Horace, maneuvering his subjects into serving as further emblematic demonstrations of the same universal feelings.

The counsel of reflection remains, too, not only in the moralizing of the whole but through the speaker's desire to project the inner workings of his lover's mind. It was a speaker with vatic claims to immortality who could hold up to their possessors for scrutiny the inner natures of Censorinus and Lollius. The far more personal voice of ode 10 anticipates future words of Ligurinus which reveal a self-awareness apparently absent from his present hauteur. Contemplation of his mind (*mens*) and spirit (*animus*), and of the relation of both to body, is something—or at least so the speaker claims for Ligurinus—that comes only with time. Yet intellectual enlightenment precludes the desire or even ability to enjoy those pleasures that passion could have once provided but no longer does.[3]

The rhetorical settings complement the point of the speaker's psychosomatic revelation. In this brilliantly compressed look at time and two lovers, the speaker's words in the poem's foreground are addressed to a Ligurinus who hears them without understanding their intent. The speaker craves present dialogue, seeking an answer in words which would mean a sexual yielding as well, neither of which

---

[3]Fraenkel (*Horace*, 415) somewhat misleadingly interprets Horace's voice here as representing "a man who cannot help looking back on the time when he was young himself." The poem is not a wistful meditation on the loss of passion which aging brings but the history (imagined or otherwise) of a very particular evolution in the sexual life of an adolescent, who, while possessed of boyish charm, refuses lovers (among them the speaker) and, once the charm has gone, experiences desires similar to those of the speaker. These cannot now be fulfilled because the speaker in his turn finds the now older, former adolescent unattractive. In neither case is passion spent, though in both it is frustrated. Cf. Quinn, *Horace*, 317–18.

is forthcoming. After the passage of time, Ligurinus will develop yearnings, perhaps even for the speaker, but will have lost his physical allure. His situation then will parallel that of the speaker in the poem's present. His imagined words will be a soliloquy since the only form of dialogue remaining, even with his newfound sagacity, is not with a reciprocating lover but with the mirror that tells him the bitter truth.[4]

This truth and the truths of the whole are concerned, as so often in these poems, with temporality and with the continuities and changes that time maintains or effects. The central change is the metamorphosis of Ligurinus. His position of power depends on his beauty, and the loss of one betokens the disappearance of the other.[5] The strengthening gifts of Venus, which foster haughtiness (*superbiae*), are documented by synecdoche, the boy's hair (*comae*) and the color of his complexion surpassing even the most brightly purpled rose (*rosae*).[6] The incessant end-rhyming that accompanies this list is bro-

---

[4]Though the literature noted above offers examples of rejected speakers looking into the future of their scornful lovers ("A time will come . . ."), in no instance does the speaker imagine the future words of his repentant *amour,* confirming, at least in his mind, the actuality of his vengeful presentment. Since the poem has an addressee, I am presuming that it is imagined, on the surface, as being overheard. If, like *eclogue* 2, it is offered to a lover at hand only in the speaker's imagination, then, like Ligurinus' quoted words, it is a soliloquy manufacturing desires rather than effecting truths. The speaker then appears bent as much on self-pity as self-satisfaction. From this viewpoint the speaker's present position of loneliness resembles that in which he imagines Ligurinus.

[5]The notion of power runs carefully through the poem. If Horace was relying on the etymology of Varro (*L. L.* 5.141), then *munera* is allied with *moenia* and *munio* (Venus' gifts are Ligurinus' momentary fortifications). Though it is also a word concerned with time's passage, *prior* (4) has the meaning "superior to" with an ablative of comparison for the first time in Latin literature (*OLD s.v.* 7c). Both words anticipate the adjective *incolumes* which is unparalleled in the sense of "beardless," "not yet shaveable" (*TLL* s.v. 979.83–84 and 980.1 calls the turn *audacius*). It is also a final reminder that in the unimpaired smoothness and color of his cheeks rests the security of his undamaged position as a love-object.

[6]To draw attention to Ligurinus' attributes Horace coins the verb *involito,* whose iterative quality emphasizes continuity in the present, and uses *insperatus* and *puniceus* for the only times in his work. For the brightness of the latter by contrast with *purpureus,* cf. Lucr. *DRN* 2.830, "*purpura poeniceusque color clarissimu' multo . . .*" (purples and crimson color, by far the most brilliant . . .).

ken at the poem's midpoint when the mutation occurs and time present becomes time future. But both synecdoche and rhyme return in the poem's, which is also Ligurinus', last word: *genae*. The chief weapon in his arsenal of charm has been his cheeks. While they were beardless his potency was unscathed. With their disappearance goes Venus' support and his magic.

The initiation of this bodily alteration, which also marks the conclusion of Ligurinus' mindless ways (at least according to the speaker's speculation), is at line 2. The arrival of down on his cheeks is unexpected (*insperata*) because he is naive, unforeseen because his pride makes him heedless of the bodily mutation that causes his charm to vanish. The word Horace uses for the down itself, *pluma*, (feather), replacing the expected *lanugo*, is a unique usage in Latin.[7] The metaphor returns our thoughts to the particulars of ode 1 where, we recall, the speaker finally dreams himself aloft in pursuit of his bird-lover (*volucrem*). I suggested that Horace might be quietly linking Ligurinus with the Ligurian Cycnus, lover of Phaethon changed into a swan. If so, then what now happens to Ligurinus is a negative variation of the earlier metathesis. The tresses, which lend him grace and still "fly" along his shoulders, further the connection with the bird Ligurinus of ode 1. But the new "plumage" he will soon sprout gives a bizarre twist to our expectations, keeping the image but reversing its thrust. No lover will track this mock-avian creature, once the airborne locks of youth have been displaced by the facial hair of manhood.

The shedding (*deciderint*) of youth's symbol (from falling out or, perhaps, under the barber's shears) means the collapse of its concomitant pride, the high loftiness (*superbia*) from which Ligurinus is deprived by time.[8] Motion downward is accompanied by complementary activity of coming (*veniet*)—the new plumage—and going (*redeunt*)—the smooth cheeks that can now "return" in thought alone. But the clearest changes are sensory. The word *hispidus*, which is first attested in Horace's *c.* 2.9, characterizes both visual and tactile

---

[7]See Kiessling and Heinze. Lewis and Short list the peculiarity (*s.v.* IIA) but *OLD* does not.

[8]*C.* 2.10.10–12 offers another Horatian juxtaposition of height, as a symbol of pride, and the collapse therefrom.

sensations. In the earlier ode the word is applied to thorny fields sodden from winter rains, and is therefore connected with the sense of touch,[9] but Pliny the Elder speaks of plants that are *aspectu hispidos,* loathsome to the sight.[10] Though Ligurinus' new beard would be potentially rough to the touch of a lover, the sight of it would already be offensive enough to turn away the literally tactile sensations Ligurinus would now, too late, try to elicit. It is appropriate, then, for Ligurinus' metamorphosis to be defined primarily through the visual. What we observe first is his pride, the smooth cheeks of a color brighter than a rose, and the flowing locks whose comeliness is apparent to others. With the fall of the one and the disappearance of the other—the smooth becomes rough and the rosily bright is darkened—there is nothing more about Ligurinus worth the glimpse of a lover such as the speaker. Another, sadder sight remains, however. Reciprocity with someone else will not be possible for the boy when at last he desires it. He must rest content with the double vision his mirror gives him, the sight of his altered form and the insights this belated self-scrutiny gives him into the willed congruence of mind and body necessary for happiness.[11]

The course of the poem documents an evolution in the life of Ligurinus caused by time's passage. This imagined alteration is so graphic among other reasons because of the continuities that precede and follow. The initial *adhuc* bespeaks the temporal extent of the boy's cruelty and the speaker's suffering. In the final lines the speaker gains his revenge in the hypothetical utterance he foresees as Liguri-

---

[9]*C.* 2.9.1–2: "*Non semper imbres nubibus hispidos / manant in agros. . .*" (Not always do rains drip from clouds onto sodden fields. . .).

Pseudo-Acron glosses *hispidos* as *sentuosos,* thorny. The second use in Latin (and the only occurrence in Virgil) is at *Aen.* 10.210 where we are told of Aulestes being borne downstream in a ship sporting a Triton "*cui laterum tenus hispida nanti frons hominem praefert, . . .*" (whose shaggy front, as it swims along, shows a man down to the waist). For the first time *hispidus* refers to a feature of an anthropomorphic body, replica of the hirsute sea-god, a usage Horace himself now imitates. It is perhaps not accidental that the preceding episode in *Aeneid* 10 describes the metamorphosis of Cycnus who (192) "*canentem molli pluma duxisse senectam. . .*") drew [to himself] hoary old-age with its soft plumage).

[10]Pliny *H. N.* 22.17.

[11]Horace employs *speculum* only here and, according to Kiessling and Heinze, the instrumental use is unparalleled in Latin until Nemesianus (*ecl.* 2.74).

nus'. Whether these words are to be taken as outspoken vatic truth or as a self-satisfying dream which twists the conclusion of ode 1, the speaker anticipates a future for Ligurinus in which he will look again and again at the galling evidence of the mirror. What will now remain constant in his life is the revelation of time's passage bringing with it a new stability of body and mind at once repelling and craving love. The use of *animis* in the last line confirms this recurrence. Though a consonantal ending is demanded by the meter to avoid *hiatus,* nevertheless the plural further demonstrates that the new intuitions and ways of thinking, which are to be the youth's enduring lot, are in fact the speaker's retribution for the persistence of his inamorato's earlier, heedless unresponsiveness.[12]

As ode 7 taught us, man on his own cannot claim for himself any part in nature's temporal renewals. The rose of our beauty fades once and for all. What endures in life, as in love, claims Horace in the tenth ode, is the constancy of suffering, of retaliation, of regret. Yet in the lyric of personal experience nostalgia can sometimes complete a cycle of return, or intensity can freeze in words the moment whose passing is beyond human efforts to offset. Two such occasions are documented in the poems that follow.

[12]Mueller comments on the absence of the expected, customary use of the singular here. Just as *puero* balances *mens* in the preceding line, so *animis* matches *genae* in line 8. Chiasmus links the two nominatives and the two datives, since both lines are equally concerned with parity, either then or now, of mind and body, thoughts and feelings, so that affections would be as equitably given as received. They are differentiated, however, as they should be because of their diverse temporal modes, by the uses of the singular, as when Ligurinus yearns for the present to be brought into the past, and of the plural, as when he wishes the past restored into present.

[11]

ODE ELEVEN

Est mihi nonum superantis annum
plenus Albani cadus, est in horto,
Phylli, nectendis apium coronis,
    est hederae vis

multa, qua crinis religata fulges;   5
ridet argento domus, ara castis
vincta verbenis avet immolato
    spargier agno;

cuncta festinat manus, huc et illuc
cursitant mixtae pueris puellae,   10
sordidum flammae trepidant rotantes
    vertice fumum.

ut tamen noris, quibus advoceris
gaudiis, Idus tibi sunt agendae,
qui dies mensem Veneris marinae   15
    findit Aprilem,

iure sollemnis mihi sanctiorque
paene natali proprio, quod ex hac
luce Maecenas meus adfluentis
    ordinat annos.   20

Telephum, quem tu petis, occupavit
non tuae sortis iuvenem puella
dives et lasciva tenetque grata
    compede vinctum.

terret ambustus Phaethon avaras   25
spes et exemplum grave praebet ales
Pegasus terrenum equitem gravatus
    Bellerophontem,

semper ut te digna sequare et ultra
quam licet sperare nefas putando   30
disparem vites. age iam, meorum
    finis amorum

—non enim posthac alia calebo
femina—, condisce modos, amanda
voce quos reddas: minuentur atrae   35
    carmine curae.

I have a full cask of Alban bettering nine years, I have in my garden, Phyllis, parsley for weaving chaplets, I have much sturdy ivy, plaited with which your hair glistens. The house smiles with silver, and the altar, bound with holy verbena, yearns for the spattering of a ewe-lamb's blood. The help all scurry, here and there girls jumbled with boys keep on the run, the flames are aquiver as they coil the sooty smoke within their whirl.

So that you might know to what festivity you are summoned, you are to celebrate the Ides, the day that halves April, month of sea-born Venus, rightly revered by me and nearly holier than my very day of birth, because from this dawn my Maecenas tallies his brimming years.

A rich and wanton girl has enthralled Telephus whom you pursue, a youth not of your station, and clutches him tethered by pleasure's trammels. Charred Phaethon frightens greedy hopes, and winged Pegasus furnishes a weighty precedent, weighted down by Bellerophon, his earthbound rider, always to quest for what fits you and to avoid the ill-matched by counting it corrupt to harbor hopes beyond the possible.

Come now, last of my loves—for hereafter I shall warm to no other woman—learn, to the full, measures which you can offer back in a voice of love. Black cares will slacken with our song.

Time stops momentarily for ritual, and it is with two different rituals that odes 11 and 12 are concerned.[1] In the first Horace's persona invites Phyllis, the last, so he later claims, of his loves, to celebrate the month of Venus and Maecenas' birthday. Festivity abstracts its participants from reality in two ways, through the excitement of the celebration which deflects the mind from life's pressing truths, and through the reasoning behind ceremony which here is a regular commemoration not of occasions past but of recurrence and renewal. The ritual of words that re-creates this vivid moment is perhaps the most explicitly plotted in Horace's lyric poetry. It fashions an appropriate mirror for the circumstances of the occasion, which counterposes a steadying litany of repetition, conveyed through the anaphora of *est,* with a bubbling of verbal activity rare even for Horace.[2]

The figural tension, which enlivens the rich immediacy of this intimate setting, begins with the opening line where the stolidity of the initial *est* is directly challenged by the continuity *superantis* implies.[3] This is the first occasion in Latin where the direct meaning of *supero* is to outlive or survive, but the ellipsis of a word for wine personifies Albanus, and the personification in turn draws to itself notions of physical potency already basic to the verb itself. The metaphor anticipates or, better, announces the attempted human triumph over time which will prove a major theme of the poem.

The tensile distinction between the static catalog of available objects and the dynamism of the objects themselves grows dramatically as the lines progress. The speaker next lists parsley available to Phyllis, appropriately, as she prepares to participate in a spring feast, for

[1]The most sensitive treatments of ode 11, to all of which I am indebted, are by Opperman, Reckford ("Some Studies," 30–31), Commager (*The Odes,* 302–4), and Boyle (181–82). Fraenkel (*Horace,* 416–17) sees the poem primarily as an honorific bow to Maecenas. Williams (*Tradition and Originality,* 87) finds the ode "frivolous."

[2]Fraenkel (*Horace,* 417 and n. 2) correctly notes the "asyndetic parallel clauses" in the opening three stanzas, their general lack of subordination, and, for lines 9–12 in particular, the "breathless bustle" produced by the verbs. Commager (303) also speaks of "bustling activity."

[3]For the first time (*OLD s.v.* 5b) notions of space and power usually associated with *supero* are also extended to time.

one whose name in Greek means "green sprout." If the present participle shows wine progressively overwhelming time, here the gerundive suggests the stimulus of prospective, purposeful action, the weaving of garlands for the wine bowls or the heads of the celebrants.

In place of climax is ivy, specifically for the girl's hair. The phrase *vis multa* to describe it is usually interpreted as meaning "a vast supply" and, even though we expect *magna,* this sense is surely part of Horace's design.[4] But since he is writing poetry not prose, we can, with equal propriety, interpret *vis multa* as "much strength," a brilliant metonymy that replaces concrete with abstract and puts special stress on the attribute.

Virgil uses the phrase eight times, once in a context of tangential bearing. At the end of the fourth *georgic* he tells the story of Aristaeus who must capture and bind the seer Proteus in order to elicit from him a revelation of the future. When Aristaeus first learns the means to success in this enterprise from the lips of his mother, Virgil uses the word *vis* twice in adjacent lines:[5]

> nam sine vi non ulla dabit praecepta, neque illum
> orando flectes; vim duram et vincula capto
> tende . . .

for without force he will not offer any directives, nor will you bend him by praying. Present hard force and bonds to the captive.

After the heroic deed is over and Proteus is in manacles, Virgil qualifies the noun *vis* with *multa:*

> . . . ad haec vates vi denique multa
> ardentis oculos intorsit lumine glauco, . . .

Upon this the seer, at last [yielding] to mighty force, turned toward him eyes burning with sea-blue gleam, . . .

[4]According to Kiessling and Heinze, *magna* with *vis* belongs to the vocabulary of prose; according to Oppermann (107, referring to Ruckdeschel, 141) the pairing is a vulgarism. Cf. the citations in *OLD s.v. vis* 8b. This verbal "binding" stands out all the more for linking stanzas noteworthy for their asyndeta.

[5]Vir. *geo.* 4.398–400; 450–51. Virgil uses the phrase *multa vi* twice in the *Georgics,* on six occasions in the *Aeneid.*

The abundance of constraining force, which Virgil allots to Aristaeus and to the shackles he applies, Horace's speaker imputes only to the ivy itself. Yet both georgic narrative and lyric invitation are in diverse ways concerned with the idea of binding. In terms of the story line, we have first the binding of Phyllis, for the hypallage of *religata,* attached to her specifically rather than to her hair, makes her whole person subject to the speaker's constraints. Then we learn of the tying of the altar with verbena. But binding in such amatory contexts, as Virgil shows us in *eclogue* 8, has a symbolic as well as a literal meaning.[6] It is part of a ritual where potent words, as well as the deeds they portray, play their part in a magic drama. *Vis multa,* therefore, is a masterly phrase not only for its figural realization of power but for the way this is graphically portrayed in its enjambment, lexically securing the first and second stanzas of the poem together. The enchaining of a strand of verses is but a further verbal exemplification of binding, in this conjuring of words that, along with the objects they denote, seize Phyllis by their own ceremony and hold her for the poet's last love-making.

The magic is beginning to work in the presentness of the metaphoric *fulges.*[7] She is already there, a crucial adjunct to other festal necessities. Her bright person is complemented by the house itself

[6]The words *verbena* (*ecl.* 8.65) and *necto* (8.77–78, three times) are in common. Virgil's witch binds an altar (64; cf. 74) and prepares *vincula* (bonds) for her lover (78; cf. Horace's double use of *vincio* at 7 and 24). *Carmina* play parallel roles in each poem. The witch, in her intercalary line repeated nine times and varied on the final occasion, when her magic may have worked, uses *carmina* for the verbal charms that are implicitly her words themselves. Horace's ode itself is the magic *carmen,* the invitation that enchants.

[7]It is quite possible, however, that Horace is using the future of *fulgo,* the archaic third conjugation form of *fulgeo,* which appears only once in Augustan poetry (Vir. *Aen.* 6.826; cf. *effulgere* at *Aen.* 8.677) and only twice thereafter in classical Latin. (Oppermann, 107, n. 10, also makes this suggestion against the majority of commentators.) If so it establishes a colloquial and archaic tone for the stanza also exemplified in *avet* and *spargier.*

Whatever the verbal form, the image of brightness is important for the evolution of the poem. Horace's women are dangerous when they glitter. They often lure lovers to their destruction through their deceptive brilliance or, at the least, set them aflame (see, e.g., *c.* 1.5.13 and note the parallel between line 5 of ode 11 and *c.* 1.5.4). But, as the myth of Phaethon reveals, the Gleamer can also come to grief and can be burned instead of burn, if he or she exceeds the bounds of reason. Better for Phyllis to warm the speaker, rather than Telephus, lest the image in her change from active to passive (*ambustus*).

which, extending the personifications that invigorate the domestic scene, gleams with its silver and smiles accordingly. Both personification and synecdoche (*argento*) further enliven this new climax that fixes on the sacrificed lamb at the altar, focal to the house, just as the preceding colon led from garden to garlands to Phyllis' hair. The altar has its special yearning, not for the lamb as much as for the scattering of blood that is its due. In other respects the language is "homely," not high-flown. Horace uses the verb *aveo* and the archaic present passive infinitive (*spargier*) elsewhere only in the *Satires*. Both usages further reflect a "humbleness" that assumes intimacy, meant to put Phyllis at her ease and lure the reader further into the simple immediacy of a happy household scene.

To all these devices Horace adds intensive alliteration and assonance in the final stanza devoted to the ceremonial setting. Sonic repetition represents aurally the vivid activities the words portray, hurrying, running, mixing, quivering, turning, but both synecdoche and personification again play important roles. This is the first use in Latin of the singular *manus* in the English sense of workman or hand.[8] The double reduction—singular for plural, part for whole—adds both intimacy and force as does the climactic personification of quivering flames that anthropomorphically tremble with excitement and bustle like the slaves dashing around them.[9] *Cursitant*, important for its iterative quality, adds also a requisite touch of *sermo cottidianus*, for again Horace's one other use is in the *Satires*.[10]

[8]The first use of the plural *manus* as "hands"—that is, workmen—is at *Aen.* 11.329 where Servius explains the word as *artifices*. Cf. *Aen.* 1.455 (where *manus* is the craftsmanship resulting from work by hand) and 1.592 where Servius rightly glosses *manus* as *vel artificis, vel ars ipsa*, the work of the artisan or his talent itself at work.

[9]Horace uses the verb *roto* here only. In combination with *vertice*, the verb enhances the idea of enclosure and enclosing, encompassing and conjunction, already suggested in the imagery of binding.

The alliteration linking *trepidant* and *rotantes* points to the syllable -*an*, its expansion, -*ant*, and reversal, -*na*, as one of the major unifying factors of the first five stanzas and, indeed, of the poem as a whole. It takes us from *annum* and *Albani*, in the first stanza, to *festinat* and *cursitant* in the third, to *natali* and the repetition of *annos* in the fifth. The poet thus has us aurally attend to the theme of time, whether passing or being renewed, even in lines where it is unstated, even in the details of a feast that would have us at once remember and forget temporality.

[10]*Sat.* 2.6.107. One of the four instances of *aveo* is at *sat.* 2.6.99. Both verbs form part of the description of another feast which that time goes humorously awry.

The fluttering fire is the cynosure of the third stanza, but the stanza as a whole is the culmination of the sentence and its tripartite rhythmic division. The verb of the poem's opening four lines is the simple monosyllable *est,* repeated twice. Lines 5–8 likewise contain three verbs, *fulges, ridet,* and *avet.* They cohere among themselves for reasons even beyond the differentiations in meaning that distinguish them from the preceding triple *est.* All are disyllabic and belong to the second conjugation. The third stanza, like the first and second, also possesses three verbs, *festinat, cursitant,* and *trepidant.* Their similarity again unifies their particular stanza—each verb belongs to the first conjugation and is trisyllabic. The expansion in syllabic length, however, from one stanza to the next, leads climactically to the explosion of vitality in the ultimate stanza where the verbs' increased syllabic length mimics the varied operations we apprehend in progress.[11] Language and desire are at one.

Behind this superb delineation lies the speaker himself, the possessive *mihi* of the opening lines. The synecdoches, energizing by compression, are his self-extensions; the personifications, animating the inanimate, reflect his own feelings. The house that smiles, the yearning altar, the trembling flames, aquiver with eagerness—all exemplify his own expressions of yearning. Their emotions are facets of his own, their suggestive magnetism is a manifestation of his own growing appetite and the words that weave its wiles.[12] Yet it is only in the fourth stanza that the speaker openly explains his invitation.

Noris gives warning that the speaker is adopting a more pensive tone after the opening stanzas' primarily sensate description, a tone that might titillate Phyllis and vicariously, perhaps, the linguist Maecenas.[13] The lines would on the surface satisfy her curiosity and

---

[11]Oppermann (106–7) also views these stanzas as a climactic structure.

[12]Commager (303) rightly observes that "the mingled sexes of the servants . . . suggests, in a minor way, the Ode's erotic intent, . . ." The replacement here of *ancilla* by *puella* is, according to Kiessling and Heinze, "ganz singulär." Is the usage, which eliminates any hierarchical intimations of mastery and enslavement (cf. *ancilla* at *c.* 2.4.1), meant to help Phyllis more easily adapt the poet's erotic suggestiveness to herself? By implication at line 22, she is a *puella.*

[13]*Noris* is a "popular" usage found elsewhere in Horace only at *sat.* 1.9.7. Horace's only other use of syncopation in the perfect of *nosco* is *nosti,* found once in the *Epodes* (17.77), once in the *Epistles* (1.2.23), three times in the *Satires,* and never in the *Odes.* (For Horace's colloquial use of such syncope in compounds of *moveo,* see Ruckdeschel, 109.) As in the case of the second stanza, the collo-

compliment her on her knowledge of wordplay, though they may in fact be the speaker's deft way of educating. The reasons for celebration are threefold. It is the Ides of April, the middle of the month of Venus and the actual natal day of Maecenas, mentioned here at the poem's center for the only time in book 4 of the odes. Horace may be thinking as he writes of an etymology for *Idus* quoted with approval by Macrobius in the fourth century, as the "day which divides [*dividit*] the month."[14] He is certainly playing, as commentators note, on the origin of "marine" Venus from the Greek Aphrodite, derived, in a tradition going back to Hesiod, from ἀφρός, sea-spume.[15]

Two births, then, are to be celebrated, of which one signals seasonal change and hints at love-making, the other honors a patron possessed by the speaker though remote from his poem's action. It is to him that one further instance of *figura etymologica* is dedicated. Something is *sollemne* "because it ought to be carried out every year" (*quod omnibus annis praestari debet*), according to Festus who derives the first segment of the word from *sollus* (synonymous with *omnis*), the second from *annus*.[16] The feast, which respects a particular day in a particular month, looks reverently to the years (*annos*) of Maecenas, but the allusion to time's passage is accomplished with great tact. It is centripetal motion, not motion away, that is a unifying image in these stanzas, incorporated into two usages novel for Horace, *advoceris* and *adfluentis*.[17] Phyllis is called to the festivity. The years flow at Maecenas who, through *ordinat,* is given the power to arrange his

---

quialism would invite Phyllis in language she might be expected to use (she must be taught *carmina*). Also, with *gaudiis* continuing the line of synecdoches and *agendae* of gerundives, the stylistic transition between the third and fourth stanzas is not as abrupt as it first appears.

[14]Macr. *Sat.* 1.15.17. Varro's (preserved) etymology is at *L. L.* 6.28. This is Horace's only use of the word.

[15]Cf. Varro *L. L.* 6.33; Ovid *F.* 4.61 (with Bömer's references); Macr. *Sat.* 1.12.12–13. Varro prefers a connection of *Aprilis* with *aperio* ("*quod ver omnia aperit*" [because spring opens everything]). This word also is found only here in Horace.

[16]Paulus-Festus 384.36 = 385.6L. Cf. 466.27: "*Sollemnia sacra dicuntur, quae certis temporibus annisque fieri solent*" (rites are labelled solemn which are wont to take place at set seasons and years).

[17]*Adfluentis* is also unique in itself as a poeticism, the first usage of *adfluo* associated with the passage of time (*OLD s.v.* 3).

own chronology and thus to regulate, rather than be regulated by, time.

Suddenly, however, we look away from the speaker's inviting setting and directly at Phyllis and her world. Her inclinations are not toward him but toward another lover, Telephus, whose abrupt naming—no verbal binding here!—adds a new dimension to the poem. The story is typically Horatian. One person is in love with someone who, in turn, is involved with a third party. Horace in fact uses the phrase *grata compede* in *c.* 1.33 which deals with exactly such amatory triangulations and their inept pairings.[18] Here Phyllis is meant to seem at odds with the object of her desire and his particular propensities. We are to presume that she cannot compete with her rival in either riches or lusty ways, and the speaker tells us forthrightly that Telephus is *non tuae sortis.* This could mean that her social position or financial circumstances, or even some vaguer "destiny," keeps them apart. But the prominence of *iuvenem* to describe Telephus, immediately adjacent to *puella,* denoting his mistress, hints delicately that the youthfulness the couple have in common may not, at least for long, be Phyllis' own.

Where she does belong the speaker leaves to the realm of metaphor. His girl has seized Telephus (*occupo* is another of the verbs that Virgil uses to describe Aristaeus clasping Proteus)[19] and holds him "chained with love's shackles." A Phyllis, properly listening, would have sensed in the introduction to the speaker's own world a very similar pattern of tying and binding mixed with yearning and eagerness.[20] If conditions exclude her from shackling Telephus, maybe the speaker's energetic, lively setting will offer appropriate provocation along with a chance for the "similarity" that, from his stance of worldly wisdom as he views her still unenlightened proclivities, he, not Telephus, might bestow.

His words further the act of seduction—which is the action of the poem—by gentle instruction in erotic compatibility. The education of Phyllis now takes a more vivid turn. Her grasping hopes, which lead her beyond the bounds of the licit, are like the desires of Phaethon and Bellerophon to tame the quenchless energy of their steeds in

[18]*C.* 1.33.14.
[19]*Geo.* 4.440.
[20]Note the repetition of *vincio* at lines 7 and 24.

the search for immortality. She is like myth's great heroic overreachers, the earthbound aiming for an airy realm not theirs by nature
and for a godlike existence not ordinarily bestowed on humankind.[21]

Yet there is something less than total seriousness in the speaker's
tone. How close, in fact, is the private world of Phyllis' sexual op-
tions to that of the mythological schemers who seek control of the
universe? Does the elegiac patterning of beautiful youths and rich
mistresses she sees for herself deserve the type of analogy reserved by
Horace elsewhere for a Virgil about to embark on epic's treacherous
waters?[22] Is amatory intrigue worthy of Plautine comedy entitled to
parallels more at home in the tragedy of Euripides, who wrote both a
Phaethon and a *Bellerophontes?*[23] Would Phyllis, hearing herself called
celestial equestrian, wring her hands from the lesson learned or have a

[21]With the dubious exception of *Culex* 282 (*cortice avara*), line 25 contains the
first instance in Latin of *avarus* standing for *avidus* used with an inanimate object
(*TLL s.v.* 1187.66–67). (If the *Culex* was written before 13 B.C., which is highly
improbable, Horace's use is still unique with an abstract substantive.) Even
though actual greed for money or property does not figure in Phaethon's tale, the
adjective still lends a touch of the literal to his, Phyllis', or anyone's (personified)
hopes. As such it supplements the insinuation of the preceding stanza, namely
that the society with which Phyllis would like to become embroiled, unlike that
of the speaker, dotes on wealth. Improper hopes lead Phaethon, whose name
("the radiant") is itself inauspicious, to death by burning (*ambustus*). One of the
poem's chief strands of imagery suggests that the appropriate fires for Phyllis to
become associated with are the literal *flammae* of the speaker's domestic hearth
which, at the poem's conclusion, are transformed into his metaphoric love (*calebo*). Her gleam, the silver's shimmer, fire's brilliance, daylight, and day itself all
complement each other.

[22]In *c.* 1.3 Virgil is implicitly compared to Daedalus, Prometheus, and Hercules, overreachers who, like Phaethon and modern man, draw Jupiter's vengeful
thunderbolt to themselves. At the beginning of ode 2, we remember, Pindar is
implicitly equated with Daedalus. Any poet foolish enough to emulate his grand
flights would suffer Icarus' fate. Among the subjects tackled by Pindar, but
unsuitable for his humble Matine successor, is the quelling of the Chimaera's
flames, Bellerophon's most notable feat (2.15–16). Any poetic overreaching on
Horace's part would parallel Phyllis' misplaced ethical ambitions. Note how the
overweening Bellerophon usurps the whole of line 28—a metrical mirror of his
pride and also, perhaps, the mock sign, in a lyric poem, of a high style unsuitable
for either a Phyllis or the speaker, whether style be a matter of sexuality, social
standing, or poetic statement.

[23]The fragments of the *Phaethon* are collected by Diggle, who deals with the
history of the myth (4–9).

good chuckle? Horace deliberately deflates his own apparently incongruous mythologizing with the play on *grave* and *gravatus*. The quick reworking of the same root in adjective and verb forms only calls attention to the change from abstract to concrete which turns an instructional paradigm of weighty intellectual moment into a question of a rider's avoirdupois.

The speaker who uses such disparate analogies to analogize disparity may at first seem to Phyllis and to his reader-hearer to lack an instinct for the proportionate and the apt. But the very ludicrousness of the image-making betrays a deeper sense of the humorous which would allow Phyllis, with a laugh at the speaker, to discern the modest grain of serious truth she shares in common with those mythic fantasists after omnipotence. The teacher, by drawing attention to himself, allows her by the wit of indirection to see one important moral similarity between herself and the Greek heroes. For both there is a pronounced discrepancy between dream and fact, between the preposterousness of her interior hopes—for Telephus, for riches, perhaps for youth—and what should be the reality of expectations. For her to laugh at him and through him at herself might be the prelude to laughing with him as well. Explicitly to avoid erotic inequities is, by innuendo, to elect his proposals of compatibility.

As if to confirm the success of his enterprise, the speaker closes with a commanding tone. The conclusion of the poem is the conclusion of his erotic experience. We assume that the trembling flames, which receive the place of prominence in the speaker's description of his domestic setting, are literal manifestations of inner warmth, fanned to one final glow by the arrival of Phyllis. Her spring bloom is the last blossoming of the speaker's love. Her arrival into this ceremony of binding sets bounds on her aging courter's sexual activity. In this poem about the intertwining of amatory and ethical restraints, her presence offers an opportunity for the speaker's final deed of amatory imprisoning, but that very deed is his own acknowledgment of self-limitation, his final fling at the stopping of time.

The poem's ruling distinction between rushing and binding, which helps illustrate how motion—and emotion—are controlled by chaplets, ritual, and, finally, song, serves also as brilliant metaphor for the tension in the life of an aging lover-poet between urgency and gratitude. We watch the immediacy of passion (the speaker's unspoken "greedy hopes"), approximated in the clinical observation of the

present moment's unique excitement, yield to a growing medi-
tativeness based on knowledge accrued through a stretch of time and
placed at Phyllis' disposal through the medium of myth, the detached
wisdom of a compendium of moments. As the metaphoric history of
a transition from eagerness to restraint, with the great sweep at the
poem's start replaced by the settled calm of love's musical exchange
at its conclusion, the ode is a study in renunciation—of physical for
spiritual, of sexuality for song. Phyllis is lured into the speaker's
world only to have herself charm the charmer and further the persistence of his magic. Literal passion may ultimately spend itself, as
life ebbs away, but on another level love is reignited forever through
the power of lyric verse.

For even with their double act of moderating, in his life and in hers,
the poem's last words anticipate something beyond such framings, a
future that embraces the foreground and background of the lyric's
protagonists. The background looks impersonally to black cares that
are lessened, not eliminated, and shared by both lovers.[24] These may
symbolize troubles outside the confines of domestic celebration or
peer closer to hand into the darkness foreordained when love's and
life's flames are spent. The future of Phyllis may look to those repeated moments (*semper*) when she can put the speaker's teachings from
myth to work in her own life. The speaker's present, by contrast, is
one last moment of love. But even this love, which has no future, is
only achieved in song, which retains the fleeting power to diminish,
though not obliterate, the poem's final blackness.

This pessimism is reinforced by two major differences between
poem 11 and other invitations from Horace's first collection of
odes.[25] The first, as I mentioned earlier, is the insistent particularity
of the setting and the frenetic vitality of its inhabitants. This seems to

---

[24]Like *calebo, atrae* also is a factor in unifying the poem, looking back to
sordidum fumum (11–12). On first reading mention of sooty smoke seems only a
further homely detail in the composition of a domestic setting. But, like the
image of fire, blackness too changes from palpable to emblematic in the poem's
course. The speaker's interior *atrae curae*, like the warmth of his final love, also
have a small literal counterpart in the *mise-en-scène* for love-making to which
Phyllis should be enticed. *Et in Arcadia ego*.

[25]Another notable difference, according to Oppermann's excellent comparison
(106), is the inclusion in ode 11 of verses 21–31, whose paraenetic quality is
unique to Horace's invitation poems.

mirror an eagerness or even impatience for the girl's acceptance and arrival not found elsewhere in Horace. A girl is often essential decoration for a party (Lyde in *c.* 2.11; Neaera in 3.14), and in two odes her singing is given special emphasis (*c.* 1.17 and 3.28), but in none is the speaker's anticipation and worry made so patent and the need for her particular presence so clear.[26]

Second, with the exception of *c.* 3.14, the "cares" to be dissipated by the poet's conviviality are those of the invited guest, not of his host. For Tyndaris (*c.* 1.17), the violence of ill-matched love, for Pompeius (*c.* 2.7) his military troubles are to be forgotten. Affairs of state will not bother Maecenas (*c.* 3.8 and 3.29), and neither the plots of foreign enemies nor the loss of what youth and grace bestow disturb Quinctius Hirpinus (*c.* 2.11). Even in *c.* 3.14, where Horace also gives his speaker the phrase *atrae curae* (13–14), the worries he voices about tumult and death by violence stem only from the external political situation. In our present ode, *atrae curae* are given place of prominence at the poem's end. Their cause and effect are left vaguely appropriate to the immediate circumstances, whether mental or physical, of both the tenderer and the receiver of the invitation.

For both these reasons, then, the reader has the ominous feeling that the speaker's inner anxieties are now at issue and that he desperately needs solace from Phyllis; she is as important for the speaker as he is to her. Especially if this is the poet's last bout of love-making, sharing is now a necessity to a persona that is no longer given to boasts of uniqueness and self-sufficiency. Instead of only receiving the troubled with philosophical concern and even, on occasion, a touch of complacency, the speaker's imaginative hearth has troubles of its own from which he needs distraction. For this reason he must do his best to reach out and make his inner world not only a haven for those with troubles of their own but also tantalizing enough to lure to it someone with the potential of relieving the speaker's own darkening sorrow.

But if *curae* has the last word, its neighbor *carmine*, to which it is closely joined in sound and sense, looks to a closer foreground and predicts another aspect of the future which, like the poem itself,

---

[26]There is never any direct mention of amatory involvement between speaker and girl in other invitation poems, though it might be suspected in *c.* 1.17 and perhaps in *c.* 3.28.

abstracts us from time. This last form of binding and bounding, the exacting rhythms of word and music that define a lyric song, works its magic now as Phyllis hears the enchanting call of the speaker's charming words. We thus initiate a new pageant of words which complements the ritualizing of the poem's present and continues in the song that re-creates it. Perhaps in this ultimate stage in the education of Phyllis the instructor is offering a final example of their harmony. She is the last of his loves, but her voice, in the poem's final prospective gerundive, will arouse love in him as his, we assume, had in her.[27] The common ground is song, *carmen:* first the ode we have before us, which is Phyllis' seducer, then the further song she is to learn in this setting, then the cyclical reproduction of that song which will entice the poet as she becomes his mouthpiece. Ceremony of words and ceremony of love-making blur into a unity, and their amalgamation in this private festival of celebration is the chief vehicle both to remember temporality and, for a brief while, brilliantly to stave off its black ravages by love and by the restorations of beauty we call art.

[27]Just as *amanda* is the ultimate in a series including four gerundives and one gerund, so *condisce* documents the poem's last moment for Phyllis to learn while also being its final colloquialism. It may also be designed as one last verbal gesture to put Phyllis at her ease despite the speaker's hortatory tone (see Ruckdeschel, 35; Smereka, 70). The *modi,* which she will learn, urge us also to think of the "modes" of love-making that the lovers, the singer-teacher and his girl, will practice in erotic fulfillment. That they are sublimated into the spiritual and enduring creation of song gives the poem's ending a surprising twist, forming a strong contrast with the preceding ode.

[12]

ODE TWELVE

Iam veris comites, quae mare temperant,
inpellunt animae lintea Thraciae,
iam nec prata rigent nec fluvii strepunt
   hiberna nive turgidi.

nidum ponit Ityn flebiliter gemens   5
infelix avis et Cecropiae domus
aeternum opprobrium, quod male barbaras
   regum est ulta libidines.

dicunt in tenero gramine pinguium
custodes ovium carmina fistula   10
delectantque deum, cui pecus et nigri
   colles Arcadiae placent.

adduxere sitim tempora, Vergili.
sed pressum Calibus ducere Liberum
si gestis, iuvenum nobilium cliens,   15
   nardo vina merebere.

nardi parvus onyx eliciet cadum,
qui nunc Sulpiciis accubat horreis,
spes donare novas largus amaraque
   curarum eluere efficax.   20

ad quae si properas gaudia, cum tua
velox merce veni: non ego te meis
inmunem meditor tinguere poculis,
　　plena dives ut in domo.

verum pone moras et studium lucri　　　　　　　25
nigrorumque memor, dum licet, ignium
misce stultitiam consiliis brevem:
　　dulce est desipere in loco.

　　The breezes of Thrace, companions of spring, who soothe the sea, now billow the sails, now meadows are not stiff and streams do not snarl from swelling with a winter's snows.

　　The hapless bird, groaning in her lament for Itys, builds her nest, an undying disgrace to the house of Cecrops because she cruelly avenged the brutish lusts of kings.

　　In the tender grass the guardians of fattening sheep sing songs on the pipe, and gladden the god who takes pleasure in the flocks and black hills of Arcadia.

　　The season has aroused thirst, Vergilius. If you are anxious to broach Bacchus pressed at Cales, my protégé of noble youths, you will win the wine with ointment.

　　A small jar of ointment will entice the cask, which now reclines in Sulpicius' vaults, expansive at giving fresh hopes and adroit at purging the bitterness of cares.

　　If you are in a rush for these festivities, come quickly with your barter. I have no thought, like a wealthy man whose house is full, to dye you, giftless, in my cups. But put aside delays and ambition for gain, and, mindful of the blackening flames, while the chance remains blend fleet folly with your wit: sweet is unwisdom opportune.

　　The eleventh ode summons the girl Phyllis to a calendrical celebration that also looks to a conclusion. While honoring the regularity of Venus' and Maecenas' birthdays, the speaker also admits the flow of time in his own life. His words of seduction and her putative accompanying song serve both to extract the protagonists from temporality and to remind them, and us, of it. The transient flames of passion harbor within themselves the bleakness of an enduring lovelessness. The book's subsequent invitation, though it is proffered to a man,

Vergilius, and centers on a drinking bout rather than a birthday celebration with erotic play, also seeks to lure the poem's addressee from his environment into that of the speaker.[1]

But, since we learn nothing of the ode's lived "present" until its fourth stanza, the initial differences between the two lyrics are as startling as the similarities. Preparations for a specific occasion, described in arresting detail, yield to impersonal, abstracted glances not at a day but at a season. A concrete "I" and "you," caught up in and, in one case, symbolically bound by a wealth of particularity, are effaced, at least for the moment, by generality of statement and an objective tone. Likewise the paratactic style of ode 11, suitable for the novelistic elaboration of a ritual's progress, is replaced by an opening series of three end-stopped stanzas, each of which offers an episodic, paradigmatic definition of spring.

We watch the influence of the brightest season on three different spheres of existence: elemental, animal, and human. The first deals with the metamorphoses spring effects in external nature, changing unruly to tame, stiff to soft, swollen to subdued. By replacing the winds we expect, warming western Zephyrs, with the cold blasts from the Thracian north, the poet reminds us that nature, even in spring, is part of a cycle and, paradoxically, that lodged within her are the unalterable seeds of her own mutations.[2] The hibernal is implicit in the primaveral. Nevertheless the very animism imparted to the inanimate speaks of a revitalization that is both calming and restorative.

Animal nature helps define spring by an even more specific metamorphosis that illustrates continuities of another sort. In an apparent instant of history destined to become myth, Procne killed her son Itys, to take revenge on Tereus, their husband and father, for raping her sister Philomela. Mythologizing makes her action exemplify forever the interrelation of sexuality and violence.[3] The demeaning

---

[1]On the Latin invitation poem and on ode 12 which, though not strictly an invitation, contains "invitational motifs," see Edmunds, 185.

[2]Horace links winter and the winds of Thrace at *epode* 13.3 and, symbolically, at *c.* 1.25.11–12; Thrace and snow at *c.* 3.25.10–11; Thrace and cold at *epi.* 1.16.13. We were taught to expect Zephyrs as the winds of spring in ode 7 (9).

[3]The plurals, *regum* and *libidines,* not only illustrate the continuity of lust in the protagonists' individual experience but by their plurality turn historical moment into myth.

transformation of Procne, the murderer of her son, into a swallow provides a further form of permanence. The unique occasion becomes timeless, the mortal creature becomes a bird who instinctively reenacts, year after year, the brooding and begetting that symbolize a shame now equally immortal. To the percipient, spring's revivification as a nesting swallow connotes an eternity of evils and deaths, a birthing that, like the landscape, contains within itself sad reminders of its own demise. The particularities of human suffering are continually renewed in the generalities of myth and in the cycles to which seasonal and animal nature are ever subject.

Vignettes of inanimate and animate nature are followed by a look at shepherds about their work of pleasing Pan. But as we reach into the human and divine realms, the previous two are not forgotten; the speaker reminds us of the springtime's tender grass and the forests of Arcadia, black with foliage, and of the fat sheep who make up the flocks in which the god delights.

As the speaker, moving hierarchically from one aspect of nature to the next, brings his catalog to a culmination in the springtime activities of men and of the god they address, his topographical allusions change from Thrace to Athens to Arcadia. But within this generic and geographical diversity there are two interconnected factors that knit together all three stanzas. The first is the common emphasis on the music of sound and song. In the opening stanza we learn that swollen streams no longer roar (*nec . . . strepunt*). I suggest that the scene of calming imposed on the sea by the breezes (*quae mare temperant*) was equally concerned with audition. Their power is parallel to that which the poet's apostrophe attributes to the muse Melpomene in ode 3 (17–18)—

> o testudinis aureae
> dulcem quae strepitum, Pieri, temperas, . . .—

and it spills over into the soothing of fresh water's tumble as well.[4] Allusion to spring's quieter resonances may explain the anomalous presence of the perpetrators of this renewed softness, the *animae Thraciae*. This is the only occasion where Horace replaces the ex-

---

[4]On *tempero* and music, cf. also Prop. 2.34.80, the conclusion of a distich which Horace also has in mind as he writes ode 3 (17–18).

pected *ventus* with *anima,* wind with its breath, but if we grant *anima* the meaning Horace regularly allows it of "life" or "spirit," then *Thraciae* can also gain a rich connotation, more apposite to spring's personified companions and her music than to winter's chill. The primary musician associated with Thrace is Orpheus whose lyre, tradition reminds us, had the power to soften the rigid, tame the wild, and change death to life. It is appropriate that emanations of his civilizing soul would serve to quicken as well as to tame nature in her moment of refreshment.[5]

If we follow the Virgilian version of his tale, tragedy inheres in the myth of Orpheus, just as winter, Horace's stanza reminds us, and its Thracian winds cling to spring's coming. Tragedy is a more explicit part of the second of Horace's three spring musics. The moaning of the swallow, even as she prepares her new nest, recalls for us a specific Procne mourning for a specific Itys. The tale of Tereus was dramatized by Sophocles, Livius Andronicus, and Accius, among other playwrights.[6] It, too, prompts thoughts of the sorrow that touches joy, of lust and slaughter tainting the mating rituals of spring, and of the bird-song that intones at once revivification and death.

The songs of shepherds to their pipes constitute Horace's final music which serves the same generic relation to pastoral poetry as the story of Procne does to tragedy. Whereas Virgil's *Eclogues* document

---

[5]The connection is also suggested by Belmont (15). *Anima* is used in synecdoche for a person by Horace at *sat.* 1.5.41, *c.* 1.3.8, 2.17.5, and 3.9.12. Orpheus is called *Threicio* by Horace at *c.* 1.24.13. Among the powers listed in *c.* 1.12 which were given Orepheus by his mother, the muse Calliope, is the ability to delay rushing streams and swift winds: "*arte materna rapidos morantem / fluminum lapsus celerisque ventos.*" In Virgil cf. *ecl.* 4.55; *Aen.* 6.120–21 and 645.

[6]Cicero attests (*ad Att.* 16.2.3 = 412SB, and *ad Att.* 16.5.1 = 410SB) that the *Tereus* of Accius was popular at least as late as July 44 B.C. Horace also mentions Procne as a subject for tragedy at *A. P.* 187.

Line 5 contains the first use of *flebiliter* in Latin poetry. The other three uses in classical Latin are all in Cicero's *Tusculan Disputations* and all in contexts devoted to tragedy. The first (1.85) introduces a fragment of the heroine's lament from Ennius' *Andromacha,* quoted by Cicero at greater length later (3.45 = *fr. sc.* XXVII 92–94 Jocelyn). In the second (2.39), Cicero describes the restrained words (he spoke *non flebiliter*) of Eurypylus to Patroclus in another play of Ennius (*fr. sc. inc.* CLXXI Jocelyn). Finally, he quotes from a speech of Odysseus, apparently from the *Niptra* of Sophocles, who weeps *perquam flebiliter,* unlike Ulysses in the parallel play of Pacuvius who, because he suppresses his emotion more, puts things "better," according to the orator (cf. Pacuvius *fr. sc.* 255ff.R).

the topic of unhappy love, regularly treated by bucolic bards who on occasion claim it as their own experience, Horace dwells on the pleasure such poetry brings. Only as his own song progresses will its touch of blackness take another form.

The other closely allied unifying factor of these three stanzas is their common rich allusiveness to past poetry. Spring's immediate, variegated harmonies are buttressed by reminiscences of other literary re-creations, other imagined musics.[7] When dealing with nature's suppression of her own winter bombast in the retoning that spring effects, Horace looks to Catullus 46, as critics have long noted, for word choice and figuration:

> Iam ver egelidos refert tepores,
> iam caeli furor aequinoctialis
> iucundis Zephyri silescit auris.

Now spring brings back chill-less warmths, now the frenzy of the equinoctial sky is hushed with the gentle gusts of the Zephyr.

Horace inserts the *comites,* the traveling companions who enter Catullus' poem at line 9 where he bids them farewell, at his poem's start to enrich the personification that lends credence to unreflective nature's studied articulations.[8] Catullus also enters the second stanza, for Horace is rehearing and re-presenting a moment in poem 65 where the speaker compares his songs of mourning for his dead brother to those of Procne "mourning the fate of Itylus torn from her" (*absumpti fata gemens Ityli,* 14).

---

[7]Because in the next two stanzas Horace is concerned with tone as well as meaning, with the "how" as well as the "what" of expression, *turgidus* may also be used here for what it says of style, swollen, like nature in winter, rather than restrained, like the sound of spring breezes. The most prominent example of the turgid style at work puffing out a wintry subject is Furius Bibaculus, the *turgidus Alpinus* of Sat. 1.10.36, whom we hear of again at *sat.* 2.5.41: "*Furius hibernas cana nive conspuet Alpis*" (Furius will bespatter the wintry Alps with hoary snow).

[8]There are several other words in common between the poems (*studium, dulcis, domus*), but ultimately, as in the case of the influence of Catullus to be examined below, the intellectual thrust is reversed. In Horace the speaker is static while the invitee takes a mental journey through varied imaginative territories to arrive at a proper home that is also a source of wise unwisdom. In Catullus the speaker is away from home and spring arouses thoughts in him that lead to the action of return.

Virgil, too, influences both stanzas. In his brief treatment of the legend of Tereus in the sixth *eclogue,* he styles Philomela, whom Roman authors regularly confused with Procne, as *infelix* (81). And one passage from the fourth *georgic,* detailing the proper time to go about renewing a moribund beehive, links the two sets of lines together (305–7):

> hoc geritur Zephyris primum impellentibus undas,
> ante novis rubeant quam prata coloribus, ante
> garrula quam tignis nidum suspendat hirundo.

This is done when the Zephyrs first stir the waves, before the meadows grow red with fresh colors, before the chattering swallow hangs her nest from the rafters.

In Virgil's vision, as in Horace's, we go from the impulse of spring winds, to meadows, to the swallow and her nest.

The third stanza is no less retrospective. Horace may have been thinking of the epigram of Porcius Licinus, quoted by Aulus Gellius, which begins[9]

> Custodes ovium tenerae propaginis, agnum,
> quaeritis ignem? . . .

Guardians of lambs, the tender offspring of sheep, are you searching for fire?

Licinus imagines the shepherd as lover, informing his colleagues directly of his passion. It is Virgil, however, who again seems to be the major influence. In the introduction to his sixth *eclogue,* he imagines Apollo offering Tityrus, the shepherd-poet, some words of advice which encompass the style as well as the content of pastoral verse (4–5):[10]

---

[9]Fr. 6 Morel, from Gellius 19.9.13.

[10]Horace uses the word *pinguis* in the same contrast between fat sheep and a stylistically "thin" mind-set at *sat.* 2.6.14–15 in his prayer to Mercury: "*pingue pecus domino facias et cetera praeter / ingenium*" (May you make the master's flock and all else fat, save his wit). In the preceding satire, Furius, about to embark on his turgid *Annales* (see above) is "distended on fat pig's stomach" (*pingui tentus omaso* [*sat.* 2.5.40]), stylistically overfed.

". . . pastorem, Tityre, pinguis
pascere oportet ovis, deductum dicere carmen."

"Tityrus, it befits a shepherd to feed a fat flock but to sing a song fine-spun."

Sheep may grow plump from browsing on tender grass, but a singer of pastorals performs on a slender reed that symbolizes both how and what he chants, hiding his song's imaginative richness under the double disguise of restraint in both style and substance.[11]

In the poem's central stanza, as the speaker turns from his detached, triple meditation on the sonic vocabulary of spring, we find ourselves at last apparently sharing his thoughts as he summons Vergilius for a visit. The season has invited thirst to its party.[12] Horace's speaker, in counterplay, invites Vergilius, but the guest who will in fact banish thirst is Bacchus of Cales, and the only way he can be co-opted into their common symposiastic design is for Vergilius in his turn to bring a jar of nard, to liberate the "freer" who will himself then free the participants from thirst—and from deeper spiritual cares.[13]

[11]Dew on tender grass (*tenera herba*) is the source of a flock's nourishment at *ecl.* 8.15 (which, with the change of initial *cum* to *et* = *geo.* 3.326). This is Horace's only mention of Arcadia, but Virgil on several occasions links Arcadia with Pan (*ecl.* 4.58–59, 10.26; *geo.* 3.392). At *ecl.* 8.22–24, we learn in Damon's song that Mt. Maenalus has a clear-sounding grove and talking pines, and that it gives ear to the loves of shepherds and to Pan, singer and sponsor of singers.

[12]Cf. *sat.* 2.8.22 and the "shades" whom Maecenas had invited (*adduxerat*) to the banquet given by Nasidienus.

[13]It has been and will be debated whether or not the addressee of ode 12 is the poet Publius Vergilius Maro, whom Horace elsewhere (*c.* 1.3.8) defines as "the half of my soul" (*animae dimidium meae*). Belmont, a recent reviewer of the problem, adopts a positive view, basing his argument on metrical considerations and on thematic parallels with Virgil's early work, many of which I also note. On pp. 5–6, nn. 19–22, he surveys the bibliography of writings both for and against. To the list of those arguing in favor of Virgil should be added the important articles by Porter ("Horace, *Carmina*, IV, 12") and Moritz who ("Some 'Central' Thoughts," 119) sees the centrality of the address in ode 12 as an honor particularly appropriate for the great poet.

Though the presence of Virgil's poetry is without doubt strongly felt in the opening stanzas, as numerous critics from Bowra on have noted, I still find the tone of phrases like *iuvenum nobilium cliens* (15) and *studium lucri* (25), which even critics advocating Vergilius as the poet must take as humorous banter, hard to measure in a poem published some six years after the poet's death. (Date of

As we leave the more abstract initial stanzas to enter the speaker's own spring, we change from Pan to Bacchus and from the Greek setting of Thrace, Athens, and Arcadia to locations in Italy of growing specificity, to wine's vintaging at Cales and to its storing in the Sulpician warehouses that stood in Rome below the Aventine near the Tiber.[14] But these very distinctions are also reminders of a continuity manifest both in style and content. Though a plot line now opens out as the speaker explains the reasons for his complex request, each of the poem's concluding four stanzas is end-stopped, which is to say it is as rhetorically self-contained as each of the initial three. Literary allusiveness likewise remains equally rich. In line 13, in which it is possibly the poet Virgil who is apostrophized, phrasing from a line in the third *georgic* (483) is turned to Horace's own purposes. There we learn that thirst shriveled the pitiable limbs of plague-ridden animals (*sitis miseros adduxerat artus*). In Horace's witty invitation, it is wine that will save Vergilius from spring's inherent dessication. Catullus, too, returns to suffer at Horace's hands a comic twist to his own cleverness.[15] His poem 13 amusingly invites Fabullus to dinner—if he will bring all the necessities with him. He can expect in return only an unguent, even though it has the amazing property of making its recipient wish to become all nose. Horace reverses both expectations and proprieties, offering for a small box of nard a jar of wine which has the magic in its own liquid bounty to

---

publication, not of writing, even if the poem is early, is the vital issue. It is the tone it sets in its published context which should be most closely evaluated.) The word *lucrum* as used by Horace regularly has negative connotations. (Cf. *sat.* 1.1.39 and 2.3.25, *c.* 2.4.19, where Phyllis is praised as *lucro aversam, c.* 3.16.12 where the house of Amphiaraus was plunged into ruin *ob lucrum,* and *epi.* 1.12.14 where Iccius remains untouched by *contagia lucri.* Even in the phrase *adpone lucro* at *c.* 1.9.14 the word suggests not what is useful—*pace* Belmont [13]—but what is gained.) Such badinage, the serious seen humorously among friends, takes on another dimension and a different degree of seriousness when response by the person teased is no longer possible.

[14]Prophyrion on *Sulpiciis* (18) comments "[*Sulpicii*] *Galbae horreis dicit*" (for the storehouses of Galba he says of Sulpicius). This is our only evidence that the *horrea Galbae,* located below the southwestern side of the Aventine and separated from the river by the *porticus Aemilia,* were also called *Sulpicia.* See under *Horrea Galbae* in Platner and Ashby for the citations, in Nash for the exact location.

[15]The interconnection is noted, among others by Rutgers van der Loeff (112–13), Ferguson (11–12), Syndikus (403), and Quinn (*The Odes,* 320), on ll. 17–20.

accommodate both the positive and negative aspects of the future, bestowing fresh hopes and abolishing cares.

Hence, because the fourth stanza imitates the rhetoric of end-stopped stanzas and continues the abundant allusiveness, especially to Catullus and Virgil, of its three predecessors, we expect that in meaning, too, it will resemble them. Syntactic self-containment demands we pause to contemplate, first, the framed meaning of each stanza, then the culmination of such units into a larger whole. It will be through common strands of allegory, as well as through rhetorical parallelism, that these apparently discrete entities are forged into a dynamic unity.

The intensity of the personification of wine, the third, crucial "guest" at the speaker's party, helps establish its deeper significance. In an earlier ode, *c.* 2.11, which is also an invitation offering wine and nard to dispel the cares of politics and time's passage, the speaker turns at the end to ask for the presence of the courtesan Lyde whose music-making and beauty will complete the setting (21–24):[16]

> quis devium scortum eliciet domo
> Lyden? eburna dic age cum lyra
> maturet, in comptum Lacaenae
> more comam religata nodum.

Who will lure from her dwelling the roaming courtesan Lyde? Off and tell her to hurry with her ivory lyre, her hair bound back into a comely knot after the Spartan manner.

In ode 12 the figure of the courtesan is replaced by the jar of wine, now "reclining" elsewhere, which can only be "elicited" by a proper reward.[17] But in another, still richer sense, the jug is equivalent to Lyde for it also takes to itself her function as singer. The jug is a metonymy for the speaker. Its potent contents stand for the magic flow of his verses which Vergilius will absorb once he has been

---

[16]Other lexical usages in common between these two poems are the words *aeternus* and *consilium,* and the phrase *dum licet,* which Horace uses in only these two instances in the *Odes.*

[17]This is the only instance in Horace of the verb *accubo.* Though Virgil applies the verb to a grove (*geo.* 3.334), Horace is the first to use it with a lifeless object which reinforces the personification engendered by the context.

seduced by "hearing" the present words of invitation.[18] The poem itself, in other words, and the further verbal "wine" Vergilius will imbibe at the speaker's table embody the speaker's own spring music, telling his guest, in its own idiosyncratic, Roman way, of feelings and thoughts as important as those we learn from pondering the sounds of water, bird-song, or shepherds about their piping.

As we draw nearer to the setting of the speaker whose home does not echo the munificence of his wine jar, we also further refine the significance that the speaker attaches to his offering. As we would expect for an object that is at once literal and figurative, Horace's wine is multivalent. Its sweetness (*dulce*) can help eliminate life's bitternesses (*amara*).[19] It can at once wash away (*eluere*) and dye (*tinguere*). It mixes into Vergilius' ordinary draughts of trite *consilia* and (apparent) zeal for the superficial a dose of foolishness and irrationality which, because it is in fact the height of wisdom, calls into question the intellectual and moral quality of his day-to-day enthusiasms. The philosophizing is gently put. Pan may claim the black forests that delight him in spring. For mortals what remains are the black flames of the funeral pyre which turn us to dust and shade. The fleeting wine of the poet's brief wisdom, toward which Vergilius is twice urged to rush, catches him between his life's drawn-out ambitions and his death's eternal finality. The invitation both momentarily stops time—through the forgetfulness wine induces—and serves as a reminder of the opposite—that human time progresses inexorably toward our final obliteration and that it is utmost ignorance to overlook the gravity of death in favor of pursuing one's ambitions.

To drink in such words is to hear in the poet's concluding verbal music a practical lesson that the permanencies of spring's earlier songs had scarcely touched on. For all their ambiguities, the cycle of the seasons, the recurrence of the swallow's tragic twittering, and the shepherds' Arcadian caroling have only indirect reference to the lived experience of our human condition. Only in the remembrance of the final truth of our mortality comes an appreciation of the need for

---

[18]On wine as poetry in Horace, see Commager ("The Function of Wine," *passim,* and *The Odes,* 264). One of the most conspicuous examples of the metaphor is the whole of *c.* 1.20.

[19]The conclusion of *c.* 2.7.27–28—"*recepto / dulce mihi furere est amico*" (For me ecstasy is sweet when a friend is received back)—offers another instance where wine, sweetness, and a madness very rationally expressed are combined.

Horace's folly of forgetfulness. The ultimate wisdom is in paradox. Forgetfulness and remembrance are carefully intertwined, and the real folly in life is to mistake what is truly somber for what is not. Retreat from the pseudo-serious to drink the poet's brief wine is in fact unblinking acknowledgment of the enduring presence of death from which the joys of wine provide only ephemeral escape.[20]

The links between the preceding invitation to Phyllis and ode 12 are careful and clear. Each of these two rituals of two centers on the speaker's *gaudia,* which the addressees are asked to share. The first poem begins with a wine jug as part of the alluring accoutrements of ceremony. In the second the jug and its contents slip easily from literal to figurative, from wine to the philosophizing it initiates and the poetry it contains. Both poems are concerned with hopes and cares that affect both sets of protagonists. But this very mutuality points up the differences between the two guests the speaker invites to his poetic festivities. Phyllis is the amatory overreacher, seeking erotic patterning elsewhere less suitable for her than the speaker's warmly receptive, suggestive domesticity. With Vergilius, the potential lover is replaced by a symposiast whose interests are distinct from the speaker's own. Vergilius seems the quintessential Roman, given to the immediacies of politics and sycophancy, a competitor for the world's goods who is addressed appropriately in the language of finance and exchange.[21] To him the speaker suggests, by means of his

[20]Horace's final words, and his poem as a whole, are therefore an ironic variation on a theme central to his first epistle (*epi.* 1.1.41–42): *"virtus est vitium fugere et sapientia prima / stultitia caruisse"* (Virtue is the fleeing of vice and to lack folly is the beginning of wisdom). As so often Horace is playing with his addressee, which means with us, his readers.

[21]Riches play a parallel role in ode 11 by helping distinguish the speaker's mode of living from that of others. At 11.23 it is a *puella dives,* not Phyllis, to whom Telephus is attracted. Horace's speaker, at 12.24, claims that he is not wealthy, as, presumably, are the *iuvenes nobiles* with whom Vergilius associates. He does, however, have one mark of affluence, wine from Cales, as *c.* 1.31.9–12 reminds us:

> premant Calenam falce quibus dedit
> fortuna vitem, dives ut aureis
>   mercator exsiccet culillis
>   vina Syra reparata merce, . . .

magic wine that leads from one sphere to the other, a substitution of the quotidian for the spiritual, of practicality for the figurations of poetry. The speaker both exemplifies his message and flatters its receiver by offering him verses of wide-ranging referentiality.

Both poems, but especially ode 12, exemplify the persistent yearning in Horace's speakers for personal company as opposed to more expansive notoriety. To try to be everyone's friend, as client of a number of noble youths, is the ultimate misstep. What matters, after all, are particulars—particular people (and beloved settings), and the particular details of careful poetry, not the generalities of politics and public life.

For all their individual distinctiveness, both odes complement each other as parallel evocations of two feasts that at once define and transcend time, suggesting retreat from its importunities. They locate the actors—speaker and hearer—in the excitement of domestic rituals that heighten the moment and also serve as reminders that the reverse of this heady particularity is the generality of death. Erotic or symposiastic play, though it may lure the participants from their own implicitly misguided lives into an education by poetry, offers but a brief stay against mortality's blackness.

It is their common interest in lived experience, in education, and in the melancholy encroachments of temporality which link these two poetic ceremonies with their brief predecessor to form the book's fourth triad. All three odes, which as a group are the book's most private and personal, are to some degree exhortations toward self-knowledge. In the invitation poems the speaker's elaboration of his very palpable context and its values provides sufficient impulse for the requisite dialectic with the outsider summoned in. For Ligurinus, his mirror occasions the pertinent introspection, assisting him into the revelation of truths from which he had hitherto averted his glance. The mirror, which demands self-scrutiny, both stops time and fosters a solitary mediation on the self in time. From this the

---

Let those trim the vine of Cales with the pruning fork, to whom fortune has granted to drain, as a rich merchant, from golden goblets wines for which he gives in exchange his Syrian wares.

But the wine is soon seen as metaphoric, its riches of another magnitude than the *merx* with which economic exchange seems at first to make it parallel.

enlightened Ligurinus can survey the disparity between mental attitude and physical desire which now rules his life.

Nevertheless, closely knit though they are, this trio of odes again follows the pattern we have traced in the preceding three groupings where the initial poem, standing more or less alone, deals with personal loss, and the second two, explicitly linked by verbal and thematic echoes, are devoted more to poetry, its content, power, and importance in the Roman community. Odes 11 and 12 share with the book's second and third poems a common interest in the poet's view of himself and his intellectual setting. They join with the more public odes 5 and 6 in serving both to describe and reenact rituals, ode 5 inducing and honoring the return of Augustus, ode 6 celebrating secularity and the speaker's own Apolline re-creation of it. Odes 8 and 9 proclaim poetry's power to immortalize its subjects; and the eleventh and twelfth poems, though far more private, look also to two miraculous rituals. For all their greater brevity and fragility, these ceremonies, too, abstract their participants from the exigencies of temporality for at least the length of the poem and the festivity renewed by its sorcery. Poems 8 and 9 claim to grant their receivers the grand consolation of immortality while the act of reading survives. Odes 11 and 12 bestow the more limited comfort of the poet's invitation, which is to say of his poetic wisdom, in the face of a cheerless reality. Each offers a moment of duplicitous, tenuous timelessness.

In concluding my survey of the penultimate group of odes, I would like to look particularly at the interrelationship of the first and third poems in each segment.[22] The common presence of Ligurinus, of course, links the first and tenth odes, as we already noted. We still see

[22]I will treat the middle poems in more detail when analyzing ode 14, but it is worth observing here that odes 2 and 11 share allusions to the myth of Bellerophon and Pegasus. Ode 2 looks to the fight with the Chimaera (15–16), ode 11 to the later, doomed flight toward divinity. For Horace to treat such a myth would be to adopt a feature of a Pindaric ode. This, in turn, would be to overreach poetically as Phyllis does erotically, by going after Telephus. In ode 14, with the utmost tact, epic bravado is imputed to Drusus and Tiberius. The post–epic, hymnic calm that frames the poem is given to Augustus. Hymn is the generic equivalent there of the ritual feast to which the speaker in ode 11, with excited restraint, invites Phyllis, charming her away from Telephus and inappropriate ambitions. Augustus, on his arrival at Rome, and a lyricist, turning from expansive lyric to hymn, have their parallels.

before us the purple color that his features share with the swans of
Venus, and the hair that flies past his shoulders is a reminder of the
birdlike swiftness with which he earlier flees the somnolent speaker.
In one sharp detail, however, matters are turned around. The cry of
heu, which the yearning speaker allows himself in ode 1, is now put
into the mouth of Ligurinus, sorrowing, in the belated wisdom his
vision brings, at what has become his own loss.[23]

Still closer even are the parallels between odes 7 and 10. The passage of time, which the seasons in their cyclicity can surmount but
which, for humans from Aeneas to the speaker and addressee, is
inexorable, takes another victim in Ligurinus. In nature's annual
round, grasses return (*redeunt*) to the fields and foliage (*comae*) to the
trees, as the earth changes (*mutat*) her changes. Mortals should not
hope for immortality (*immortalia ne speres*). For us there is no recovery
of our losses once we have fallen down (*decidimus*) to the domain of
shades. Only proper handling of the "sum of today" (*hodiernae . . .
summae*) can be of avail, without any worrying concern for
tomorrow.

Because his hopes have been naive (*insperata*) and he has misused
his present (*hodie*), Ligurinus' metamorphosis (*mutatus*) provides a
direct example of the point argued more impersonally in poem 7.
When the human "foliage" of his hair has "fallen" under the trim-
mer's shears (*deciderint comae*), there will be no restoring the more
youthful time of flowing locks. And when he has at last realized too
late that his beauty and his desires must be compatible, then his
bearded face can return (*redeunt*) but only in fantasy, not in fact, to its
former handsome estate. Although he is still young, metaphor nevertheless gives his growing-up a negative twist. In the life of Ligurinus autumn's purple ripeness has given place to the ugly roughness of
winter's deadening because, however clear his thinking and strong
his desire, in neither case can they any longer be brought to fruition.[24] He has now become kindred with the speaker he had scorned
in the book's initial ode.

In the poems on personal loss and on the varied manifestations of
time's havoc, the tenth ode, therefore, seems most closely linked to

---

[23]Another echo of ode 1 in ode 10 is the association of *munera* and *potens* at
1.17–18 and 10.1.

[24]Purple is the color of autumnal ripeness at *c.* 2.5.12.

the seventh. It is not surprising that the last poems in these contiguous trios should also be related. When, at 12.22–23, Horace has
his speaker forewarn Vergilius

> . . . non ego te meis
> inmunem meditor tinguere poculis . . . ,

he is reminding his reader of what a strangely similar speaker had told
Lollius three poems before (9.30–31):

> . . . non ego te meis
> chartis inornatum silebo . . .

The earlier ode presents material for writing, become writings themselves, as the means for immortalizing the character of Lollius. In the
later poem, the goblets that contain the speaker's vintage philosophy
tempt Vergilius to a symposium that is also a schooling in self-
understanding. The overarching connection, however, is the poems'
mutual concern with poetry. Poem 9 pits the speaker against the
various "muses" of past poets to illustrate his imagination's originality; in turn such documentation assures continuous life for the
subjects with which it deigns to deal. The twelfth ode, in contemplating the motley musics that spring evokes, offers Vergilius wine to
drink in the form of a poem to be both read and heard, spoken and
sung. Goblets and writing papers, which diverge as metaphor and
metonymy, are in fact emblems of the same multiformed art, meditation on which, in the climaxes of this spiritual architecture, always
has the last word.

Finally, we must look at one powerful personage who also looms
behind these poems, the figure of Callimachus. While assessing the
influence of Catullus and Virgil on ode 12, I reserved for mention
here one of the most striking examples of the presence of the poetic
past. As Horace writes of shepherds about their chanting, he is thinking back, as we have seen, to Virgil's sixth *eclogue* where Apollo
inculcates in "Tityrus," who has grander schemes afoot, a poetics of
refinement. The tradition for this polarity begins with the great Alexandrian poet who also imagines himself listening to the words of
poetry's god:[25]

---

[25]*Aet.* 1.fr.1.23–24Pf.

". . . ἀοιδέ, τὸ μὲν θύος ὅττι πάχιστον
θρέψαι, τὴ]ν Μοῦσαν δ᾽ ὠγαθὲ λεπταλέην ·. . . "

". . . poet, nourish a victim to be as fat as possible, but, friend, keep
the Muse slender."

We have already seen the specific importance of Callimachus'
Aetia, Hymns, and *Epigrams* for the third ode. The influence of his
second hymn, to Apollo, on Horace's sixth ode, addressed to the
same god, is more general but Horace would have learned from him
an emphasis on the act of performance and on the self-consciousness
of the poet as writer, teacher, and leader of song which is absent from
the Homeric hymn to Apollo, the prototype for both.

It remains to mention the boast that initiates ode 9 where the
speaker proclaims that his deathless words have been broadcast
"through artistry never before revealed to the public" (*non ante vol-
gatas per artis*). Horace would have good reason to make such a claim
for his poetic artifacts, be it in his skillful adaptation of Greek
rhythms to Aufidian resonances or, more expansive, in his originality
of thought and expression. It is ironic, however, that this phrase,
central to the speaker's accounting of his pride, smacks of someone
else's words and of allegiance to a stylistics not of his own making.
Variations of the statement are represented throughout the corpus of
Callimachus' writings. We find its sense at the end of the hymn to
Apollo where the god himself rebukes Envy and, using language that
symbolizes different genres of poetry as well as styles of writing,
contrasts the filth carried by epic's broad Euphrates with the purity of
the water carried by Demeter's priestesses and Callimachean poets.[26]
Originality, concentration, and refinement are inseparable in his poetics. Likewise, in one of his epigrams when he announces "I despise
all things connected with the mob" (σικχαίνω πάντα τα δημόσια),
his words apply to any expression of vulgarity, be it cyclic poetry, a
road too well traveled, or a vagrant lover.[27] Last, we should recall the
verses that, in the *Aetia,* follow immediately on Apollo's exhortation
to his poet to fatten a corpulent offering but to keep his muse slender.
His admonition continues:[28]

[26]*H.* 2.108–12.
[27]*Epi.* 28.4Pf. = *AP* 12.43.4.
[28]*Aet.* 1.fr.1.25–28Pf.

"πρὸς δέ σε] καὶ τόδ᾽ ἄνωγα, τὰ μὴ πατέουσιν ἄμαξαι
    τὰ στείβε]ιν, ἑτέρων ἴχνια μὴ καθ᾽ ὁμά
δίφρον ἐλ]ᾶν μηδ᾽ οἶμον ἀνὰ πλατύν, ἀλλὰ κελεύθους
    ἀτρίπτο]υς, εἰ καὶ στε[ι]νοτέρην ἐλάσεις."

"This also I command you: tread a path which carriages do not trample, do not drive your chariot on tracks common to others, nor along a broad route, but on untrodden ways, though you drive a narrower course."

Callimachus, therefore, takes his rightful place not only with Catullus and Virgil as an influence on ode 12 but as a major coalescing force on the four diverse, brilliant statements on poetry which crown each trinity of odes as the book builds toward its final climax.

PART FIVE

Sorcery and Song:
Odes 13–15

For most of us, there is only the unattended
Moment, the moment in and out of time,
The distraction fit, lost in a shaft of sunlight,
The wild thyme unseen, or the winter lightning
Or the waterfall, or music heard so deeply
That it is not heard at all, but you are the music
While the music lasts . . .

T. S. Eliot, "The Dry Salvages"

[13]

ODE THIRTEEN

Audivere, Lyce, di mea vota, di
audivere, Lyce: fis anus; et tamen
   vis formosa videri
     ludisque et bibis inpudens

et cantu tremulo pota Cupidinem   5
lentum sollicitas: ille virentis et
   doctae psallere Chiae
     pulchris excubat in genis.

inportunus enim transvolat aridas
quercus et refugit te, quia luridi   10
   dentes, te quia rugae
     turpant et capitis nives.

nec Coae referunt iam tibi purpurae
nec cari lapides tempora, quae semel
   notis condita fastis   15
     inclusit volucris dies.

quo fugit venus, heu, quove color, decens
quo motus? quid habes illius, illius,
   quae spirabat amores,
     quae me surpuerat mihi,   20

felix post Cinaram notaque et artium
gratarum facies? sed Cinarae brevis
    annos fata dederunt,
      servatura diu parem

cornicis vetulae temporibus Lycen,   25
possent ut iuvenes visere fervidi
    multo non sine risu
      dilapsam in cineres facem.

The gods have heeded my prayers, Lyce, the gods have heeded, Lyce: you have become a crone. Yet nevertheless you wish to appear pretty, and brazenly you cavort and carouse, and, besotted, you accost limp Cupid with shaky serenade. He lies sentinel before the lovely cheeks of youthful Chia, clever on the lyre. For, an omen of ill, he flies across shrivelled oaks and flees back from you because yellowed teeth, because wrinkles, because a hoary head disfigure you. Neither the purpled silks of Cos nor precious gems now bring back the seasons which the winged day has once locked up in the prison of a calendar well-known.

Where has your Venus fled, alas, or where your mien, where the grace of your step? What do you claim of her, of her who breathed loves, who snatched me from myself, fortunate successor to Cinara and famed for her beauty and her pleasing arts?

But the fates, which gave short years to Cinara, will preserve Lyce on and on to equal the seasons of the beldame crow, so that seething youths could see, not without many a smirk, your pine-torch smouldered into ash.

The eleventh ode commemorates a specific date with a ceremony built around an erotic scenario. Its successor, a more general "spring" poem, uses elements of the symposium as the basis for its own variation of the invitation poem. Nevertheless both odes are similar in their use of poetry to dramatize, and in a sense to become, rituals that abstract their guests from the black and bitter cares, present and potential, that human existence harbors. For the present, Phyllis, amatory overreacher, and Vergilius, zealous for economic gain, both need to share in poetry's enlightenment, though for diverse reasons. But the looming future melds all the protagonists, speaker and guests alike, together as fleeting allies—she for a final bout of love-making with her host-poet, he for a brief session of shared un-wisdom, to escape time's demands into poetry's fragile dreams.

The opening of ode 13 dramatically reverses this stance of a speaker offering his words as education and comfort against life's exigencies. His magic now takes the form of prayer shading into curse, and its result is a hastening, not an impeding, of time's encroachments. If Phyllis and Vergilius accept his invitation, which is to heed the power of his verses, he will have engineered for each a metamorphosis away from the unsuitable and the tawdry, and into a fecund instant of spirituality. Poetry, for a fragile moment, might make an equally momentary future bearable. At the start of ode 13, as hope now reaches fruition and future becomes past, a wish has indeed been granted and a mutation effected, but one quite different from those contemplated by the previous odes. The speaker prays not to a woman or to a man for a love or friendship that would be mutually beneficial. Instead he has turned to the gods and can announce to his addressee, Lyce, that together they have turned her youth to old age and her beauty to ugliness. The combination of chiasmus and sequential order in the opening lines places special emphasis on the pivotal *vota* that have been fulfilled, while the syntactical insistence of repetition and especially of the striking initial anaphora suggests a dual tonality. The speaker appears amazed, with his iterations perhaps meant to mimic former successful prayers. Yet his doublings have a touch of *Schadenfreude* about them. Restatement implies not only pride in how verbal wizardry can produce physical results but rejoicing in the truth itself.[1] In both cases repetition further secures and reassures the reality that the speaker announces to Lyce.

Lyce, however, does not wish to understand this affirmation. The speaker's initial astonishment implies a preceding stretch of time for prayer in which he has not seen Lyce. His present imagined vision of her confirms, by sudden sight, the actuality that he had requested in words. But, as the poet's marvelous sonic play, which takes us from *fis* (the first word of the revelation) to *vis* (which begins the next line), to *videri* (which ends it) makes clear, she does not accept this highly visible fact. Desire still triumphs over possibility, seeming over being, appearance over reality in her mental world. For the speaker, time's course and its accompanying supplication have actuated his

[1]Fraenkel (*Horace,* 415) finds a "jubilant note" in the poem's beginning.

negative desire. For Lyce, on the other hand, temporality has as yet no meaning. The result is that, although we see the truth about her through the speaker's eyes, she does not wish to see herself. And this deliberate lack of self-perspective provides Horace with an occasion for censure.

In the preceding two poems wine and music were fitting attributes for settings that took careful note of time and for an instant preached retreat from it. Here foolish drinking and singing in the hope of seducing desire are small infelicities that stem from the larger inde-corousness of refusing to face time and to behave in accordance with its dictates. Cupid's yearnings lie elsewhere. While Lyce presses her demands on him, he keeps watch on Chia's beauty.[2] In response to the importunities of Lyce's quivering song, he remains unconcerned. To the proper music of "green" Chia, whose artistry suits her young years, he metaphorically plays the *exclusus amator* who is simul-taneously the slave guarding his mistress. *Ille* distances Cupid from Lyce and at the same time helps foster the distinction between her and Chia.

Chia's youth we learn by metaphor, her training and beauty we literally hear and see. She is what Lyce would be but is not, an image of the fitting interaction of youth, talent, charm, and desire. The poem's words also craft the mirror of truth for Lyce herself to gaze upon. Her metaphors, both visual and tactile, are antonymical to Chia's green freshness. The leaves of Lyce's oak are dry, her teeth yellowed, her hair snow-white.[3] Spring is Chia's season. Winter's hoar and chill have come upon Lyce. And the winged Cupid who flies over her wizened limbs is *inportunus* in richly varied senses. Toward Chia he is importunate, asking for love in the poem's third solicitation. He is *inportunus* to Lyce, first, if we look to the word's

---

[2]This is Horace's only use of *excubo*. Though Caesar uses the verb of ships (*B. C.* 2.22.3), this is its first use in Latin with an abstraction. As such it supports the personification of *Cupido*. Horace does use *excubiae* at *c.* 3.16.3, to describe guardian dogs posted before the door of imprisoned Danae (*Inclusam*), whom golden Jupiter easily outwits. Ovid imagines *Cupido* as the excluded slave of love in *Am.* 3.11.12.

[3]*C.* 1.9.1–17 mixes *nive, virenti,* and *canities* in defining youth and old age, and at *c.* 1.25.17–19 *virenti* is contrasted to *aridas*. Quintilian (8.6.17) found the meta-phor involved in *capitis nives* both harsh (*dura*) and far-fetched (*a longinqua similitudine*).

root meaning, because he no longer finds in her oaks the same in-gratiating resting place he has discovered on Chia's cheeks. In a more abstract sense, he is stubborn, unyielding to her advances. Finally, with a deft twist in meaning, he is a bird of ill-omen who in his flight does indeed approach Lyce, but with relentless pronouncements on her aging, nor with the persistent wooings of a suitor.[4]

Attribution of the catalog of lines 10–12 remains ambiguous. It could epitomize Cupid's documentation of her ugliness, the thump-ing iteration that thrusts on her the reality of herself. But the speaker himself, as the first stanza reveals, is also given to similar acts of restatement. If there we learned twice over that the gods heeded his curses, we now have the evidence for this perception enumerated, as the speaker, too, accosts Lyce with the truth. In each instance repeti-tion validates and substantiates, in the first place supporting her gen-eral metamorphosis, in the second both announcing its resolution in detail and furthering the curse through a brief litany of its potent results.

The description of time's alterations is followed by an enumeration of Lyce's attempts to hide them, and these, too, the power of anaph-ora doubly denies. Romans of the Augustan period much prized garments of Coan silk. Horace himself and his earlier contemporaries viewed them as signs of affluence and of sexuality (they were di-aphanous). This is the first occasion where they are said to be dyed purple. Though the metonymy is not new, this is also its initial Latin use in the plural.[5] The double novelty underscores the futility of Lyce's gestures. Wealth and superficial attempts to appear seductive will not hide the truth. In the context of ode 13 there is further significance to the emphasis on purple. As a color of youth as well as emblem of artificiality it signifies Lyce's continuing futile attempt to regain what "green" Chia possesses naturally and what her own whiteness proves in her case to be irrecoverable.

The precious stones she wears also project the same ambiguity. On

---

[4]Porphyrion (on lines 9–10) correctly remarks that *inportunus* is an example of witty irony. It is curious that two out of Virgil's three uses of *inportunus* involve ill-omened birds (*geo.* 1.470; *Aen.* 12.864). Cf. also *sat.* 1.8.6 (*inportunas volucris*).

[5]Smith (on Tibullus 2.3.53) discusses in detail Roman fondness for Coan fab-rics. They are mentioned in Latin poetry before ode 13 by Horace himself (*sat.* 1.2.101), Propertius (1.2.2, 2.1.5–6, and possibly 4.2.23, 4.5.23 and 57) and Tibullus (2.3.53, 2.4.29). For the plural *purpura,* see *OLD s.v.* 3a.

the one hand, such costly adornments would be thought the attempts of a misguided mind to mask the ravages of time and to entice new lovers. For a Roman, the truth of time's progress would be seen not only in inscriptions carved on sepulchral monuments (*lapides*) but in calendrical *fasti,* the most famous of which, the so-called Fasti Capitolini, were probably carved on the inner walls of the Arch of Augustus some five years before Horace published his fourth book of odes.[6] These are the stones on which time's irretrievable advance would be recorded.[7] They invoke a lapidary permanence that Lyce's baubles would wish away in a transient, trite gesture against the inevitable.

The details of this, the poem's central stanza, build toward an extraordinary paradox. Time and love are interactive entities. Both share the ability to fly—both are emblems of swiftness—and both can imprison: Cupid plays sentry before the cheeks of Chia, the rushing day confines time's forward impulse in the solidity of characters on stone. Love's fleetingness is a reflection of time's quickness to vanish. Cupid speeds past Lyce (*refugit*), and, no matter what ruses she employs, she cannot call back (*referunt*) those times whose evanescence offers but a grander manifestation of the reasons for love's departure. Yet, for all its volatility, time is also a steadfast lover, far more steadfast than Cupid. Its minion, the swift day, can and will enclose her in the archives that chronicle time's passage for a longer period than Cupid will watch over Chia. Chia, too, will age, and lust again prove volatile. The dialogue between motion and stability will continue on in all lives. Yet for all its changeableness the grasp of time is eternal, steadying and immortalizing its subjects in its transience.

The initial stanzas of the ode made no direct connection between the speaker and Lyce. Yet as the poem begins to draw to a conclusion, we learn of this intimacy. For the revelation both tone and rhetoric change. As the speaker becomes retrospective, his sigh of sadness evinces sorrow at the visible inroads of time on Lyce's comeliness. Venus has fled, like her offspring. Gone, too, as we have seen,

---

[6]Tibullus (1.3.54) offers a good poetic example of *lapis* as funeral stele with *notae* inscribed on it. L. R. Taylor dates the engraving of the Capitoline *Fasti* to between June, 18 B.C. and June, 17 B.C. ("The Date" and "New Indications," *passim*).

[7]Both *includo* (OLD s.v.) and *condo* (OLD s.v. 14) are regularly connected with the act of writing.

is quality of appearance, to be replaced by the truth of white hair and the sham of purple clothes. Charm has been succeeded by the indecorous (*inpudens*). In sum, the appearance of Lyce in her youth, when she manifested talents in singing, lyre playing, and dancing, which ingratiated her to her former lover, has become that of a crone. She who was known for her beauty has now become "known" in the calendars that fix such mutations.

But the speaker's altered tone betrays his own participation in the exclamation of sadness they both should share. Retrospection in her life means the same in his own. And as present curse, successful over time, becomes yearning for the past, the insistent rhetoric, which established the actuality of appearances (and the forcefulness of the speaker's prayers), becomes now an equal insistence on repeated questions accompanied by another siege of anaphora. Initial restatements may have denoted wonderment at the efficacy of the speaker's words and the reality they produced. His concluding iterations query what has happened. Has she really aged? What has become of her loveliness? What does this mean for the speaker himself? Perhaps time, too, has passed in his own life and he is no longer as attractive as he once was when given to a life of passion. Through his rhetoric of interrogation for a moment he becomes her and thus links them both as young lovers in time past, imitating her present inability to accept the truth of time's fickleness.

Distance and immediacy intermingle in this moving moment whose heightened diction reflects an emotionality built on the excitement of the lived past as well as on the multifaceted bitterness of its recollection. In his backward glance, especially in the asyndetic repetition of *illius,* the speaker may be thinking of Catullus who can characterize Lesbia to his friend Caelius as[8]

> . . . Lesbia nostra, Lesbia illa,
> illa Lesbia, quam Catullus unam
> plus quam se atque suos amavit omnes, . . .

. . . our Lesbia, that Lesbia, that Lesbia whom alone Catullus loved more than himself and all his own, . . .

[8]Cat. 58.1–3. Catullus uses the word *angiportum* only at 58.4, Horace only at *c.* 1.25.10, a poem also on his mind as he wrote ode 13.

The former Lesbia was truly loved by Catullus. The present is whore to Rome. The change registers the difference between the complexity in Catullus' approach to love, which combines intense piety with intense eroticism, and the directness of Lesbia's present physicality. The change Horace portrays is much more a factor of time alone. Lyce, as her name implies, has always been a courtesan.[9] It is just that now the beauty and charm with which "that" Lyce abounded have vanished.

If the excited iteration of *illius* looks directly to the Lyce who once was, the more analytic phrase *quae me surpuerat mihi* (who snatched me from myself) takes us into that past itself. The phrase is glossed by two moments in Horace's initial book of epistles. The first comes at the opening of the fourteenth "letter," addressed to the bailiff of his Sabine farm and dedicated to the differences between them, when "Horace" speaks of his beloved plot of land as "giving me back to myself" (*mihi me reddentis*).[10] The second instance is near the end of epistle 18 where, listing for Lollius some philosophical debates in which he should take an interest, the speaker asks,[11] ". . . *quid minuat curas, quid te tibi reddet amicum,* . . . ?" ("What lessens cares, what gives you back as friend to yourself, . . . ?"). The separation of self from self can come about from the madness of city life or from plain thoughtlessness. In ode 13, it is erotic involvement with Lyce that took away the self-distance which is at the basis of self-understanding and self-respect. Yet once again the protagonists have similarities. The speaker's backward glance sees in the results of his former feelings for Lyce a parallel with Lyce's own powerlessness now to face her aging. Neither character had, or has, sufficient detachment to analyze the involved self. In both cases passion—to make love when young, to seem young when old, and still to make love—gets in the way of reason. For the speaker, but not for Lyce, this self-distance has accrued with time and with the ability to philosophize which longevity sometimes brings.

But this passionate look at passion, at a past time when irrationality sundered the speaker's selves, disappears with the suddenness of its

---

[9]Quinn (*Horace: Odes,* on II.1–6), among others, notes the punning connection between λύκη, invented feminine from λύκος, and *lupa,* a Latin word for prostitute recorded first in Plautus.

[10]*Epi.* I.14.I.

[11]*Epi.* I.18.101.

inception. The remainder of the poem pursues the speaker's biography with a tone as aloof as the preceding lines had been demonstrative. Cinara and Lyce are looked at not as erotic objects but simply as creatures who lived short or long lives. And Lyce herself, who has until this point played a vital role as the poem's addressee, is now relegated to the third person, contemplated still but no longer apostrophized directly. Not that she leaves the poem. The poem's last image of preservation evokes her, remanded not by the swift day but by fate itself into an old age that hovers between Cinara's brief years and her own looming demise. She also takes to herself the image of a bird, previously allotted to *Cupido,* in order to approximate not eager lover but the crow, symbol of age, darkly squawking of darkness.[12] And the brilliant final vignette of torch slipping to ashes epitomizes her career, taking us from body to bodiless, light to dark, warmth to chill, youth to age, and, in the final instance, to death.[13]

Lyce leaves the poem as an immediate presence, but the speaker also distances himself from youth. Though he experienced it deeply once, he places himself now as far from its fervor as he does from the ugliness and indecorousness of Lyce's old age. And with distance from their ardent ways goes an equal remoteness from their mockery. This does not mean that we were wrong to hear a tone of derision in the speaker's opening words. But an ode that purported then to be a monologue with an addressee imagined listening has in the end proved, or at least become, a soliloquy. Only those ignorant of the passage of time would ridicule someone like Lyce, whom time has made so obviously its prey. Only someone insensitive to his own appearance would laugh at a creature bent on so patent and pathetic a

[12]The crow is an appropriate emblem for Lyce. Not only does it symbolize old age from Hesiod on (fr. 304M), it also is known for the harshness of its singing (see, e.g., Lucr. *DRN* 5.1084, 6.751–52) and for its role as persistent augur of rain (e.g., *c.* 3.17.13, Vir. *geo.* 1.388), with all its implications.

[13]*TLL s.v.* 1074.11ff. lists instances of *cinis* as a metonymy for death. For *fax* as attribute of *amor,* see *TLL s.v.* 401.80–84, 402.1–6. Propertius (4.11.46) uses the phrase *inter utramque facem* to define the period between marriage and death, between the torch of the wedding ceremony and the torch that ignites the funeral pyre. No doubt we are also meant to remember the "black fires" of the preceding poem—the funeral pyre with its dark smoke of death. We should note, too, the punning connection assonance creates between Cinara and *cineres, facies* and *facem.* Her name, which gave her reality, and the face that was so significant a feature of that reality have become only ash.

dissemblance. Final intellectual aloofness from both Lyce and the youths who scoff at her on the part of a speaker who is heart-whole again suggests the absence of such derision. Nevertheless her implicit attendance at the start suggests that an element of mockery is also present and that the poem's progress is also a final education of the speaker into the imperturbable acceptance of his own old age with grace of statement, which is to say grace of feeling as well.

Critics are right to compare ode 13 with two poems from Horace's earlier collection, *c.* 1.25 and 3.15, for they share many elements in common. The first is a macabre parody of the standard *paraclausithyron*. The usual beautiful mistress, imagined secure within her dwelling and unresponsive to the plight of her excluded suitor, is replaced by an aging courtesan whose door no longer moves to the pleas of lovers and who will soon tearfully take her unsatisfied longings to lonely alleyways. Green ivy belongs to the young. Lydia is linked with dry leaves and Thrace's chill Hebrus, companion of winter, not spring. The second ode is addressed to Chloris, attempting to join her daughter in storming the houses of gallants but only thereby publicizing her gracelessness by insistence on an all too revealing association with the young. Both poems look at the effects of time on an aging courtesan and at how these are manifested, first, in the ugly metamorphosis of desired into desirer, second in the indecorousness of the pretense at youth.

Elements of both Lydia and Chloris enter into the portrait of Lyce, but the differences reinforce a primary enlivening tension we find in the poem itself between physicality and reflection. Compared to the earlier poems, ode 13 is vividly biographical. The details of the arrival of senescence upon Lyce are more worthy of a diatribe such as *epode* 8, which also catalogs with almost repugnant abundance of detail the reasons why an old woman's body repels the deliverer of the harangue. Yet we learn a good deal about the speaker himself whose erotic history has led him from Cinara to Lyce to (contemplation of) Chia (lust emanating from her and manifested for her is left to Cupid). The speaking "I" is strongly involved in looking at himself and others, as if life's immediacy was slipping from his grasp. It is as if what he notes in the superficies of Lyce and Chia was a reminder of then and now, of youth and age, in his own experience. The action of the poem at once betrays the galling effects of age on former lovers, including the speaker, and pretends to purge them, at least from himself.

The opposite pole of this palpable emotionality is a philosophizing tendency also absent in the earlier odes and perhaps lent to the speaker by the intervening book of epistles. For all its scrutiny of human corporeality the poem also studies, as we noted, the difference between seeming and being, between appearance and reality in our lives, and between myopia and awareness in dealing with the truth of ourselves. Though Lyce's beauty once made the speaker unphilosophical, he has learned detachment during the lapse of time that the poem documents. This attitude, after snatching the veil off her self-deceptions, at the end provides a distance from the pathology of both her unenlightened aging and youth's ignorant ridicule of her, which may in fact be his method for knowledgeably coping with his own pressing realities.

The speaker is, of course, an electric presence, insisting, pronouncing, yearning, withdrawing. He is fascinated by the effects of speech and sound, of Lyce's and Chia's music, of the importunities of Cupid and the laughter of the young. But the speaker's dynamic rhetoric is not merely descriptive or evocative. Lyce roused feelings in him the origins of which are not elucidated but which are strong enough to make him curse her before the gods. But his is no ordinary curse. It is the prayer of a former lover who happens also to be a poet with the ability to spellbind with verses. His orisons move the gods who engineer the transformation of Lyce, but his words have a further power. The author of a curse has jurisdiction over the processes of temporality. He can not only bring about aging, he can imaginatively fix his victim in the time-frame he desires. Detachment, or at least its appearance, controls the speaker's emotional self, which mutates over time, but the charm of a poet's words controls time itself. His language creates and affirms a verbal calendar that schedules both Lyce and the speaker, who initially reviles her, into a perpetuity both including and triumphing over age itself.

The speaker's leave-taking from Lyce is also the poet's farewell to the lyrical uses of elegy. Here, too, in each instance the craftsman's power is evident. I will presume that the Lyce who appears in Horace's last amatory poem is the same Lyce who is addressed in *c.* 3.10. There, in her pride, she is as oblivious to time's negative potential in her life as she is to the harsh elements in nature which beset her suitor, the suppliant speaker, waiting patiently on her threshold. In the literary time, which is a metaphor for the emotional, human time that has passed between the two odes, the speaker has gained his revenge.

The final exemplification of power also involves a look beyond the confines of Horace to the third book of Propertius' elegies which we have seen, from time to time, exerting a varied influence on Horace's final collection. It is appropriate that the particular resonances in Horace's ultimate poem devoted to private eroticism stem from the concluding two poems of Propertius' book, 3.24 and 25. They form a continuum engaged with the *forma,* the enticing beauty, of Cynthia. The first recounts his praisings of an allure from whose toils he finally slipped. The second looks directly at Cynthia and anticipates the results of the advent of age on her charms. As the elegy draws to a close he catalogs the possibilities: the pressing of hidden years, the "sinister" furrow, the white hairs to be plucked from the roots, then furrows again, as the mirror cackles its delight. Propertius' speaker concludes with a curse and a command:[14]

> exclusa inque vicem fastus patiare superbos,
>   et quae fecisti facta queraris anus!
> has tibi fatalis cecinit mea pagina diras:
>   eventum formae disce timere tuae!

Shut outside, may you in your turn suffer the disdains of pride and, become a crone, may you grieve for what you did. My page has sung these curses of fate upon you. Learn to dread the outcome of your beauty.

In terms of plot line, Horace begins where Propertius left off. The prediction has come true as future time becomes present. Even though Lyce has not yet accepted the reality of her aging, and therefore, we presume, no fear of the possible loss of her beauty has stricken her, nevertheless she has become old. The potentiality of her

[14]Prop. 3.25.15–18.

aging (*facta anus*) has become its truth (*fis anus*).[15] Horace's speaker
has effected what was only predicted by Propertius'. His words have
the ability to consummate a curse, which is also to perform a metamorphosis. But the creator of such a dynamic protagonist exhibits a
strength of his own. By continuing and concluding Propertius' design, Horace is also co-opting the elegist's imagination and refiguring
it to his own purposes.

Although such incorporation evidences a certain triumph over a
poetic predecessor, it implies a compliment to him as well. Imitation,
however original, marks the worth of its model. And the bow takes a
particular form here. The linear leap from one poet to another may
often signify that the second means to prove his genius by transcend-
ing the first. But, in this instance at least, the later poet also carefully
parallels his predecessor. Both poems are conclusions. Propertius
ends a poetry book that is arguably his finest achievement.[16] Horace's
ode, his last on an erotic theme, smacks as much of the immediacies
of Roman subjective elegy as any of his lyrics. We may assume
Horace's pride in his poem's brilliant novelties, but the ode stands
clear as an act of homage as well, closing a phase of his poetic activity
with matter and manner close to those Propertius had adopted for the
same purpose.

Yet, for all its backward glances into Horace's previous writing
and reading, the particular forcefulness of ode 13 comes from its
position of closure within the fourth book of odes itself. Its themes
follow smoothly after the preceding two odes which also deal with
time's forward march and its effects on addressees who associate with
the young, as if this promised rejuvenation, and on speakers who
appreciate its abbreviating ways. Yet, for all this somberness, odes 11
and 12 propose festivities as ceremonies of escape, bouts of lyric
intensity to celebrate repetition rather than sequentiality. By contrast
ode 13 looks unblinkingly at the incursions of temporality on Lyce,
the addressee, while quietly acknowledging that the speaker, too, has

[15]Among several other links between the poems we might note the presence of
laughter, in Propertius at the beginning (*Risus eram*), in Horace near the end
(*risu*). I noted above that the word *speculum* appears in Horace only in ode 10 (6).
One of Propertius' three uses is at 3.25.14 in a remarkably similar context.

[16]I have defended the quality of the book as a whole in "Propertius' Third
Book."

experienced a rich emotional life that is now a thing of the past. As the book's final ode about temporality and individual human lives, it is the capstone of a series of poems that initiate each of the five triads of the book.

Common "biographical" elements tend to merge the speakers of odes 1 and 13 into one and bring the book full circle. Cinara once figured in "Horace's" amatory life and personifications of Venus and Cupid appear prominently in each ode. In ode 1 the goddess of love is a conspicuous force in the speaker's life while in the later poem the now dispassionate, though wistful, speaker can watch as she and her wily son act their mercurial parts in the drama of old Lyce and young Chia.[17] Yet, during the transition from one to the other of these defining poems, the speaker has undergone a remarkable change. The aging lover, doubly praying Venus away and yet in the end yearning for youth, has now gained a voice both authoritative and philosophical, announcing twice over that the gods have heard his curse against Lyce who, suspiciously like his alter ego in the initial ode, is foolishly attempting to stay young. Both poems use *decus* and *artes,* felicitous, seemly grace and the uses of artistry that accompany it, as touchstones for behavior. The speaker of ode 1 knows full well that Venus belongs with Paulus Fabius Maximus, whose characterization forms the center of the poem. He is young, *decens,* a clever speaker, boy of a hundred arts (*centum puer artium*). He will use his architectural and sculptural skills fittingly, to monumentalize his goddess under a citron-wood roof by the Alban lakes. He is responsive to her sensibilities, furnishing incense to smell, music for her ear, dances to delight the eye. The aging speaker, in a contrast that is melancholy and humorous at once, has, while delivering himself of ten extraordinary stanzas, lost his one talent. By inappropriately yearning for young love, his tongue, vehicle for speaking words of courting and poems about love, has fallen into an unseemly silence.

In ode 13 time has moved on apace. Paulus Maximus, paragon of present elegance, suitable young lover, gives place to old Lyce who was once the protégé of Venus when she had *decens motus* and was known for her alluring arts (*gratarum artium*), the practice of music and dance that attracted her paramours. She has now lost her external

---

[17]We move, of course, from Venus, winged on her purple swans, and swift Ligurinus in ode 1 to aleate Cupid and swift day in 13.

decus but not gained the inner self-understanding and the penchant for philosophy that time should bring to replace unseemly eroticism. Yet, in contrast to his former self, the speaker has forgone any inane desire to be like her (or to be like himself in the initial ode). His newfound realism has regained his rhetorical skill for him, and with it he can move heaven, reveal Lyce to herself, and manipulate time.

Ode 4, the second poem in this sequence, leaves behind private amatory foibles for the expansive public world of Rome, and the continuity assured to it by Augustus' education of the Nerones. Yet however grand its reaches into past history and present politics, the poem ends with a seven-stanza monologue by Hannibal which draws our sympathy. The brothers Drusus and Tiberius, epitomes of Roman freshness and integrity, have their parallel to Hannibal and Hasdrubal. Yet the day whose dawn dispelled darkness from Rome brought the opposite for Carthage, the setting, in Hannibal's words, of all hopes (*occidit, occidit spes omnis*) because of the death of Hasdrubal.[18] Rome's enemies are the historical equivalent of suitors in private elegiac time. They die just as aging lovers finally do. Yet the youth of Rome, incorporated in the Nerones, is gifted with grander longevity than a Paulus Maximus or a Chia. In the analogies Horace imparts to Hannibal, Rome takes to itself the image of ilex or hydra, part of nature herself, easily revivified after history's futile onslaughts. A Lyce may for a moment be an oak, but what they seem briefly to have in common is only a dryness leading to human death, not an inner solidity or the instinct for annual revirescence. Rome springs a phoenix from its embers. When our human torch has sunk to ashes there is no renewal.

The same holds true, as the next poem in the series varies the image, when we have become dust and shade. Ode 7 reminds us that even Roman historical characters (Aeneas, Tullus, Ancus), as well as those presently among the living (Torquatus, with his rhetorical prowess and his piety), or mythic lovers with immortal paramours (Hippolytus or Pirithous) have no recourse against death. Here it is the pattern of flight and return that anticipates poem 13:

> Diffugere nives, redeunt iam gramina campis
> arboribusque comae; . . .

[18]Ode 4.71. Hopes and their loss figure in odes 7 (7) and 10 (2) as well as 11 (26) and 12 (19).

Nature has its own cyclicity, inexorable yet self-renewing. When Cupid (*refugit*) and Venus (*fugit*) flee past Lyce, there is no bringing back lost time (*nec referunt*). The snows of winter may melt and the naked Grace (*Gratia*) dance her pleasure at nature's resuscitation, but when Lyce has lost her "graceful" arts and the persistent snows of age have settled on her head, the only immortality left her is the poet's portrait of her decline.

Finally there is Ligurinus. Poem 10, whose opening "still" (*adhuc*) suggests that we read it as partially a continuation of ode 1, also serves as a bridge between the earlier lyrics and ode 13. The cry of *heu*, be it indicative of the speaker's own sadness or of Ligurinus' realization of what has passed him by, is common to all three poems.[19] All three take note of the cheeks either of speaker or addressee which offer intimations of love or of age, and in the final two poems facial features and the complexion color of Ligurinus and Lyce are scrutinized for the same reason.[20] One rich line combines metaphors of foliage and flying, varied in its kindred poems, as the speaker tells of a time for Ligurinus when "*. . . quae nunc umeris involitant, deciderint comae, . . .*" (3). I noted earlier how closely this last phrase reminds us of the major theme of ode 7. It looks ahead also to Lyce as withered oak, suffering her own form of senescence. *Involitant* also anticipates Cupid's flight past those same trees (*transvolat*) and the imprisoning power of swift day (*volucris dies*) just as it looks back to swift Ligurinus in ode 1 (*volucrem*), soaring ahead of his pursuing lover.

But Lyce is both *quercus* and *cornix,* and both tree and bird as often as not in these poems are emblems of nature's vigorousness and continuity.[21] Winged Venus and Ligurinus in ode 1, flying Cupid in 13, may be labeled emblems of love's transience, but by the same token Venus and Cupid stand for love itself and for the continuous mating of love and youth which becomes incongruous only when youth loses its bloom. In the second ode the endurance of poetic artistry is made equivalent to nature's perpetuation as Pindar becomes

[19]See 1.33, 10.6, 13.17.

[20]*Genae* (1.34, 10.8, 13.8), *facies* (10.5, 13.22), *color* (10.4, 13.17). Perhaps the tears on the cheeks of the speaker at 1.34 are at once a manifestation of yearning and a sign that it cannot be fulfilled even in a dream of pursuit.

[21]Horace's recourse to imagery of birds and trees throughout the book is schematized by Porter ("The Recurrent Motifs") under the headings "The Motif of Birds and Flying" (202–5) and "The Motif of Trees and Flowers" (220–23).

a swan and more "humble" Horace a bee. (The speaker's humility is gently mocked in the next poem as he hints that Melpomene might give the sound of a swan even to a mute fish like himself.) The fourth ode opens with Drusus, hope of Rome's future, as an eagle, immortal servant of an immortal Jupiter who happens also to rule Rome.

What then of Lyce who, like Rome, part eagle, part *ilex,* takes to herself images of oak and crow? I maintained earlier that we may be meant to think of the aridity of the oak's leaves, not the permanence of its trunk, as appropriate for Lyce just as greenness is fitting for youthful Chia. I suspect, however, that permanence is also a pertinent aspect of these symbols.[22] As he prepares for his two magnificent concluding public poems, Horace reminds us that Lyce—shriveled by time, unseeing of self—has something in common with mighty Rome. Each is given its immortality by a poet. In the case of Lyce the imagery takes a negative turn since both tree and bird symbolize an eternal expansion of longevity, while Rome remains ever young. Nevertheless both are made fixtures of nature by words that, though they may dictate spheres of temporality, also allow their subjects to transcend time.

---

[22]If the oak symbolizes Lyce's withered appearance, then *quercus* stands for *frondes* in a synecdoche of whole for parts (*frondes* is the noun used with the adjective *aridus* at *c.* 1.25.19). For the oak as symbol of longevity, cf. Vir. *geo.* 3.332 and *Aen.* 4.441 (*annoso validam . . . robore quercum*) with Pease's list. In his earlier Lyce poem Horace had used the image to suggest her "hardness" in the face of a lover's pleas (*nec rigida mollior aesculo, c.* 3.10.17). He turns this here into a symbol of the fixed rigidity of her loveless age.

[14]

ODE FOURTEEN

Quae cura patrum quaeve Quiritium
plenis honorum muneribus tuas,
    Auguste, virtutes in aevum
        per titulos memoresque fastus

aeternet, o qua sol habitabilis   5
inlustrat oras, maxime principum,
    quem legis expertes Latinae
        Vindelici didicere nuper,

quid Marte posses. milite nam tuo
Drusus Genaunos, inplacidum genus,   10
    Breunosque velocis et arces
        Alpibus inpositas tremendis

deiecit acer plus vice simplici,
maior Neronum mox grave proelium
    conmisit immanisque Raetos   15
        auspiciis pepulit secundis,

spectandus in certamine Martio
devota morti pectora liberae
    quantis fatigaret ruinis,
        indomitas prope qualis undas   20

exercet Auster Pleiadum choro
scindente nubis, inpiger hostium
　　vexare turmas et frementem
　　　　mittere equum medios per ignis.

sic tauriformis volvitur Aufidus,　　　　　　　　　　25
qui regna Dauni praefluit Apuli,
　　cum saevit horrendamque cultis
　　　　diluviem meditatur agris,

ut barbarorum Claudius agmina
ferrata vasto diruit impetu　　　　　　　　　　　　30
　　primosque et extremos metendo
　　　　stravit humum sine clade victor,

te copias, te consilium et tuos
praebente divos. nam tibi quo die
　　portus Alexandrea supplex　　　　　　　　　　35
　　　　et vacuam patefecit aulam,

Fortuna lustro prospera tertio
belli secundos reddidit exitus
　　laudemque et optatum peractis
　　　　imperiis decus adrogavit.　　　　　　　　　40

te Cantaber non ante domabilis
Medusque et Indus, te profugus Scythes
　　miratur, o tutela praesens
　　　　Italiae dominaeque Romae.

te fontium qui celat origines　　　　　　　　　　　45
Nilusque et Hister, te rapidus Tigris,
　　te beluosus qui remotis
　　　　obstrepit Oceanus Britannis,

te non paventis funera Galliae
duraeque tellus audit Hiberiae,　　　　　　　　　50
　　te caede gaudentes Sygambri
　　　　conpositis venerantur armis.

What concern of senators or what of citizens, with full reward for honors due, can immortalize your prowess for time to come, through eulogy and mindful chronicle, O greatest of princes, where the sun surveys the settled earth, whose strength in war the Vindelici, shareless in the Latin law, recently discovered! For with your soldiery keen Drusus, in manifold requital, hurled down the Genauni, an unquiet race, and the swift Breuni and their bulwarks bastioned on the fearsome Alps. Soon the elder Nero with favorable omens engaged the heavy fray and beat back the giant Raeti. He was conspicuous in Mars' struggle for the mighty thrusts with which he exhausted hearts dedicated to a free death, much as the South wind, when the choir of Pleiades cleaves the clouds, wearies the untamed waves, eager to harass the hordes of foes and to urge his roaring steed through the fires' midst.

Just as bull-formed Aufidus whirls his flooding course past the kingdom of Apulian Daunus, when he rages and schemes dreadful deluge for the tended fields, so Claudius with spreading on-rush swooped on the armored ranks of the savages, and, scything the first and last, victoriously strewed the ground, with nothing lost. You offered the forces, offered your wisdom and your gods. For on the very date when contrite Alexandria spread wide her harbors and her empty palace to you, kindly Fortune, after fifteen years, allotted again a favorable outcome for warring and assigned the praise and glory craved for discharging your commands.

At you the Cantaber marvels, not tamable before, the Mede marvels, the Indian, and the fleeing Scythian, O indwelling guardian of Italy and of mistress Rome. You the Nile heeds, who cloaks the sources of his stream, and the Hister, you the sweeping Tigris, you the beast-ridden Ocean that bellows at the far-off Britons, you the land of Gaul, terrorless before death, and of rugged Hiberia; you the Sygambri, whose gladness is in slaughter, worship, their weapons laid aside in peace.

In the final private poem of book 4, Horace's persona can effect time's passage and then freeze it in the life of Lyce. His valedictory to eroticism is a charm that at once curses his subject with aging, immortalizes that age, and, in the end, dissociates him from what he has created. The book's concluding poems reach outward again, to the public themes of Rome and Roman grandeur. Both are variations of panegyric, addressed to Augustus and paired by content and meter (this is the only occasion in the book where Horace uses the same

[238]

meter, here his favorite alcaic, in adjacent poems). Ode 14 looks back, as we would expect given the book's patterning, to the two previous poems most directly concerned with the emperor, odes 2 and 5.[1] It also claims close association with the fourth ode, sharing a common focus on the offspring of Tiberius Claudius Nero and their epic sweep. But where in the earlier poem the speaker cut himself off from detailing the prowess of Drusus after only two lines, he now allows himself to luxuriate in the heroic exploits of both brothers against Alpine Gallic tribes in 15 B.C. The opening period, which takes us briskly from stepfather to stepsons, extends, with only brief pauses, over six stanzas, in rhetoric that turns from interrogation to exclamation to expansive documentation.

In passing from the *curae* that afflict humankind in their quotidian affairs and the *munera* that lovers or symposiasts exchange to the "care" of an entire people for its charismatic leader and the rewards it plans to offer him, Horace broadens his purview to enclose, in his final poems, the larger world of Roman politics. But even as he does so he has his speaker vary a major point of the preceding ode. Lyce's senescence is fixed forever in a poetic calendar that all can notice. The endurance of Augustus and his significance depends on the inscriptions that publicize his deeds and dates, and give them the stability of stone. But in taking note of the same feats, the poet gives them his special form of permanence. His poem will prove a *titulus* more enduring than that attached to any statue. The hyperbole of the speaker's panegyric extends space to a sun's view of the world and time to eternity, but, beyond this, his words have the power to furnish incipient immortality.

The choice of the verb *aeterno* (5) accentuates the point. It contains the noun *aevum,* which appears in line 3, in its meaning, as if doubly to forewarn the reader that the manipulation of time is once more the speaker's province. The address to Augustus manifests power of another sort. This is the only point at which Horace apostrophizes the emperor with the designation that Augustus took to himself in 27 B.C. (instead of Romulus, some said). In a context so taken with

---

[1]Ode 14 is the least discussed poem of book 4. It has been studied recently in detail only by Doblhofer (103–5). Fraenkel (*Horace,* 431–32) sees the poem primarily as documentation for the constitutional position of Augustus vis-à-vis his stepsons. The ode is not mentioned by Commager.

temporality, the honorific title reminds us of renewals and new beginnings, of majestic inaugurations that herald a series of individual fresh starts. Together, as the epithet's basic etymology from *augeo* implies, these increase and augment the prosperity of an empire dependent for its constancy on the august stature of the emperor himself.[2] For the recipient of such a name is both passive and active, drawing due symbols of respect to himself but also nurturing his people and sharing his ability to preserve his domain with those worthy to enjoy the boon.

By the end of the poem the speaker will have revealed another, still more transcendent example of incantatory legerdemain. In the second ode Augustus is away fighting the Sygambri. He is the distant subject of concern to Iullus, who sings his epic praises, and to the speaker who offers a smaller poetic sacrifice. In the fifth ode he is addressed directly, as kindly leader sprung from kindly gods, whose physical and moral universe is in good order save only that it lacks his presence. By ode 14 this deficiency has been remedied. Augustus is at last *tutela praesens* (43), a guardian imagined at hand to secure his empire.[3] In the course of book 4 Horace has defined the lapses of time in the private lives of his seemingly autobiographical speaker and of his other creatures, capping it with a poem that faces time's ravages and makes them forever static in poetry. But in his Augustus poems

---

[2]The connection of *augustus, augur,* and *augeo* is discussed at length in Ernout-Meillet *s.v. augeo*. It is already made in Suetonius (*Aug.* 7), who quotes Ennius' juxtaposition of *augustus* and *augurium* (*Ann.* 502V³).

[3]*Praesens* is an example of wordplay doubly suitable to ode 14. It means, literally, that Augustus is to be imagined having returned home to Rome, bringing to fruition the prayer of ode 5 and, we should note, without the triumph in which the speaker of ode 2 anticipates taking a humble share. More figurative, but appropriate for a poem in the tradition of Hellenistic panegyric, *praesens* is equivalent to ἐπιφανής. Augustus is now to be treated as a god on earth, having fulfilled the conditional prophecy of *c.* 3.5.2–4:

> . . . praesens divus habebitur
> Augustus adiectis Britannis
> imperio gravibusque Persis.

Augustus will be considered a god in our midst, when the Britains and the menacing Persians have been added to the empire.

Cf. also *epi.* 2.1.15 with Brink's discussion (49–53).

Horace exerts his charm to another end. The sequence of odes devoted to the emperor is a major *revocatio,* which, if only in his imagination, brings Augustus home. With this passage in odic time, over literal and verbal space, comes not the abidingness of individual aging, but the public assurance of Rome's constant renovation, through might well employed to preserve peace.

Augustus' own dynamism is clarified in the first of two striking prolepses in these lines, unparalleled elsewhere in Horace. Though a variation of synecdoche furthered by metonymy, the "whom" that the Vindelici learn about is in fact what Augustus can accomplish together with Mars, namely in war. This switch from a person to the potential embodied in that person is continued as the abstraction takes concrete form in the troops who incorporate such might. This further synecdoche is an imaginative complement to Roman political *Realien:* the omnipotent emperor was seen as sharing his power and his good fortune with his generals in the field. They are his self-extensions, and just as he lent them the abilities that are really his, so he gains the credit for their heroics which, again, are merely his *virtutes* exploited by someone else.[4]

The movement from *Marte* to *milite,* which assonance expedites, is extended as Augustus' generalized soldiery lend their strength to his particular envoys, first Drusus, then Tiberius, who between them occupy this and five more stanzas. As the initial sentence builds to its climax, Horace introduces the metaphor of horses, gently at first, then more intensely until at the end, as image becomes reality, we find Tiberius spurring on his roaring steed through battle's flames. It begins with the Genauni, an untamed race awaiting Rome's tutelage, and the swift Breuni who need Rome's training. It even impinges on

---

[4]See Fraenkel, *Horace,* 431–32: "Under the new regime it was the Princeps to whom the *auspicia* belonged and who had the supreme command of all troops in the Empire; he alone, with a few exceptions in special cases, was entitled to the triumph. This state of affairs is perfectly reflected, in general, in the fact that Horace's triumphal ode for Drusus has no addressee and the ode for Tiberius is addressed to Augustus, and, in particular, in the expressions 14. 9 *milite . . . tuo* and 14. 33f. *te copias, te consilium et tuos praebente divos.*" I would object only to the designation of 14 as an "ode for Tiberius." The poem is as much for, as to, Augustus who lends Tiberius his vitality and yet forecloses on it at the end, extracting a lyric hymn from the speaker once the need for epic narrative, however lyricized, is past.

the picture of Drusus overthrowing their Alpine citadels. For Horace may wish us to think of his earlier treatment of the battle between the Olympian gods and the giants Otus and Ephialtes—those brothers

> . . . tendentes opaco
> Pelion inposuisse Olympo.

aspiring to burden Pelion on to shady Olympus—

and of the appropriate reversal in the fate of Enceladus who forever endures Etna weighted on him (*inpositam Aetnen*).[5] But *deicere* can also mean to throw from a saddle, so even here the suggestion remains that dismantling the mountain fortresses of the barbarians is like unhorsing them from their source of unbridled energy.[6] These new "giants" opposing the new Jove and his minions will have as little success as their mythical paradigms.

Many of these same rhetorical and imagistic motifs persist in the longer description of Tiberius.[7] If *milite tuo* represents the sharing of power with Drusus, *auspiciis secundis* is the emanation from the emperor offered to his elder stepson. Verbally their intimacy seems close for other reasons. *Auspiciis* itself, as a word, involves at least a partial sharing of Augustus' name, as well as his good fortune, with Tiberius, and though the immediate meaning of *maior* is "elder," it connotes a physical grandeur (absorbed metaphorically into the "heavy" battle he offers) and a stature nearer to that of Caesar himself who eight lines earlier was characterized as *maxime principum*. This kinship is emphasized syntactically as Tiberius is allotted the poem's

---

[5]*C*. 3.4.51–52 and 76. There are also other parallels between the two poems.

[6]For *deicio* in the sense of "un-horse," see Vir. *Aen.* 11.642 and 665, 12.509; and Livy 2.17.3. The repeated *c* sounds in line 13 make it a sonic example of the "sharpness" it is detailing in the life of Drusus. Cf. Quintilian 1.11.4–5, on letters like *c* and *t* which should be pronounced with great bite to them (*acriores*) but are too often softened to *g* and *d*.

[7]Curiously, according to *TLL s.v. gravis* (2298.58), line 14 offers the first example of the phrase *grave proelium* after its initial appearance in a fragment of Q. Claudius Quadrigarius (*HRR* fr. 51 Peter), and its only occurrence in poetry. Is the phrase *grave proelium conmisit* meant to have a touch of the prose documentary about it? *Habitabilis* (5, and see further below) is also used before Horace only in Cicero.

other powerful prolepsis, running from *spectandus* to *ruinis*. Not only is the second more expansive than the first, it encloses and in a sense supersedes it as well, because *in certamine Martio* marks the realization of what *quid Marte posses* implies. Tiberius, through the poet's language and grammar, attracts and manifests the emperor's authority even more dramatically than does his younger brother.

The speaker also embellishes Tiberius' doings with an elaboration of the horse metaphor hinted at earlier. This can best be illustrated by a Virgilian parallel. Early in book 6 of the *Aeneid* the titular hero meets the Sibyl who is to foretell his future. She is the mouthpiece of Apollo, but in order for her to voice his sayings she must first be tamed, her equine fervor reined in by his demanding order:[8]

> At Phoebi nondum patiens immanis in antro
> bacchatur vates, magnum si pectore possit
> excussisse deum; tanto magis ille fatigat
> os rabidum, fera corda domans, fingitque premendo.

But the priestess, not yet tolerating Apollo's sway, storms dreadfully in her cave, if she might shake out the grand god from her breast; so much the more does he tire her raving lips, taming her wild heart, and fashions her by tightening.

Horace may be listening to these lines. *Immanis* anticipates Horace's *immanis Raetos* (15), while *pectore, fatigat,* and *domans* look to *pectora, fatigaret,* and *indomitas* which, as in Virgil, follow contiguously.[9] The barbarians apparently play the Sibyl to Tiberius' Apollo. Just as the god of prophecy must bridle his vatic seer, constraining her to pattern his ideas through her words, so Tiberius must "break" his Alpine tribes, wearing down their opposition to Roman imperatives.

He is nearly a force of nature opposed to another natural power, the south wind "driving" waves it has yet to tame. The suggestion, through simile, that each of the opponents is elemental and therefore from one viewpoint parallel, is carried over into the reality that the simile ornaments. Tiberius' enemy is particularized as *hostium turmas,* throngs of cavalry, but he himself is also on horseback, harnessing

[8]*Aen.* 6.77–80. The metaphor is continued at 100ff.
[9]Virgil uses *fatigo* for horse riding also at *Aen.* 1.316 and 11.714.

animal energy for his own purposes, but likewise sharing in that energy itself.

This two-sided look at Rome's users of its might, where negative reappraisal lies just beneath the surface eulogy, causing a friction that enriches the poetry considerably, has a Virgilian ring to it. If we look specifically at Virgil's symbolism of the horse we find, out of many examples, horse-winds that must be caged for the emblem of piety to continue on his way,[10] a Carthaginian queen whose mission it is to "rein in" proud peoples through justice,[11] or an omen of four white horses which means war, if untamed, the possibility of peace, if they suffer the yoke.[12] Horace, learning from his friend, offers us in Tiberius as Roman horseman a double-edged figure, human civilizer at first sight, but also participant in animalistic wildness as he accomplishes his mission. The poet has prepared us for this tonal metamorphosis by already conjoining wind simile with horse riding in the fourth ode, to describe Hannibal and the relief that came to Italy

> dirus per urbis Afer ut Italas
> ceu flamma per taedas vel Eurus
> per Siculas equitavit undas.

since the fell African galloped through the cities of Italy like fire through pitch-pines or East wind through Sicilian waves.

Equitavit, of course, goes literally with Hannibal, racing through the peninsula, but its placement also lends a metaphorical touch to his riding, like the East wind through Sicilian surge.

This ambiguous glance at the figure of Tiberius helps explain the speaker's preceding outburst of sympathy for the peoples whose hearts are devoted to a free death, who are willing, in other words, to offer their lives for their freedom. Against the Romans they practice the very Roman custom of *devotio*, vowing their lives to the gods to guarantee success in battle and the liberty it might ensure.[13] In satisfaction of our expectations of panegyric, then, Tiberius is presented as the civilizer of the barbarian, organizing Roman might to demolish

[10]*Aen.* 1.52–63, *passim.*
[11]*Aen.* 1.523. Cf. 12.568.
[12]*Aen.* 3.537–43.
[13]The antiquity of the Roman tradition of *devotio* is traced by Latte (125–26).

its opponents' massive brutality. Yet Horace offers us a deeper level of meaning which reverses such presumptions, showing the barbarians adopting Roman customary procedure and the Romans assimilating a physicality that propaganda would more readily associate with its enemies. Paradoxically, to civilize barbarians is also to destroy the urge for and possibility of *libertas,* which in turn is to undermine one of the bases of civilization.

The same ambiguity pervades a second, more elaborate simile that occupies the center of the poem and serves as transition back to Augustus. Here, too, we are not disappointed in what we await generically. Tiberius, East wind (*Auster*) in the preceding stanza, is now become water, the element in which the barbarians previously shared. He resembles the Aufidus, in the course of its irresistible rampaging. This new force of nature, with its devastating onrush, carries all before it in ruin, even armored battle lines, reaping the first and the last of the enemy without any reciprocal harm.[14]

But the very hyperbole of this omnipotent conduct forces us to review with a more quizzical eye the preceding lines. The association of rivers with bulls is long-standing in ancient thought, but the effect of the word *tauriformis,* coined by Horace and used only here, is to associate Tiberius not only with river but with animal as well.[15] The innate savagery of each is translated into rage. And once again the poet's wordplay allows his assumed meaning to be easily twisted into its more suggestive opposite. In the panegyric's "plot line" it is ranks of barbarians which Tiberius mows down. In the simile that reinterprets and revises history, cultivated fields (*cultis agris*) furnish proof of civilization's effectiveness. These fields are the ironic counterpart of the barbarian hordes, while, with equal irony, Rome the supposed civilizer is represented by the destroying stream that vents its natural anger against man's attempts at order.

---

[14]Servius twice refers to lines 27–28 from *horridamque* to *agris,* at *geo.* 3.153 and *Aen.* 4.171 (where he replaces *horridamque* with *et horridam*). In each instance he glosses *meditatur* with *exercet,* a reading that would bring it into close conjunction with Horace's use of the word at line 21. For *exerceo* and horse riding, see *Aen.* 7.782 (and cf. *exercentur* at 7.163).

[15]Porphyrion sees the connection between bulls and rivers based on the "forward rushing and roarings" (*impetus et fremitus*) of the latter. The two are linked as early as Homer (*Il.* 21.237) where the Scamander roars like a bull. For further details see *RE* 12.2780–82 *s.v. Flussgötter.*

Once again Horace's bows to his poetic past may help clarify his intent. The focal contrast between *cultis* and *barbarorum* Horace would have seen in Virgil's first *eclogue* where a dispossessed shepherd-farmer, Meliboeus, exclaims in sorrow to the lands from which exile is forcing him:[16]

> en umquam patrios longo post tempore finis
> pauperis et tuguri congestum caespite culmen,
> post aliquot, mea regna, videns mirabor aristas?
> impius haec tam culta novalia miles habebit,
> barbarus has segetes?

Lo, will I ever after a long time marvel at my paternal lands and the roof of my lowly hut, piled high with sod, looking hereafter at those few ears of corn, my kingdom? Will a blasphemous soldier possess these fields I have nurtured, a barbarian, these crops?

Virgil encloses within three adjacent lines *regna, culta,* and *barbarus,* words that Horace spreads over four (*regna, cultis, barbarorum*), but the influence of the earlier master is strongly felt. In his bitterness Meliboeus aligns himself with culture in the form of his kingdom of cherished ploughlands, and imputes impiety and incivility to the Roman soldier who is annexing his property. Some of the same irony spills over into Aufidus-Claudius, manifestly obliterating his Gallic adversaries but in the act of war evidencing in fact a deeper, more instinctive primitivism that bears some kinship with his opponents' presumed feelings.

Irony is also a salient characteristic of Horace's other major influence on these lines, the sixty-fourth poem of Catullus. If Virgil furnishes the image of fields destroyed by deluge, Catullus helps make the transfer from fields to the more specific grain they produce, as the metaphorical comparison narrows from landscape to the people it nourishes. The *epithalamium* for Peleus and Thetis, sung by the Fates toward the end of Catullus' great epyllion, is, on the surface at least, a song of praise to the married couple and to the quality of their union. But the central part of the song is devoted to the *virtutes* (348), the manly instincts of their child Achilles, which, for all the immediate

---

[16]*Ecl.* 1.67–71.

glory they generate, contrast carefully with the domestic *concordia* that frames their accounting. Even in the detailing of his exploits Catullus allows irony. So great is Achilles' heroism that, even after his death, he can demand the sacrifice of Polyxena on the heaped-up barrow of his tomb. The image is anticipated in the piles of slaughtered dead with which in life, thanks to his *magnis virtutibus* (357), Achilles had blocked the course of the Scamander, and, still earlier, in his depiction as grim reaper of a harvest of enemies. It is this startling vision that Horace has in mind:[17]

> namque velut densas praecerpens messor aristas
> sole sub ardenti flaventia demetit arva,
> Troiugenum infesto prosternet corpora ferro.

For just as a reaper, grasping the thick grain, mows down the yellowing fields under a burning sun, so he will lay low bodies of Trojan born with his grim sword.

The heroism of Tiberius, as latter-day Achilles, is magnificent for the sheer numbers he annihilates. But since they are visualized in relation to him as grain to mower, scarcely an equitable contest, his humanity is called in question at the same moment as his glory is extolled.

Hence the double thrust of literary heritage, be it in the words of Virgil's exiled farmer looking at Rome's expropriating soldiery and the civil discord that motivates their actions, or in the utterance Catullus gives to the Fates, lauding the idealism of a wedding that produced a symbol of war's realistic violence, magnifies a negative tone running through the poem's core stanzas. At the least we can see this tone as commentary on the violence necessary for Roman subjugation of the unruly elements in its world, an act of placation which brings culture's learning and law in its wake. Interpreted more severely Horace might be said to suggest a certain unthinking inhumanity in Rome's own militaristic behavior which, for the very scope of the decimation it causes, proclaims its own form of barbarism.

Nevertheless, if we leave aside the bias his literary past brings to

---

[17]Cat. 64.353–55. *Meto* is also used for Aeneas (*Aen.* 10.513) on the rampage after the killing of Pallas. The parallel with Catullus is noted by Quinn (*Horace: Odes*), in his comment on lines 25–34.

the poem, we would be at least partly justified in viewing Horace's hyperbole as a normal adjunct to encomium. But the interpretative difficulty raises questions of tact on the author's side and of responsibility on the emperor's, which are inseparable. The reader, educated in literary tradition, might sense a deeper prejudice on the speaker's part, imposed by his creator. The emperor, one hazards, would have perceived a poetic act of more immediate diplomacy. Just as the Drusus ode quickly turns from the fledgling hero to Augustus' success as educator, so the present look at the elder Claudian, though duly elaborating Tiberius' feats at arms, is in fact addressed to his stepfather. The emperor is, in three final metonymies, an essential ingredient in his stepson's activities. The soldiery and good auspices earlier divided between Drusus and Tiberius are rounded out in the supplies, counsel, and, in place of climax, gods lavished on the second. In so acting the emperor is both fully and partially responsible for the Gallic campaigning—fully, because the positive outcome would have been impossible without his good offices, partially because no physical activity and certainly no brutality are imputed to him. Tiberius, who performed the deeds, receives no direct praise. The emperor, who did nothing, is the subject of eulogy.

Horace structures his poem so as to ease us away from the deepening accusation of its central history. He follows, in fact, the pattern of both Catullus and Virgil, the first of whom, as we have seen, frames the wildness of Achilles with the theme of marital bliss, while the pastoral poet begins and ends his extraordinary first *eclogue* with two sketches of the idyll preserved for the happy shepherd Tityrus and lost by Meliboeus. Renewed use of metonymy returns us from the actual exploitation of power to its source, to Augustus, to Rome and its continuities.

The poem's final metonymy, *peractis imperiis* (39–40), the final sharing of power now carried through to completion, stems from Fortune's assignment of praise and grace strictly to Augustus. The *laudatio* that belongs to the victor and the *decus* attached to all the actors deserving of glory in its various manifestations throughout these poems are here a fitting accompaniment for the *honores* announced as due Augustus at the poem's start. But these stanzas also look to the poem's beginning for their common emphasis on time, and especially its anniversaries. If book 4 documents a grand renewal based on the return of Augustus, poem 14 particularizes that renewal by dwelling on repetitions in Augustus' own life. Exactly fifteen years have passed between the surrender of Alexandria to Octavian and Tiberius' final vanquishing of the Rhaeti. Such a happenstance suggests a systematic recurrence, the re-giving (*reddidit*) of good fortune in political affairs that will benefit Rome because it happens to Augustus. To inscribe not one but two dates on Rome's calendar of remembrance is to imagine continuing circularity, not linearity, moments of refreshment, not peterings out, for Rome's bastion of power and for Rome itself. In Augustus' conclusions lies Rome's constant incipience.

Even at this moment in the poem there is a gentle reminder that war has its costs as well as its gains, that winning by definition means also loss, perhaps someone else's, perhaps even one's own. The royal palace at Alexandria opened without resistance to Octavian on August 1, 30 B.C., because on that same day first Antony and then Cleopatra had committed suicide. Virgil, as so often, schools us in the deeper implications. The only previous occurrence in Latin of the phrase *vacua aula* is in the fourth *georgic* where Virgil is teaching methods for dealing with civil warring in a beehive. His remedy smacks of allegory, abetted not least by the word *aula* itself, anomalous for a hive, proper for a handsome human dwelling:[18]

> Verum ubi ductores acie revocaveris ambo,
> deterior qui visus, eum, ne prodigus obsit,
> dede neci; melior vacua sine regnet in aula.

But when you have called back both leaders from the battle-line, the one who seems the lesser, him surrender to death lest his prodigality be a hindrance; let the better reign in the empty hall.

If you are an apiarist the chief way to put an end to the internecine strife of your charges is, according to Virgil, to kill the lesser king and let the better leader reign without competition. But what if the bees stand for mankind and there is no suitable "keeper" to calm our squabbles? Our civil strife, it seems, ends either in murder or self-slaughter. That Virgil, in his allegory, was thinking of the strife between Octavian and Antony is made plausible by the reference, at

[18]*Geo.* 4.88–90. Cf. also *Aen.* 2.528.

the end of the same book, in the last lines of the *Georgics*, to Octavian in Asia "thundering at the deep Euphrates," after the settlement of Alexandria.[19] The aftermath of civil war for bees is one thing, for man another, but in both instances lives are lost. In the case of Octavian and Rome, Antony and Cleopatra had to die for war to end. *Vacua aula* reminds us that they did.

But, even accepting the allusion to civil war, it is possible, indeed essential, to read these lines in a positive light. The campaign at Alexandria terminated Roman civil war. Fifteen years later to the day Tiberius successfully completed his engagement against the Rhaeti. It was not until two years later that Augustus himself returned to Rome, after winning victory over the Sygambri. But, as we learn in ode 15, that triumph included a double peace, first over internal enemies (for the defeat of Antony, though in Egypt, was a civil

---

[19]The facts are recounted in C. D. 51.18. The allusion to Virgil, then, may have a double meaning in that the *Georgics* were finished and presumably published in the same year, 30 B.C.

This is Horace's only mention of Alexandria, but the implicit allusion to Alexander the Great, with whom Augustus carefully linked himself, would not be out of place in panegyric. For the connection see Blumenthal (122) and Kienast (*passim*), among others, and for Virgil's use of Alexander panegyrics in formulating his encomium of Augustus at *Aen.* 6.791–805 see Norden, *passim.*

In a passage in *epi.* 2.1 of importance to ode 14, lines 229–59, Horace almost equates Augustus with Alexander. Virgil and Varius would therefore be high-class versions of Choerilus of Iasus, the poetaster who sang the "splendid deeds" of Alexander. Horace is incapable of any such thing for Augustus, he protests, who is worthy only of what his more competent friends have produced. What he will not create for Augustus is, as virtually all commentators note, remarkably similar, down to the words themselves, to what in fact he does accomplish in odes 14 and 15, as he tells (252–56) of

> . . . arces
> montibus inpositas et barbara regna tuisque
> auspiciis totum confecta duella per orbem
> claustraque custodem pacis cohibentia Ianum
> et formidatam Parthis te principe Romam, . . .

citadels placed on mountains and barbarian kingdoms and wars concluded throughout the world under your auspices, and bars closing in Janus, warden of peace, and Rome dreaded by the Parthi, with you as *princeps.*

He is, after all, and with his usual understatement, in the tradition of the Alexander panegyrists, and Augustus is his worthy target.

matter, whatever later propaganda insisted), then over external. The implication is that the new Augustan cycle is to be one of peace sufficiently thoroughgoing, as a result of the enduring *virtutes* of its sponsor, to last, like his deeds and their poetic recounting, *in aevum*— for as long as memory stalls time's advance.

Certainly the end of the poem, like the historical progress of Rome, proposes enduring peace after the shifts of war. We turn from a lyric accounting of epic deeds to the more unfettered eulogy of the lyric as hymn. In its concluding stanzas Horace's panegyric most closely follows the usual pattern that leads from martial deeds to the conqueror as bringer of peace to the enumeration of defeated enemies. Even here, however, he makes an important alteration to literary tradition for the many aspects of the defeated world are observed to be not downtrodden and suppliant but awestruck and reverent.[20] Lexically as well as generically there are novelties in these final stanzas. Not only does Horace mention four proper names unused by him elsewhere (Gallia, Hister, Indus, and Tigris), he also invents two words, one of which (*beluosus*) never occurs again in classical Latin. The other, *domabilis*, will help us further fuse the concluding litany with the poem as a whole.

First a word on the variety of the catalog itself. We begin, in lines 41–42, with individual tribesmen, Cantaber in the west of the empire, Persian and Indian in the east, and Scythian standing for the northeast.[21] The subsequent stanza deals with rivers whose geo-

[20]See Doblhofer (104). The facts of the specific occasion, whereby the Sygambri surrendered to Augustus without his recourse to arms, are recounted by C. D. at 54.20–21.

[21]The *profugus Scythes* makes an earlier appearance of interest to students of ode 14. At *c.* 1.35.9 *profugi Scythae* are among those peoples, barbarian or Latinized, who have proper dread of *Fortuna* (the poem's cast of characters, including Caesar, overlaps frequently with that of ode 14), and who hymn her accordingly (*te Dacus asper, te profugi Scythae* . . .). *Fortuna*, as we have seen, appears in the preceding stanza of ode 14, a powerful figure in plotting the repetitions of the Augustan principate; but the hymn is now addressed to the emperor himself. By the comparison he could be said to have taken over the role of *Fortuna,* just as he does that of Faunus in ode 5, if we look back to *c.* 1.17. It is Augustus, in the guise of good fortune, who brings to an end both the civil wars and the potential foreign wars to which, in *c.* 1.35, *Fortuna* subjects the world.

On the altar of *Fortuna Redux* and Augustus, see n. 23 to ode 4. Augustus both was and is "Fortune returned," and his *virtutes* still remain worthy of a people's, and a poet's, honors.

graphical distributions are, if anything, even more diverse, involving all the points of the compass, south (Nilus), northeast (Hister), east (Tigris), and northwest (Oceanus bordering Britain). The last, climactic stanza is more focused, looking only to Spain and Gaul, and allotting the most prominent displays of emotion to Rome's enemies. The reason is Augustus himself. Aside from a journey to the east where, in the spring of 20 B.C., he received back from the Parthians the standards of Crassus, the emperor's only post-Actian sallies from Rome before Horace published book 4 were against the Cantabri in northern Spain, in the mid 20s, and from 16 B.C. to 13 B.C., into Gallia Transalpina. On hearing of his advent the Sygambri retired beyond the Rhine, made peace, and gave hostages. As in his earlier dealings with Parthia there was no need for the emperor to resort to arms.

The compliment to Augustus, then, is many-sided. In this grand litany, where *te* is reiterated seven times, he serves as divine center for the world's diversity.[22] Individual tribesmen, synecdoches for their entire clans, are succeeded by rivers who stand for the strength and fertility of the lands through which they pass (a reminder, perhaps, of the Aufidus and the undefeatable Tiberian energy it symbolizes). But the universality of the submission both offer, with individual names and special identities always tugged back to the godlike addressee, is particularized in those areas whose capitulation, with the relenting of passions it implies, would have given the emperor most personal pride. It is with them that the poem ends.

In the course of the final stanzas the poet also allots to Augustus and his Rome an image we have seen earlier associated both with the Nerones and with the tribes they subdue, namely that of horses and their taming. We find it first attached to the premier item listed, the Cantaber who was not "tamable" before Augustus (the uniqueness of the word *domabilis* complements the uniqueness of the exploit). We

---

[22]The sound *te* rings throughout the passage, most pronouncedly in the word *tutela,* the only noun in the last three stanzas which stands for Augustus.

The submission of variety to singularity in political affairs is complemented by lexical choice. Of the two coinages in these last stanzas, one, at least, *beluosus,* is an adaptation from Homer (μεγακητής). It is the last in a row that includes *tauriformis* and the Ennian *ferrata.* Just as there is no need, as the poem draws to a close, for further Claudian deeds of valor, so too epic language is absorbed into the language of prayer.

find it almost immediately again in *domina Roma,* mistress Rome, tamer of tribes, reiner in of the wild. There is one last instance. Though the ocean may roar around the Britanni, it becomes quiet, like Gallia and Hiberia, in order to heed (*audit*) Augustus' rule. But the verb *audio* has also one important association with horses in earlier Latin literature. At the end of the first book of his *Georgics* Virgil portrays a world gone mad, with east and west, the Euphrates and Germany, making war and unholy Mars raging in their midst. His analogy for this sad turn of events, with which he concludes the book, is a chariot race in which "the driver, tightening the bridle in vain, is borne along by his horses nor does the chariot listen to the reins:"[23]

> . . . frustra retinacula tendens
> fertur equis auriga neque audit currus habenas.

The end of the *Georgics* shows the situation reversed with Octavian, after Actium, now thundering against the Euphrates, as we previously noted. The fifteen-year leap to the present moment finds not just Rome but the earth at large giving obedient ear to Augustus, the bringer of peace. If there is one final reminder in the ultimate stanza that the tribes of Gaul have no fear of death as they fight for their lives against Rome, nevertheless the last line puts the stress where it always has been, on the majesty of Rome going about her work of pacification and education.[24]

Allusion to the Sygambri looks back to their only other mention by Horace, at line 36 of the second ode where Augustus is imagined in triumph, leading those fierce tribesmen up the Capitoline during his festive procession. In the course of Horace's book the future has become the present, the Sygambri have been conquered, Augustus has been lured home by the poet's words, and Roman epic militarism

---

[23]*Geo.* 1.513–14. Line 514 offers an example of *figura etymologica* in the near juxtaposition of *auriga* and *audit.* Paulus-Festus (8L), *s.v. aureax,* connects *auriga* (his gloss for *aureax*) with the ears (*aures*) of the horse to which reins were attached.

[24]Syndikus (419) is quite correct when he speaks of how, in the final stanza, "der bisher vorwiegend kriegerische Charakter der Ode gemildert wird." I would argue only that this amelioration begins with the initiation of the *tu*-formula, at line 33.

has been tamed to Horace's lyric hymn. This metamorphosis can also be illustrated by looking at the way Horace alludes to Propertian elegy, for it, too, is a unifying factor in Horace's structuring. In analyzing the second ode we noted, along with the pervasive influence of Pindar, that Horace had the situation of the fourth elegy of Propertius' third book in mind as he wrote. Each deals with a speaker contemplating the prospect of an Augustan triumphal procession and verbalizing his response to its implications. Though Propertius' tone is more ironic and detached, nevertheless both authors espouse a "smaller" genre, be it elegy or lyric, to offer less than total allegiance to Augustan epic pretension.

As he rounds off his book, Horace is thinking in his next-to-last poem of the influence which he had acknowledged in his second. Among other verbal links between ode 14 and Propertius 3.4, we should note that the elegist uses the phrase *in aevum* without a qualifier for the first time in Latin, a usage Horace here borrows.[25] Each poet mentions the Tigris River only here in his poetry, and the word *titulus,* prominent in Horace's opening stanza, occurs in Propertius' first three books only in poem 4.[26] Equine imagery is basic to Horace's central stanzas and Propertius mentions horses three times within a twenty-two-line poem.[27] Finally, where Propertius begins his elegy with *arma,* contemplated by Caesar in his putative campaign against the Parthi—"*Arma deus Caesar dites meditatur ad Indos . . .*" (Caesar, the god, is pondering arms against the rich Indi . . .)— Horace ends *conpositis armis,* with arms "composed," now that the north as well as the east have succumbed to the dominion of Rome.

But Horace also casts a glimpse at Propertius' subsequent elegy, companion piece to the fourth and meant to be read closely with it. Horace and his contemporary, for instance, share the striking phrase *Pleiadum chorus,* which Propertius here invents (Horace mentions the Pleiades only in ode 14).[28] But it is Propertius' opening line that most

[25]Prop. 3.4.19; ode 14.3.
[26]Prop. 3.4.4, ode 14.46 (Tigris); Prop. 3.4.16, ode 14.4 (*titulus*).
[27]Prop. 3.4.8, 14 and 17.
[28]Ode 14.21 and Prop. 3.5.36. It is a matter of curiosity that Virgil seems to invent the phrase *scindit nubes* at *Aen.* 1.587. If so, lines 21–22 offer a microcosmic example of two of the major influences on Horace as he wrote: Propertius' third book of elegies and the *Aeneid.*

commands our attention: *"Pacis Amor deus est, pacem veneramur amantes . . ."* (Love is a god of peace, we lovers worship peace . . .). Both sentiment and verbal choice look complementarily to the opening line of the preceding elegy. Each poem molds dissimilar material for parallel intellectual purposes. If the first demeans Augustan militarism on the narrative level (the speaker, we remember, watches the procession while leaning on the lap of his girl), the second does so through considerations of genre. Make love, honor war from a distance, becomes write physiology, not epic, as the speaker disavows thoughts of raising his literary sights toward Augustan themes, when amatory material is no longer tractable, in favor of the impersonal and the didactic.

But for the student of Horace it is *veneramur* that stands out. Horace has taken words from each of Propertius' initial lines—the first noun from one, the key verb from the other—and claimed them for his final verse. But there are appropriate changes as we move from beginnings to end, from elegist writing probably in 22 B.C., to lyricist publishing in 13 B.C. Arms, disapproved of by the elegist for their ongoing use, can now be seen in last place, their utility blessedly past, and veneration, which lovers bestow on peace, is now the final due of Augustus for pacifying Rome's foreign enemies and making them her metaphorical lovers.

Yet the word *veneror* has a more restricted sense in these contexts. The most recent dictionary gives the original meaning of *venus as perhaps "propitiatory magic."[29] In Propertius, lovers verbalize this concept by offering obeisance to peace. Yet the elegist may here also be tingeing his expression with irony. In the penultimate couplet of the preceding poem, in the same line where he coins the phrase *in aevum*, Propertius has the following prayer: *"ipsa tuam serva prolem, Venus"* ("Venus, keep safe your offspring").[30] The goddess of love is to guard her progeny, Augustus, as he goes about his eastern cam-

---

[29]See *OLD s.v. veneror*. The speaker may be cleverly hinting that Venus is preparing to take over the Roman world and become his final subject. With the exception of mention of the *campus Martius* in ode 1, ode 14 contains the only references to Mars in book 4 (ll. 9, 17). He is not named in the final poem. The contiguity of *veneratur* and *Veneris* at *c. s.* 49–50 proves Horace was aware of the etymological connection.

[30]Prop. 3.4.19.

paigning. Venus herself, however, Propertius seems to assert, lies more essentially in *veneramur,* in the ritual offering we lovers make to a power that segregates us from life's confusions.

But the end of ode 14 is different. In a grander, public act of eroticism, the Sygambri are made by Horace to propitiate Augustus. The gesture is based on a concept active in his own much publicized descent from the goddess of love which leads him to enact universal dramas of conciliation and affection. By the concluding line of the poem that follows, Horace's last lyric utterance, the abstraction inherent in etymology has suffered metamorphosis into a personification that is at once divine, mythic, and historical. In the very same place in the poem and in the line *venus becomes Venus:

> . . . et almae
> progeniem Veneris canemus.

we will sing fostering Venus' progeny.

The reverence granted Augustus by the world becomes the goddess herself, presiding over Rome's destiny from Aeneas to Augustus, and bringing it to a larger peace that can at the last evoke the lyricist's unstinted praise.

We can now determine more precisely the relationship of ode 14 to its predecessor, the first of the final triad, and to the other odes that come second in their respective triads, namely, 2, 5, 8, and 11. The thirteenth poem, we remember, shows the speaker in a private setting, able to bring his vows to fruition and implement the process of aging in the self-deceiving Lyce. He effects his sorcery not only by affixing to her fitting symbols of senectitude but also by showing us a glimpse of her in the calendar of his own erotic life and in the generalized *fasti* into which she now fits. Poem 14 also deals with calendrical arrangements, but in it the poet dons his public mask in order to bring the ever mindful Augustus back to Rome and set the deeds of his stepsons, and the vision of a world at peace as a result of his heroism, into the immortal ledger of poetry.

But like the speaker's culminative "biographical" survey in the preceding poem which extends back to the initial ode, the *revocatio* of Augustus is also accomplished over poetic time. To document this we must turn back briefly to ode 2, where it begins.[31] Augustus' triumphal moment, with his enemies dragged behind him, would seem better than if the times were to return (*redeant*) to their initial golden perfection. The days will be happy, the city festive, when his long-craved return (*inpetrato reditu*) has taken place. The speaker will sing of the beautiful, glorious sun on the occasion when Caesar is accepted back (*recepto Caesare*).[32] The poetic votive offering, which the modest speaker is prepared to sacrifice if his prayers for Augustus' restoration are granted, is only a calf. The better equipped singer of this magnificence is Iullus, Pindar *redivivus*, vower of twenty cattle, soaring Theban swan, we assume, to Horace's humble Matine bee.

The self-irony evaporates over the course of the book. The presence of Pindar is strongly felt, of course, in ode 4, especially in the grandiloquent opening similes and in the transition into the center of the poem by which an appeal to reticence deflects the poem's progress from further contemplation of Drusus' heroizing. After this the poem turns to Augustus as educator and to Hannibal's monologue, which is as much lament as *laudatio*. Horace's grandest Pindarizing is in ode 14.[33] The raging stream, that in ode 2 is Pindar but not Horace, the speaker now incorporates as subject of his own verses in the form of the Aufidus. It tears threateningly along like Pindar, rolling down his new words in bold dithyrambs. Pindar's rhythmic freedom (*numeris . . . lege solutis*) has its parallel in the barbarians, hitherto shareless in Latin law (*legis expertes Latinae*), whom Tiberius-Aufidus must eject from their Alpine citadels.

Prosody also plays a part in forming this expansive poetic accomplishment. In the act of writing Horace is also displaying a nearly Pindaric poetic bravura. If we look to lexical choice, in ode 14 he uses nineteen words for the only time in his career. Of these, four (*beluosus, domabilis, inplacidum, tauriformis*) are coinages, two others (*arrogo, ferratus*) are given new meanings for the first time, and still another

---

[31]Porter ("The Recurrent Motifs," 226, n. 74) considers the motif of return to be minor, but lists many of its occurrences.

[32]Ode 2, 39, 43, and 47.

[33]Syndikus (414 and n. 8) distinguishes the Pindarizing of odes 4 and 14 on the basis of "Einzelformungen" (4) and "Sprachductus" (14). (See also 319–20 for Pindaric elements in ode 4.) I would expand his point only to say that both concepts are operative in both poems.

(*aeterno*) is used but once elsewhere in classical Latin.[34] If we turn to matters of grammar and meter, the expansive prolepses at lines 7–9 and 17–19, as we noted, have no precedent elsewhere in Horace, and line 17 itself is one of two in all of Horace's alcaics which lacks a caesura.[35]

To embrace Pindar stylistically is to accept Augustus politically. The passage of poetic time over the course of book 4 may fulfill the poet's vows—his words perform their magic—but that passage also transforms the ironic speaker, joining only in the throng's response, preparing only a single calf as sacrifice, into public eulogizer of Augustan accomplishments. Not that his words lack their Virgilian sting, for the speaker observes the shortcomings as well as the glories inherent in omnipotence. But, in a singular form of lyric courage, the speaker now directs his irony not at himself but at the deeds themselves which he lists. Our final impression is of Horace's open, honest espousal of the *pax Augusti*. The sun does not simply dawn on a happy day but surveys (*illustrat*) the whole of the habitable world. And geographic expanse easily shades into extent of time as the moment of celebration, anticipated in ode 2, becomes a very particular day that, by looking back three *lustra* into Augustus' past, announces a form of repetition as vital for Rome's futurity as the return of Augustus' tutelary presence.

It is the excited mood of anticipation of that return which makes ode 5 such a powerful link in this chain of inevitability. The fathers and the fatherland whose care, in ode 14, will properly eternalize Augustus, are here still awaiting his homecoming. Like a mother making vows for her absent son, the state yearns for the suns and bright spring days that his features will beam on Rome and that figure in the universal stability Rome is seen to abet in ode 14. There is morality at home and peace abroad. It is no accident that two of the

---

[34]*Arrogo* is also used in the sense of "assign" or "attribute" at *epi* 2.1.35 and *A P.* 122. Varro (in Nonius, 75M) makes the only other recorded use of *aeterno,* which, together with *aevum,* Smereka (68–69) considers an archaism. *Ferratos* (30) appears in Horace at *sat.* 1.4.61 where he is in fact quoting Ennius. In the *Annales* the word means "bound or covered with iron." According to *OLD s.v.* 2, *ferratus* has the sense of "armored" here for the first time in Latin. *Habitabilis* (5) occurs before Horace only in Cicero at *T. D.* 1.45 and 68 (where it is connected with *orae*).

[35]The other example is *c.* 1.37.14.

four foreign locales alluded to in its seventh stanza, Scythia and Hiberia, are mentioned again toward the end of ode 14 (and the others, Parthia and Germania, are only renamed through synecdoche as Medus and Sygambri). Although they are rhetorical, that stanza is phrased as a series of questions: Who need fear the Parthian? Who need have a care for war emanating from wild Hiberia? By the conclusion of 14, interrogation is replaced by declarative statement, tentative settlement by assured stability.

There is another parallel between the conclusions of the two poems which accentuates another major difference. Each poem ends in celebration that takes the explicit form of a hymn, with the second-person pronoun appropriately reiterated in each case. What distinguishes ode 14 is the complete absence of a first-person narrator in the telling. In the second ode the speaker remains attached to a larger "we," shouting "*io triumphe*" and burning incense, slipping into the singular "I" prominently only at the end as he attends to his oblation. In the fifth he is part of a "we" who utter once, and yet again, with words repeating the cycle of days, a prayer for an extended celebration in Caesar's honor. The speaker is clearly placed in each instance, either in the Roman crowd watching the triumphal procession pass or in the country, sharing with the viticulturist a common delight in wine from vineyards whose ordering is reassured by the Augustan peace. The narrator of ode 2 hesitates to give himself fully to a Pindaric encomium of Augustus. The speaker of the fifth, in the final analysis, contemplates the effect of Augustanism on a georgic idyll where private feasts, not public receptions, are in order. The poetic gesture is still limited. No framing ego with thoughts and postures of its own intervenes in ode 14. Through this semblance of self-effacement, the poet allows the deeds of Augustus and his surrogates to speak for themselves and, as it were, fully yields himself to his subject.

But a glance back at the third in this series, ode 8, around which the book pivots, reminds us, as it might have reminded Augustus, that, whatever ruse he adopts to feign its disappearance, the poet's crafting intelligence is the source of endurance for his subjects, even when no "I" seems directly involved. Augustus is not mentioned in either poem 8 or poem 11, but both remain concerned with the power of poetry and with the rituals by which poets celebrate and mold their world. Though ode 8 omits the emperor, it still proves what the poet could do for him. We read, at the opening of ode 14, of the *munera* that the fathers and citizenry of Rome are pondering for Augustus. But the poem itself is a *munus,* as ode 8 twice over represents to us. The speaker's poetic "gifts" (*munerum*) surpass Greek statuary, and he knows full well how to place a value on such a reward (*pretium dicere muneri*), a witty way of saying that his work is a type of artifact, only impalpable and therefore more prone to immortality, and to immortalize, than the canvasses and statues of Parrhasius and Scopas.

But when the poem takes a Roman turn, it embraces a particularity that looks more immediately to ode 14. Greek artists may attempt to eternalize through statuary. Romans, with greater practicality though less imagination, may seek to preserve the memory of their great through inscriptions:

> . . . incisa notis marmora publicis
> per quae spiritus et vita redit bonis
> post mortem ducibus, . . .

marbles carved with entries plain to all, through which breath and life return to noble leaders after their demise, . . .

It is to these, in their special guises as *tituli* and *memores fastus,* notations under statues and calendrical citations, that the opening of ode 14, we remember, refers. But ode 8 states what 14 adumbrates only indirectly—that the poet's muse is a stronger guarantor of the continuing return of life after death than any tangible monument, even one devoted to the inscribed word. Yet there is one essential difference. Ennius' writings preserve forever the mortal Scipio, and other authors have salvaged for eternity the memory of Romulus, Aeacus, Hercules, and the Dioscuri. The poetic *munus* that Horace's odes bestow on Augustus, a *munus* that incorporates and enhances other visible *munera,* is divinization in his lifetime. In ode 5 he is the new Romulus, having the same relation to Rome as Castor and Hercules do to mindful Greece. But it is the fourteenth ode that, in positing the renewed presence of Augustus, perpetuates Rome's own renewals. Bacchus, in the last line of ode 8, may, from his new divine estate, bring vows to happy completion: "*Liber vota bonos ducit ad exitus.*" The "favorable outcomes" (*secundos exitus*) that, in ode 14, *Fortuna* gave back to Rome, as defeat of the Sygambri reinforces defeat of Antony and Cleopatra, are really Augustus' restorative enterprises given unique form by his death-defying bard. Augustus and Rome are the great beneficiaries of the power of self-renewal granted by a poet whose personality, though seemingly subsumed into the matter at hand, is in the process of creating the verbal artifact on which they depend for their resilience.

It remains to place poem 11 within this spiritual grouping. The speaker here is neither the self-confident artisan of lapidary words, who boasts the ability to monumentalize his subjects for perpetuity, nor a characterless worshiper before the courage of Augustus who enfolds, one by one, the world's diversity within the "you" whom all now hymn. He is, instead, a lover, inviting Phyllis, last of his amours, to a feast. Yet, for all the personal, private tone differentiating it from the poems that deal with Augustan heroics, the ode shares basic elements with them. Though more modest, perhaps, than anticipations of triumphs or remembrances of Alexandria, it too looks to a specific celebratory event, the birthday of Maecenas on the Ides of April. In the process it also shunts aside the pressures of temporality. However much slighter the challenge it presents, the ode's course opposes time's advance in two ways: by honoring Maecenas' nativity, which in one respect means that he is annually reborn, and by abstracting the ceremony's participants out of life's ongoing troubles into a moment of festivity, diminishing time's cares. Cyclicity wins over inexorability fleetingly at the end, as Phyllis is ordered to give back to the speaker the songs he has taught her. The brief round of poetry analogizes the round of the year it salutes.

The lyric summoning of Phyllis also, in its small way, reflects the grander homecoming of Augustus which is spread over the course of a poetry book. Even here the speaker's vatic magic is at work—animating, alluring, philosophizing, teaching—aiming to seduce, perhaps, but to memorialize as well, and in the celebration of remembrance, as in the making of love and of song, triumphing, in however limited a way, over the fugitive and the ephemeral.

[15]

ODE FIFTEEN

Phoebus volentem proelia me loqui
victas et urbis increpuit lyra,
 ne parva Tyrrhenum per aequor
  vela darem. tua, Caesar, aetas

fruges et agris rettulit uberes   5
et signa nostro restituit Iovi
 derepta Parthorum superbis
  postibus et vacuum duellis

Ianum Quirini clausit et ordinem
rectum evaganti frena licentiae   10
 iniecit emovitque culpas
  et veteres revocavit artis,

per quas Latinum nomen et Italae
crevere vires famaque et imperi
 porrecta maiestas ad ortus   15
  solis ab Hesperio cubili.

custode rerum Caesare non furor
civilis aut vis exiget otium,
 non ira, quae procudit ensis
  et miseras inimicat urbis;   20

non qui profundum Danuvium bibunt
edicta rumpent Iulia, non Getae,
   non Seres infidique Persae,
     non Tanain prope flumen orti;

nosque et profestis lucibus et sacris   25
inter iocosi munera Liberi
   cum prole matronisque nostris
     rite deos prius adprecati

virtute functos more patrum duces
Lydis remixto carmine tibiis   30
   Troiamque et Anchisen et almae
     progeniem Veneris canemus.

When I yearned to discourse of battles and cities won, Phoebus Apollo on his lyre protested against consigning my tiny sails through the
Tyrrhenian sea. Your era, Caesar, has ushered back lush harvests to the
land, and restored to our Jupiter standards torn from Parthians' haughty
doors, and firmed shut the Janus of Quirinus, void of warrings, and cast
reins on license roaming free of meet design. It has eliminated reasons
for our blame, and resummoned the ancient arts whereby the repute of
Latium, and Italian vigor, have grown, and the grandeur of imperial
rule was extended to the risings of the sun from his western rest.

    While Caesar shields our world, neither the wildness of citizenry nor
main force will exile leisure, nor will wrath, which hammers out
swords and sets sad towns to hating. Not those who drink the deep
Danube, not the Getae, not the Seres and treacherous Persae, not the
offspring of the Don's neighboring course will rend Julian mandates.
And we, on dawns whether routine or hallowed, amid the munificence
of Bacchus' joy, having first in company with our children and our
wives rendered due prayers to the gods, our melody remingled with
Lydian flutes, we will sing of heroes, as was our fathers' wont, who
have proven their courage, and of Troy, and Anchises, and fostering
Venus' progeny.

Ode 15 and Its Inheritance

Horace's final ode, his richest meditation on Augustan Rome and
the intimacy his poetry possesses with it, is structured both sequen-

tially and chiastically. Read as a continuum it divides into neat halves. The first four stanzas, with eight verbs in the perfect tense, look to past time, to what not Caesar but his age has accomplished. They take our thoughts from the end of war and the elimination of public immorality to the renewal of "ancient arts." Our eye scans from fields once again fertile, to the Capitoline, sacred center of Rome, where the restored standards of Crassus were housed prior to their final resting place in the Forum of Augustus. It leaps from there down to the shrine of Janus Quirinus, with the twin faces of its statue oriented east and west, on the north side of the Forum Romanum, and out from this center to Latium, Italy, and the bounds of the Roman empire, measured by the eastern and western precincts of the sun.

Caesar is apostrophized directly in the poem's opening stanza. In the fifth stanza, which initiates the ode's second half, the name of Rome's ruler is absorbed into an ablative absolute construction that could connote causality (since) or duration (while, so long as), or even hint at conditionality (if). Generalizations that look to the pre-sent—anger that now and always sets cities against each other, people who continually drink the Danube—are left to relative clauses while all the main verbs in the final stanzas (*exiget, rumpent, canemus*) fore-shadow future events. Cities, too, figure in both the first and fifth stanzas. In the first Apollo's chiding has arrested the speaker's desire to sing of their conquering (*victas urbes*); in the fifth, the anger that ordinarily activates warring among them will no longer expel *otium*. Whatever his propensity, the speaker will not allude in detail to events that happened in the past, and Augustus' guardianship will not allow the historical circumstances, which might inspire such songs, to recur again.

Looked at linearly, then, and in terms of temporal modulations, the poem documents an instant of poise, equally balanced by opening past and closing future. What is present and will ever remain so is the address to Augustus, which is to say the words of the poem them-selves, representation in song of a lived moment that ever looks backward in retrospect and forward in anticipation.

The repetition of *vires* and *vis* in the central, pivotal stanzas encour-ages us to view the ode chiastically as well. Like the *Aeneid,* Horace's last ode also meditates on the idea of force, used to good effect as Rome expands the majesty of her empire, but employed disastrously when coupled with madness and wrath to drive citizen against citizen in domestic strife. It is the proper exercise of *vis* (Horace adorns the ethical point with *figura etymologica*) which engenders the *virtus* of the leaders whose careers, we learn as the poem closes, will be the basis of the speaker's future *carmina*.[1]

For, if power is at the hub of the poem and of the Augustan achievement, song is at its circumference, as the singer ponders what he cannot and what he will sing. Though Augustan might is the ode's main theme, it is in fact the dynamism of poetry which frames, and therefore both monumentalizes and preserves, that magnificence. As we have come to expect from its position, ending the book's final trinity, Horace's final ode is essentially about poetry itself, its contents and its astonishing potency to immortalize by celebration. We will survey the ode's extraordinary originality from several points of view, beginning with its outer bounds: the overarching chiasmus takes us from an "I," blaming Apollo for stopping his incipient epic, to a "we" about to sing of *duces,* Troy, Anchises, and the offspring of Venus—namely, both Aeneas, Rome's founder, and its renewer, Augustus.

The tradition from which the opening *apologia* stems has a venerable history.[2] It begins with the introduction to Callimachus' *Aitia.* There the Alexandrian poet takes note of his detractors who expect of him "one continuous poem" after the model of Homer, dealing with "either kings or heroes."[3] But what remains for Callimachus essentially a declaration of style and content—he has not written epic but a poetry, he claims, far more refined—takes a more immediate turn in the Roman poets. Virgil is apparently the originator of the personalized *recusatio* at the famous opening of the sixth *eclogue* where he refuses to sing the praises of Varus which would mean "to compose sad wars" (*tristia condere bella*):[4]

---

[1]For the etymology, see Ernout-Meillet *s.v. vir.* The juxtaposition of *vis* and *virtus* for purposes of paronomasia is common in Virgil (e.g., *Aen.* 5.454–55, 7.257–58, 12.912–13).

[2]The Roman variations on this Callimachean theme are dealt with by Wimmel, *passim* (see esp. 290–91, n. 2, for detailed discussion of Propertius' influence on ode 15). Brink (532, n. 5) points out that it is Virgil, at the opening of *ecl.* 6, who politicizes and individualizes what to Callimachus remains essentially a stylistic matter.

[3]Call. *Aet.* 1.fr.1.3–5Pf. (ἢ βασιλ[η . . . ἢ . . .] . . . ἥρωας).

[4]Vir. *ecl.* 6.3–5. See above, 204–205, for the influence of *ecl.* 6 on ode 12.

cum canerem reges et proelia, Cynthius aurem
vellit et admonuit: "pastorem, Tityre, pinguis
pascere oportet ovis, deductum dicere carmen."

When I would sing of kings and battles, Apollo plucked my ear and
warned: "Tityrus, it befits a shepherd to feed a fat flock but to sing a
song fine-spun."

Kings and battles, and Varus' martial exploits, are not suitable topics
for the singer of slender pastorals. The element of topicality is added
to stylistic considerations as Virgil turns aside Varus' putative request.

The *recusatio* thus formulated is also varied earlier in the Horatian
career, most closely in *c.* 1.6 where the "thinness" (*tenues*) of his own
poetic self is seen as capable of embracing Agrippa's epic sublimity
(*grandia*). But it is the influence of Propertius, writing in the decade
after the publication of the *Eclogues,* that is most strongly felt in the
opening lines of ode 15. To the Callimachean–Virgilian past he adds a
major political element that brings with it a concomitant ethical concern. Propertius, elegist with his own bias toward Callimachus, must
deal with, or at least imagine, a speaker who wishes to confront the
problematics of an *Augustiad,* the epic praises of the emperor himself.

Propertius' first *recusatio* comes in the opening elegy of his second
book, one of the two poems he addresses to Maecenas. Were the fates
to have given him the strength "to lead bands of heroes into arms,"
he assures his patron, he would have sung not of gods against Titans,
or of Xerxes or even of Marius, but of Caesar:[5]

bellaque resque tui memorarem Caesaris, et tu
Caesare sub magno cura secunda fores.

I would recall the battles and deeds of your Caesar, and you would be
my next responsibility after mighty Caesar.

The list that follows, of places and times not to be treated, takes us
from Mutina and Philippi to Naulochus, Perusia, Alexandria, and the
final triple triumph—in other words, from Octavian's early cam-

[5]Prop. 2.1.25–26.

paigns after Julius Caesar's death through the aftermath of Actium. But it is not only stylistic or generic unfitness that precludes the elegist from turning to an emperor's epic. The speaker also feels a repulsion from the subject matter briefly but tellingly put. We sense it first in the description of Philippi as *civilia busta,* a Greek town become, via bitter metonymy, tombs of Roman citizens slaughtering each other. It appears again in the description of the seige of Perusia, a scene all the more striking for being out of chronological order, as "the overturned hearths of the ancient Etruscan race" (*eversos . . . focos antiquae gentis Etruscae*).[6] Once more metonymy helps recreate not Octavian's success but the horrors that war brings in annihilating the centers of domestic stability. It requires no great mental leap to move from Propertius to the conquered cities (*victas urbes*) viewed as pitiable (*miseras*) for their association with madness of citizenry (*furor civilis*). This is a phenomenon with which any persona of Horace's invention, plotting an epic traversal of Augustus' military deeds, would have to deal.

Propertius' other two *recusationes* come from his third book, the importance of which for Horace as he wrote his final sequence of odes we have already often observed. The first example is found in Propertius' third elegy where the speaker imagines himself following the lead of Ennius and writing of the kings of Alba and their regal deeds:[7]

> cum me Castalia speculans ex arbore Phoebus
>   sic ait aurata nixus ad antra lyra:
> "Quid tibi cum tali, demens, est flumine? . . ."

when Apollo, regarding me from his tree at Castalia, leaning against his cave speaks thus on his gilded lyre: "What have you to do with such a stream, madman?"

The verbal parallels, where in contiguous lines *Phoebus* and *lyra* serve as demarcations for endings in Propertius, for beginning and conclusion in Horace, leave little doubt that Horace had Propertius' "refusal" in mind as he wrote. The battles, which a Muse much like Calliope recounts for the poet to avoid, as the poem reaches its finale,

6Ibid., 2.1.29.
7Prop. 3.3.13–15.

run from Marius' northern campaigning to warfare at the Rhine. This
flows with Suevian gore as a result of campaigning that took place
two years after the victory at Actium and hence brings vicarious
credit to Octavian.

The second *recusatio* in book 3 comes, not unexpectedly, in the only
other poem Propertius addresses to Maecenas, elegy 9. It begins as
follows:[8]

> Maecenas, eques Etrusco de sanguine regum,
>   intra fortunam qui cupis esse tuam,
> quid me scribendi tam vastum mittis in aequor?
>   non sunt apta meae grandia vela rati.

Maecenas, knight sprung from the blood of Etruscan kings, who desire
to live within your fortune, why do you launch me on to so boundless a
sea of writing? Huge sails are not suitable for my bark.

Again the verbal echoes—reiteration of *aequor* and *vela* in adjacent
lines, the antonymy of *grandia* and *parva*—suggest that in ode 15
Horace has been pondering Propertius. Once more he is imagining a
specific refusal to sing of Augustus. Just as Maecenas in his ethos of
living remains within his means, so Propertius' speaker should con-
fine his Muse to suitably refined topics. Only if his patron should lead
the way—but he will not, if he is as sensible toward literary as toward
economic matters—would he find a plausible subject for his song in a
tale extending from Romulus and Remus, to Parthians in flight, and
Antony's suicide, while Alexandria is overrun by Roman weaponry.

What Horace has learned from Propertius may be studied by comparing his *recusatio* with *eclogue* 6 and with the contents of epic as
summarized in the *Ars Poetica:*[9]

---

[8]Prop. 3.9.1–4.

[9]A. P. 73–74. The language is close to that used by the first-person narrator at
Aen. 7.41–45:

> . . . dicam horrida bella,
> dicam acies actosque animis in funera reges,
> Tyrrhenamque manum totamque sub arma coactam
> Hesperiam.

res gestae regumque ducumque et tristia bella
quo scribi possent numero, monstravit Homerus; . . .

The deeds of kings and dukes, and sad wars—Homer showed in what
meter they could be written; . . .

Horace's formulation embraces the kings and heroes who appear in
Callimachus, in Virgil (just kings), and in the more elaborate presen-
tations of Propertius.[10] *Bella* are mentioned in *eclogue* 6 (7) and are
nearly synonymous with their metonymy, *proelia,* earlier in the same
poem (3) and in the opening line of ode 15, as well as in the several
occasions in Propertius. What remains absent from Horace's opening
recusatio are the kings (*reges*) of *eclogue* 6, expanded into *regumque
ducumque* of the *Ars Poetica* definition. They are replaced, in Horace's
most prominent novelty, by *victas urbes.* Honestly to elaborate the
deeds of Augustus' coming to power, as Propertius tells in the not
telling, would be to dwell on Italian as well as foreign cities conquered, on the strife of civil along with the glories of external wars
brought to conclusion. The cynical might say that it was a *rex,* the
new Romulus with a different title, who had led the way.

Propertius plays a notable part in these lines, but Virgil is also
subtly present. At the opening of the *Aeneid,* in words given to their
antagonist Juno, the Trojans are sailing on the "Etruscan sea" (*Tyrrhenum aequor*), bringing Troy and its conquered gods to Italy.[11] For
Horace to embark on the epic of Augustus would be, metaphorically
though not literally, to contemplate a new *Aeneid.* As in the case of
Propertius, Horace would have to analyze not only Augustan heroism per se but also the metaphysical and ethical supports for that

---

I shall tell of dreadful wars, I shall tell of battle lines and of kings driven to
mortal combats by their emotions, of the Etruscan squadron and all of
Hesperia forced under arms.

There are no conquered cities yet. Instead we have, later in the book, the more
predictable vision of cities renewing their arms, with anvils in place (*positis
incudibus,* 629).

[10]In Propertius we find *reges* (2.1.33; 3.3.3, 9.1 and 51), *duces* (3.9.47), and
proelia (2.1.45; 3.3.43, 9.38).

[11]*Aen.* 1.67–68.

heroism. Such a task would entail scrutinizing Augustus and his history under the bright glare of that poem's insights, built around the tension between ideal and real, the personal and the public, suffering and duty, passion and control, between force as civilizer and as bringer of chaos.

What follows in ode 15 is one of the most brilliant ellipses in this highly elliptical poet. The reader, schooled in poetic tradition from Callimachus to Propertius, expects an epiphany of the reproving god of poetry or, in the case of Propertius 3.9, implicit dialogue with a more human patron. As a result of any such exchange the poet will himself state or hear from his inspiring source that he should suppress his desire to write epic and turn to more appropriate matter, "slender" content in the case of Callimachus; pastoral and erotic elegy instead of encomiastic epic, and its equally turgid style, for Virgil and Propertius. Horace's imaginative leap over this anticipated denial is unparalleled.12 What is more remarkable still, however, is that the subject matter before and after the ellipsis, as we turn from *recusatio* to encomium, remains the same: Augustus and his time. Virgil will renounce the possibility of an epic on Varus in order to continue reshaping his pastoral modes. Propertius, at Apollo's insistence, imagines forgoing an epic on Augustus for an elegist's more personal themes. Horace remains with Caesar.

But, though subject matter may form a continuum that completes the poem's jolting initial sequence, the implications of generic change, from epic contemplated to a lyric achieved for us to hear and read, must not be minimized. Lyric eulogy of the same subject for whom epic is denied presumes that we are in a post-epic world, that epic linearity can be domesticated to the resonant "now" of odic praise, and that such a present will have an uninterrupted future through the good offices of Augustan mores and the resilience of the speaker's lyric voice. Horace is not only making the Callimachean point that epic's grand sweep through time is unsuitable to his refined Muse, he is also saying something explicit about Augustus and his fellow Augustan poets.

In the late 20s, when Propertius published his third book and Virgil was finishing the *Aeneid,* the ambiguities of Augustus' rise to authori-

---

12The particular force of *tua aetas,* unexpected from several points of view, is recognized by Syndikus (423).

ty would have remained vividly before the poetic geniuses who had come of intellectual age with his solidification of political primacy. Virgil can make his moral points universal by resorting to the stratagem of allegory. Aeneas is, or is not, a prototype for Augustus only according to the individual reader's inclination. Propertius simply claims he is stylistically unfit to write of Augustus in words that hint at moral repugnance as well. In keeping Augustus as his theme but switching from epic's reticence to lyric's unvarnished proclamations, Horace can dispense with the politics of force exerted (and imagined as poetically extolled) over epic time and embrace an ardent present. There poetic time stops to contemplate what an Augustan Age has done to deserve lyric assertion of its futurity in song. In the year 13 B.C. he can speak out reassuringly on the quality of the Augustan peace in ways his colleagues could not have, even a few years earlier.

Just as the initiation of Horace's valedictory to lyric through a refusal to sing epic startles the reader, so also the conclusion of this allusive chiasmus has its share of surprises. From the opening *recusatio* we would not expect to find, in the vista of future song with which the ode ends, either *duces* or what seems another *Aeneid,* spanning from Troy to Aeneas-Augustus. Yet how we are to understand Horace's speaker singing of such subjects generically is the crucial issue, and here the ambiguous placement of *more patrum* may assist interpretation. It goes readily, of course, with *functos* to describe the earlier leaders of Rome who have lived a life of *virtus* according to ancestral custom. But the phrase can, in a displacement not unprecedented in Horace, also serve as further explanation of *canemus*.[13] As

---

[13]R. D. Williams and Syndikus (432, n. 66) would restrict the meaning of *more patrum* purely to the context of line 29. Syndikus gives three reasons: verse 29 makes sense in itself, all clauses after 29 are self-contained, and Horace offers no examples elsewhere of such a separation. Leaving aside the undue restrictions such treatment puts on poetic statement, we should note that a self-enclosed verse 29 only makes logical sense when translated "leaders who have fulfilled their heroic *virtus* according to the customs established by their fathers." But just as Horace returns to origins in the lines that follow about the Julian *gens,* so we presume here that he must also allude to the original fathers themselves, the initial creators of what was to become the *mos maiorum,* as well as to their emulators.

As for the displacement, we might compare the separation of *te* and *vetulam* at *c.* 3.15.13–16 which is virtually the same length as here. In fact the linkage between *nos* and *canemus* by means of *more patrum* is masterly, keeping present, past, and future together in our thoughts.

the poem's opening "I" becomes a more general "we" and private refusal becomes public acceptance, the speaker is absorbed into a community whose songs will also share in a procedure as customary to Rome, or at least so the speaker imagines, as the *virtutes* of its past heroes.

I say imagine because we have no evidence save the nostalgia of later writers that such *carmina* existed. Cicero more than once bemoans the fact that we lack the songs which, according to Cato in his *Origines,* men sang at banquets to praise the virtues of famous heroes (*clarorum virorum laudes atque virtutes*), and Varro, too, speaks of the songs of old (*antiqua carmina*) that were sung as encomia to past elders.[14] Horace, therefore, would have known the tradition of delivering these songs "to the flute" (*ad tibiam,* Cicero) or "with a flute player" (*cum tibicine,* Varro), but would not have possessed the *carmina* themselves, if in fact they were ever delivered, much less preserved in writing. It is masterstroke to reinvent, or at least reenliven, that putative heritage. But even here, as he concludes his lyric career by redevising an ancient Roman melic genre, he surprises us with the generically unexpected. Ode 15 does not only imagine the performance of such lyric eulogies; in itself it is the Horatian version of such a *carmen* as Cato hypothesizes was delivered at Roman banquets in eras past. Yet Horace's speaker is exalting a living hero and his song is to be incorporated in future celebration, a song within songs, praising the past of the Julian *gens* and assuring its constant vivification. The double compliment would not have been lost on the emperor himself.

I emphasize the word lyric. Horace is not proposing to rewrite the *Aeneid* but to transfer, and thus transform, the people of Julian story from an ostensibly detached to a passionate medium, to exchange expansive narrative of events in progress for the intense figuration of

---

[14]The evidence, drawn largely from Cicero (*Brutus* 75; *T. D.* 1.3, 4.3) and Varro (*De Vita Populi Romani* 2, quoted by Nonius *s.v. assa* [107–82]) is analyzed by Momigliano who believes that such *carmina* did exist (111, 113) and that they did not disappear before the end of the fourth century B.C. He takes the "hymns" that Dionysius of Halicarnassus (1.79.10) claims were still sung by his contemporary Romans to honor Romulus and Remus as implying only their mention "in passing in some religious hymns" (111). Dionysius' mention of Coriolanus (8.62.3) as a person still praised and hymned remains equivocal. Does his second verb refer to specific hymns or merely to the suitable retelling of his tale?

an immediate world and its leading characters. He is modulating the same point his opening verses make. He places us again, and finally, in a post-epic, ceremonial setting where first-person eulogy replaces third-person novelistic expansiveness and controls the far-flung within the bounds of an ode's brief instancy.

The substitution of epic voyaging over the Tyrrhenian sea with lyric supported by Lydian flutes is not a discontinuous activity. Their mediation tracks the poem's course. The allusive trailing of the Etruscans from their Italian resting place back to their supposed homeland in Asia Minor is a metaphor not only for generic *recusatio* but perhaps even also for the search for poetic origins.[15] We may be meant to fancy ourselves in a Hellenic context of pre-epic lyric songs of praise, prayer, and thanks to the gods for their helpful intervention in human affairs. If so, the covert bow to Augustus is enormous. It is a sufficient obeisance to the emperor, I think, to watch Horace proposing the reinvention of a Roman poetic tradition and placing Augustus and his forbears in a Republican lyric setting, with a past formed of valorous deeds and a future of their renewal in familial, symposiastic song, not in the supposedly impersonal elaboration of epic.

This is a remarkable conclusion for a lyric career in one other generic respect. The reader schooled in the endings of Horace's earlier books of odes, especially in the seal poems of the second and third collections, expects a pronouncement on the singular accomplishment of the speaking "I" who turns into an immortal swan in the first ode and adopts in the second the posture of lyric *princeps,* supreme for the enduring quality of his monument.[16] We expect nothing less in the *sphragis* of book 4 where novelty of content and revisions of earlier lyric codes are at least as grandly inventive as in Horace's preceding books. Instead, individuality seems exchanged for a social

---

[15]Aristotle, for instance, reminds us (*Poetics* 1448b) of the antiquity of the tradition of hymn in Greece.

We should note in passing how much the buoyant atmosphere of ode 15 stems from the complex of direct references not only to return and renewals but to origins and originators, of the sun (*ortus*), of those born near the Don (*orti*), of wives, fathers, and children and, in the place of honor, the duplex *progenies* of Venus herself.

[16]In his standard survey of seal poems (Horace is discussed on 117–21), Kranz does not touch on the peculiarities of the poet's final ode.

"we," and self-effacement, in the midst of public celebration, re-places any prideful boasting of unique mastery. Yet these very meta-morphoses, from previous books' finales to this particular ending and from the opening of ode 15 to its closure, point up an irony of which students of literary history more than watchers of the Augustan prin-cipate would take notice. Horace's handling of the initial *apologia* and of the *sphragis* as a whole, by varying the tradition of previous poets and confounding the reader's expectations arising from the poet's own past performance, is in fact a boldly innovative stroke. It fur-nishes evidence of a formidable imagination at work, however much its surface plot may suppress the responsiveness of the individual "I" in favor of the larger ethos of a public "we."

The return to origins, therefore, with a forceful, unique speaker apparently subsumed into a generalized plurality of praisers, helps define one of the most original accomplishments in Latin letters. The framing sequences of ode 15 offer a study in the remaking of lyric genres, and their subtypes, the refusal and the seal poems. What seems an homage to the emperor is in fact an opening out, and a hypothetical renewal, of poetic vistas. The ode is a seal poem that, instead of postulating a conclusion, proposes the continuity of song (the poem's last word) under the aegis of immortal Phoebus Apollo (its first). Horace's speaker apparent yields his individuality to a com-munal celebration of the Augustan Age, but in reality his inventive-ness in the telling is what will preserve his subject matter. On the one hand the emperor and his times dominate the poem. On a more subtle level, the ironically recessive speaker, in putting his special marks on the poetic past, is maintaining Augustus by the sweep of his own originality. It is the emperor who will prove beholden not for immediate encomium but for the grander gift of remembrance.

The originality of the poem's framing statements permeates the body of the poem, and to this we must now return. It is appropriate that Horace, as he begins his elaboration of Augustan renewals, should look first to the land and its fertility. As he writes the phrase *fruges agris uberes* he may be thinking of *divitis uber agri,* the rich fertile land that, in Virgil's words, Latinus tenders to the Trojans on their arrival in Latium but that is not to be theirs because of Juno's machi-nations and an unwanted war.[17] Since the fighting between Trojans

---

[17]The phrase *ager uber* also occurs in line 5 of Catullus 46, a poem about which Horace often thought as he wrote his fourth book.

and native Italians is ultimately a form of civil war, are we meant to see Augustus returning his world to a parallel time of prosperous peace before any communal strife? Certainly the *Aeneid* is much in Horace's mind as he writes of the temples of Jupiter and Janus Quirinus, and his alterations of Virgil are, as always, instructive.

The standards of Crassus, rightfully returned to the Capitoline through Augustus' good offices, are "torn from the proud doorposts of the Parthians" (*Parthorum superbis/postibus*). Virgil uses the last phrase, with the same enjambment between lines, at *Aeneid* 8.721–22 where, in the description of the triple triumph of 29, Octavian, as he sits on Apollo's gleaming threshold

> dona recognoscit populorum aptatque superbis
> postibus . . .

acknowledges the gifts of nations and fits them to the proud doorposts . . .

In the context of *Aeneid* 8, Virgil allows the reader to sense a dubious as well as a noble pride in Caesar's doings because not long before he has spoken of the "proud door-jambs" (*foribus superbis*)[18] affixed by the monster Cacus with faces dripping gore. Horace divests Augustus of any moral ambiguity by imputing *superbia* to Parthia and allotting its proper humiliation to Rome. The ethical dilemmas that Virgil senses in Augustus' management of power now prove negligible to Horace, while the pride that, according to Anchises in *Aeneid* 6, Rome should beat down, appropriately characterizes her enemies, not herself and her leader.

The next accomplishment, of which Augustus himself boasted in similar words,[19] in the closing of the temple of Janus: ". . . *et vacuum duellis/Ianum Quirini* . . ." The tradition looks back to Ennius' *Annales* where the poet speaks of a period "after ugly *Discordia* has broken open the ironed posts and doors of War":[20]

> postquam Discordia taetra
> Belli ferratos postes portasque refregit . . .

[18]*Aen.* 8.196.
[19]*R. G.* 13.
[20]Enn. *Ann.* 266–167V³ quoted by Horace at *sat.* 1.4.60–61.

Virgil thought of Ennius, within the time-frame of his own epic's events, when he has Juno dash open War's gates and set Latium on fire with war:[21]

> tum regina deum caelo delapsa morantis
> impulit ipsa manu portas, et cardine verso
> Belli ferratos rumpit Saturnia postis.

Then the queen of the gods, slipping down from heaven, herself with her hand dashed open the sluggish gates, and the daughter of Saturn breaks the ironed doorposts as they turn on their hinge.

But at an earlier moment in the poem, glancing ahead to an Augustan present, Jupiter expands on the symbolism:[22]

> . . . dirae ferro et compagibus artis
> claudentur Belli portae; Furor impius intus
> saeva sedens super arma et centum vinctus aenis
> post tergum nodis fremet horridus ore cruento.

The gates of War, grim with tight fastenings of iron, will be closed, and unholy Wrath, sitting within upon fierce arms, bound with a hundred brazen knots behind his back, will roar dreadfully with bloody mouth.

For Virgil's Jupiter, looking to the era of Augustus, the gates of War will be closed and *Furor impius* enchained within. For Horace's speaker, by contrast, the gates of Janus' temple will be shut, but it will be empty of all wars. Within there will be no potential violence, domestic or foreign, to cause disruption to Rome. As we soon learn, while Caesar is guardian of Rome's affairs no *furor civilis* will drive out the restored quiet that has long been her due (or at least so the poet hypothesizes). Horace revises Virgil similarly in what must have been a nearly contemporary epistle to Augustus. As we noted in discussing ode 14, he would tell, if he had the power, of wars concluded throughout the world under his auspices, "and bars closing in Janus, warden of peace" (*claustraque custodem pacis cohibentia Ianum*).[23]

[21]*Aen.* 7.620–22.
[22]*Aen.* 1.293–96.
[23]*Epi.* 2.1.255.

The *Aeneid* itself stands as a warning that fury is only imprisoned and that, given the requisite circumstances, it will readily burst forth again. Horace, sensing perhaps a greater stability to the *pax Augusti*, can reverse his friend's great image, exiling fury from the land, and enclosing peace, not madness, within War's gates. Writing some two decades later, with direct allusion to the Augustan peace, Ovid borrows Horace's, not Virgil's, imagery. His narrator asks of Janus:[24]

> "at cur pace lates motisque recluderis armis?"
>   nec mora, quaesiti reddita causa mihi est:
> "ut populo reditus pateant ad bella profecto,
>   tota patet dempta ianua nostra sera.
> pace fores obdo, ne qua discedere possit;
>   Caesareoque diu numine clausus ero."

"But why do you remain quiet in time of peace and reopen, when war is declared?" Without delay he responded to my question: "So that possibility of return remain open to the people when they have set off to war, our whole threshold remains open, its latch unbarred. In peace I bar my doors, lest she have the power to depart; under Caesar's protection I will remain long closed."

Earlier, in dwelling on former times when "the earth endured the presence of the gods," Ovid has Janus look at himself in relation to peace and war:[25] "*nil mihi cum bello: pacem postesque tuebar . . .*" (I had nothing to do with war. I was protecting peace and my doors . . .). In guarding his doorposts he is also preserving peace. The zeugma is one that Horace would have well understood.

If his allusions to the haughty doorposts of the Parthians and to Janus Quirinus, empty of wars, revise Virgil in order to glorify Augustus, in his subsequent look at Augustan moral reforms Horace is refashioning himself, with the same result. He now looks back to *c.* 3.24, an impressive, strategically placed ode openly critical of the behavior of modern Roman man. "What avail bitter laments," the speaker asks at one point, "if wrong (*culpa*) is not cut back by penalties? What profit in empty, unprincipled laws, if . . . ?" Before this

[24]*F.* 1.277–82.
[25]*F.* 1.253.

outburst he indirectly throws down the gauntlet to the emperor himself:[26]

o quisquis volet impias
  caedis et rabiem tollere civicam,
si quaeret pater urbium
  subscribi statuis, indomitam audeat

refrenare licentiam,
  clarus postgenitis, quatenus, heu nefas,
virtutem incolumem odimus,
  sublatam ex oculis quaerimus invidi.

O whosoever wishes to do away with unholy slaughter and the madness of citizens, if he seeks to have Father of Cities written under his statues, let him, famous to our progeny, dare to rein in untamed license, since (alas, the crime) in our envy we hate virtue while she lives, and we look for her when she is torn from our eyes.

The challenge, with its reproach scarcely hidden, is a strong one. Although the ode that follows, addressed to Bacchus and mentioning Augustus openly for the last time in the third book, announces inspiration to sing of Caesar's noble exploits still untold, the poem shies away from its own responsibility and remains hypothetical in tone, concerned with the power to sing, not with the actual telling of deeds themselves. Our final memory of Augustus in the third book rests, therefore, on a dual contingency. He can be entitled *pater urbium,* if he can bring about proper moral reforms and the restoration of *virtus.* He already inspires the poet to sing, but where is the encomium itself?

   The double resolution comes in the fourth book of odes, especially in poem 15. *Culpae* have now been removed, and *furor civilis,* kin of *rabies civica,* is no longer a threat. Renewed *virtus* and the proper use of *vis* can again be the subject of song and, in the most striking metaphorical parallel, license, unbroken in the earlier ode and wandering free, now has its animal wildness tugged in. The present age restrains public immorality the way Tiberius reined in the barbaric

[26]C. 3.24.25–32.

tribes in the preceding ode. The reason is, of course, Augustus. Just as the words of the poem announce a moral revolution by comparison to *c*. 3.24, so the poem itself fulfills the implicit promise of *c*. 3.25. Inspiration has borne fruit in a final panegyric. We would expect the emperor, at last, also to be worthy of the title *pater urbium,* or, as it turns out, *pater patriae.* He is, as we will later see.

In the final, most expansive item on the list of the accomplishments of the Augustan Age Horace may also be thinking back to Virgil, not to alter negative to positive but to transform predicted future into past reality. At the end of Anchises' disquisition in the underworld to his son on the coming brilliance of Rome he lists vocations—sculptor of metal or stone, orator, astronomer—in which his descendants, unlike their Greek ancestors, will not excel. A Roman's superiority will lie elsewhere:[27]

> "tu regere imperio populos, Romane, memento
> (hae tibi erunt artes), pacique imponere morem,
> parcere subiectis et debellare superbos."

"You, o Roman, remember to rule nations with your sway—these will be your arts—and to impose the tradition of peace, to spare the humbled and crush the proud."

The proper imposition of *imperium* on the world, the regularization of peace, will come about through the uses of political artistry, climaxing, to quote earlier words of Anchises,[28] in

> "Augustus Caesar, divi genus, aurea condet
> saecula qui rursus Latio regnata per arva
> Saturno quondam, super et Garamantas et Indos
> proferet imperium; . . ."

Augustus Caesar, offspring of a god, who will establish a golden age again in Latium in fields once ruled over by Saturn, and will bring to bear imperial might over both Garamantes and Indi; . . .

---

[27]*Aen.* 6.851–53. Cf. 6.663 mentioning, after priests and poets, those in the underworld "who have enhanced life by the arts they discovered" (*inventas . . . qui vitam excoluere per artis*).
[28]*Aen.* 6.792–95.

Anchises merely predicts what will happen, expanding his vision of Rome's rule from Latium to the ends of the earth. Horace sees the prophecy come true. And unlike human souls in ode 7 who cannot claim a parallel in their lives with the rotation of the seasons or the sun's daily round, Rome can assert its equivalence to this grandest of celestial objects. Since her bounds are its *termini,* Rome, according to the poet's innuendo, is now a force of nature, sharing, by verbal sleight of hand, in her unaltering alternations.

There may be another allusion to temporality operating in these lines with a more specific tribute behind it. In ode 5, Augustus, whose face is like spring, even in his absence brings fertility to the fields and banishes blame (*culpa*). He has now returned and with his presence presumably the seasonal analogy can be considered still more firm as a time ode 2 predicts to be even better than golden takes its start.

The tripartite progress that lines 13–16 outline is usually, and rightly, seen as sketching steps toward world domination. Its references begin with Rome's sharing her rights with the Latins in the limited *ius Latii,* continue as she extends her scope and her political rewards to the Italian *socii,* and conclude as she reaches a posture of universal sway.[29] It is worth remembering that two Iulii played important technical roles in this evolution. Lucius Julius Caesar, second cousin of the dictator, in 90 B.C., at the end of the so-called Social Wars, promulgated the *lex Iulia de civitate Latinis et sociis danda,* that gave full citizenship to both Latins and allies. Julius Caesar himself saw passed, some four decades later, the *lex Iulia de civitate Transpadanis danda,* which extended civic rights to the whole Italian peninsula.[30] Whether or not Horace means to remind us of these two steps, the final compliment and the grandest manifestation of power, as the relative clause expands to its conclusion, belong to Augustus. Emulating his idol Alexander, he has extended Rome's reputation, with all that that implies, to the bounds of the civilized world. He has done so through the grandest display yet of Julian artistry, renewing his country's particular genius that had fallen into desuetude as the result of a century of civil warring.

[29]As noted, e.g., by Kiessling and Heinze on line 13 ("die drei Etappen der römischen Weltherrschaft"). Cf. also Juno's language at *Aen.* 12.826f.

[30]See C. D. 41.36.3, on the year 49 B.C.

The *artes* by which Rome acquired her broad hegemony are, of course, neither the fine arts (to one of which Anchises alludes) nor the art of poetry (which, for a spate of reasons, Virgil does not have him mention). But we should pause for a moment, before turning to the poem's second half, to watch the unassuming verbal artistry that articulates and gives permanent form, at least in the imagination, to Roman political cleverness. I would like to make two points only here. Fraenkel correctly observes the piling up of words with the prefix *re-: rettulit, restituit, revocavit.*[31] These contrast with vocabulary suggesting centrifugality (*evaganti, emovit*) and form a tiny cycle of their own. Yet the words and the renewals and restorations they evoke are small constituent parts not only of the larger *aetas,* now recurring, but also of the poetry of secularity and its book of restorations which, in bringing about the return of Augustus, is in itself the greatest magical agent of renewal. The origins of Rome, at the poem's conclusions, are complemented by reference to the initiation of communal lyric practice, and the Augustan renewal, in the hands of Horace, has its own poetic revivals and new beginnings. The poet is the agent of both transformations, lending the power of his own imaginative originality to his version of Augustus' ethical fresh start.

Second, we should take note of the words *duellis* and *evaganti.* The first is an archaism, the second is used in a figurative sense for the first time in Latin.[32] Together they define one of the poet's major tasks. Just as he is both the preserver of Roman, and now Augustan, traditions and their imaginative reinventor for the future, so he is also the guardian and invigorator as well as the redirector of poetic forms and language. Never in Horace do content and means of expression complement each other as profoundly as in this poem. He is to poetry what Augustus is to Roman political institutions, but the final power to perpetuate Augustus by imaginative reinvention lies with the verbal, not the political, artist.

[31]Fraenkel (*Horace,* 450) who interprets the cluster of words as symptomatic of Augustus' desire to have his rule appear but a "restoration of the true *res publica.*"

[32]Trisyllabic *duellum,* though apparently an Ennian coinage, would have been an archaism to Horace who uses it twice elsewhere in his lyric poetry (*c.* 3.5.38 and 3.14.18), as opposed to nineteen instances of *bellum,* and three times in his *Epistles.* See Clausen, *passim.*

For the importance of the poet's duty to revive and preserve words, see *epi.* 2.2.109–25. The poet guards and renews language just as the *princeps* does customs and public morality.

As we turn to the poem's second half, and to the future of Rome and of the poet's music, we can again divine something of Horace's ideological intent by tracing his patterns of retrospection and the mutations he works on the poetic past. Here, too, he teaches us by glancing back, first, at Virgil (this time at the *Georgics*), then at his own past. Not unexpectedly he is looking at the book endings of that splendid poem where the tensions between past and present, nostalgia and reality, life as it might be lived and as it must, come together. The initial *georgic* closes with a prayer to the gods to help Rome and its young Caesar. The world's morality is inverted by war. There is no honor given to the plough, no workers are left for the fields[33]

> et curvae rigidum falces conflantur in ensem.
> hinc movet Euphrates, illinc Germania bellum;
> vicinae ruptis inter se legibus urbes
> arma ferunt; saevit toto Mars impius orbe, . . .

and curved pruning-hooks are forged into the stiff sword. On this side the Euphrates, on that Germany moves war; with their laws broken between them neighboring cities take up arms; unholy Mars rages throughout the world.

Virgil uses similar language toward the end of *georgic* 2 where, after conjuring up an idyllic Rome of the Saturnian past with men living happily together on the land, he concludes:[34]

> necdum etiam audierant inflari classica, necdum
> impositos duris crepitare incudibus ensis.

for not yet had they heard clarions blown, nor yet swords clang when laid on hard anvils.

The forging of swords, and the eating of meat, tug us into the age of Jupiter when the land is held in disrespect and warring is the norm. Last, though the parallel is less forthright, we should look at the *envoi*

[33]Vir. *geo.* 1.508–11.
[34]Vir. *geo.* 2.539–40.

of the poem itself where Caesar's militant thundering in the east contrasts with the singer's Neapolitan leisure:[35]

> Haec super arvorum cultu pecorumque canebam
> et super arboribus, Caesar dum magnus ad altum
> fulminat Euphraten bello victorque volentis
> per populos dat iura viamque adfectat Olympo.
> illo Vergilium me tempore dulcis alebat
> Parthenope studiis florentem ignobilis oti, . . .

This I sang about the care of field and flocks and about trees, while great Caesar thunders in war at the deep Euphrates and as a victor gives laws to willing peoples and assays a road to Olympus. At that time sweet Parthenope nourished me, Virgil, flourishing in the arts of inglorious ease, . . .

Horace makes a series of points by his plethora of allusions to Virgilian endings.[36] Caesar's fighting days are over. There is no further need to force ploughshares into swords and set cities against each other. The rule of law, with no little help from *edicta Iulia,* is reestablished at home (the tactful stanza deals primarily with abstractions and symbols) and abroad, where concrete places and names can allude unabashedly to non-civil wars fought and won.

At the end of *georgic* 4 the poet's *otium,* the tranquillity that is the basis of civic peace and is needed by an artist for contemplation and creativity, seems present, in part because of the statesman's distant acts of jurisprudence. In the second *georgic's* expansive vision of an idealized countryside apparently possible, we learn at the end, only in time past, *quies* and *otium* are listed as fundamental requirements of a Roman Eden.[37] Perhaps Horace's suggestion is that with the resolution of domestic and foreign conflict Rome has regained, and will maintain, an *otium* that Virgil, with the natural pessimism of an observer of war's constancy, shifts either to the Bay of Naples or into an imagined paradise. Rome's Saturnian heritage can now be revived as

---

[35]Vir. *geo.* 4.559–64.

[36]And there may be still others—*Aen.* 7.629–40, for example—where within twelve lines we have one line ending with *urbes* (629) and two (636 and 640) with forms of *ensis.*

[37]Vir. *geo.* 2.467–68.

a vital element of the renewed golden age that the reader of the *Aeneid,* though he can scarcely trust to its realization in light of the deeds that occupy the epic's final foreground, can at least anticipate from hopeful words predicting the future.[38]

But these two stanzas also reach back to the bounds of the Horatian lyric career. Horace means to recall to our attention both the matter and manner of *epode* 7 which, because of its plausible dating to the early 30s B.C., is one of the earliest, if not the earliest, Horatian poem.[39] (I use here the label lyric in the wider, modern sense. The ancient reader would have classified alternating iambic trimeter and dimeter lines in the tradition of Archilocus as invective.) Horace's speaker there takes the posture of rhetor, haranguing the people and denouncing them at the start as villains (*scelesti*), because of the swords they hold, and still driven, we learn at the end, by the crime (*scelus*) of Romulus' murder of Remus. Roman blood is being spilled, cries the preacher, not to tame Carthage or enchain the Briton, but so that this city (*urbs haec*) should perish suicidally, according to the wish of the Parthians. Then he propounds a question that they cannot answer:[40]

> furorne caecus an rapit vis acrior
> an culpa? responsum date.

Does blind rage or a more bitter force or blame grasp you? Give a response.

At the conclusion of his career, as encomium replaces caustic de-nunciation, Horace exchanges a single speaker, aloof from Rome's tainted citizenry, for another who joins with mothers and children to sing of the continuous singing of Rome's progress from Troy to Augustus. The metamorphosis is clear and intentional. At the end of the twenty-five years or so that separate the dramatic date of *epode* 7 from the publication of *Odes* 4, cities are no longer at odds—Rome

---

[38]Even here, as he continues to look at his poetic past, Horace coins a new word, *inimico* (20), and at 21 *Danuvius,* the river Danube, is mentioned for the second time in Latin literature and the first in poetry (the only previous reference is Caes. *B. G.* 6.25.2).

[39]For the dating see Fraenkel, *Horace,* 56, n. 3.

[40]Hor. *epode* 7.13–14.

against her own—nor are swords still forged out of anger. *Culpae* have been exiled, and *furor* and *vis* do not now seize Rome in their grip. The reason is Caesar, whose virtuosity has engendered parallel changes in the poet's own response.

The next stanza, because of the double allusion to the Seres and to the river Tanais in contiguous lines, recalls another, much later masterpiece, ode 29 of Horace's third book, placed prominently in the penultimate position in the first collection. The poem, which invites Maecenas to the country and a banquet, urges the statesman to leave behind the smoke, commercialism, and noise of Rome—and his worries as *éminence grise*. The good shepherd has the sense to guide his flock to shelter when the sun's warmth grows treacherous, yet Maecenas stays in life's glare:[41]

> tu civitatem quis deceat status
> curas et urbi sollicitus times,
>   quid Seres et regnata Cyro
>   Bactra parent Tanaisque discors.

You worry over what situation befits the state and, troubled for the city, you fear what the Seres and Bactra, reigned over by Cyrus, and the rebellious Tanais are up to.

Maecenas should learn from the speaker. The man who is honestly self-reliant and independent of mind cares nothing about the swirl of alternations around him—the river of life running on the rampage or with gentleness, the sun now bright, now dark, fortune ungenerous or kindly. He is immune to the world's temptations because of his inner security.

A spiritual revolution of sorts has taken place in the writer between this poem and its parallel moment in ode 15. The earlier ode would

---

[41]*C.* 3.29.25–28. Mention of the Danube in line 21 of ode 15 reminds us of how idealizing is Horace's vision of the realities of Augustus' Rome of 13 B.C. The very next year Tiberius was dispatched to deal with troubles in Pannonia. And, looking elsewhere in the poem, we should remember that the standards of Crassus were not snatched away from the Parthians but restored by diplomacy. Augustus' propaganda could boast that he had not resorted to force in their retrieval, but the cynical might speculate on whether or not force would have been successful had it proved necessary.

seem to denigrate Maecenas' concerns and place the speaker's self-confident, aloof poise, and the pastoral metaphor that bolsters it, as the touchstone of moral quality. By the time ode 15 was written the specific cares that burdened Maecenas had evaporated. But the poet who speaks about their departure is one who, instead of retreating away from public cares into his mind's private reassurances, now openly embraces Rome and the accomplishments of its leader. In this instance at least, Horace seems to use Virgil to illustrate the ethical change that has come about in Rome and the possibility of realizing in the Augustan present what the older poet had imagined true only for an idealized past. He cannibalizes his own previous writing to illuminate his personal volte-face toward Rome and Augustus. The passionate praiser of community replaces the reserved, critical, solipsistic watcher of politics from his inner distance, whose pride, at the end of *Odes* 3, is in himself, not in anyone else, as *princeps*.

If, then, we survey the complex referentiality in these stanzas to Virgil's and to his own literary career, we see Horace by the act of remembrance showing how much both Rome and his attitude toward Rome have altered over the quarter-century of his writing. Nevertheless, for all the forthrightness of this ideological change, the language in which it is presented sounds a litany of negation. Six uses of *non* in eight lines serve a double effect. They remind us as much of what has happened in the Roman past as of what, one trusts, will never occur again in her future. The opening *recusatio* looked at what the (supposedly willing) speaker would have to chant, were he to enumerate the battles and conquered cities that were landmarks on Augustus' road to the principate—epic praise bestowed on what might come hard for an ethical imagination to glorify. The poem's counterbalancing second look at Caesar, present words promising future realities, also has its parallel irony. Caesar's rise to national and international omnipotence has occurred against a backdrop of national and international madness. Its nonrecurrence in fact is assured, but only by its verbal restatement in the speaker's tolling.

Alliteration links the sixfold repetition of *non* with *nosque* which initiates the poem's penultimate stanza and final sentence, and the sound of *non qui profundum* may be meant to reecho in *nosque et profestis*. But, though resonance secures the interconnection of the verses, the element of negativity so pronounced in lines 17–24 is now totally eliminated as the poem reaches a conclusion that proclaims firm commitment to Augustan Rome. We will look at these crucial lines again, from several points of view, beginning for one final time with a backward glance into the literary past. I am particularly interested in the words *progeniem* and *canemus,* and in how, taken together with *aetas,* which appears so prominently in the sentence that begins the poem's nonapologetic core, they recast crucial moments in the Virgilian and Horatian past.

The first point of reference is the astonishing fourth *eclogue,* one of the most revolutionary and influential poems in Latin. After introductory lines, in which the singer announces that he intends to broaden the scope and appeal of pastoral poetry, he proclaims:[42]

> Ultima Cumaei venit iam carminis aetas;
> magnus ab integro saeclorum nascitur ordo.
> iam redit et virgo, redeunt Saturnia regna,
> iam nova progenies caelo demittitur alto.

> Now the last age of Cumaean song has come. The great line of the ages is born anew. Now even the Virgin returns, the kingdom of Saturn returns. Now a new race is sent down from heaven above.

Many of the major poems of the Augustan era comment on this manifesto, but it is only in the final poem of Horace's career that its idealizing message is heralded as a reality. Though Virgil announces that the new age is at hand, the body of the poem sees its advent in the future, as the boy, whose birth trumpets its arrival, passes through three stages. Though the last of these anticipates a time when the earth is all-productive and nature gives man spontaneously the emoluments he might ordinarily have to acquire through competition, the intermediate stretch is a time of renewed crime and deceit in the world, a time for the boy to test his *virtus* as wars recur and "great Achilles will again be sent to Troy." The dramatic setting for the poem is only the birth of the boy, presided over by Diana and Apollo, and the poem ends with the infant looking on its mother with a smile that implies future apotheosis.

In his final ode Horace presumes the passage of literal and imaginative time from the moment *eclogue* 4 was composed until the year 13

[42]Vir. *ecl.* 4.4–7.

B.C. It makes little difference whether Virgil's *puer* was actual or fictitious, the offspring of a political figure who might implement the poem's dream or merely its symbol. For Horace the boy has become Augustus, the offspring of nourishing Venus (*almae progenies Veneris*), and his *aetas*—the word is placed conspicuously at the end of line 4 in both poems—has in fact brought about what Virgil only prophesies. The antisecular period of Achilles, as ode 6 carefully sketched, has passed, and Apollo can change from a god of war to a divinity along with his sister, welcoming the new era and supporting its inspired poet. The final ode, as it runs its course from *aetas* to *progeniem,* documents the palpability of this recurrence, with war's energies spent and the Roman macrocosm revitalized, with its artistry renewed not only in its landscape but in its moral and political values.

It is plausible to speculate, as I did earlier, that Horace's wholehearted embrace of Augustus and his achievement came about because of the acceptance and fulfillment of the commission to write the *Carmen Saeculare* for the celebration of the secular games in 17 B.C. Certainly there are previous moments in Horace's writing devoted to the same themes which cast a far less positive eye on the situation of contemporary Rome. The first is the famous sixteenth *epode* which in all likelihood is an objective response to the aureate glow with which Virgil illuminates the Rome of 40 B.C., the year of the pact Octavian made with Antony at Brundisium. Two years later, despite the treaty signed at Puteoli the year before, Octavian was at war with Sextus Pompeius, reigniting what would by then have seemed the unquenchable flames of civil war. But no specific event need have triggered Horace's appraisal of his times which begins with Rome misusing her *vis*[43]—

> Altera iam teritur bellis civilibus aetas,
> suis et ipsa Roma viribus ruit.

Now another age is worn away with civil warrings, and Rome herself collapses from her own strength—

and continues with an indictment of her impiety:

[43]*Epode* 16.1–2, 9–10.

inpia perdemus devoti sanguinis aetas
  ferisque rursus occupabitur solum; . . .

An unholy age with our blood cursed, we will perish and our earth will be tenanted again by beasts of the wild.

The only recourse for the pious remnant is to escape from Rome under the speaker's vatic tutelage into the dreamworld of the blessed islands where a holy race exists, sequestered by Jupiter when he stained gold with bronze and then hardened the ages with iron.

This vision remained with Horace during the construction of the so-called Roman odes, the cluster of six poems devoted largely to ethical concerns which opens the third book of odes. There are moments that look to a productive future (Augustus will be considered a god, if . . .), but the conclusion of this impressive sequence, the final stanza of ode 6, is one of the more gloomy moments in Horace:[44]

damnosa quid non inminuit dies?
aetas parentum peior avis tulit
    nos nequiores, mox daturos
    progeniem vitiosiorem.

What has our cursed age not demeaned? The era of our parents, worse than their fathers', has borne us, more evil, soon about to bear offspring yet more depraved.

This ode was probably written in 28 B.C. and published in 23 B.C. In the ten years that intervene before he released his last book of odes, Horace suffered a dramatic change of heart, as the close verbal parallels and sharp moral differentiation between the endings of the two poems show. The age is now one of renewal, not begetting progeny of a still more decadent sort than its predecessor but itself the work of Venus' offspring (*progenies*), Augustus, who directly links Rome with the gods. It projects rejuvenation, not moral collapse.

The beginning of the sequence of "Roman" odes, which purports to deal with the setting and presentation of what follows, also has bearing on the way Horace chooses to end his final ode:[45]

[44]*C.* 3.6.45–48.
[45]*C.* 3.1.1–4.

Odi profanum volgus et arceo.
favete linguis: carmina non prius
audita Musarum sacerdos
virginibus puerisque canto.

I loathe the profane mob and avoid it. Keep a holy silence: priest of the Muses, I chant songs never before heard to virgins and youths.

Once again the metamorphosis of the earlier into the later singer is readily documented. The individual, priestly "I," disdainful of the common man, reciting songs to children presumably for them to memorize and reiterate, has become in ode 15 part of a communal society. He joins in celebration, singing not to the unwed but to mothers and their offspring who, we presume from the evidence of the *Carmen Saeculare* and the sixth ode of book 4, will continue the process of renewing Rome with progeny as well as in song.

But the word *canemus,* in itself one of the most moving concluding words in literature, looking as it does to constant futurity in song, to new beginnings, not finality, has its own history. Perhaps we are meant to think again of the opening of the fourth *eclogue:*[46]

Sicelides Musae, paulo maiora canamus!
non omnis arbusta iuvant humilesque myricae;
si canimus silvas, silvae sint consule dignae.

Muses of Sicily, let us sing of a somewhat loftier theme. Hedge and lowly tamarisk do not delight everyone. If we sing of woods, let the woods be worthy of a consul.

The two instances of the first-person plural present of *cano,* the first subjunctive, the second indicative, may also look to Horace's final lyric utterance. But one of Virgil's poems ends with exactly the same word as Horace's, namely the ninth *eclogue,* and this equally emotional use of *canemus* the later lyricist would certainly have had in mind. The poem concerns two shepherds expelled from their fields and making their way to the city in the face of night and rain. They ease their journey not by inventing new songs, for the horrors of their life make creativity no longer possible, but by attempting to

[46]Vir. *ecl.* 4.1–3.

recall the songs of their fellow shepherd-singer, the absent Menalcas. He, we learn from one of the protagonists, was heard to have saved the land by his songs. But the other disabuses his comrade of the hope for such a turn of events: their songs have as much force pitted against the weapons of Mars as doves confronting eagles. Nevertheless the poem ends with the prospect of Menalcas' return:[47]

> Desine plura, puer, et quod nunc instat agamus;
> carmina tum melius, cum venerit ipse, canemus.

Say no more, lad, and let us be about what now hangs over us. We will sing songs better then, when he himself has returned.

From antiquity on commentators have usually allegorized Menalcas as a representation of Virgil himself, away in Rome, uttering *carmina* for the survival of the landscape and the life of the mind it stands for.[48] By the time Horace came to write his last odic verses, the Menalcas figure had returned, brought about equally by historical circumstances and by a poet's *revocatio*. He is no longer emblem of a poet but a patron of poets, someone who, like his divine protector Apollo, can now dispense with the weapons of war for the artistic arms of peace. He can bring restored fertility to the earth of Italy and inspire at least one sublime poet not only to recollect the factual and imaginative past but also to frame a poem of great originality from it and from his own inspiration. By such a creation he can assure a future for his song and through it for those of whom he sings, including the savior. He will preserve, for a future the emperor seems to have understood, the peace-bringer himself. For Horace, too, is Menalcas, the singer of recovery incorporated into his own song.

Ode 15 and the Structure of Book 4

Much of the originality of ode 15 can be perceived by projecting it, as I have striven by example to do, against Horace's contemporary literary background and against his own past lyric accomplishment.

---

[47]Vir. *ecl.* 9.66–67.

[48]As, for example, Servius and Servius *auctus* on *ecl.* 9.10: "that is your Vergilius, because of whom their fields were returned to the inhabitants of Mantua" (id est vestrum Vergilium, *cuius causa agri Mantuanis redditi sunt*).

It is the superb conclusion of a career, and of a moment, in Latin letters. (No lyrics of comparable quality will be written in Latin for four hundred years until the Christian hymn begins its flowering through the very different genius of St. Ambrose.) But its particular specialness is felt as the carefully wrought climax of book 4. Let us return to the poem to examine its culminating force in two ways, first, as the rounding off of the book's last triad, second, as finale of a still more expansive trinity that embraces the book as a whole. For ode 15 has close associations with odes 1 and 8, the book's initial and central poems, associations that secure its position as linear climax and round out the book into a cycle whereby beginning and end continually review and reinterpret each other.

First the final triad. The book's last grouping follows and reshapes a pattern that we have seen Horace vary in all the earlier segments. In general, the initial ode of each trinity is private and personal in tone, sensitive to the pressures of human time and, in particular, to the loss of desire and desirability which temporality brings to present and former loves and especially to the speaker as lover. By slipping an apparent exception, ode 4, into this scheme, Horace succeeds in stressing not only the importance of Augustan *doctrina* in the education of the Claudii but also the individual bereavements of Hannibal. In words given to the latter, which take up one third of the ode, the Carthaginian is Hercules while Rome is ever regenerative, and monstrous.

The second poem in each series takes a more public turn. With three poems (2, 5, and 14) devoted to Augustus and a fourth (8) concerned with *duces* and their eulogies in poetry, Horace seems to be looking toward the Roman heroic present, reforming and rethinking ways of constituting it in odic verse. Once more the evident exception to this pattern, ode 11, has something to tell us about itself by its apparent deviation. It is a private poem, with a speaker caught up in life's trials and love's ending, but, like its colleagues, it also documents a festive celebration. Though Maecenas' birthday, which comes in the middle of Venus' month, cannot claim prestige equal to the return of Augustus, nevertheless it too generates a moment of rejoicing. Ode 11 solemnizes a continuity that in fact abstracts its protagonists from contemplating human decline and locates them in the excitement of the calendar's cyclical renewal.

Finally we have poems specifically devoted to poetry. We begin, in ode 3, with the poet's vocation as Roman *vates* with Callimachean leanings (Callimachus, as we have seen, makes regular appearances in all these boundary poems). We then turn to the patronage of Apollo and the re-creation of secularity through charismatic song, to the immortalizing of Lollius through the singer's eternal resonance, to—and here again an anomaly that only proves richly congruous—an invitation to Vergilius to drink the heady, evocative wine of the poet's spring music with the commitment to his mental world that this implies.[49]

The final triad reaffirms and transmutes this arrangement, putting special emphasis on the passage of time, on age, aging, and eternity. Because it is the last in a sequence that ode 1 initiates, ode 13 not unexpectedly looks back to the book's opening. The common mention of Cinara and the brooding presence of Venus give the poems a mutual flavor of "biography" which the parallel ideas—the presence or absence of *decus* in the lives of Fabius, of the speaker of ode 1 and of Lyce; the *artes* of Fabius and of Cinara in 13—and imagery, especially of birds and of color, confirm. But both the tone and the potential of the speaker are radically different in the two poems. The first ode is wistful and retrospective, attempting to reclaim what is forever lost (and belongs elsewhere, in any case). Although the speaker in ode 13 momentarily revives past emotion, he ends on a note of clinical detachment. Moreover, while the speaker may be thought of as aging because of his sequence of loves and because of time's passing in Lyce's erotic biography, he himself is now the initiator of the process. He has the power to cause by prayer, and the will to document in further words, the senescence of Lyce. Horace adds an ironic twist to one of his book's major claims, that man's imagination can triumph over nature's tendency toward diminishment and that poetry's longevity is victorious over life's brevity: he stretches individual time and secures it in the calendar at the moment of old age. Lyce, by the poet's metamorphic witchcraft, is forever old.

The poet's power takes a public turn in the penultimate poem. In bringing Augustus home and framing Claudian epic deeds by lyric prayer, the speaker accomplishes the Pindarizing of the emperor that he had treated ironically in the book's second ode. He also promises

---

[49]The importance of Callimachus for Horace, notably in the structuring of the "Roman" odes, has been finely analyzed by Ross, chap. 7, esp. 139–52.

immortality to the *virtutes* that he celebrates by asking, with a play, as we saw, on the etymology of *aeterno,* "What endeavor will eternalize your heroism, Augustus, into eternity?" (*Quae cura . . . tuas, Auguste, virtutes in aevum . . . aeternet?*). The fathers have their way of fixing Augustus' deeds into *fasti* that will retain them as part of the people's calendar. The poet's imaginative calendar, with prayers answered, an epiphanic, living god venerated, *imperium* extended and stabilized, proffers a more considered immortality.

Poems 14 and 15 are meant to be read as a pair. Both are in alcaic meter (as noted earlier, the book's only adjacent poems in the same meter) and both detail accomplishments of the emperor. Both begin, or nearly begin, with age, poem 14 with the *aevum,* the eternity that secular and artistic schedules bestow, the final ode with *aetas* itself, the age that, for what its past achieved, offers reason for its endurance in song.

This eulogistic posture is one of poise between past and future, recollection and anticipation, memory and desire. The vision is enormously effective not only for the positive portrait of the time's military and political vigor as well as its moral quality, but also for the brilliance of the poetry in which it is couched. If the standard of the Augustan Age is measured against its past achievements and its future potential, the poet whose artifact makes this excellence palpable is also constantly measuring his own design against poetry's past and future, by retrospect into tradition and by the prospect that originality ensures. A poem that begins with allusion to Callimachus, the sixth *eclogue,* Propertius' third book and the *Aeneid,* continues with a plethora of bows, especially to Virgil and Horace's own past lyric performance, and ends by repeating the final word of the ninth *eclogue,* is bent on summarizing the poetic past and bringing its dynamic essence to bear on a subject of the greatest importance. But this recapitulation of poetry's heritage, phrased from time to time in deliberately archaic language, is in fact as a whole splendidly new, constantly surprising with generic, lexical, or ideological novelty. The poem is therefore in a sense an extraordinary metaphor for the Augustan Age itself, combining the traditional with the unprecedented, renewing and modifying past poetic performance just as the Augustan Age, as Horace would have us see it, re-created and re-energized the world of Rome.

The compliment to the emperor is a special one. In telling of

Augustus Horace will do in and for poetry what the Augustan Age has done for the Roman present. His final ode refurbishes the Roman poetic imagination for the future just as Augustus, in the speaker's imagination, has reassured the political and ethical prospects of Rome. The art of one echoes the artistry of the other. But the firm authority for survival rests with the imagination that incorporates and reinvigorates the secular restorer himself. The poet's sorcery, the futurity of his song, has the final say. His inventiveness in summarizing and revising the poetic past assures the preservation and rebirth of the age whose renovations and renewals, conservatism and originality, he has singled out for his ultimate praise.

The culminating force of this final trio accrues still further vigor if we expand our scope and watch the momentum the book gradually gains through its whole course. To see this we must look to the larger trinity of initial, central, and final poems, returning first to the opening. I noted earlier that one of the more subtle links between the last two odes was the presence of Venus in the same position in the last line of each poem—in ode 14 in the scarcely hidden etymology of *venerantur*, in 15, *in propria persona*. The first looks to the propitiatory magic due the new Roman god, his conquering days now over. The second consolidates this magic in the form of the goddess herself, nourishing mother of Aeneas and of his august descendant. In touching on the historicizing of the goddess of love, of which Virgil had taken full advantage in the *Aeneid,* Horace, as he concludes, may be thinking of the opening lines of another Roman poetic masterpiece, *De Rerum Natura:*

> Aeneadum genetrix, hominum divumque voluptas,
> alma Venus, . . .

> Begetter of the sons of Aeneas, pleasure of men and of gods, fostering
> Venus, . . .

Lucretius' prayer is that Venus, animating spirit of creativity, will lull into quiescence the disruptive energies of Mars, and that this act of symbolic eroticism will affect not only the natural world but the historical activities of human nature. Only if this other calming takes place can Memmius, the poem's apparent dedicatee, replace his commitment to the safety of Rome with contemplation of the poet's message of philosophical peace. The poem gives no hint that this dream is fulfilled, and in fact its powerful look at the truths of our inner and outer worlds suggests its impossibility in a way not dissimilar, finally, to Virgil's. In completing this other grand cycle, Horace uses his allusion to imply that Lucretius' prayer of some forty years before has been answered in the form of a new offspring of Venus. He has calmed war's fury and encouraged a new time of *otium* with which Lucretius would have been deeply sympathetic.

But Horace is also carefully completing a cycle of his own and here too the figure of Venus is focal. It has often been observed that the second word of ode 1 and the penultimate word of ode 15 is *Venus,* and that Horace, by this explicit balance, plots a poetic course from a serio-comic au revoir to the goddess of love to final acknowledgment of the fostering presence of a divinity who is both the mythical source of the Julian *gens* and a vital symbol for the peace that bears the name of its most notable scion.[50] But there is another cluster of verbal parallels an analysis of whose interaction will deepen still further our appreciation of Horace's book as a whole. To illustrate this I must quote again, as a reminder, the concluding stanzas of ode 15:

> nosque et profestis lucibus et sacris
> inter iocosi munera Liberi
>   cum prole matronisque nostris
>   rite deos prius adprecati
>
> virtute functos more patrum duces
> Lydis remixto carmine tibiis
>   Troiamque et Anchisen et almae
>   progeniem Veneris canemus.

As we have seen, Horace creates one of the great moments of retrospection in Latin letters, bringing historical and poetical origins (however hypothetical) from past to present, renewing the old through the ongoing act of ritual celebration. What I have not hither-

---

[50]The metamorphosis is discussed most recently by Porter ("The Recurrent Motifs," 207, with references). The *mater Cupidinum* has become someone whose offspring is Aeneas. Among other lexical parallels in the two poems we might note that Horace's only two uses of the verb *revoco* in his lyric work are at 1.8 and 15.12.

to observed is that in this process of refabricating customary song for future performance Horace coins two new words, *adprecor* and *remisceo,* blending as he regularly does throughout book 4, the crucial, novel ingredient into what purports to be traditional but is in fact a virtuoso demonstration of inventiveness.[51]

These two examples of new lexical usage hark back to Horace's employment of the simple form of each verb in ode 1. The only occurrences of *precor* in book 4 are in the initial poem's second line—

> Intermissa, Venus, diu
> rursus bella moves? parce precor, precor.

The double praying away of a goddess whose untimely advent is bittersweet for the speaker is, at the book's conclusion, replaced by appropriate prayer to gods which precedes songs to the heroes of Rome and ancestral background of Augustus. The earlier use of *misceo* is more complex and occurs in one of the central stanzas of ode 1 where the speaker is reminding Venus of the olfactory and aural delights that she will share when crafted in marble by the lakeside Alban villa of Paulus Fabius Maximus:

> illic plurima naribus
> duces tura lyraque et Berecyntia
> delectabere tibia
> mixtis carminibus non sine fistula; . . .

The passages are clearly meant to echo each other, and their very positions, at the beginning and end of the collection, at the center of one poem and the conclusion of the other, have something to tell us about the book as a whole.

Each cluster of words documents an instance of ritual celebration, a major motif of the collection but never so clearly formulated as on these two occasions. From the first situation the speaker is debarred. The festivity for a monumentalized Venus at the core of ode 1 cele-

---

[51]For all its novelty, *remisceo* (which Horace also employs at *A. P.* 151) is also climactic and cumulative as the last of many instances of the prefix *re-* in book 4. The recurrence of festival song signifies also the recurrence of the Horatian poetry that not only exemplifies such a hymn (the *Carmen Saeculare*) but also imagines its iteration in a stable context of ritual (as here and ode 6).

brates the appropriateness for young love of Paulus Fabius Maximus, with his grace, fluency, and love of the arts. Her institutionalization by Fabius seems to mirror requisite moral stability in his own life. By contrast the speaker, aging but yearning still to be youthful, bemusedly pursuing an amour that flees his grasp, is indecorous, tongue-tied, and in flight, because of his unseemly behavior, away from the pivot of his Roman life. Central stability and framing disintegration are at odds, and ritual confirmation belongs with the former.

By the time we reach the finale of the book, celebration comes at the poem's conclusion and is participated in (and, on another level, created by) the speaker, whose inspiration of communal song is the focus of the ceremony. A speaker imagined to be removed from society for reasons of incongruity has mutated into one who shares in a chanting that is at the heart of decorousness. The metamorphosis from one moment to the other epitomizes *in magno* what we have seen replayed in each different trinity of poems throughout the book. The transformation in Venus from goddess of love to historical ancestress of Rome and exemplary divinity of the Augustan peace is metaphoric for alterations in the personae Horace chooses to adopt and in the poetry that describes them.

In ode 1 nature deludes the speaker, taunting him with evanescent dreams of regaining a lost love or, better, a lost ability to love. And beyond love's longings lies death. In ode 15, poetry, triumphing over human fallibility, creates its own world in which the practical arts of politics are revived and reaffirmed by the poet's more permanent artifice. The imagination, fully committed to Roman *realien,* envisions an age without age, endlessly refreshed by the poet's continuous song. The change from the book's beginning to its conclusion, as private becomes public and personal trials yield to public, historical occasions, defines a sublimation of the individual's amatory cravings, ever a victim of time's flow, into the larger, more constant love of Rome and the communal rituals of song which betoken her eternity. It also seems to assure the poet-speaker a continuity in art which nature's linear inexorability patently denies.

In the first ode, misguided sexuality appears to silence speech, which is to say its expression in song. In the fifteenth all is finally music, lavished on Roman ethical, political, and, not least, literary orderings. The initial ode furnishes one last instance of the lover's metaphoric *bella* before life's eroticism dwindles into hallucination.

The final ode finds real *proelia* at an end as the Venus of the speaker's private "warfare" becomes the Venus of public peace. But the end of actual battling means not only the revival of civic community but the beginning of continuous, post-epic song, in the lyric of secular recurrence which offers the final illusion—to Rome directly, to the speaker vicariously—of immortality in words. Hence, as Horace's speakers replace worry about time's flight with concentration on Rome's, and poetry's, persistence, his lyric mode alters from elegy to eulogy. It moves from poetry of bitterness or, at least resignation, before the inroads of temporality to praise of the strength of poetry, of Rome, and, especially in poems 6, 15, and, for the individual Roman, 9, of their impressive combination.

Read as a linear continuum, then, Horace seems to be presenting us with a developing sequence of poems which preaches the triumph of art over life, of intellect over nature. But by pointedly recalling for his reader the first poem in the conclusion of the last, Horace reminds us that his poetry is also a self-renewing cycle. This reintegration serves two purposes. It promotes the centrality of Paulus Fabius Maximus, whose attributes of nobility, *decus, facundia,* and aestheticism are basic to Rome and to poetry about Rome. But it also encourages the paradox that, in the hands of Horace, poetry about private loss is as immortal as poetry of Roman magnificence. As we read and reread his final masterpiece, we sense a linear thrust from poetry of sadness to poetry of rejoicing, but the cycle forces us to see the alternation of both in poetry and in life. If the last poem looks toward Rome's futurity in song in its final miraculous word, the book as a whole movingly immortalizes the human creature named Horace behind this extraordinary round of fifteen poems, reading the signs that point toward his own decay but, with paradoxicality allowed a bard, pronouncing the furtherance of Rome and, in so doing, of himself.

The penultimate ring of the book's cycle, formed of poems 2 and 14, looks to Augustus. In the first Horace is directly concerned with poetry, brilliantly playing Pindar while disclaiming the ability to treat Augustus in Pindaric terms—which would be to embrace in lyric the details of Augustan valor. Its counterbalancing poem appears in fact to do exactly that, but it, too, is a gentle form of *recusatio,* more generic than stylistic. By dealing with the heroic *gesta* of the Claudii in the third person and by framing the poem with apostrophes to an

Augustus in the foreground, Horace restrains epic linearity to the immediate confines of prayer's outburst of thanksgiving. As we reach ode 8, the focus of this concentricity and middle segment of the book's spanning trinity, our expectations are at first disappointed. The cycle of odes 2 to 14 and the horizontal movement that presses from the second to the fifth poem lead us to anticipate a grand hymn to the emperor himself. He is present, but in the most impersonal, objective manner. The *dux bone,* the "good leader" whose double apostrophe binds ode 5 into a whole, is absorbed into the *bonis ducibus* whose immortality is assured by incorporation into the imaginings of poets. The speaking poet and the dynamism of poetry are at the core of Horace's thoughts. Meditation on a monument more enduring than bronze and loftier than the pyramids ends the earlier trilogy of books. Here at the center of Horace's last poems, at the apex of his final grand spiritual triangulation, is a poem on poetry and its capability.

More specifically, and more important for our present purposes, it is a poem on artistry and the meaning of art. In the final ode of his first collection Horace had used bronze and pyramids as analogies for endurance. The very tangibility of artistic fabrications in metal or stone makes them subject to the corruption of the elements and of time in a way that poetry is not. This strong distinction between artifacts that survive and those that vanish is gently modified in ode 8. There are those who do give bronzes as gifts, and Horace's speaker would reward Censorinus with the stone statuary of Scopas or the colorful paintings of Parrhasius if such were his talent and the recipient's pleasure. Poetry is to be preferred to the fine arts as a creator's "gift" because examples of the latter are *deliciae,* toys that give the receiver immediate delight but, we assume, do not possess the persisting charm of song to gladden and to lengthen the life of its subject.

Variation of equivalence, not distinction, is behind the poem's second comparison between the fine arts and poetry, namely, between the likenesses that statuary and painting convey and the descriptive words that vocal parchments contain:

> non incisa notis marmora publicis
> per quae spiritus et vita redit bonis
> post mortem ducibus, . . .
> . . . clarius indicant
> laudes quam Calabrae Pierides. . .

The key word here is *clarius*. Statuary images of great heroes serve as icons of remembrance before the public eye, and the plaques underneath, which list their deeds, not only repeat the same marble medium as the effigies, but make use of the very stuff of poetry, words, in pursuit of one of poetry's major functions, the rekindling of memory to link past with future. Even the root meaning of Horace's verb, *indicant,* to show, which is at the basis of its kindred *dicere* and the Greek cognate δείκνυμι, is as suitable for statues and their inscriptions as for poetry. It is just that poetry's demonstration has the edge in all that *clarus* stands for—imaginative brightness, sharpness, the self-pride that lends fame to others. Though the point is more subtly put than in *c.* 3.30, it also has time on its side. A contemporary of Horace could examine busts of the Scipios with their accompanying eulogies and compare, if he wished, the strength of their ability to survive through time with the potentiality of Ennian verse to grant eternity to the same figures. He could not, however, see Romulus, let alone Aeacus and the shapes that the poet extricates from mortality; he could only imagine them in the mind's eye as re-created not by inscriptions but by words formalized into a more illustrious order. It is no accident that, as we saw earlier, two of the Greek personages, the demigods Castor and Hercules, to whom the singer prays along with the implicitly deified Augustus at the conclusion of ode 5, reappear among those listed at the end of ode 8 on whom the singer of songs bestows eternal charm. Augustus need not now be mentioned (nor need Horace, as first-person speaker, enter the poem), but he would have understood the poet's message. If Augustus is worthy of apotheosis, it is a poet's special honoring and not his own *res gestae* which will effect the miracle.

Whatever the carefully modulated distinction between the fine arts and poetry in poem 8, the former make their presence felt at two other important junctures in the book's development. The first is in the initial ode where, we remember, among the many manifestations of artistic taste Paulus Fabius Maximus exhibits is the positioning of a marble statue of Venus under a roof of citron wood. An appreciation of sculpture and architecture is among the hundred *artes* that make up Fabius' mental world from which the aging speaker imagines himself excluded.[52] The other appearance

[52]In the interaction of odes 1 and 8 the uses of *ponere* at 1.20 and 8.8 are notable: each is concerned with statuary, the first with its literal placement, the second with its composition.

of the fine arts, both more subtle and more splendid, is in the book's final poems, especially the last.

The eighth ode looks to poetry's immortalizing power and the ninth shows this power explicitly at work with a speaker born near the loud-roaring Aufidus eternalizing his contemporary, Marcus Lollius. The speaker as monumentalizer fashions his figures and their attributes, assuring them a future by granting them poetry's art. This power grows stronger still in the last three poems. It causes one creation, Lyce, to age, brings another, Augustus, back home, with epic deeds seen in progress become prayer for their conclusion. Finally, it expands this particular *revocatio* into the broader cycle of an age of gold ever renewing itself. In all cases the speaker manipulates temporality, even to the point of asserting the future.

One detail is constant between the first two of these poems, as we have seen. The *fasti,* the calendrical records on stone which allegorically document time's swift inroads into Lyce's beauty, become the realistic *titulos memoresque fastus,* the statuary inscriptions and calendar records, with which the fathers and citizens of Rome will eternalize the virtues of Augustus. Poem 8 speaks of *incisa notis marmora publicis,* marbles carved with evidence for the public to read, which poetry surpasses.[53] Ode 14 muses on what *tituli* and commemorative inscriptions in the Roman world can grant Augustus while itself supplying poetic evidence for their contents. But the final poem, with its paratactic style complementing a dazzling enumeration of the accomplishments of Augustus, stands as a poetic model. It is itself one grand *titulus* of the emperor, furnishing the evidence, which ode 8 suppresses, for why poetry excels mere inscriptions in guaranteeing immortality, and exemplifying what the fathers of ode

---

[53]The thesis that these *marmora* refer to the *elogia* under the statues of the Augustan Forum was espoused by Kiessling and Heinze until their seventh edition where (on 13) they write: "Die Triumphatoresstatuen auf den Augustusforum, die erst etwa ein Jahrzehnt später aufgestellt werden, kann H. schon deshalb hier nicht im Auge haben, weil seine Auesserung dann eine Kritik an des Kaisers Plan bedeuten würde." Pasquali (758), writing in 1920, believes that Horace may be anticipating the statue inscriptions, but Degrassi (*Inscriptiones,* 1) dismisses any connection. To my knowledge no critic has made an interconnection among the forum's *tituli,* the *marmora* of ode 8, and the language of ode 15, whether we look to the specific wording of the poem's ending or to the cast of the whole.

14 might do, were they gifted with Horace's brilliance, in the way of encapsulating the evidence for the greatness of the Augustan Age.

But Horace does something still more specific. In the concluding, climactic lines of his *elogium*—

> Troiamque et Anchisen et almae
> progeniem Veneris canemus—

he incorporates the type of genealogy which would form the beginning of an actual *titulus* (once again we have evidence for finality that in fact initiates, for endings that are fresh starts). Except for the poetic replacement of Aeneas by the ambiguous *progenies,* which allows both Aeneas and Augustus, originator and renewer of Rome, to be equally understood, the language is similar to that in which Livy has the arrival of the Trojans reported to Latinus. He heard, says Livy, "that the throng were Trojans, their leader Aeneas, son of Anchises and Venus" (*multitudinem Troianos esse, ducem Aeneam filium Anchisae et Veneris*).[54] It is also close to Dido's exclamation on first beholding Aeneas:[55]

> "tune ille Aeneas quem Dardanio Anchisae
> alma Venus Phrygii genuit Simoentis ad undam?"

> "Are you that Aeneas whom nourishing Venus bore to Trojan Anchises
> at the wave of Phrygian Simois?"

It is equally parallel to the opening of what now seems certain to have been the *titulus* under the statue of Aeneas which stood in the Forum of Augustus: "Aeneas, son of Venus and Anchises, who led to Italy the Trojans who survived the war in which Troy was captured" (*Aeneas, Veneris et Anchisae filius Troianos qui capta Troia bello superfuerunt in Italiam adduxit*).[56]

---

[54]Livy 1.1.8.

[55]Vir. *Aen.* 1.617–18.

[56]The *elogia* of the Forum Augustum have been collected most recently by Degrassi (*Inscriptiones,* 1–36). The *elogium* of Aeneas is usually reconstructed from a *titulus* for Aeneas found in the forum at Pompeii (Degrassi #85, pp. 69–70; *CIL* 10.808, and see *CIL* 1.1, p. 189, #I). The *titulus* that Degrassi posits for him in the Forum (#1, p. 9) cannot be his, first, because the base on which it is

Looking in summary, then, at the book's beginning, middle, and end, we contemplate a pyramidal architecture that takes us from a poem out of whose central world of Fabian artistry the speaker is exiled to one in which the speaker creates verbal effigies of Republican worthies more brilliant than bronze or stone artifacts, to one, finally, in which the poetry configures, in deed and in idea, the greatest hero of them all. Ode 15 creates for Augustus an extraordinary *titulus* in a placement at once climactic and closing, honorific and fulfilling poetic space. If Horace, in the process of finishing this poetic monument in his medium of words, is in fact anticipating Augustus' magnificent forum, as I argue in the appendix, the allusions only confirm the design of his own poetry book, his mental architectonics. His final ode is the poetic equivalent of the detailed iconography and general spatial layout of an architectural form, rich in individual ideas enmeshed in a composition of great originality. Even on the assumption that aspects of the forum were still under discussion as he wrote, the emperor is soon to pay Horace the enormous compliment of concretizing what in the poetry remains abstract. He will use the hints in which Horace's *elogium* abounds not to tell of himself specifically—two words suffice for his literal *titulus*—but, by larger gestures to the eye, to teach the onlooker to think of the Roman past and present in a context that seems to reassure its future. This is exactly what Horace accomplishes, as well as much more, because he is incorporating and revising his own poetic heritage as well, in his final lyric memorial to Rome, Augustus, and, to the percipient, himself.

The individual trinities, whose linear progress builds toward the final trio, can thus be once more seen as synecdoches for the grander signposts of 1, 8, and 15. Each has a different thrust. We have poems on the speaker's literary self-placement, on his role as teacher, monumentalizer, sequesterer from time, and, finally, stationer in and of time. But each trio mirrors the book in its entirety as the physical yields to the metaphysical, the erotic to the aesthetic, and poems on the decay of human beauty and the waning of bodily passion give place to odic eulogies of the permanence of the poetic self and its artistry. The paradoxical but uplifting progress of the book, in the

---

found shows no evidence that it held a statue, second, because the inscription itself is both too short and attributes the designation *rex Latinorum* to Aeneas for which there is no parallel (see Zanker, 32, n. 88).

part and in the whole, is from aging to the birth and rejuvenation, whether implicit or explicit, of the poet-speaker in odes 3 and 9, of the children of the moment of secularity in 6, of spring and the singer's subtle melodies in 12, of the offspring of Venus (*progeniem Veneris*) at the end of 15. Or if we survey the specific interaction between the initial and final odes, we watch the change from a speaker who quite decorously sings of his lack of rhetorical skill (*decus* enhances the appropriate aestheticism of Fabius Maximus) to a poem that musters exceptional energies of the spirit to expound the ethical artistry of Augustus and ends with a speaker peering confidently into the hereafter of his, and Roman, song.

The comforting, if delusive, message is that art, specifically poetry and the musics of its song, can abstract its creator and audience from time, or looked at from another vantage, can allow history and its time-riddled protagonists to share in resuscitations vouchsafed only ordinarily to nature about her quotidian or annual cycles. There is scarcely a poem among these fifteen that does not allude to or describe stretches or instants of celebration which glorify the present and recall the past in order to help time stop or effect its recurrence. These ritual festivities are contained within and reenacted by the rituals of the poetic artist, those crafty words that in hymning perpetuate a series of enchanted moments, whether public or private.

Augustus is the lucky beneficiary of these liturgies that both stabilize and refresh language. The monumentalization of the one career is the consummation of the other. The confirmation of one is the finalization of the other, and, cryptically, as one is continued and revived, so is the other perpetually reborn. The myth of Rome's political and ethical triumphs achieved, of foreign and domestic orderings effectuated, is bolstered by allusion to a double past, to Rome's history and Horace's literary inheritance, whether self-generated or absorbed from others. The development of one is paralleled in the development of the other. Assurance of the Augustan peace allows Horace, in his imagination, to step beyond his legacy of pessimism from Virgil, in whose epic individual desire constantly challenges and in the end prevails over idealistic ideological schemata. He can surmount the irony of a Propertius toward politics and politicians, a stance not unlike his own in the earlier collection of odes. The habitual egocentrism of the lyric speaker, which tends existentially to respond to life's trials and joys, seems lost in communal praise, as epic's impersonal historicity and elegy's private hurts and acts of evasion are mutated into the odist's public song of acceptance and multifaceted reconciliation.

Yet the final mythmaker of self and its world, eternalizing each at once, is the writer himself, the "I" pretending to be subsumed into a larger "we," nudging the past into the future by the potent immediacy of words and their powerful orderings of order. The book's cyclical affirmations and linear thrusts toward final climax both confirm the poet's projection of the efficacy of his own imagination. Augustus may renew the civilizing strength of Rome's political artistry, but it is an *ars poetica* as practiced by the genius of Horace which has helped preserve that civilization and its values, and make it part of a larger sweep than even Augustus may have foreseen.

CONCLUSION

But Poets . . . are not only the authors of language and
of music, of the dance, and architecture, and statuary, and
painting; they are the institutors of laws, and the founders
of civil society, and the inventors of the arts of life, and the
teachers, who draw into a certain propinquity with the
beautiful and the true, that partial apprehension of the
agencies of the invisible world which is called religion.

SHELLEY, *A Defence of Poetry*

We should begin an overview of Horace's accomplishment in his
final book of odes by a brief comparison of the continuities and
disjunctions from his first, more acclaimed collection. The great lyric
themes, however varied, remain constant in each group—erotic mutability, seasonal change, imminence of death. The need persists for
moments of revelry to relieve life's tedium and worries, and we sense
the same pervasive ethos of moderation and restraint called upon to
regulate human actions in so many of the earlier odes. What changes,
and changes most dramatically, is the poet's stance toward history,
politics, and the wider public circumstances of his world.

Not that power and those who wield it are absent from the earlier
collection. Poetry of retreat and privacy, voicings of a self-sufficient
mind devoted to solitude, stillness, and the need for inner contemplation, are ever in counterpoint with meditations on statesmen about
their work of forging an empire, on ambition, on fortune's fickleness, on our moral limitations. Sometimes the two spheres merge in a

masterpiece like the fourth "Roman" ode where Augustus, tired from his martial activities, is urged to yield to the sway of the Muses, which is to say, to the singer's encouragement of counsel in the manipulation of might. As often as not, the realm of public ethics is troubling to speakers who remain aloof from it. It is to be fretted about from the escapist remove of a landscape signifying devotion to the *vita contemplativa* that shudders at the prospect of life at large.

Nor is concern for important social issues missing from the younger Horace. Rather, his speakers direct their rhetoric toward such issues from a distance, not as participants living them out in actuality. The spiritual leap from the persona behind the seventh *epode*, haranguing the viciousness of the criminal Roman populace, to the speaker of the first "Roman" ode ("I loathe the profane mob and avoid it") is not so grand as may at first appear. Though we hypothesize the first voicing his chagrin with immediacy from a podium and the second singing to a select audience of impeccable initiates, they share a tone of hauteur. The speaker is in each case profoundly troubled by public immorality, and in fact the "Roman" odes as a group, deep though their indictment goes, could only have been written by a poet earnestly committed to the very institutions and inherited standards of behavior which he sensed in jeopardy. Even the masterly penultimate poem of the first collection, as we have seen, urges Maecenas away from the "smoke, commercialism and noise of Rome," and from his disquiet over the situation abroad, to drink with Horace in his Sabine sanctuary. The habitual Horatian moral is there: take life easy, my friend; don't brood too much over fortune's volubility; emulate my economic and psychic independence of body and mind.

But this circumscribed stance, valuable as it is and typical of Horace's passion in his odes for spiritual balance as the best countermeasure to life's distress, could only have been bought at the expense of caring for what would have been Maecenas' no doubt honest anxieties for the immediate situation of Rome. Horace's sense of responsibility to the inner life of himself and his associates allows him to formulate only a largely negative appraisal of Rome and Romanness. As book 3 rounds out its cycle from "Roman" odes to covert lecture to Augustus (24) and overt seduction of Maecenas away from the troubled metropolis for a private *causerie*, Horace remains the mordant critic of society at large. In the complex tension between the urban and the pastoral which enlivens so much of his lyric verse, Horace opts, regularly though by no means totally, for the seclusion and spiritual autonomy that define the latter, leaving the former in its decline to suffer his scorn. Rome is not ready for his poetic embrace.

The metamorphosis in Horace's thinking in the ten years that intervene between the two lyric collections is astonishing. Perhaps changes in Rome itself gave Horace impetus for his reversal. Whatever his reasoning, he now not only brings into being but sustains through odic praise the world of power and the individuals who possess it, a Fabius Maximus, a Lollius, especially an Augustus. The aloof individualist, complaining of Rome's spiritual dissolution, becomes the whole-hearted participant in responsibility for her grandeur and well-being, the creator of public odes often about the act of communal song and the shared values it represents.

Not that all the old themes are absent. We still have a series of poems about the private losses that individual human time entails. In one instance the theme of deprivation is incorporated within an otherwise grandly Pindaric encomium. But their very structuring into the emotional rhythms of that complex verbal action we call a poetry book serves again and again to prepare for, and hence underscore, the more numerous poems on societal, historical time that they introduce. They are melancholy punctuations in a series whose general tonality is positive, granting assurance to Rome and its contemporary military and ethical heroes of a future through song. The recurrent odes on human temporality only reinforce the speaker's new dedication to the immediacies, and to the immortalizing, of Augustan Rome. We focus now not on the singer but on the song.

In terms of ideology, these poems mark a moment of reversal in a more extensive sequence of pessimistic literary events that make up a negative apocalyptic tradition for Rome. This heritage begins, apparently, with the conclusion of Catullus 64 and its searing indictment of contemporary immorality, echoed also in *De Rerum Natura,* and continues in Sallust's *Catiline* where present decadence is condemned through a contrasting vision of a past society living uprightly on the land. *Eclogue* 4 and *epode* 16 are two sides of this coin, the one painting a rosy picture of return to a noble style of living after a period of strife, the other preaching escape to a never-never land as the only solution to present difficulties. The *Aeneid* looks, in its teleology, to an aureate future under Augustus, while its foreground ultimately appraises human nature, even the nature of those placed in positions of dominance, more realistically. The first collection of odes, as we have seen, draws near its conclusion with a negative look at contemporary Roman values, but also with the intimation that matters might change for the better if Augustus learns from his poets.

One major figure who passes through these poems is Achilles, emblem of cruelty without clemency in Catullus and of war's necessity in *eclogue* 4. In the *Aeneid* he appears in at least three guises—in his own person in the series of brutalities that adorn Dido's temple to Juno, under the surrogate of his son Pyrrhus, whose ugly slaughter of Priam is one of the epic's most dramatic moments, and as the titular hero himself. For as Aeneas goes about his final deed of killing Turnus, his victim is meant in part to resemble the suppliant Hector of *Iliad* 22. The essential purging of Achilles occurs at last in ode 6 of the fourth book. With his going Apollo can relinquish the martial arts to reespouse poetry, and the new *saeculum* can commence in the poet's song. The future visions of *eclogue* 4 and the *Aeneid* become present realities, and the negative or, at best, hesitantly hopeful tone of the foreground in the *Aeneid* and in the earlier odes concerned with Augustus and Rome, can now be dispensed with. Looking at the span of the book as a whole, we see that the new age predicted in ode 2 to surpass even a restored golden age, when Augustus will come home to be greeted by festivity and song, becomes a reality in the final two poems, with Augustus returned and the era of his rule proved both morally and aesthetically exalted. As so often in this poetry, acts of completion and origination, of brilliant conclusions and equally miraculous fresh starts in historical, religious, and poetic events, are commensurate and indistinguishable.

In these great poems of reconciliation, where the hitherto private poet accepts a public role because, among other reasons, the dubieties of epic's ethos have been replaced by lyric of celebratory renewal, other ingredients kept distinct in Horace's earlier mental world can now be harmonized. One is the antinomy between Rome and the Sabine landscape as emblems of ways of thinking. The second ode, for instance, finds the small bee-artisan-poet feeding on thyme, fashioning toilsome, carefully wrought songs around the grove and banks of wet Tibur. By the end of the poem the bee-poet has been displaced by his metonymy, the heifer-poem, growing young, as does all great verse, not old, on expansive grasses (size is a metaphor for quality, not quantity, for the scope of artistic vigilance in construction, not for any overextended grandiloquence). But both now are at the service of Augustus, singing songs at Rome and "sacrificed" to the deified Augustus on his triumphant reappearance.

But the union of literal-figurative landscape, Tiburtine, and of the mind, with the reality of Rome is most apparent in ode 3, in a way the most "biographical" of the collection and the first in which the speaker's consorting with divine sources of inspiration prepares us for his ability to make his subjects divine. Sculptured Horace is fashioned by Tibur; her fertility and thick foliage are metaphoric for his resultant poetic richness and density. Tibur grants him spiritual nobility; Rome bestows his *dignitas*. She documents and secures the excellence that only comes to poets and poetry from judgmental appreciation by readers after the act of writing. The poet sees himself as a breathing, pleasing fabrication, perhaps "placed" in effigy among choirs of bards, certainly pointed out, in his steadied monumentality as Apolline lyre player to Rome, by those who pass him by. Poetry and poet, artifact and artificer, are one, fashioned by the secluded natural landscape of Tibur but now needing the accolade of the larger public context of the city and its denizens to affirm his permanence in his art. The complexity of this interdependence of country and city, creator and audience, inspiration and its stimuli, will only be revealed as the book unfolds and Horace perseveres in suiting Rome and Romans to his own imagination.

If the concluding ode provides an *elogium* for Augustus which in fact looks constantly to Horace's poetry and poetics, ode 3, especially when taken in company with its predecessors, provides a spiritual *titulus* for the poet himself by touching on many themes that will gain further prominence in the subsequent odes. The poet who, in the conclusion of each trinity of poems, will go on to write odes to Apollo and the song of secularity, on his origin by the roaring Aufidus and the subsequent affect on Lollius' longevity, on spring's musics and their siren call to Vergilius, on Apollo and communal eulogy of the emperor, has much to tell us even here about himself, as Melpomene presides at a spiritual birth that outlasts any physical death.

We might first pause on the notion of artistry itself which is much more on Horace's mind here than in earlier works, as if the various modes of imaginative expression and their differing methods of monumentalizing their subjects were of special interest as his talent reached final maturity. Artistic expression takes a range of guises in these poems, from the mere gracefulness of looks and perhaps performance in dance and in music of the young Lyce (*artium gratarum facies*) to the ancient arts (*veteres artes*) of politics Augustus successfully revived. But even at the start the fine arts directly take their place in the world of Paulus Fabius Maximus, *centum puer artium,* graceful, eloquent, aesthete inclined to the appropriate in statuary and architecture. Implicit even here is a comparison with the ways and means of poetry: the amusedly ironic speaker, for all the elegance of his presentation, claims to lack the grace and rhetorical prowess he imputes to Fabius.

The conjunction of eloquence and aestheticism, thematic foil to the speaker's elegiac biography in poem 1, is varied to become the major concern of ode 2. In a poem now directly about poetics, the speaker sees his métier as both similar to and distinct from a craftsman's. To emulate Pindar is to play Icarus to the Theban poet's Daedalus, to be an artificial re-creator, not a natural genius, an imitator, not an originator. Yet, as the poem opens out, the question becomes one as much of degree as of kind. For all the soaring singularity of the Pindaric swan, Horace's humble bee is still, if scarcely, airborne. Pindar's words are a greater gift than one hundred signs of palpable artistry, yet comparison with the fine arts is the way in which the greater permanence of poetry is measured. Soon, therefore, Horace seems to turn irony against himself. He is a tiny sculptor doing what Pindar does not, making his own lapidary songs, that are *operosa,* involving much effort but elaborately wrought and smacking of artificiality. But by switching from a realistic comparison—poems versus statues—to metaphor, Horace takes the intelligence, not the products, of Daedalus to himself. And by the end of the poem, in his final symbolic act, Horace's poetic vow will be as natural as can be, a heifer whose horns imitate the moon.

In sum, then, Horace may make use of the "arts" (8.5) of Parrhasius and Scopas to boast of his own verses' ability to withstand time, and of the metaphor of artist to show off his craftsmanly gifts. He may even have the best of both worlds and be himself and his poetry at once, sculptured in Tibur and lionized in Rome. But the "arts" that he will practice and that he will expend on Lollius (9.3) have not been previously publicized. Together they forge his own version of the "art of song" (*artem carminis*, 6.29–30) that is Apollo's special gift.

A major supporting motif to the idea of artistry in these poems is the dual theme of eloquence and its counterpart, wordlessness, and of music and sound with their parallel opposite, silence. Augustus may practice political "arts" and extend the Latin "name" over the globe, but the poet's magic act of "naming," which stems from Apollo's other gift, his own *nomen poetae,* can only come from exerting the combination of words and music that is the essence of lyric. To look first at ode 3 again, if "Horace" is to be transfigured as the player of the Roman lyre, it is because of Melpomene's gift of melody which is a compromise between extremes. She grants swan song to voiceless fish, that is, she can make the mute tellingly articulate, yet she also tames the sweet roar of the lyre itself. Her benison is the combination of brilliantly natural song with the ability to temper the lyre's dulcet din. The speaker who in *c.* 3.29 sought to lure Maecenas away from the noise of Rome to his own reasoned landscape, has become in his way the champion of the city, bringing to it a *strepitus,* a resonance that here is poetical not practical, elevating not repellent.

Music as a metaphor for ways of hearing life through a poet's words is worked out most elaborately, as we have seen, in ode 12, but words and music become song and, publicized in the act of singing, are touched upon in poem after poem. In ode 1 we find the songs, and the three instruments accompanying them, that will delight Venus in her sensuous new shrine. Poetics aside, the "occasion" of ode 2 is the anticipated triumphant return of Augustus at which both Iullus and the speaker will sing. The fifth ode ends with a double act of speaking (*dicimus, dicimus*) and with a snippet of song itself which will celebrate Augustus' advent, but, as another poem about the act of singing, it too is a *carmen* in Augustus' honor. An even more explicit song about song is the sixth ode, as lyre-playing Apollo teaches his Roman deputy to educate in turn his own charges into the continuities of secular harmony. In ode 9 the reechoing of the Aufidus which accompanied "Horace's" birth assures Lollius of eternal reverberation through his words. Only upon learning the speaker's measures and *carmen,* which are and are not the poem itself, can the Phyllis of poem 11 lessen life's dismal troubles. The reverse magic operates for Lyce in poem 13 where the speaker's words of curse leave her voice with the quivering rasp of age while approving green

Chia's talent on the harp. Finally we have the book's ultimate word, *canemus,* the singing about the subject of song which is, for one last time, the *carmen* itself, the melodious charm that renews self and subject at once.

Closely allied with quality of song throughout book 4 is quality and endurance of speech. Ode 1 suggests that Paulus, because he is eloquent as well as graceful, will succeed in love where the tongue-tied speaker, falling into awkward silence, will not. But there is a stronger suppressor of voice even than love. We learn from ode 7 that his *facundia,* his persuasiveness as a rhetor, will not extricate Torquatus from the clutches of death. What might save him, the next poem makes abstractly clear, is the sound flowing from the poet's pages that, if they were silent, could allow Censorinus to slip into oblivion, as would Romulus if silence, envious of the power of speech (*taciturnitas invida*), had had its way. In ode 1, the tongue of the foolishly lovesick, aging speaker proved impotent. It is now the "tongue of powerful bards" (*lingua potentium vatum*) which saves their protégés from time. The next poem offers an example. Though Lollius may be both a *vindex* and a *iudex,* someone who uses speaking to guarantee justice, it is the election of his own sacred poet to speak on his behalf ("I will not in silence leave you unadorned in my pages") which secures immortality for his very excellence as a rhetor. Finally, we remember ode 6 as a study in the perversity and creativity of speech, taking us from a boastful Niobe, a lying horse, and an Achilles who would murder a still voiceless infant even in its mother's womb, to the metamorphic utterances of Venus and Apollo and the poet's song of secularity. These voices are more symbolic versions of the words imagined as sung for Augustus' return and for the renewings it postulates, from the second ode to the last.

Scarcely separable from the themes of song and speech, the theme of festivity is closely associated with another subject long noted to be a constant concern of the poet's in book 4—even more than in the first collection—time and its passage. I have already listed the acts of celebration these poems incorporate. They run from the reception of Venus in ode 1, to the differing celebrations for Augustus' return in 2 and 5, to the training and continuing teaching of the ritual of secularity in ode 6. Poems 11 and 12 are invitations to Phyllis and Vergilius to share the speaker's moment of rejoicing and escape, which is to say, his poetry and its richness. Finally ode 15 is one grand hymn to Augustus, ending with the futurity of ritual song ennobling the futurity of Rome and its heroes.

Sometimes a specific calendrical date is in question—the day that Hasdrubal was defeated at the Metaurus, the birthday of Maecenas bisecting the month of April, the date of the fall of Alexandria taking on further significance in the life of Augustus fifteen years later. Sometimes the occasion is commended through its own manifestations of brightness. In ode 2 the "happy days" (*laetos dies*) that Iullus will glorify become the "handsome sun" (*sol pulcher*) that the speaker will extol. In the second stanza of ode 5, Augustus' *lux*, his bright gleam, is inextricable from the days (*dies*) and suns (*soles*) that glisten in its honor. And, as the poem proceeds, we learn first, that the blessing of Augustus allows the farmer to "bury the day" (*condit diem*) on his own hills, second, that he remains on their minds when the day is in full vigor (*integro die*) or when the sun is beneath the ocean. The magic here is that, through Augustus and through the regularity of chants in his praise, man keeps within his control the cycle of the day, with the poet allowing himself no opportunity for commentary on the divergence of human and natural time. The same holds true for ode 6 where the praises of Diana, going about her monthly tasks of bringing prosperity to crops, are closely associated with the "festive lights" (*festas luces*) that the *saeculum* brings back.

Honest appraisal of human time comes, of course, with ode 7 where the temporal frame in which mortals live out their lives is set in contradistinction to nature's system of loss and regeneration, be it revealed in the seasons of the year, the moon's monthly restorations, or the cycle of the day by comparison with which our "setting" is into deathly permanence. And human loss, especially loss of beauty and hence of love, in the change from youth to age, afflicts the protagonists in other crucially placed poems throughout the collection—the speaker in ode 1 fatuously hankering after youth and youthful love, Ligurinus voicing in ode 10 his own self-anagnorisis as he watches his adolescent bloom fade, Lyce in ode 13, aged by the poet's inimical sorcery.

Countering these odes on time's ineluctability are poems on a poet's time and time-making so placed as to end both the book as a whole and its individual segments on a confident note. Ode 3 outlines how the poet's birth under the supervision of Melpomene assures him a place as lyric artisan and artifact of Rome, and ode 9 takes the speaker's birth by the roaring Aufidus as evidence for the death-lessness of his subjects (the sacred bard can overcome for his ad-dressee the "long night" of forgetfulness). Occasionally positive and negative views of time are kept in delicate balance within a poem. The prime examples here are the marvelous odes 11 and 12. Each is an invitation to a moment of conviviality, the one dedicated to a day, Maecenas' birthday, the other to a season, spring. Each is engaged with sound and song, the first with Phyllis' singing, the second with the varying sonorities of spring encased in the poet's own subtle music. (If they listen carefully both Phyllis and Vergilius will learn much about themselves. To accept the speaker's invitation is to yield, as well, to his imagination.) Yet in each case the image of blackness tinges the sparkle of the day and its joviality. In the ode to Phyllis the darkness is at once literal, allegorical, and symbolic, in the black smoke that curls amid the hearth flames, in the charred body of Phaethon, the Gleamer who overreaches toward his ancestral sun, and in the black cares that song will lessen but not dispel. It is because of Vergilius' awareness of the underworld's black fires, ode 12 tells us, that he should quaff the genial unwisdom of the poet's primaveral wine.

Ode 4 is the most extensive example of this concatenation of themes and its sometimes ambiguous tonality. It begins with the juxtaposition of youth and spring that the next, closely related, poem will also utilize. In the fifth ode's initial similes, Augustus' face is like spring while he himself is a youth yearned for by Rome, his mother. The more elaborate analogy that opens ode 4 finds the eagle Drusus launched from his nest by Youth (*Iuventas*) and taught by spring breezes to make its first swoops. As well as youth and its season (a condition and a time continuous, we assume, for Augustus and his *saeculum*), poem 4 celebrates a calendrical day that is also visualized as a moment of brightness. The day "smiles" in its glimmer just as in ode 11 the host's house "smiles" as its silver glimmers at the prospect of Phyllis' advent. Hannibal, by contrast, has brought to Rome the total darkness (*tenebrae*) that ode 7 associates death, and, paradox-ically, fire (*flamma*) as well. But his is a blaze that rather than help-ing to brighten a festive moment (as in ode 11) would destroy like the flames Achilles uses to menace unborn children in ode 6 or the fires of the underworld which, in ode 12, are both black and blacken-ing. Yet in the final third of the ode, the poet allows us to enter the

[316]

mind of Hannibal through his spoken words. From them we learn not of death inflicted but of a double death suffered—of the actual death of Hasdrubal, and of the "setting" (*occidit, occidit*) of the general's hopes and fortunes. Augustus and his heroic stepson may be associated with seasons, days, and festivals that bespeak recurrence. Hannibal links himself with mortal time. History is therefore twice-over adapted to lyric as it attends to moments of rejuvenation and of privation.

I have been speaking about certain interests that permeate the book as a whole, a concern with art and artistry, with speech and silence and its kindred pair, naming for posterity and consigning to the unremembered. We have traced the poet's concentration on festivity and the parallel importance of ritual, and we have watched him analyzing time from a multitude of vantages, not least for its eternalizing congruence with art and ritual and for its destructive dominance of the human and the mortal. These interests are inextricably associated with other patterns of development and transformation we have traced as we read the book in appropriately linear fashion. Chief among these is the triumph of permanence over transience, of public over private, of values of the community over personal fancies and misfortunes. In tones that constantly press toward affirmation rather than denial, Horace proclaims the social function of poetry through his commitment to Rome and to the refreshment and stability of her civilization. At the conclusion of his career Horace, like the fatherland in ode 5, stricken with yearning for the absent Augustus, writes poetry about a love that transcends mere individual eroticism. The fulfillment of lyric desire comes now in wider contexts, both poetic and social, artistic and moral, in the self-assurance of the poet, in the renewal of quality in Roman life, and in the transcendence of both over the tugs of mortality by the power of poetry itself.

As a book about desire, it dwells on the figure of Venus and, in particular, on her metamorphosis from goddess of human sexuality into divine progenitor of Rome. From deity of love, a constant, ruling reminder of the irreconcilability between sexuality and the passage of personal time, she becomes mother goddess, steady symbol of historical continuity and of the magnificence of Augustus' Rome and its heritage. But Horace idealizes this maternity by eliminating the presence of Venus' Roman husband, the war-god Mars, from his concluding poem. He thus tells us that his poetry, in prejudicing our view of her, may also be romanticizing Augustan glory. The poet's magic, his version of Venus, brings old age to Lyce and seems to say of Rome that, unlike aging prisoners of Venus' emotionality such as Lyce, it will, in an assured future, be ever young, fertile, artful.

A mythic Venus may have made Rome possible and have inspired her greatest lyric poet and his poetry. Yet this poetry itself captures in seemingly ageless verse what was in fact a brief, shining moment, and claims to make it eternal thereby. It is poetry instinct with Venus, not the Rome engendered by Venus, which insists on immortality and the ability to immortalize. *Odes* 4 is the authoritative proof of Horace's claim, in the final ode of his earlier collection, to have made Greek lyric his own. It is this extraordinary Romanization, among other factors, that distances him from Propertius who restricts his Muse to amatory verse as a means of avoiding the responsibilities as well as the pitfalls of public poetry.

To reassess, then, our list of the book's major themes: this is poetry about art and about the need for grace in its implementation, yet it is itself an example of the most elegant poetic craftsmanship, showing great allegiance to its heritage and yet great originality in summoning up the past, predicting the future, molding the immediate. The social metamorphoses in the Roman present—of war into peace, of disintegration into restoration—become absorbed in the transvaluation of literature as lyric triumphs over Propertian elegy or Virgilian epic, and text assimilates and masters context, whether that of the Roman historical present or of the literary past, transforming it into something as novel as the ethical renewal it describes and augments.

Horace is concerned within his poems with eloquence and muteness, yet his poetry is a marvelously articulate example of the power of words and the potential of language to foster and re-create its world. And if his poems go readily about the task of naming others, augmenting poetry's role as verbal memory and its function as a rite of preservation, they also illustrate the great act of self-naming as they create their own larger figural continuity into which their subjects are absorbed. Horace is fascinated with festivities, celebrations, and their accompanying rituals, vatically declaring the return of Augustus, or secular renewal, or momentary retreat from the menacings of temporality. Yet the poetry itself is a complex, magical ceremony that, if in the imagination alone, through the cycles and rhythms of words, dismisses mutability and brings about the very restorations of which it tells.

Horace's intense Pindarizing in book 4 not only betokens his increased interest in the possession and possessors of power but also stands as metaphor for the enhanced intensity of his poetry itself through heightening of the lyric genre. Ultimately, of course, either irony or a quieter tone, equally metaphoric, deflates the pretensions of political capability and incorporates them within lyric of restraint, but this is only to claim final potential for poetry not politics, for the capability of the imagination not the sword.

Finally, these odes are about time. Not only does the matter of poetry tame history by acts of specification which hold time still, but the poetry itself, because it is lyric, by definition solemnizes the "now" of its own foreground, joyously asserting its independence from the impersonal distance of epic narrative or from elegy's penchant for the nostalgic or the unattainable.

I presume that, even with its careful dashes of irony, Augustus would have sensed in Horace's fourth book of odes the most heart-whole appraisal from any of his poets of his regime and the realities of its accomplishment. The background of the *Aeneid* anticipates a glorious history for Augustan Rome, but the struggle between moderation and madness in its protagonists offers little solace to those who seek from it a positive assessment of future Roman, or human, modes of behavior. In his final ode Horace recalls the *Aeneid,* modifying it in one essential respect. At the end of Virgil's epic we find Aeneas readying to kill Turnus, "afflamed by frenzy and frightening in his wrath" (*furiis accensus et ira terribilis*). By the time Horace concludes his career, his sense is that the abstractions which rule Aeneas' emotions at the climax of his tale have been banished from a Rome now under the guardianship of Augustus. *Furor* and *ira,* so he claims, no longer have a place in Rome's moral environment. In Rome the era of war, especially civil war, is now over, and the acts of brutality which dot the emperor's rise to power are things of the past.

In this poetry of historical and spiritual returns and renewals time can now stop and begin anew. And the genre that authenticates this singular occasion is lyric not epic. What Horace presents to Augustus is not poetry that blazons *virtutes* in action but that chants in odic form the character behind deeds long done, for future admiration. It is poetry imagined as written in, and ultimately of, *otium.* But

Rome's rebirth and its futurity are coextensive with the advent and longevity of a poet who now, as Rome triumphs, wins, through acts of co-optation into poetry, a series of more intimate poetic skirmishes with the mortal time that encroaches on the private, lyric "I." For a poet such as Horace to embrace Rome is to attach his imagination to a historical entity that might not at first seem suitable material for the lyricist's more limited enterprise. But, as private evanescence yields to public *continua* in the flow of his thought, by taming epic potentiality to the devices of lyric, Horace controls Rome and fashions it to conform to his own genius. For this act of authority Augustus and we, his readers, are handsomely in his debt.

I have been reading Horace's final book as, I suspect, would his ancient audience, traversing it as a sequence that carefully and climactically develops its emotional and ideological patterning over the whole. Various structures help modulate this poetic dynamism and I have laid special stress on Horace's arrangement of poems in groups of three. Other schemes are both plausible and revelatory. If we look at clusters of five, the first and last pentads each end with two poems devoted to Augustus. Of these pairs the first is more generous with the details of history, the second more paratactic and enclosed, given to a litany of restorations subsequent to the necessary acts of power that the preceding odes outline and manipulate.[1] Or, if we double our figure and trace numberings by decades, we find that poems 1 and 10 center on Ligurinus and the problematics of aging, while the odes that frame the book's final such grouping, 6 and 15, begin with Apollo, symbol of Rome's change from war to artistry and teacher-protector of the poet who at once monumentalizes and immortalizes the metamorphosis and its creators, Augustus and his poet.

But the analysis of structures is a means, not an end, only one of the many tools at the critic's disposal as he searches out quality in poetry and attempts to describe it. Its value lies, first, in directing and redirecting the reader's attention to essential ideas, modes of expression, rhythms of tone, sense, or even sound which recur throughout a poetry book but which a mind of Horace's brilliance is forever varying and scrutinizing from different angles. Yet even by so doing structure is the covert servant of a linear reading, raising or

[1]This pairing is discussed in detail by Dahlmann, 344–45.

modifying expectations, confirming or reshaping patterns of order, and pushing the reader, in ways he or she may only dimly sense on first study, inexorably toward the book's conclusion which in the case of *Odes* 4, is the capstone of Horace's lyric career.

Ode 15, then, holds a place of enormous prestige, as the closing poem of the sequence of odes which forms book 4, itself the grand closure of a larger sequence embracing the lyric poet's whole oeuvre. We may ourselves conclude with a brief search for parallels in later poetic careers. Since in these poems private diminution is always superseded by certainty of the survival of poetry and through it of the poet and his chosen milieu, we lack both the romantic poet's frantic attempts to stave off the losses of individual time and the modern artist's nihilism or deliberate avoidance of responsibility. Though poetry of its author's high maturity, it neither pessimistically decries its world nor dispenses hoary wisdom from Olympian isolation. We lack the tiredness and resignation of Robert Lowell's last collection, *Day by Day;* nor do we find poems on essences and silences, on the imagination and the solitudes of interiority, which make Stevens' "The Rock" so moving. Though past time and the ongoing life of the mind are Horace's obvious concerns, the tone we sense from these poems is neither regretful nor solipsistic. It is not given to rage or to self-isolation.

But there are poets of the last two centuries whose careers end in ways that illumine and are illumined by Horace's final lyrics. Keats is one example. If we read his odes sequentially and congruently, as Helen Vendler has taught us, we progress climactically through these masterworks of 1819 until we reach the ode "To Autumn," written in September of that year and Keats' final poem of any scope.[2] It is an ode to fruition and its boon companion, loss, to a time of year which embraces at once expansion and subsidence, creativity and decay. The second of these dichotomies we do not find in Horace who dwells, in his moment of closure, not on thoughts of finality but of renewal. The distinction can be seen even in an area where, paradox-

---

[2]The ode "To Autumn" was "composed" (letter of Keats to John Reynolds, September 21) on Sunday, September 19, 1819. In all probability Keats' tuberculosis, which was to kill him by February 1821, was in the active stage by early that same month (Bate, 616). He would have known the symptoms well.

Lipking (180–84) criticizes with sensitivity what may have been his last verses, "This living hand . . ."

ically, the two poems overlap, namely their ultimate attention to music—Keats, in his last stanza, listening to the sounds of gnats and lambs, hedge-cricket, red-breast, or swallow; Horace, in his final verses, to the songfulness of "we" singers, by whose iterations poetry's past and present lives on into the future. For in the midst of his hymn to nature's resonance, Keats urges our eye to contemplate the soft-dying day and our sense of touch to feel the wind that "lives or dies," on whom the "wailful choir" of gnats depends. Even the "gathering swallows" whose twitter records the landscape's final music can be interpreted in two ways, as the last item in a series that looks to natural and artistic continuity, or as the concluding reminder that day precedes night, autumn winter, and life death, and that death-in-life is as basic to nature's cycles as it is to human linearity.

If a melancholy tinges the actuality of Keats' music which is not found in Horace's last allusion to song, nevertheless on a subtler level of poetics, as the imagination in the act of creation looks to itself and its inheritance, both poets are remarkably akin. Both final poems are rich gestures of retrospection. Vendler has demonstrated not only how "To Autumn" is the culminating statement of ideas that circulate through the preceding odes but that it looks to Keats' earlier work and to Coleridge, Wordsworth, Milton, Shakespeare, and Spenser as well.[3] What seems a meditation on a day and a season is also an act of homage to the past, concentrating its power on the present act of originality. The same is true for Horace. For under the superficies of a highly particularized eulogy to Augustus, culminating in the promise of rituals of revival through song, is a deep study of the Greco-Roman literary past, especially of the near contemporary work of Virgil and Propertius, by which Horace tests his own novelty and lends it the forceful backing of his intellectual forebears.

Looking to more recent literature, we also find analogies between Horace's envoi and the Yeats of Last Poems. If the operative form in our comparison of Horace to Keats is music, here it must be sculpture. Horace ends his final ode with words about song, but implicitly even in poem 15 and openly many times throughout his book, as we have observed, he compares himself to a sculptor and his poetry to the fine arts in the competition for permanency. Yeats also creates a series of speakers who see their transcendence into the changelessness

[3]Vendler, chap. 7, esp. 234–43.

of art take the visible form of statuary. In "Lapis Lazuli," for instance, we find a speaker who delights "to imagine" three stone
figures who, presumably not unlike the poet himself, combine age
and gaiety in their stability. "The Statues," another poem that resorts
to imagery of artifact to support the possibility of immortality
through pattern and form, tell us of Phidias and his peers—

> . . . the men
> That with a mallet or a chisel modelled these
> Calculations that look but casual flesh . . .

Then there is the last poem itself, "Under Ben Bulben." It is appropriate that this act of closure read like an epitaph, penned for a poet
whose "limestone" solidity, coldly scorning life and death, gives the
reader in its course the *ars poetica* of W. B. Yeats himself ("Irish poets,
learn your trade, . . .").

But if late Yeats shares with late Horace the notion of art's transcendence, the two poets diverge, sometimes sharply, in their treatment of the immediacies of the human setting. On the question of
eroticism, for Horace the private cravings of the private self are never
far off as a subject for poetry, yet over the course of the book they are
spasmodically and then completely metamorphosed into yearning for
Augustus and devotion to poetry, especially poetry that is at the
service of Rome. By contrast, Yeats' final poems on sexuality and
social conduct, on desire, and on history, betray a knowledge of
human violence that Horace's idealism wishes away. His book's initial poem, "The Gyres," speaks of the "numb nightmare" in which
we live out our lives, and even "The Statues" shows despair at the
situation of political man (the "formless spawning fury" of "this
filthy modern tide") that contrasts with Phidias' talent at devising the
beautiful. As for the erotic, I need only quote "The Spur":

> You think it horrible that lust and rage
> Should dance attention upon my old age;
> They were not such a plague when I was young;
> What else have I to spur me into song?

And, if recent research is correct that the last collection should end
not with "Under Ben Bulben," which Yeats may have intended to

set first, but with "Politics,"[4] then his final lyrics would have concluded with the lines

> But O that I were young again
> And held her in my arms!

This would give pride of place not to the artifices of eternity or even
to the turmoil of social experience but to the very human, individual
desire of the aging to relive their youth. Yeats would end his last
collection where Horace begins and have our final remembrance be
desire itself, not a poetics that subsumes it. Horace, by contrast, can
accept and celebrate his present moment in history by conforming its
ceremonies of recurrence to poetry's, co-opting larger reaches of time
into the imagination's superior affections.

It is not Yeats but Eliot, I would suggest, whose career ends with
matter and manner that Horace would have found sympathetic. "Little Gidding," Eliot's last major poem and the final movement of *Four
Quartets,* deals, like its three predecessors, with time and temporality.[5] The earlier three segments look to our gains and losses from
time's movement, to solar, seasonal, or geological time and how
these affect man's accomplishment and contrast with his own psychic
chronology, to the poet's own past and its sense, mirrored in the flow
of the river, the strong brown god near which he was born, and in the
timeless, boundless ocean that receives it. "Little Gidding" suddenly
takes on a very moving historical specificity, remembering Nicolas
Ferrar and the religiosity of Reformation England, but dwelling also
now on an exact moment and its meaning. The time is 1941 in
England, the season is midwinter spring, the hour is the instant between dusk and dawn or, more circumstantially, between an air raid
and the sounding of the all-clear. This concatenation of instants engenders Eliot's grandest meditation on the passages and permanencies
of time, on the losses and continuities of civilization, on the interdependence of poetry and civility with poetry given the power to pre-

---

[4] The point is made by Rosenthal and Gall (136–45) in the course of reading
Last Poems as a modern "sequence." See also Lipking, 152.

[5] It is a curiosity that Eliot became fifty-two in September 1940, the year before
"Little Gidding" was written and that Horace turned fifty-two in 13 B.C., the
most plausible year for the publication of book 4.

serve and even reconstitute the artistic achievements of self and world.

I will quote his final words. After a moving *ars poetica,* on the relation of word to poem and of poem to the deeds it hedges against time, Eliot concludes:

> We shall not cease from exploration
> And the end of all our exploring
> Will be to arrive where we started
> And know the place for the first time.
> Through the unknown, remembered gate
> When the last of earth left to discover
> Is that which was the beginning;
> At the source of the longest river
> The voice of the hidden waterfall
> And the children in the apple-tree
> Not known, because not looked for
> But heard, half-heard, in the stillness
> Between two waves of the sea.
> Quick now, here, now, always—
> A condition of complete simplicity
> (Costing not less than everything)
> And all shall be well and
> All manner of thing shall be well
> When the tongues of flame are in-folded
> Into the crowned knot of fire
> And the fire and the rose are one.

As with Horace, this is poetry that, paradoxically, in its conclusion begins again, returns to origins and starts time—and poetry—over. And because this finalizing is also an act of origination, Eliot's words constitute another of the great lyrics of reconciliation, of self with self and with human and historical time and with death, as the self approaches redemption. Reaffirming simplicity, the poem leads us through the refining fire of purgation into the paradisal rose where the good, at last, are united in God's love.

But what seems a suitably direct, unadorned statement accompanying a return to religious and philosophical simplicity is in fact one of Eliot's most complex and allusive statements. These lines glance back into "Little Gidding" and into the other three members of *Four Quartets,* summarizing and harmonizing the design of the whole. By dwelling on his earlier poetry ("New Hampshire") and plays (*The Family Reunion*), Eliot draws his past into his final present. But the poetry also looks out and beyond its author. It touches on Mallarmé and on Yeats, Eliot's nearest rival in the grand tradition of English poetry, whose influence is also felt prominently earlier in the poem, with its reference to fire (we think of the "sages standing in God's holy fire" in "Sailing to Byzantium"). It reaches back into Eliot's English intellectual inheritance, especially to the legacy of mysticism. The passage is introduced by a quotation from *The Cloud of Unknowing* and near the end Eliot reiterates phrases from Juliana of Norwich which he had used twice earlier in the poem—

> And all shall be well and
> All manner of thing shall be well.

Above all, in his ending that is also a beginning, he looks to the most important of his spiritual origins, to Dante, especially Dante of the *Divina Commedia,* whose utterance of the ineffable, in the greatest poetic act of faith in Western letters, was Eliot's constant guide.

In the final lyrics of both Horace and Eliot, then, fragments of the poet's intellectual past are fused into a new whole of enormous originality, with a concentrated power rare in poetry. But what is so moving and what helps secure the bond between these two very different masters is that in each case the imaginative novelty supports the documentation of moments of deep spiritual renewal and return to essential sources. For Eliot it is to imagine himself placed within the ultimate origin of God's goodness. For Horace it is to catalog the moral re-creation of Augustan Rome, as he chooses to mythologize it, in its own detail and by reference both to the larger rite of secularity, by which the new age can start again ethically refreshed, and to the smaller acts of celebration in which song redeems the past. But for each it is the valedictions and summary brilliance of poetry which in their farewells assure the survival of poet, poetry, and, if only in the mind, the civilizations, that their allegiance cherished, into future time. For each it is poetry's ritual of words which sweeps its subjects from the movement of becoming into the stasis of being and which, through its intense spirituality, persists in reprieving them from the ravages of time.

APPENDIX: ODE 15
AND THE MONUMENTS

If the allusion to the Forum of Augustus in the concluding lines of ode 15 is direct, then Horace may wish us to associate his final lyric gesture with the last architectural masterpiece of the Augustan regime. To offer evidence that this is the case, I will look at the poem itself for one last time. Before this it is right to mention briefly the monument with which the fourth book of odes has been most closely and correctly connected, the *Ara Pacis Augustae*. As we have seen, the major structural framings of book 4, whether linear and climactic or chiastic and cyclical, all point to the return of Augustus and the primacy of his ancestress, Venus Genetrix. They focus on poem 15. If we look at the book's penultimate ring, we find that in ode 2 the speaker leaves to Iullus Antonius the privilege of singing about the moment when Augustus will lead in triumph the fierce Sygambri up the Capitoline's sacred slope. In the book's next to last poem, in its next to last line, the speaker himself tells of the Sygambri, whose subjugation was the prime reason for his campaigning in the northwest and who now worship an Augustus imagined back within range of the speaker's invocation. The forward thrust of the book also takes us from an absent Augustus in poem 5 to his presence in the book's final odes.

Now we know that on July 4, 13 B.C., the Senate decreed that an *Ara Pacis Augustae,* an altar honoring the peace that shares Augustus' name, be erected, and it is natural to assume, as have most critics, that this is the very date of the emperor's reentry into Rome.[1] The con-

[1]The assumption of Fraenkel, for example (*Horace,* 449, n. 2).

temporaneity, then, of Horace's carefully orchestrated poetry book and the most dazzling remnant of sculpture from the Augustan Age lends cogency to the search for intellectual bonds between them.[2] As first of these we might put the notion of ceremony and its details. The long friezes on the north and south walls of the altar precinct depict the procession of consecration, oriented, on each side, toward the entrance to the altar on the west.[3] Along with the members of the royal family accompanying Augustus, Livia, and Agrippa, were probably Iullus Antonius, Octavia's stepson, who had wed her daughter (and therefore Augustus' niece) in the year 21 B.C. Among the several figures we may conjecture the presence, with that of her husband, of Marcia, Augustus' first cousin, who had married Paulus Fabius Maximus around the year 15.[4] Horace had already given them place of prominence in his initial odes as, respectively, singer of Augustus' hypothetical triumph on the same occasion of his return from Gaul and enshriner of his ancestress Venus. Horace's own final ceremonial for Augustus is more general and more continuous, performed on festal and nonfestal days alike, as long as odic *laudatio* has a future.

One aspect of both "monuments" has particularly captured attention, namely the alternation of peace and war or, as it is perhaps better put, the reminder of war's potentiality even during a time of peace. On the *Ara Pacis* this balance is illustrated in the reliefs that flank the rear, eastern doorway to the altar. They show, on the left, a female figure with two children in her lap and animals at her feet, accompanied on either side by shapes whose attributes are a swan and a sea monster. On the right is the figure of Roma, seated on a heap of

[2]The connection has been suggested, among other recent critics, by Norberg (105–6), Doblhofer (100, n. 5), and especially Syndikus (420, n. 2; 421, n. 5; 424), on the *Ara Pacis* and the "Stimmung" of ode 15. The discussion by Benario of the link between the two monuments, both in detail and in its overview of Augustan ideology, is especially helpful.

A parallel between the way we "read" the *Ara Pacis* and a reading of the "Roman" odes has recently been suggested by Witke (14–16, 50–52).

[3]The authoritative discussion of the *Ara Pacis* is that of Simon *Ara Pacis Augustae*. See now also Torelli, chap. 2 ("A New Start: The *Ara Pacis Augustae*"), 27–61, especially 31–38 on the connection of the *Ara Pacis* and the temple of Janus Quirinus.

[4]The date is Syme's (*History*, 144) who, following Bradshaw, sees evidence of an epithalamium in ode 1.

weapons. It has been traditional to label the left figure Tellus or Italia, but in recent decades strong arguments have been advanced in favor of Venus.[5] Her many mentions in the fourth book, and not least her place of prominence framing its opening and closing, strongly support this attribution. Critics note in *Odes* 4 a counterpoint between poems 4 and 5, as a pair, and 14 and 15, as if the first of each set dealt with war, the second with peace.[6] But, to look only at the final ode, we remember Horace's catalog as much for its absences—no madness, no anger, no tribes breaking the *edicta Iulia*—as for its positive accolades. Rome sitting on weaponry reminds us not only of her power but of the means she uses to maintain it, available to others to tear it down. And omissions in poetry's listings of negation stand to prod, not lull, the memory. As for the facts of history and the tenuousness of the literality of Horace's prediction, already by the winter of 13 B.C. Agrippa was advancing against Pannonia, that is, toward the very Danube whose peoples, according to our poet, will not now violate the Augustan world peace.[7]

Nevertheless, the idealization that both sculpture and poetry project is what is meant primarily to stay with us. The *Ara Pacis* documents a specific ceremony celebrating peace after war, a ceremony to be repeated annually, whose artistic setting was an even more constant iconographic reminder that the ritual of consecration on Augustus' return looked to still grander renewals—future rituals that Horace's final poem of restoration also movingly documents.

It is my suggestion that ode 15 is also closely linked with the sculptural and architectural program of the Forum Augustum. The chronological relationship here of poems with monument is far more problematical than that with the *Ara Pacis*. Octavian vowed a temple to Mars Ultor at the battle of Philippi in 42 B.C. and, as Augustus, dedicated both the temple and the forum that it dominates on August 1, 2 B.C. We know from Suetonius that the forum was opened before the temple was finished because of a pressing need for further space in which to hold trials,[8] and Macrobius recounts an anecdote whose

---

[5]The idea was proposed contemporaneously in 1966 by both Booth and Galinsky ("Venus in a Relief"; cf. *Aeneas, Sicily, and Rome*, 191–241), and has recently been supported by Thornton.

[6]Doblhofer, 99–100.

[7]C. D. 54.28.1–2.

[8]Suet. *Aug.* 29.

point is Augustus' impatience with the slowness of his architect.[9] On this evidence alone it is impossible to pinpoint accurately when the emperor's plan for his grandest public monument would have been outlined. Some scholars have conjectured a date as early as 27 B.C. and sought a direct relationship between the statuary (which I will discuss in a moment) and the parade of heroes Anchises marshals in the sixth book of the *Aeneid*.[10] Even a conservative estimate for the chronology puts the opening of the forum around 6 B.C. with building commencing in 12 or 11.[11] If this is the case, then it seems a reasonable working hypothesis that the artistic organization of forum and temple would be very much under discussion, if not actually formulated, as Horace put the capstone on his own final memorialization of Augustus. Both works complement each other, whether by design or intuition.

Let us begin, where Horace ends his poem, with the *tituli* and the statues that they labeled.[12] We have every evidence that Augustus worshiped, at least for propagandistic purposes, the heroes of Republican Rome, seeing their lives as patterns for him and his successors to emulate. To this end, according to Suetonius, he set up their statues in his forum:[13]

Proximum a dis immortalibus honorem memoriae ducum praestitit, qui imperium p. R. ex minimo maximum reddidissent. Itaque et opera cuiusque manentibus titulis restituit et statuas omnium triumphali effigie in utraque fori sui porticu dedicavit.

Next to the immortal gods he offered honor to the memory of the leaders who raised the empire of the Roman people from the smallest to the largest. Therefore he both restored the works of each with their remaining *tituli* and dedicated statues of all in triumphal garb in each portico of his forum.

[9]Macr. *Sat.* 2.4.9.

[10]This dating was first proposed by Frank as well as by Rowell ("The Forum," 139ff., "Vergil and the Forum," *passim*).

[11]Suggested by Degrassi ("Virgilio") in a critique of Frank and Rowell.

[12]In the pages that follow I am indebted to the description of the *Forum Augustum* by Paul Zanker for both specific and general points. See also J. C. Anderson, Jr., chap. 2, "Forum Augustum" (the sculptural program of the forum is discussed at 80–88).

[13]Suet. *Aug.* 31.

Ovid provides further evidence of their deployment when, in the *Fasti,* he imagines the titular divinity himself in the newly opened forum, gazing (from his temple?) at the statuary flanking either side of the forum with his majestic shrine at its back:[14]

> hinc videt Aenean oneratum pondere caro
> et tot Iuliae nobilitatis avos,
> hinc videt Iliaden umeris ducis arma ferentem,
> claraque dispositis acta subesse viris.

Hence he sees Aeneas, weighted with his dear burden, and so many ancestors of the Julian nobility, hence he sees the son of Ilia carrying the weapons of the leader on his shoulders and their famous deeds set beneath heroes placed in order.

When this literary evidence is combined with archaeological discoveries, we gain the following picture. There were two porticoes with open colonnades on the eastern and western (more precisely northeastern and southwestern) sides of the quadrangular forum, each of which opened out into *exedrae* as one neared the forum's back. Their walls, which bounded the forum, contained niches in which statuary was placed, each statue, apparently, with two inscriptions, a shorter one on the plinth furnishing names and *cursus honorum,* and a longer one inscribed on a plaque affixed to the wall underneath, celebrating *res gestae.* The eastern side, both portico and hemicycle, held figures of the *summi viri* of the Republic with a larger niche at the center of the *exedra* wall reserved for Romulus shouldering the *spolia opima.* The western side also held effigies of Republican *duces* in its portico, but the *exedra* was set aside for the ancestors of the Julian *gens* and for the kings of Alba Longa, with the middle niche, corresponding to that of Romulus on the forum's opposite side, containing a statue of Aeneas.

The parallelism with Horace is noteworthy. As he ends his ode we find him prepared to sing in future celebration first of *duces,* then of Troy, Anchises, and the offspring of Venus, namely the Julian line, from Aeneas and his son Iulus to their formidable contemporary descendant. Horace will glorify in poetry what a visitor to Augustus'

[14]Ovid *F.* 5.563–66.

forum would see monumentalized in sculpture as he passed within
the enclosing colonnades from south to north, watching—and reading about—the sequence of past Roman heroes culminating in one
exedra with Aeneas carrying Anchises and leading Iulus, in the other
with Romulus. Though the media are different, the message of each
is the same—the imaginative glorification of the Roman past in form
that seems to warrant its special longevity. (That Horace postulated
greater endurance for his bright words than for pieces of sculpture
does not undermine my point. Augustus would have been shrewd
enough to foster for himself any means at his disposal to dissemble
his immortality.)

   To work backwards in Horace's design is to look upwards in that
of Augustus' architect. Above the colonnades of the flanking porticoes, on the outer walls supporting the roofs, were rows of caryatids.
Their symbolism, at least in Roman monumental architecture, is made
clear from a reference in Vitruvius' *De Architectura,* a work dedicated to
Augustus. Vitruvius is explaining the revenge taken by the Greeks
against the Peloponnesian city of Carya for medizing:[15]

> Itaque oppido capto, viris interfectis, civitate declarata matrones eorum
> in servitutem abduxerunt, nec sunt passi stolas neque ornatus ma-
> tronales deponere, uti non una triumpho ducerentur, sed aeterno ser-
> vitutis exemplo, gravi contumelia pressae poenas pendere viderentur
> pro civitate. ideo qui tunc architecti fuerunt aedificiis publicis desig-
> naverunt earum imagines oneri ferendo conlocatas, ut etiam posteris
> nota poena peccati Caryatium memoriae traderetur.

> The town was captured; the men were killed; the state was humiliated.
> Their matrons were led away into slavery and were not allowed to lay
> aside the garments and ornaments of *matronae.* In this way, and not at
> one time alone, were they led in triumph. Their slavery was an eternal
> warning. Insult crushed them. They seemed to pay a penalty for their
> fellow-citizens. And so the architects of that time designed for public
> buildings figures of matrons placed to carry burdens, in order that the
> punishment of the sin of the Cariatid women might be known to pos-
> terity and historically recorded.

[15]Vitr. *Arch.* I.I.5 (trans. Granger). The symbolism is discussed by Zanker,
12–13.

Horace's equivalent is the contents of his third stanza from the end, the peoples who drink the Danube or originate near the Don, the Getae, Seres, or treacherous Persae, synonymous with the Parthians. Conquered by the military efforts of Augustus, they will no longer resist his might but will remain suitably pacific. All such individuality is lost in their architectural counterpart, the scarcely distinguishable caryatids in their long lines. But, however different the emphasis in poet and architect, the symbolism of each is complementary. Both reader and viewer would ponder the effect of Roman martial triumphs over foreign peoples, whether it be through metaphor that sees Julian edicts enforcing bondage or through artistry in stone emblematic of eternal, fixed enslavement.

To continue our retrograde survey of Horace's ode means, now, to cast our eye out into the bustle of the forum proper. Horace is concerned with the absence of *furor,* of domestic strife, in a Rome under the stewardship of Augustus. The emperor, too, was apparently at pains to keep similar thoughts before the eyes of visitors to his forum. This time his means of symbolism was painting, not sculpture. We know from Pliny the Elder that Augustus placed two paintings by Apelles in his forum, each portraying Alexander the Great:[16]

mirantur . . . Romae Castorem et Pollucem cum Victoria et Alexandro Magno, item Belli imaginem restrictis ad terga manibus, Alexandro in curru triumphante, quas utrasque tabulas divus Augustus in fori sui celeberrimis partibus dicaverat simplicitate moderata; . . .

[Among the paintings of Apelles, people] admire at Rome a Castor and Pollux with Victory and Alexander the Great, also a picture of War, hands tied behind its back, with Alexander the Great in triumph in his chariot. Each of these two paintings Divine Augustus had dedicated, with openness yet restraint, in the most frequented portions of his forum.

The second painting, and the area of location, are further specified by Servius in his comment attempting to locate the famous figuration of *Furor* imprisoned which Jupiter, in the first book of the *Aeneid,* envisions as symbol of Augustus' suppression of war. According to Ser-

[16]Pliny *N. H.* 35.93–94 (and cf. 35.27).

vius, it is not to be found, as some maintain, within the temple of
Janus,[17]

> sed in alia in foro Augusti introeuntibus ad sinistram, fuit bellum pic-
> tum et furor sedens super arma devinctus eo habitu quo poeta dixit.

> but in another [shrine], in the forum of Augustus toward the left as one
> entered, was a picture of war and *furor* in bonds, sitting on weaponry, in
> that guise which the poet described.

Augustus would have wished himself remembered, visually as well
as in words, as the person who had at last enchained the demon of
civil madness, for it takes little imagination to make the allegorical
leap Augustus would have expected and equate Alexander the Great
in triumph with his own Roman role as bringer of peace through
might.

The second half of Horace's ode runs from Caesar to Venus, from
fury replaced by *otium* to the communal songs this restored "leisure"
will make possible. The first movement of the poem ends not with
the enclosure festivity postulates but with the eye following the *maiestas imperi* that Augustus has secured from the sun's western bed-
chamber to his risings in the east. Here, too, architecture has its
parallel that once again Vitruvius is a help in elucidating. In his dedication to Augustus, he tells us that he conceived the idea of bringing
his writings before the attention of the emperor[18]

> Cum adtenderem te non solum de vita communi omnium curam pub-
> licaeque rei constitutionem habere sed etiam de opportunitate pub-
> licorum aedificiorum, ut civitas per te non solum provinciis esset aucta,
> verum etiam ut maiestas imperii publicorum aedificiorum egregias
> haberet auctoritates, . . .

> When I noticed that you not only had a care for the common life of all
> and the constitution of the republic but also about the suitable impor-
> tance of public buildings, so that the state was not only augmented by
> [new] provinces but that the majesty of the empire was also expressed
> through the extraordinary quality of public buildings . . .

[17]Servius on *Aen.* 1.294.
[18]Vitr. *Arch.* 1. *Praef.* 2.

The grand examples of Augustan architectural monumentalization would serve as a visual reminder at home of the expansive geographical scope of Roman might under Augustus, of further provinces domesticated by her sway.

The Caryatids supporting the roof of the porticoes of the Forum of Augustus are emblems of one aspect of this power in operation. For visual imagery of the extent of *maiestas imperi* we can turn to another synecdoche, the material used in construction.[19] The huge precinct wall of the forum was made of tufa from Gabii, east of Rome on the slopes of Mons Albanus, with travertine, from quarries between Rome and Tibur, utilized at points of stress.[20] Peperino, dark grey tufa from near Marino, also on the edge of the Alban mount (hence its ancient name, *saxum Albanum*), was used for the cella wall of the temple of Mars Ultor. This was lined with marble probably from Luna (modern Carrara) which was also the source of the exterior columns of the temple (the interior were of *breccia corallina,* provenance unknown).[21] The columns and pilasters of the *exedrae* were of *cipollino,* marble from Carystus in Euboea.[22] The pavement of the forum proper consisted of designs in yellow (*giallo antico,* ancient *marmor Numidicum*) with the dark blue tones of *africano.* To these were added *pavonazetto,* cream-white marble from Phrygia, in forming the composition of the temple's floor.[23]

The visitor, then, aware of architectural construction and with open eyes, would ponder elements from as near as a few kilometers away from Rome and as far as the eastern Mediterranean. He would note that Augustus drew on the resources of the Alban hills, of Luna north along the Tyrrhenian sea, of Africa and Numidia. He would thus have before him a lavish accretion of tangible evidence for the same extent of Augustan political artistry through which Horace verbally takes us—from Latium, to Italy, to the bounds of the empire. Paralleling an analogy from the construction of the forum and temple themselves, which works outward from a core of sturdy local stone on which a veneer of more exotic materials is laid, Horace begins appropriately with the proximate and original on which Augustus, and Rome, based their valor. We remember, finally, that the

[19]I draw the comparison from Zanker, 12 and 30, n. 42.
[20]Blake, 47 and 167.
[21]Ibid., 178 and 57.
[22]Ibid., 58.
[23]Ibid., 56–57.

gens Octavia came from Velitrae on the southern slopes of Mons Albanus, quarry for the core of Augustus' monument and major sanctuary for the Latins as far into the past as evidence takes us.

The connection with the forum of the poem's third stanza, to which we have now come in our backward glance, has been touched upon earlier. In ode 24 of the third book, an ode probably datable to the early 20s, Horace alludes impersonally to someone who, if he seeks to have *pater urbium* written under his statues, should dare to rein in untamed *licentia*. Octavian is the scarcely hidden subject. By the time Horace came to write his final ode Octavian, now Augustus, in his own person has fulfilled the earlier condition and bridled license. If we follow out the implication of Horace's logic, Augustus would now be worthy to have the near equivalent of *pater urbium* inscribed beneath his effigies. This in fact did happen in the year 2 B.C. when, according to Augustus himself, the Senate, equestrian order, and people voted to have *pater patriae* written on the base on which stood the *quadriga* already set up by the Senate in his honor, near the center of his forum, in front of the temple of Mars Ultor.[24]

We have a description of how Augustus received this award in Suetonius who makes the proceedings sound unpremeditated, with a spontaneous offering first from the commons, then from the Senate.[25] With the help of Horace's earlier poem we could take a more calculated viewpoint. As early as the year 28 B.C. Horace would have sensed, perhaps even known, Octavian's wish to have the words *pater patriae* attached to his name. By 13 B.C., according to Horace, he deserved them; by 2 B.C., they were his—two short words attached to the most prominent piece of statuary in the forum. The *titulus* may be brief by contrast with the *elogia* given to the many Republican worthies, Julian and otherwise, whose statues were placed against the forum's sides. But with the exception of the statues of Aeneas and Romulus which may have been larger,[26] all these figures would have been uniform, and uniformly within the shade of portico and *exedra*. Augustus in his chariot stood unique and central. I will hazard the guess that eleven years before his forum officially opened Augustus knew that both statue and inscription were to be his, and that Horace here predicts as much within his own more lasting *titulus*.

[24]Aug. *R. G.* 35.
[25]Suet. *Aug.* 58.
[26]Zanker, 18.

Working backwards again we come to the subject of the poem's second stanza, the standards of Crassus, lost at Carrhae and returned by the Parthians through the efforts of diplomacy in 20 B.C. Restored to "our Jupiter" may simply mean that, because of Augustus, they once again came under Roman sway,[27] or, more particularly, that they were housed temporarily in a small temple to Mars Ultor on the Capitoline and hence lay within the protection of Capitoline Jove until the completion of the temple of the same name in Augustus' forum.[28] Augustus tells us himself that he placed the restored standards in the inmost part of the forum's temple, and we know from another source that the temple was meant by Augustus to house all other standards recovered in later campaigns as well as the scepters and crowns of later *triumphatores* whose statues in bronze were also to be erected in the forum proper.[29]

Finally, as we survey the poem from its opening apostrophe to Caesar to the final allusion to Venus, we remember that Augustus had himself named on the architrave of the Mars temple and that effigies of his divine ancestress appeared not only on the temple's pediment but among the three cult statues housed within the cella.[30] In between, to summarize from beginning to end, we look to the Parthian standards, to reasons why Augustus should be entitled *pater patriae,* to *maiestas,* to the sequestering of *furor,* to conquered tribes, to Republican *duces,* and to the history of the Julian *gens* from the mating of Anchises and Venus in Troy to the triumph of their descendant in Augustan Rome. All of these objects figure, whether literally (*signa*), emblematically (representative statuary), or symbolically (*maiestas*), in the program of Augustus' forum.

The most telling absence from Horace's poem is the most obvious, Mars Ultor himself. With the exception of reference to the *campus Martius* in ode 1 and to Romulus as *Mavortis puer* in 8, the only mentions of the god of war in the fourth book are both in the penultimate poem. Horace there refers to the power Augustus possesses from Mars (*Marte* 9), that is, metonymically, in the potency of pre-

---

[27]Cf. Prop. 3.4.6.

[28]The evidence is collected by K. Fitzler and O. Seeck in *RE* 10.1.135 *s.v. Iulius (Augustus).*

[29]C. D. 55.10.2–4.

[30]For Augustus' self-naming on the architrave, Ovid *F.* 5.567–68; for Venus, Zanker, 18–20.

sent Roman military practice. This power is magically conveyed to Tiberius, his self-extension, who, from his prowess on the battlefield (*in certamine Martio*), is simply the working proof of Augustus' military talent. Nevertheless, as we have seen earlier, Horace exploits chances for irony against the emperor's stepson and ends his poem with weaponry in a position of rest and with a veiled allusion to the ascendancy of Venus.

The final poem does not reverse this trend. If, throughout ode 15, Horace seems willingly to accept major themes of the Augustan principate which were to take visual shape in the magnificent forum, he nevertheless asserts his spiritual independence in a dramatic form by omitting that other divine ancestor of Rome, raper of Ilia and father of her twins left to be suckled by a wolf. Horace is denying admission into his design to the god who not only presides over Augustus' forum but appears with she-wolf, Romulus and Remus on the relief to the left of the entrance of the *Ara Pacis* and, in all likelihood, on the cuirass decoration of the idealizing Prima Porta statue of Augustus, dating probably from a few years before the altar's *constitutio*.[31] He is omitting, therefore, a major ingredient of Augustan propaganda, symbol of the dominating power of war and, in his guise most palatable to a pacifist temperament, of the might necessary to achieve and preserve peace (with the hint at vengence to be pursued against those foolish enough to resist or rebel).

Even this last interpretation of Mars is intolerable to a poet bent on celebrating both Caesar and *otium* at once. Apollo, god of the bow and the lyre, of heroism and of poetry, his contesting days over with the victory at Actium, can order the speaker to renounce the enumeration of *proelia*, leaving the temple of Janus Quirinus bereft of wars (*vacuum duellis*). As a result Mars Ultor, whatever his importance to the aesthetic and moral ideology of Augustus, cannot be accepted into the imaginative edifice Horace raises to the emperor. The gods of the renewal of peace, of the secularity that Horace had celebrated four years before in his *Carmen,* are not Mars but Apollo and Diana. The new golden age that restores crops and rehabilitates artistry does not find its authority in war but in *otium* fostered by Venus and her offspring. His sixth ode had reminded us of his importance as creator of Apolline secularity, of the magic words that bring it into being and

[31]For Mars, see E. Simon, "Sterngottheiten," 266, and, for the idealization, ibid., "Zur Augustusstatue," *passim.*

reassure its continuance. His final ode imputes this renewal to Caesar, the offspring of Venus, and proclaims its celebration in future song. But once again, in what he chooses to emphasize and to let pass, Horace exerts his own mastery over his material, which is to say, over Augustus. In our act of reading we prove him, not Augustus, the final renewer, and impute to song, and to its creator's own magic reinvigoration of his varied traditions, the final artifice of preservation.

BIBLIOGRAPHY

Acron. *Pseudacronis: Scholia in Horatium Vetustiora*. Edited by O. Keller. 2 vols. Leipzig, 1902–4.

Ahl, F. M. "Amber, Avallon, and Apollo's Singing Swan." *AJP* 103 (1982), 373–411.

Ambrose, J. W., Jr. "Horace on Foreign Policy: Odes 4.4." *CJ* 69 (1973), 26–33.

——. "The Ironic Meaning of the Lollius Ode." *TAPA* 96 (1965), 1–10.

Anderson, J. C., Jr. *The Historical Topography of the Imperial Fora*. Collection Latomus, no. 182. Brussels, 1984.

Anderson, R. D., P. J. Parsons, and R. G. M. Nisbet. "Elegiacs by Gallus from Qaṣr Ibrîm." *JRS* 69 (1979), 125–55.

Andreae, B. *The Art of Rome*. New York, 1977.

Austin, R. G., ed. *P. Vergili Maronis Aeneidos: Liber Primus*. Oxford, 1971.

Babcock, C. L. "*Carmina operosa*: Critical Approaches to the 'Odes' of Horace, 1945–1975." *ANRW* II. 31. 3 (1981), 1560–1611.

Balestrazzi, E. di F., L. Gasperini, and M. Balestrazzi. "L'emiciclo di Pratomedes a Cirene: la testimonianza di un culto aniconico di tradizione Dorica." *Quaderni di Archaeologia della Libia* 8 (1976), 109–91.

Barnes, T. D. "The Victories of Augustus." *JRS* 64 (1974), 21–26.

Barra, G. "Sul quarto libro dell' Odi di Orazio." *AFLN 8* (1958–59), 19–42.

Bate, W. J. *John Keats*. Cambridge, Mass., 1963.

Bayet, J. *Les origines de l'Hercule romain*. Paris, 1926.

Becker, C. *Das Spätwerk des Horaz*. Göttingen, 1963.

——. "Donarem Pateras." *Hermes* 87 (1959), 212–22.

Belmont, D. E. "The Vergilius of Horace, *Ode* 4.12." *TAPA* 110 (1980), 1–20.

Benario, J. M. "Book 4 of Horace's *Odes:* Augustan Propaganda." *TAPA* 91 (1960), 339–52.

Bergson, L. "Zu Horaz, Carm. IV 5." *RhM* 113 (1970), 358–63.

Blake, M. E. *Ancient Roman Construction in Italy.* Washington, 1947.

Blumenthal, F. "Die Autobiographie des Augustus. I." *WS* 35 (1913), 113–30.

Borzsak, S. "Dive, quem proles Niobea . . . Ein Interpretationsversuch zu Hor. C. IV 6." *GB* 5 (1976), 25–36.

Bowra, C. M. "Horace, *Odes* IV. 12." *CR* 42 (1928), 165–67.

Boyle, A. J. "The Edict of Venus: An Interpretive Essay on Horace's Amatory Odes." *Ramus* 2 (1973), 163–88.

Bradshaw, A. T. von S. "Horace, *Odes* 4.1." *CQ* 64 (1970), 142–53.

Brink, C. O. *Horace on Poetry: Epistles Book II.* Cambridge, 1982.

Bundy, E. L. "Studia Pindarica I: *The Eleventh Olympian Ode.*" *CPCP* 18, 1 (1962).

Burkert, W. "Apellai und Apollon." *RhM* 118 (1975), 1–21.

Cairns, F. "Five 'Religious' Odes of Horace." *AJP* 92 (1971), 433–52.

Cameron, A. "The First Edition of Ovid's *Amores.*" *CQ* 62 (1968), 320–33.

Campbell, D. A. *Greek Lyric.* Vol. 1, *Sappho Alcaeus.* Cambridge, Mass., 1982.

———. *Greek Lyric Poetry: A Selection.* London, 1967.

Carettoni, G. "Due nuovi ambienti dipinti sul Palatino." *Boll. d'Arte* 46 (1961), 189–99.

———. *Das Haus des Augustus auf dem Palatin.* Mainz, 1983.

———. "Terracotte 'Campana' dallo scavo del tempio di Apollo Palatino." *Rendiconti Pont. Acc. Rom. Archaeologia* 44 (1971–72), 123–39.

Chirassi Colombo, I. "Heros Achilleus-Theos Apollon." In *Il Mito Greco,* edited by B. Gentili and G. Paioni, 231–69. Rome, 1977.

Clausen, W. "Duellum." *HSCP* 75 (1971), 69–72.

Coarelli, F. "Il sepolcro degli Scipioni." *Dialoghi di Archeologia* 6 (1972), 36–106.

Collinge, N. E. *The Structure of Horace's Odes.* London, 1961.

Commager, S. "The Function of Wine in Horace's Odes." *TAPA* 88 (1957), 68–80.

———. *The Odes of Horace: A Critical Study.* New Haven, 1962.

———. "Some Horatian Vagaries." *SO* 55 (1980), 59–70.

Cook, A. B. *Zeus.* Vol. 2. Cambridge, 1925.

Crotty, K. *Song and Action: The Victory Odes of Pindar.* Baltimore, 1982.

Dahlmann, H. "Die letzte Ode des Horaz." *Gymn.* 65 (1958), 340–55.

Degrassi, A., ed. *Inscriptiones Italiae.* Vol. 13, *Fasti et Elogia* (Fasc. 3: *Elogia*). Rome, 1937.

———. "Virgilio e il Foro di Augusto." *Epigraphica* 7 (1945), 88–103.

Deonna, W. "Le groupe des trois Grâces nues et sa descendance." *Rev. Arc.,* ser. 5, 31 (1930), 274–332.

＊Dettmer, H. *Horace: A Study in Structure.* Altertumswissenschaftliche Texte und Studien, No. 12. Hildesheim, 1983.

Diggle, J., ed. *Euripides: Phaethon.* Cambridge, 1970.

Doblhofer, E. *Die Augustuspanegyrik des Horaz in formalhistorischer Sicht.* Heidelberg, 1966.

Dornseiff, F. "Eine Sphragis des Horaz (c. IV 8)." *Philologus* 95 (1942), 166–71.

Duckworth, G. E. "*Animae Dimidium Meae:* Two Poets of Rome." *TAPA* 87 (1956), 281–316.

Dyer, R. R. "*Diffugere Nives:* Horace and the Augustan Spring." *G & R,* ser. 2, 12 (1965), 79–84.

Edmunds, L. "The Latin Invitation-Poem: What is it? Where did it come from?" *AJP* 103 (1982), 184–88.

Elter, A. *Donarem Pateras . . . Horat. Carm. 4, 8.* Bonn, 1907.

＊Estévez, V. A. "*Quem Tu, Melpomene:* The Poet's Lowered Voice (C. IV 3)." *Emerita* 50 (1982), 279–300.

Farnell, L. R. *The Cults of the Greek States.* Vol. 4. Oxford, 1907.

＊Ferguson, J. "Catullus and Horace." *AJP* 77 (1956), 1–18.

Flach, D. *Das literarische Verhältnis von Horaz und Properz.* Diss. Marburg. Giessen, 1967.

Fraenkel, E. "Das Pindargedicht des Horaz." *SHAW Philos.-hist. Kl.* 23 (1932–33), 2 abh.

———. *Horace.* Oxford, 1957.

Frank, T. "Augustus, Vergil, and the Augustan Elogia." *AJP* 59 (1938), 91–94.

Franke, P. E. *Die antiken Münzen von Epirus.* Wiesbaden, 1961.

Frazer, J. G., ed. *Ovid's Fasti.* 5 vols. London, 1929.

＊Freis, R. "The Catalogue of Pindaric Genres in Horace *Ode* 4.2." *CA* 2 (1983), 27–36.

Führer, R. "Ein Altersgedicht des Horaz: C. IV 7." *GB* 8 (1979), 205–18.

Gagé, J. "Apollon impérial, Garant des 'Fata Romana.'" *ANRW* II. 17. 2 (1981), 561–630.

———. *Apollon romain.* Paris, 1955.

Galinsky, G. K. *Aeneas, Sicily, and Rome.* Princeton, 1969.

———. *The Herakles Theme.* Oxford, 1972.

———. "Venus in a Relief of the Ara Pacis Augustae." *AJA* 70 (1966), 223–43.

Giacomelli, A. "The Justice of Aphrodite in Sappho Fr. 1." *TAPA* 110 (1980), 135–42.

Grimal, P. *Le lyrisme à Rome.* Paris, 1978.

Highbarger, E. L. "The Pindaric Style of Horace." *TAPA* 66 (1935), 222–55.

Horn, H.-J. "Zur Deutung von Horazens Pindarode 4, 2." *Helmantica* 28 (1977), 233–39.

Johnson, W. R. "The Boastful Bird: Notes on Horatian Modesty." *CJ* 61 (1965–66), 272–75.

———. *The Idea of Lyric*. Berkeley, 1982.

———. "Tact in the Drusus Ode: Horace, Odes, 4.4." *CSCA* 2 (1969), 171–81.

Kambylis, A. *Die Dichterweihe und ihre Symbolik*. Heidelberg, 1965.

✳ Kennedy, N. T. "Pindar and Horace." *AC* 18 (1975), 9–24.

Kienast, D. "Augustus und Alexander." *Gymn.* 76 (1969), 430–56.

Kiessling, A., and R. Heinze, eds. *Q. Horatius Flaccus: Oden und Epoden*. 8th ed. Berlin, 1955.

Kissel, W. "Horaz 1936–1975: Eine Gesamtbibliographie." *ANRW* II. 31. 3 (1981), 1403–1558.

Klingner, F., ed. *Horatius: Opera*. 3d ed. Leipzig, 1959.

Kranz, W. "Sphragis. Ichform und Namensiegel als Eingangs- und Schlussmotiv antiker Dichtung." *RhM* 104 (1961), 3–46, 97–124.

Künzl, E. "Der augusteische Silbercalathus im Rheinischen Landesmuseum Bonn." *Bonner Jahrbücher* 169 (1969), 321–92.

Küthmann, H. "Actiaca." *Jahrbuch des römisch-germanischen Zentralmuseums, Mainz* 4 (1957), 73–80.

Kukula, R. C. *Römische Säkularpoesie. Neue Studien zu Horaz' XVI. Epodus und Vergils IV. Ekloge*. Leipzig, 1911.

Lachmann, K. *Kleinere Schriften zur Classischen Philologie*. Edited by J. Vahlen. Berlin, 1876.

Lambrechts, P. "La politique 'apollinienne' d'Auguste et le culte impérial." *NClio* 5 (1953), 65–82.

La Penna, A. *Orazio e l'ideologia del principato*. Turin, 1963.

Latte, K. *Römische Religionsgeschichte*. Munich, 1960.

➤ Lee, M. O. "Everything Is Full of Gods." *Arion* 9 (1970), 246–63.

———. *Word, Sound, and Image in the Odes of Horace*. Ann Arbor, 1969.

Lefèvre, E. "Rursus bella moves? Die literarische Form von Horaz, c. 4, 1." *RhM* 111 (1968), 166–89.

Levin, D. N. "Concerning Two Odes of Horace: 1.4 and 4.7." *CJ* 54 (1959), 354–58.

Lipking, L. *The Life of the Poet: Beginning and Ending Poetic Careers*. Chicago, 1981.

Lowenstam, S. "The Meaning of IE *dhal-." *TAPA* 109 (1979), 125–35.

Luck, G. "Sextus Propertius." In *The Cambridge History of Classical Literature*. Vol. 2, *Latin Literature*, 413–15. Cambridge, 1982.

Ludwig, W. "Die Anordnung des vierten Horazischen Odenbuches." *MH* 18 (1961), 1–10.

MacKay, L. A. "Horace, *Odes* IV, 5, 17–20." *CJ* 33 (1937–38), 359–60.

✻ Minadeo, R. "Vergil in Horace's *Odes*." *CJ* 71 (1975–76), 161–64.

Momigliano, A. M. "Perizonius, Niebuhr and the Character of Early Roman Tradition." *JRS* 47 (1957), 104–14.

Moritz, L. A. "Horace's Virgil." *G & R,* ser. 2, 16 (1969), 174–93.

———. "Some 'Central' Thoughts on Horace's *Odes*." *CQ* 62 (1968), 116–31.

Mueller, L., ed. *Q. Horatius Flaccus: Oden und Epoden*. St. Petersburg, 1900.

Nagy, G. *The Best of the Achaeans*. Baltimore, 1979.

Nash, E. *Pictorial Dictionary of Ancient Rome*. London, 1961–62.

Newman, J. K. *Augustus and the New Poetry*. Collection Latomus, no. 88. Brussels, 1967.

Norberg, D. "La divinité d'Auguste dans la poésie d'Horace." *Eranos* 44 (1946), 389–403.

———. "Le quatrième livre des Odes d'Horace." *Emerita* 20 (1952), 95–107.

Norden, E. "Ein Panegyricus auf Augustus in Vergils Aeneis." *RhM* 54 (1899), 466–82.

———, ed. *P. Vergilius Maro: Aeneis Buch VI*. 5th ed. Darmstadt, 1970.

Ogilvie, R. M. *A Commentary on Livy: Books 1–5*. Oxford, 1965.

Opperman, H. "Maecenas' Geburtstag (Horat. c. IV 11)." *Gymn.* 64 (1957), 102–11.

✻ Pasquali, G. *Orazio lirico*. Florence, 1920.

Pease, A. S., ed. *Publi Vergili Maronis: Aeneidos Liber Quartus*. Cambridge, Mass., 1935.

Perret, J. *Horace*. Translated by B. Humez. New York, 1964.

Pfeiffer, R., ed. *Callimachus*. Vol. 1. Oxford, 1949.

———. *History of Classical Scholarship from the Beginnings to the End of the Hellenistic Age*. Oxford, 1968.

———. "The Image of the Delian Apollo and Apolline Ethics." *J. Warb. Inst.* 15 (1952), 20–32.

Picard-Schmitter, M.-Th. "Bétyles hellénistiques." *MMAI* 57 (1971), 43–88.

Platner, S. B., and T. Ashby. *A Topographical Dictionary of Ancient Rome*. London, 1929.

Pöschl, V. "Die Dionysosode des Horaz (c. 2, 19)." *Hermes* 101 (1973), 208–30 (= *Kunst und Wirklichkeitserfahrung in der Dichtung* [Heidelberg, 1979], 209–31).

———. "Horaz und die Politik." *SHAW Philos.-hist. Kl.* (1956), 4 abh. (= *Kunst und Wirklichkeitserfahrung in der Dichtung* [Heidelberg, 1979], 145–77.)

Porphyrion. *Pomponi Porfyrionis: Commentum in Horatium Flaccum.* Edited by
A. Holder. Innsbruck, 1894.

Porter, D. H. "Horace, *Carmina,* IV, 12." *Latomus* 31 (1972), 71–87.

———. "The Motif of Spring in Horace, *Carmina* 4.7 and 4.12." *CB* 49 (1972–
73), 57–61.

———. "The Recurrent Motifs of Horace, *Carmina* IV." *HSCP* 79 (1975),
189–228.

Putnam, M. C. J. *Essays on Latin Lyric, Elegy, and Epic.* Princeton, 1982.

———. "Propertius and the New Gallus Fragment." *ZPE* 39 (1980), 49–56.

———. "Propertius' Third Book: Patterns of Cohesion." *Arethusa* 13 (1980),
97–113 (= *Essays on Latin Lyric, Elegy, and Epic,* 208–24).

Quinn, K., ed. *Catullus: The Poems.* London, 1970.

———. ed. *Horace: The Odes.* London, 1980.

———. *Latin Explorations.* London, 1963.

Reckford, K. J. "The Eagle and the Tree (Horace, *Odes* 4.4)." *CJ* 56 (1960–
61), 23–28.

———. *Horace.* New York, 1969.

———. "Some Studies in Horace's Odes on Love." *CJ* 55 (1959), 25–33.

Reinsch-Werner, H. *Callimachus Hesiodicus.* Berlin, 1976.

Rosenthal, M. L., and S. M. Gall. *The Modern Poetic Sequence: The Genius of
Modern Poetry.* New York, 1983.

Ross, D. O., Jr. *Backgrounds to Augustan Poetry.* Cambridge, 1975.

Rowell, H. T. "The Forum and Funeral *Imagines* of Augustus." *MAAR* 17
(1940), 131–43.

———. "Vergil and the Forum of Augustus." *AJP* 62 (1941), 261–76.

Ruckdeschel, F. *Archaismen und Vulgarismen in der Sprache des Horaz.* Diss.
Erlangen. Munich, 1910.

Rudd, N. "Horace." In *The Cambridge History of Classical Literature.* Vol. 2,
Latin Literature, 370–404. Cambridge, 1982.

Rutgers van der Loeff, A. "Quid Horatio cum Catullo?" *Mn.,* ser. 3, 4
(1936), 109–13.

Schoonhoven, H. "Purple Swans and Purple Snow." *Mn.,* ser. 4, 31 (1978),
200–203.

Scodel, R. "Hesiod Redivivus." *GRBS* 21 (1980), 301–20.

Seel, O. "Maiore poeta plectro." In *Antike Lyrik,* edited by W. Eisenhut,
143–81. Darmstadt, 1970.

Seidensticker, B. "Zu Horaz, C. 1, 1–9." *Gymn.* 83 (1976), 26–34.

Simon, E. "Apollo in Rom." *Jahrb. d deutschen arch. Inst.* 93 (1978), 202–27.

———. *Ara Pacis Augustae.* Greenwich, Conn., 1967.

———. "Sterngottheiten auf zwei augusteischen Panzerstatuen." *WJA* n.f. 5
(1979), 263–72.

———. "Zur Augustusstatue von Prima Porta." MDAI(R) 64 (1957), 46–68.

Smereka, J. "De Horatianae vocabulorum copiae certa quadam lege." In *Commentationes Horatianae,* 65–91. Cracow, 1935.

Smith, K. F., ed. *The Elegies of Albius Tibullus.* New York, 1913.

Steinmetz, P. "Horaz und Pindar. Hor. carm. IV 2." *Gymn.* 71 (1964), 1–17.

Syme, R. *History in Ovid.* Oxford, 1978.

———. *The Roman Revolution.* Oxford, 1939.

———. "Some Notes on the Legions under Augustus." *JRS* 23 (1933), 14–33.

Syndikus, H. P. *Die Lyrik des Horaz: Eine Interpretation der Oden.* Vol. 2, *Drittes und viertes Buch.* Impulse der Forschung, no. 7. Darmstadt, 1973.

Taylor, L. R. "The Date of the Capitoline 'Fasti.'" *CP* 41 (1946), 1–11.

———. "New Indications of Augustan Editing in the Capitoline *Fasti.*" *CP* 46 (1951), 73–80.

Thompson, D. B. *Ptolemaic Oinochoai and Portraits in Faience: Aspects of the Ruler Cult.* Oxford, 1973.

Thornton, M. K. "Augustan Genealogy and the Ara Pacis." *Latomus* 42 (1983), 619–28.

Torelli, M. *Typology and Structure of Roman Historical Reliefs.* Ann Arbor, 1982.

Troxler-Keller, I. *Die Dichterlandschaft des Horaz.* Heidelberg, 1964.

Vendler, H. *The Odes of John Keats.* Cambridge, 1983.

Waszink, J. H. "Horaz und Pindar." *A und A* 12 (1966), 111–24.

Wehrli, F. "Horaz und Kallimachos." *MH* 1 (1944), 69–76.

Weinreich, O. "Religionswissenschaftliche und Literaturgeschichtliche Beiträge zu Horaz." *ZKG* 61 (1942), 33–74.

Wili, W. *Horaz und die augusteische Kultur.* Basel, 1948.

Wilkinson, L. P. *Horace and His Lyric Poetry.* 2d ed. Cambridge, 1951.

Williams, G. *Figures of Thought in Roman Poetry.* New Haven, 1980.

———. *Horace.* Greece and Rome, New Surveys in the Classics, no. 6. Oxford, 1972.

———. "Phases in Political Patronage of Literature in Rome." In *Literary and Artistic Patronage in Ancient Rome,* edited by B. K. Gold, 3–27. Austin, 1982.

———. *Tradition and Originality in Roman Poetry.* Oxford, 1968.

Williams, R. D. "Horace, *Odes* iv. 15. 29." *CR,* n.s. 10 (1960), 6–7.

Wilson, P. "Pindar and His Reputation in Antiquity." *PCPhS* (1980), 97–114.

Wimmel, W. "Recusatio-Form und Pindarode." *Philologus* 109 (1965), 83–103.

———. *Kallimachos in Rom.* Hermes Einzelschrift, no. 16. Wiesbaden, 1960.

BIBLIOGRAPHY

Wissowa, G. *Religion und Kultus der Römer*. Munich, 1912.

Witke, C. *Horace's Roman Odes: A Critical Examination*. Mnemosyne, Supplement no. 77. Leiden, 1983.

Woodman, A. J. "Horace's Odes *Diffugere nives* and *Solvitur acris hiems*." *Latomus* 31 (1972), 752–78.

Zanker, P. *Forum Augustum*. Tübingen, 1968[?].

Zetzel, J. E. G. "The Poetics of Patronage in the Late First Century B.C." In *Literary and Artistic Patronage in Ancient Rome,* edited by B. K. Gold, 87–102. Austin, 1982.

Zuntz, G. "Baitylos and Bethel." *Cl. et Med.* 8 (1946), 169–219.

INDEX

Accius, 202

Achilles, 117–20, 123–26, 246–47, 287–88, 310, 314, 316

Acron, 87

Actium, 15–16, 127–28, 253, 267–68, 338

Aeacus, 152–53, 171, 260, 301

Aeneas, 19–20, 27, 43, 95–96, 120, 138, 140–41, 144, 163, 212, 233, 247, 256, 265, 271, 295–96, 303, 310, 319, 331–32, 336

Agamemnon, 118–19, 166

Agrippa, 17, 155, 266, 328–29

Albanus, Mons, 97, 336

Alcaeus, 28, 161, 165–66

Alexander the Great, 57, 280, 333–34

Alexandria, 249–50, 261, 266, 268, 315

Algidus, Mons, 97

Ambracia, 126–27

Ambrose, St., 292

Anacreon, 39, 45, 161–62

Anchises, 94, 265, 279–81, 303, 330–32, 337

Ancus, 138, 140, 144, 233

Andromache, 164

Antony, 15–16, 127, 249–50, 261, 268, 288

Apelles, 333

Apollo (Phoebus), 18–20, 45–46, 53, 55, 65, 117, 119–29, 134, 204, 211, 213–14, 243, 264–66, 270, 274, 287–88, 291, 293, 310–11, 313–14, 320, 338

Apollodorus, 163

Apollonia, 126

Apollonius Rhodius, 121

Apuleius, 93

Ara Pacis, 56, 99, 327–29, 338

Arcadia, 201, 205–6, 208

Archilochus, 284

Aristaeus, 187–88, 192

Aristokleides, 53

Athens, 201, 206

Aufidus, 160–61, 245–46, 252, 257, 302, 311, 316

Augustus Caesar (Octavian), 9, 15–17, 19–30, 43, 53, 56–60, 62, 64–66, 71, 76, 85–86, 90, 92–94, 96–100, 103–14, 117, 122, 124, 126–30, 134, 140, 143, 151, 155, 160, 171–72, 211, 224, 233, 238–42, 245, 248–61, 263–71, 273–89, 292–95, 297–305, 308–15, 317–20, 322–23, 327–30, 332–33, 335–38

Automedon, 178

Aventinus, Mons, 206

Bacchus, 153, 205–6, 278

Bellerophon, 53, 192–93, 211

Breuni, 241

Brundisium, 16

Cacus, 275

Caelius, 225

Cales, 205–6

Callimachus, 28, 55–56, 60–62, 72–74, 77, 84, 89, 105, 153, 213–15, 265–66, 270, 293–94

Calliope, 267

Cantabri, 59, 251–52

Capitolium, 65, 74, 264, 275, 337

Caryatids, 332, 335

Cassius Dio, 169

Castor, 112, 153, 172, 260, 301

Cato the Elder, 272

Catullus, 25, 39–41, 76–77, 110, 141–42, 161–62, 203, 206–7, 213, 215, 225–26, 246–48, 309–10

Censorinus, 149–50, 152, 154–56, 160, 179, 300, 314
Centaurs, 53
Ceres, 112
Chia, 222–24, 228–29, 232–33, 235, 314
Chimaera, 53, 193
Choerilus, 250
Cicero, 98, 104, 151–52, 202, 242, 258, 272
Cinara, 35, 227–28, 232, 293
Cleopatra, 15, 127, 249–50, 261
Coleridge, 322
Commager, S., 9
Corinth, 65, 68
Crassus, 16, 252, 264, 275, 285, 337
Cupavo, 43–44
Cupid, 222–24, 227–29, 232, 234
Cycnus, 44–45, 181–82
Cynthia, 230, 232

Daedalus, 51–52, 56, 193, 312
Damophilus, 96
Dante, 326
Danuvius, 264, 333
Deiphobus, 163, 166, 168, 170
Demeter, 214
Demodocus, 163
Diana, 18–19, 97, 122, 125–26, 134, 141, 153, 170, 287, 315, 338
Diocles, 178
Dionysius of Halicarnassus, 272
Dis, 125
Donne, 26
Drusus, 21, 23, 27, 85–91, 93, 99, 107, 109, 129, 211, 233, 235, 239, 241–42, 248, 257, 292, 299, 316

Eliot, T. S., 217, 324–26
Ennius, 103–4, 106, 118, 150–51, 202, 240, 258, 260, 267, 275–76, 281, 301
Euphrates, 250, 253
Euripides, 193
Eurydice, 113
Euterpe, 74

Faunus, 108, 143, 251
Faustitas, 107–8
Ferrar, Nicolas, 324
Festus, 191
Forum of Augustus, 264, 327–39
Fraenkel, E., 9
Frost, Robert, 26
Furius Bibaculus, 203

Gallia, 251, 253
Gallus, 58, 73

Ganymede, 86
Gellius, Aulus, 90, 204
Genauni, 241
Germania, 109, 253, 259
Gracchus, Tiberius, 15
Graces, 121, 134–35, 234

Hannibal, 91–99, 128–29, 134, 151, 171, 233, 244, 257, 292, 316–17
Hasdrubal, 92–93, 98–99, 172, 233, 315, 317
Hector, 166, 168, 170
Helen, 153, 163–64, 168
Hercules, 97–99, 112, 117, 172, 193, 260, 292, 301
Hesiod, 71–72, 74, 77, 163
Hesychius, 160
Hiberia, 109, 253, 259
Hippolytus, 141, 170, 233
Hister, 251–52, 333
Homer, 26, 85, 118–20, 125, 160–62, 164–68, 170, 173, 265, 269
Horace: Ars Poetica, 268–69; Carmen Saeculare, 16, 18, 20–22, 29, 122, 125–26, 128, 155, 288, 290, 297; Epistles 1: 67, 139–40, 226; Epistles 2: 21, 111, 250; Epodes, 26, 190, 284, 288–89, 309; Odes 1–3: 9, 17–18, 42, 52, 59, 67, 70, 89, 107–8, 136–37, 182, 207, 209, 229, 240, 242, 277–78, 285, 289–90; Satires, 189
Horae, 136
Hyginus, 163

Icarus, 51, 55, 61, 193, 312
Idomeneus, 163
Indi, 251
Itys, 200, 202–3
Iullus Antonius, 51, 55–57, 60–61, 64–65, 240, 257, 313, 315, 327
Iulus, 332
Iuventas, 99–100, 107, 112, 316

Janus Quirinus, 264, 275–77, 338
Johnson, Samuel, 15
Juliana of Norwich, 326
Julius Caesar, 58, 106, 111, 126, 155, 267, 280
Juno, 95, 269, 274, 276
Jupiter, 19, 86, 98, 105, 120, 193, 235, 275, 289, 333

Keats, 321–22

Latinus, 274, 303
Latium, 276, 280
Lesbia, 225–26

Leto, 119
Leuconoe, 89
Ligurinus, 37–38, 41, 43–46, 55, 178–83, 210–12, 234, 315
Livia, 85–86, 328
Livius Andronicus, 202
Livy, 144, 151, 303
Lollius, 56, 155, 160, 164–69, 171, 178–79, 293, 302, 309, 311–13
Lowell, Robert, 321
Lucius Julius Caesar, 280
Lucretius, 138, 150, 295–96, 309
ludi saeculares, 15–16, 122, 125, 155
Lyce, 69, 221–26, 228–29, 234–35, 238–39, 256, 293, 302, 312–13, 315, 318

Macrobius, 124, 191, 329
Maecenas, 17–18, 67–68, 70, 74, 143, 186, 190–91, 196, 199, 261, 268, 285–86, 292, 308, 313, 315–16
Mallarmé, 326
Marcella, 56
Marcellus, Marcus Claudius, 93–94
Marcellus, Marcus Claudius, son of Octavia, 94
Marcia, 328
Marcus Livius Salinator, 100
Marius, 266–67
Mars, 17, 90, 241, 253, 291, 295, 317, 329, 335–38
Meleager, 178
Melissae, 55
Melpomene, 46, 64–66, 69–71, 74–75, 129, 154, 173, 235, 311, 313, 315
Memmius, 295
Menalcas, 291
Menelaus, 163
Mercury, 204
Meredith, G., 131
Metaurus, 92–93, 98, 100, 315
Mezentius, 87
Milton, 322
Minos, 140, 171
Mutina, 266

Naulochus, 266
Nemesianus, 182
Nero, Gaius Claudius, 91–92, 97, 100
Nilus, 252
Niobe, 117, 119, 123, 314
Nymphs, 134

Octavia, 328
Octavian. *see* Augustus Caesar
Odysseus, 119
Orcus, 54–55

Orion, 153
Orpheus, 113, 202
Ovid, 61, 105, 191, 277

Pacuvius, 202
Pallas, 247
Pan, 201, 205–6, 208
Paris, 118, 163, 165
Parrhasius, 147–48, 260, 300, 312
Parthi, 16–18, 58, 109, 251–52, 259, 268, 275, 277, 284, 333
Paulus Fabius Maximus, 36–40, 43, 54, 64, 75, 232–33, 293, 297–99, 301, 304–5, 309, 312, 314, 328
Pegasus, 53, 211
Peleus, 119, 125, 246
Pelops, 153
Perusia, 266–67
Phaethon, 44, 181, 188, 192–95, 316
Phidias, 323
Philippi, 266–67
Philomela, 200, 204
Phyllis, 186, 188–97, 199, 209, 211, 220–21, 261, 313–14, 316
Pindar, 46, 51–57, 60–62, 64–65, 70, 76–77, 84–86, 88–89, 96, 98, 117, 148, 153, 161, 164, 172, 193, 211, 234, 254, 257–59, 293, 299, 309, 312, 319
Pirithous, 53, 141, 170, 233
Plancus, 67
Plato, 152
Plautus, 92, 193, 226
Pliny the Elder, 333
Pollio, 16, 35
Pollux, 153, 260
Polyhymnia, 74
Polyxena, 247
Porcius Licinus, 204
Porphyrion, 92, 206
Priam, 124
Procne, 200–204
Prometheus, 153, 193
Propertius, 10, 26–28, 58–60, 72–74, 77, 105–6, 223, 230–31, 254–56, 266–71, 294, 305, 318, 322
Proserpina, 125, 153
Proteus, 187, 192
Pytheas, 88

Quadrigarius, Q. Claudius, 242
Quinctius Hirpinus, 196

Reckford, K., 9
recusatio, 17, 25, 266, 270, 299
Regulus, 136, 166
Remus, 268, 272, 284, 338

Rhaeti, 249–50
Romulus, 67, 104, 106, 152, 172, 239, 260, 268, 272, 284, 301, 331–32, 337–38

Sallust, 309
Sappho, 25, 39–41, 45, 61, 69, 76–77, 160–63, 165, 168, 177–78
Saturn, 16, 282–83
Schiller, 131
Scipio Aemilianus, 150–51
Scipio Africanus, 150–52, 154, 170, 260, 301
Scopas, 148, 260, 300, 312
Scythia, 109, 251, 259
Servius, 44, 92, 153, 333–34
Sestius, 143
Sextus Pompeius, 127, 288
Shakespeare, 175, 322
Shelley, 307
Sibyl, 243
Silvanus, 112
Simonides, 161
Sophocles, 202
Spartacus, 60
Spenser, 322
sphragis, 25, 274
Stesichorus, 153, 161, 165
Stevens, Wallace, 31, 321
Sthenelus, 163
Suetonius, 9, 20–22, 90, 169, 240, 329–30
Sygambri, 56, 240, 251–53, 256, 259–60, 327

Tantalus, 153
Telephus, 188, 194
Tereus, 200, 202, 204
Teucer, 163
Thalia, 121
Thebes, 55, 97
Theocritus, 178
Theognis, 178
Theseus, 53, 141, 153, 170
Thetis, 125, 246
Thrace, 201–2, 206, 228
Tiberius, 21, 23, 27, 90 91, 93, 107, 109, 129, 211, 233, 241–50, 252, 257, 278, 285, 292, 299

Tiberius Claudius Nero (father of Tiberius), 85–86, 239
Tibullus, 223
Tibur, 55–56, 65–68, 70, 75, 311–12
Tigris, 251–52, 254
Tityos, 117
Torquatus, 139–40, 144, 171–72, 233
Troy, 27, 96, 99, 118, 124, 126, 265, 269, 271, 284, 287, 331
Tullus, 138, 140, 144, 147, 233
Turnus, 137, 310, 319

Valerius Maximus, 152
Varius, 17, 250
Varro of Atax, 73
Varro of Reate, 123, 180, 191, 258, 272
Varus, 265–66, 270
Velleius Paterculus, 169
Vendler, Helen, 321–22
Venus, 17, 19, 36–43, 45, 64, 75, 120, 143, 178, 180, 186, 191, 199, 212, 224, 232, 234, 255–56, 265, 289, 293, 295–99, 301, 303, 305, 313–14, 317–18, 327–29, 331, 334, 337–38
Vergilius, 200, 205, 207–9, 213, 220–21, 293, 311, 314, 316
Via Sacra, 66
Vindelici, 85–86, 88–89, 91, 241
Virgil, 26–27, 44, 85, 95, 143–44, 179, 193, 205–7, 215, 223, 244, 248–50, 254, 258, 265–66, 270–71, 294, 296, 305, 318, 322, 334; *Aeneid,* 10, 20, 27, 43–45, 85, 87, 94–97, 124, 127, 138, 153, 163, 166, 182, 243, 264, 268–69, 272, 274–77, 279, 284, 294–95, 303, 309–10, 319, 330; *Eclogues,* 16, 60, 110, 125, 178, 188, 204, 213, 246–47, 265–66, 269, 286–87, 290–91, 309–10; *Georgics,* 110, 113, 187–88, 192, 202, 204, 249, 253, 282–83
Vitruvius, 332, 334
Vulcan, 143

Wordsworth, 322

Yeats, W. B., 79, 322–24, 326

Xerxes, 266